T0207339

Lecture Notes in Computer Science

Lecture Notes in Artificial Intelligence 14694

Founding Editor

Jörg Siekmann

Series Editors

Randy Goebel, *University of Alberta, Edmonton, Canada*
Wolfgang Wahlster, *DFKI, Berlin, Germany*
Zhi-Hua Zhou, *Nanjing University, Nanjing, China*

The series Lecture Notes in Artificial Intelligence (LNAI) was established in 1988 as a topical subseries of LNCS devoted to artificial intelligence.

The series publishes state-of-the-art research results at a high level. As with the LNCS mother series, the mission of the series is to serve the international R & D community by providing an invaluable service, mainly focused on the publication of conference and workshop proceedings and postproceedings.

Dylan D. Schmorrow · Cali M. Fidopiastis
Editors

Augmented Cognition

18th International Conference, AC 2024
Held as Part of the 26th HCI International Conference, HCII 2024
Washington, DC, USA, June 29 – July 4, 2024
Proceedings, Part I

 Springer

Editors
Dylan D. Schmorrow
Soar Technology Inc.
Orlando, FL, USA

Cali M. Fidopiastis
Katmai Government Services
Orlando, FL, USA

ISSN 0302-9743   ISSN 1611-3349 (electronic)
Lecture Notes in Artificial Intelligence
ISBN 978-3-031-61568-9   ISBN 978-3-031-61569-6 (eBook)
https://doi.org/10.1007/978-3-031-61569-6

LNCS Sublibrary: SL7 – Artificial Intelligence

© The Editor(s) (if applicable) and The Author(s), under exclusive license
to Springer Nature Switzerland AG 2024

This work is subject to copyright. All rights are solely and exclusively licensed by the Publisher, whether the whole or part of the material is concerned, specifically the rights of translation, reprinting, reuse of illustrations, recitation, broadcasting, reproduction on microfilms or in any other physical way, and transmission or information storage and retrieval, electronic adaptation, computer software, or by similar or dissimilar methodology now known or hereafter developed.
The use of general descriptive names, registered names, trademarks, service marks, etc. in this publication does not imply, even in the absence of a specific statement, that such names are exempt from the relevant protective laws and regulations and therefore free for general use.
The publisher, the authors and the editors are safe to assume that the advice and information in this book are believed to be true and accurate at the date of publication. Neither the publisher nor the authors or the editors give a warranty, expressed or implied, with respect to the material contained herein or for any errors or omissions that may have been made. The publisher remains neutral with regard to jurisdictional claims in published maps and institutional affiliations.

This Springer imprint is published by the registered company Springer Nature Switzerland AG
The registered company address is: Gewerbestrasse 11, 6330 Cham, Switzerland

If disposing of this product, please recycle the paper.

Foreword

This year we celebrate 40 years since the establishment of the HCI International (HCII) Conference, which has been a hub for presenting groundbreaking research and novel ideas and collaboration for people from all over the world.

The HCII conference was founded in 1984 by Prof. Gavriel Salvendy (Purdue University, USA, Tsinghua University, P.R. China, and University of Central Florida, USA) and the first event of the series, "1st USA-Japan Conference on Human-Computer Interaction", was held in Honolulu, Hawaii, USA, 18–20 August. Since then, HCI International is held jointly with several Thematic Areas and Affiliated Conferences, with each one under the auspices of a distinguished international Program Board and under one management and one registration. Twenty-six HCI International Conferences have been organized so far (every two years until 2013, and annually thereafter).

Over the years, this conference has served as a platform for scholars, researchers, industry experts and students to exchange ideas, connect, and address challenges in the ever-evolving HCI field. Throughout these 40 years, the conference has evolved itself, adapting to new technologies and emerging trends, while staying committed to its core mission of advancing knowledge and driving change.

As we celebrate this milestone anniversary, we reflect on the contributions of its founding members and appreciate the commitment of its current and past Affiliated Conference Program Board Chairs and members. We are also thankful to all past conference attendees who have shaped this community into what it is today.

The 26th International Conference on Human-Computer Interaction, HCI International 2024 (HCII 2024), was held as a 'hybrid' event at the Washington Hilton Hotel, Washington, DC, USA, during 29 June – 4 July 2024. It incorporated the 21 thematic areas and affiliated conferences listed below.

A total of 5108 individuals from academia, research institutes, industry, and government agencies from 85 countries submitted contributions, and 1271 papers and 309 posters were included in the volumes of the proceedings that were published just before the start of the conference, these are listed below. The contributions thoroughly cover the entire field of human-computer interaction, addressing major advances in knowledge and effective use of computers in a variety of application areas. These papers provide academics, researchers, engineers, scientists, practitioners and students with state-of-the-art information on the most recent advances in HCI.

The HCI International (HCII) conference also offers the option of presenting 'Late Breaking Work', and this applies both for papers and posters, with corresponding volumes of proceedings that will be published after the conference. Full papers will be included in the 'HCII 2024 - Late Breaking Papers' volumes of the proceedings to be published in the Springer LNCS series, while 'Poster Extended Abstracts' will be included as short research papers in the 'HCII 2024 - Late Breaking Posters' volumes to be published in the Springer CCIS series.

I would like to thank the Program Board Chairs and the members of the Program Boards of all thematic areas and affiliated conferences for their contribution towards the high scientific quality and overall success of the HCI International 2024 conference. Their manifold support in terms of paper reviewing (single-blind review process, with a minimum of two reviews per submission), session organization and their willingness to act as goodwill ambassadors for the conference is most highly appreciated.

This conference would not have been possible without the continuous and unwavering support and advice of Gavriel Salvendy, founder, General Chair Emeritus, and Scientific Advisor. For his outstanding efforts, I would like to express my sincere appreciation to Abbas Moallem, Communications Chair and Editor of HCI International News.

July 2024   Constantine Stephanidis

HCI International 2024 Thematic Areas
and Affiliated Conferences

- HCI: Human-Computer Interaction Thematic Area
- HIMI: Human Interface and the Management of Information Thematic Area
- EPCE: 21st International Conference on Engineering Psychology and Cognitive Ergonomics
- AC: 18th International Conference on Augmented Cognition
- UAHCI: 18th International Conference on Universal Access in Human-Computer Interaction
- CCD: 16th International Conference on Cross-Cultural Design
- SCSM: 16th International Conference on Social Computing and Social Media
- VAMR: 16th International Conference on Virtual, Augmented and Mixed Reality
- DHM: 15th International Conference on Digital Human Modeling & Applications in Health, Safety, Ergonomics & Risk Management
- DUXU: 13th International Conference on Design, User Experience and Usability
- C&C: 12th International Conference on Culture and Computing
- DAPI: 12th International Conference on Distributed, Ambient and Pervasive Interactions
- HCIBGO: 11th International Conference on HCI in Business, Government and Organizations
- LCT: 11th International Conference on Learning and Collaboration Technologies
- ITAP: 10th International Conference on Human Aspects of IT for the Aged Population
- AIS: 6th International Conference on Adaptive Instructional Systems
- HCI-CPT: 6th International Conference on HCI for Cybersecurity, Privacy and Trust
- HCI-Games: 6th International Conference on HCI in Games
- MobiTAS: 6th International Conference on HCI in Mobility, Transport and Automotive Systems
- AI-HCI: 5th International Conference on Artificial Intelligence in HCI
- MOBILE: 5th International Conference on Human-Centered Design, Operation and Evaluation of Mobile Communications

List of Conference Proceedings Volumes Appearing Before the Conference

1. LNCS 14684, Human-Computer Interaction: Part I, edited by Masaaki Kurosu and Ayako Hashizume
2. LNCS 14685, Human-Computer Interaction: Part II, edited by Masaaki Kurosu and Ayako Hashizume
3. LNCS 14686, Human-Computer Interaction: Part III, edited by Masaaki Kurosu and Ayako Hashizume
4. LNCS 14687, Human-Computer Interaction: Part IV, edited by Masaaki Kurosu and Ayako Hashizume
5. LNCS 14688, Human-Computer Interaction: Part V, edited by Masaaki Kurosu and Ayako Hashizume
6. LNCS 14689, Human Interface and the Management of Information: Part I, edited by Hirohiko Mori and Yumi Asahi
7. LNCS 14690, Human Interface and the Management of Information: Part II, edited by Hirohiko Mori and Yumi Asahi
8. LNCS 14691, Human Interface and the Management of Information: Part III, edited by Hirohiko Mori and Yumi Asahi
9. LNAI 14692, Engineering Psychology and Cognitive Ergonomics: Part I, edited by Don Harris and Wen-Chin Li
10. LNAI 14693, Engineering Psychology and Cognitive Ergonomics: Part II, edited by Don Harris and Wen-Chin Li
11. LNAI 14694, Augmented Cognition, Part I, edited by Dylan D. Schmorrow and Cali M. Fidopiastis
12. LNAI 14695, Augmented Cognition, Part II, edited by Dylan D. Schmorrow and Cali M. Fidopiastis
13. LNCS 14696, Universal Access in Human-Computer Interaction: Part I, edited by Margherita Antona and Constantine Stephanidis
14. LNCS 14697, Universal Access in Human-Computer Interaction: Part II, edited by Margherita Antona and Constantine Stephanidis
15. LNCS 14698, Universal Access in Human-Computer Interaction: Part III, edited by Margherita Antona and Constantine Stephanidis
16. LNCS 14699, Cross-Cultural Design: Part I, edited by Pei-Luen Patrick Rau
17. LNCS 14700, Cross-Cultural Design: Part II, edited by Pei-Luen Patrick Rau
18. LNCS 14701, Cross-Cultural Design: Part III, edited by Pei-Luen Patrick Rau
19. LNCS 14702, Cross-Cultural Design: Part IV, edited by Pei-Luen Patrick Rau
20. LNCS 14703, Social Computing and Social Media: Part I, edited by Adela Coman and Simona Vasilache
21. LNCS 14704, Social Computing and Social Media: Part II, edited by Adela Coman and Simona Vasilache
22. LNCS 14705, Social Computing and Social Media: Part III, edited by Adela Coman and Simona Vasilache

23. LNCS 14706, Virtual, Augmented and Mixed Reality: Part I, edited by Jessie Y. C. Chen and Gino Fragomeni
24. LNCS 14707, Virtual, Augmented and Mixed Reality: Part II, edited by Jessie Y. C. Chen and Gino Fragomeni
25. LNCS 14708, Virtual, Augmented and Mixed Reality: Part III, edited by Jessie Y. C. Chen and Gino Fragomeni
26. LNCS 14709, Digital Human Modeling and Applications in Health, Safety, Ergonomics and Risk Management: Part I, edited by Vincent G. Duffy
27. LNCS 14710, Digital Human Modeling and Applications in Health, Safety, Ergonomics and Risk Management: Part II, edited by Vincent G. Duffy
28. LNCS 14711, Digital Human Modeling and Applications in Health, Safety, Ergonomics and Risk Management: Part III, edited by Vincent G. Duffy
29. LNCS 14712, Design, User Experience, and Usability: Part I, edited by Aaron Marcus, Elizabeth Rosenzweig and Marcelo M. Soares
30. LNCS 14713, Design, User Experience, and Usability: Part II, edited by Aaron Marcus, Elizabeth Rosenzweig and Marcelo M. Soares
31. LNCS 14714, Design, User Experience, and Usability: Part III, edited by Aaron Marcus, Elizabeth Rosenzweig and Marcelo M. Soares
32. LNCS 14715, Design, User Experience, and Usability: Part IV, edited by Aaron Marcus, Elizabeth Rosenzweig and Marcelo M. Soares
33. LNCS 14716, Design, User Experience, and Usability: Part V, edited by Aaron Marcus, Elizabeth Rosenzweig and Marcelo M. Soares
34. LNCS 14717, Culture and Computing, edited by Matthias Rauterberg
35. LNCS 14718, Distributed, Ambient and Pervasive Interactions: Part I, edited by Norbert A. Streitz and Shin'ichi Konomi
36. LNCS 14719, Distributed, Ambient and Pervasive Interactions: Part II, edited by Norbert A. Streitz and Shin'ichi Konomi
37. LNCS 14720, HCI in Business, Government and Organizations: Part I, edited by Fiona Fui-Hoon Nah and Keng Leng Siau
38. LNCS 14721, HCI in Business, Government and Organizations: Part II, edited by Fiona Fui-Hoon Nah and Keng Leng Siau
39. LNCS 14722, Learning and Collaboration Technologies: Part I, edited by Panayiotis Zaphiris and Andri Ioannou
40. LNCS 14723, Learning and Collaboration Technologies: Part II, edited by Panayiotis Zaphiris and Andri Ioannou
41. LNCS 14724, Learning and Collaboration Technologies: Part III, edited by Panayiotis Zaphiris and Andri Ioannou
42. LNCS 14725, Human Aspects of IT for the Aged Population: Part I, edited by Qin Gao and Jia Zhou
43. LNCS 14726, Human Aspects of IT for the Aged Population: Part II, edited by Qin Gao and Jia Zhou
44. LNCS 14727, Adaptive Instructional System, edited by Robert A. Sottilare and Jessica Schwarz
45. LNCS 14728, HCI for Cybersecurity, Privacy and Trust: Part I, edited by Abbas Moallem
46. LNCS 14729, HCI for Cybersecurity, Privacy and Trust: Part II, edited by Abbas Moallem

https://2024.hci.international/proceedings

Preface

Augmented Cognition research innovates human-system interactions for next-generation adaptive systems in diverse fields such as biometrics, cybersecurity, adaptive learning system design, and health informatics. Advancements in psychophysiological sensing and data analyses have led to major breakthroughs in the real-time assessment of a user's psychophysical signatures as input to human-systems leading the way for better human-system collaboration. More importantly, the use of Augmented Cognition methods and tools for studying elusive brain constructs such as cognitive bottlenecks (e.g., limitations in attention, memory, learning, comprehension, visualization abilities, and decision making) significantly contributes to a better understanding of the human brain and behavior, optimized reaction time, and improved learning, memory retention, and decision-making in real-world contexts. Each contribution paves the way for practical innovation in many fields dependent on the symbiotic relationships of human system integration.

The International Conference on Augmented Cognition (AC), an affiliated conference of the HCI International (HCII) conference, arrived at its 18th edition and encouraged papers from academics, researchers, industry, and professionals, on a broad range of theoretical and applied issues related to augmented cognition and its applications.

The papers accepted for publication this year reflect emerging trends across various thematic areas of the field. Our understanding of cognitive processes and human performance is furthered by submissions exploring topics such as impostor syndrome, academic performance, cognitive bias, cognitive-motor processes, emotional responses to music, phishing susceptibility, and the influence of educational and entertainment videos in frontal EEG activity. In addition, technological approaches for advancing cognitive abilities and performance were addressed in several articles across various contexts including cybersecurity training, situational awareness enhancement, cooperative learning, vehicle recognition, human-robot teaming, and human cognitive augmentation. A considerable number of papers discussed recent technological advancements in the AC field, exploring the impact of Artificial Intelligence and Machine Learning technologies, such as Convolutional Neural Networks and Large Language Models. Finally, applications of AC in various contexts were presented, providing insights into the challenges and opportunities in the field.

Two volumes of the HCII 2024 proceedings are dedicated to this year's edition of the AC conference. The first focuses on topics related to Understanding Cognitive Processes and Human Performance, and Advancing Cognitive Abilities and Performance with Augmented Tools. The second focuses on topics related to Advances in Augmented Cognition Technologies, and Applications of Augmented Cognition in Various Contexts.

The papers accepted for publication in these volumes received a minimum of two single-blind reviews from the members of the AC Program Board or, in some cases, from members of the Program Boards of other affiliated conferences. We would like to extend a heartfelt thank you to all the members of the AC Program Board and other affiliated conference program boards for their invaluable contributions and support. The groundbreaking work presented in this volume would not have been possible without their tireless efforts.

July 2024

Dylan D. Schmorrow
Cali M. Fidopiastis

18th International Conference on Augmented Cognition (AC 2024)

Program Board Chairs: **Dylan D. Schmorrow**, *Soar Technology Inc., USA*, and **Cali M. Fidopiastis**, *Katmai Government Services, USA*

- Martha E. Crosby, *University of Hawai'i at Mānoa, USA*
- Fausto De Carvalho, *Altice Labs, Portugal*
- Rodolphe Gentili, *University of Maryland, USA*
- Monte Hancock, *WE Global Studios, USA*
- Kurtulus Izzetoglu, *Drexel University, USA*
- Benjamin J. Knox, *Norwegian Cyber Defence, Norway*
- Chang Nam, *Kettering University, USA*
- Arne Norlander, *NORSECON AB, Sweden*
- Stefan Sütterlin, *Östfold University College, Norway*
- Suraj Sood, *Autism Behavior Consultants, USA*
- Ana Teixeira, *Polytechnic University of Coimbra, Coimbra Education School, Coimbra, Portugal and Institute of Electronic Engineering and Telecommunications of Aveiro, (IEETA, UA), Aveiro, Portugal and InED - Center for Research and Innovation in Education, Portugal*
- Martin Westhoven, *Federal Institute for Occupational Safety and Health, Germany*
- Ren Xu, *g.tec, Austria*

The full list with the Program Board Chairs and the members of the Program Boards of all thematic areas and affiliated conferences of HCII 2024 is available online at:

http://www.hci.international/board-members-2024.php

HCI International 2025 Conference

The 27th International Conference on Human-Computer Interaction, HCI International 2025, will be held jointly with the affiliated conferences at the Swedish Exhibition & Congress Centre and Gothia Towers Hotel, Gothenburg, Sweden, June 22–27, 2025. It will cover a broad spectrum of themes related to Human-Computer Interaction, including theoretical issues, methods, tools, processes, and case studies in HCI design, as well as novel interaction techniques, interfaces, and applications. The proceedings will be published by Springer. More information will become available on the conference website: https://2025.hci.international/.

General Chair
Prof. Constantine Stephanidis
University of Crete and ICS-FORTH
Heraklion, Crete, Greece
Email: general_chair@2025.hci.international

https://2025.hci.international/

Contents – Part I

Contents – Part II

Understanding Cognitive Processes and Human Performance

Not All Victims Are Created Equal: Investigating Differential Phishing Susceptibility

Matthew Canham[1]([envelope]) [iD], Shanée Dawkins[2] [iD], and Jody Jacobs[2] [iD]

[1] Quantum Improvements Consulting, Orlando, FL 32803, USA
`mcanham@quantumimprovements.net`
[2] National Institute of Standards and Technology (NIST), Gaithersburg, MD 20899, USA

Abstract. Repeat clickers refer to individuals who repeatedly fall prey to phishing attempts, posing a disproportionately higher risk to the organizations they inhabit. This study sought to explore the potential influence of three factors on repeat clicking behavior. First, building from previous research, we examined the impact of individual characteristics such as personality traits (Big 5 and Locus of Control), expertise (security and phishing knowledge), and technology usage. Second, social engineering tactics were considered as a potential factor, based on the specifications of the NIST Phish Scale, a metric for rating an email's human phishing detection difficulty. Third, the impact of contextual factors, such as world events, were investigated. Data was collected from study participants via a survey on their individual differences, followed by campaigns in which they were emailed a total of eight messages (four phishing and four controls) over a four-week period of time. Repeat clickers were found to spend less time working online, check email more often, have a more internally oriented locus of control, and a lower need for cognition than the comparison groups. The Phish Scale resulted in difficulty scores closely corresponding to observed click-rates in phishing emails, suggesting that it is an effective metric of evaluating human phishing detection difficulty in a university environment.

Keywords: Repeat Clickers · NIST Phish Scale · Phishing Susceptibility · Security Awareness · Human-centered Cybersecurity

1 Introduction

Phishing is a form of email-based social engineering attack [1, 2], which continues to pose the most pressing security challenge to the human attack surface [3]. Repeat clickers, a subset of individuals who repeatedly fall prey to phishing attempts, pose a disproportionately higher risk to the organizations they inhabit [2, 4–8]. This study sought to clarify some of the contributing factors underlying repeat clicking behavior.

The ground truth in real-world phishing attacks can be extremely difficult (if not impossible) to establish, because cyber criminals often undertake significant measures to conceal their presence on a network [2] Simulated phishing exercises, which send mock phishing email campaigns, are a form of training intended to inoculate users against

© The Author(s), under exclusive license to Springer Nature Switzerland AG 2024
D. D. Schmorrow and C. M. Fidopiastis (Eds.): HCII 2024, LNAI 14694, pp. 3–21, 2024.
https://doi.org/10.1007/978-3-031-61569-6_1

phishing susceptibility and help them recognize phishing attacks [9]. While the efficacy of these simulations has been called into question [10], these training exercises currently provide the best source of data for understanding real-world phishing susceptibility. Details on both detrimental user actions, including clicking an embedded hyperlink, downloading an attachment, or replying to the sender, as well as beneficial user actions, such as reporting the simulated phish, are also recorded. Simulated phishing campaigns can serve as effective proxies for studying real-world phishing attacks because they closely mimic actual attacks (sometimes the emails are neutered copies of real attacks), and users are not typically warned in advance that a simulated email campaign is about to be launched.

Here, in Sects. 1.1 through 1.3, we highlight the need for understanding the repeat clicker phenomenon and the underlying causes in their behavior. Section 1.4 goes into deeper detail about the NIST Phish Scale metric and its purpose for use in this investigation.

1.1 Differing Patterns of Phishing Susceptibility

Research studies examining these simulated phishing campaigns find that "failures" (clicking a link, responding to the sender, or entering credentials) are Pareto distributed, meaning that most users fail a maximum of one or two campaigns, but that a subset fail three or more within a given timeframe. One study found that this subset, the 'repeat clickers,' present approximately three times the risk exposure of other users [5]. These findings were corroborated by another study that observed that a small portion of employees fell for phishing emails multiple times in a similar "long-tail" Pareto distribution of simulation failures. Understanding why these users present a significantly elevated risk exposure is critical to reducing the overall human attack surface for an organization [8].

Little scientific research has examined the underlying causes of this repeat clicker phenomenon, with most studies being industry reports on quantity of occurrence but little explication of user characteristics [10, 11]. Li et al. [7] found that the best predictor of phishing susceptibility was previously falling prey to a phishing email, and that repeat clickers did not respond to training interventions. As part of a study focused on the efficacy of phishing training interventions, researchers explored repeat clickers peripherally, identifying three clicking patterns which they termed as: all-clickers, non-clickers, and everyone else. The researchers found that the all-clickers failed the phishing simulations due to "an interest in the subject matter and lack of careful attention" [4]. Interestingly, most had no memory of identifying anything suspicious in the emails. The all-clickers performance did not improve in response to the training interventions introduced by the researchers. These patterns of responses may suggest that these actions might result from default habituated responses to email, rather than being driven by security knowledge.

1.2 Working to Unravel the Mystery of Repeat Clickers

A key consideration in understanding phishing victimization hinges on discerning the individual differences between persons who occasionally fall prey to phishing emails, and those who repeatedly fall prey to them. Within the context of this study, individual traits refer to personality traits such as locus of control (LOC), a need for cognition, the Big 5, expertise with information technology and security, or prior victimization.

LOC describes the degree to which an individual feels that they can affect change or direct the course of their own fate [15]. The need for cognition refers to an individual's intrinsic need to question and evaluate the information that they a being provided in relation to a message, which may impact their critical evaluation of phishing messaging. The Big 5 personality dimensions (Openness, Conscientiousness, Extraversion, Agreeableness, and Neuroticism) [28] have been found to influence phishing susceptibility in other studies [29–31] suggesting that certain personality dimensions may predict repeat clicking. While the impact of information technology expertise on phishing susceptibility has been mixed [30–32] some suggest that this may play a role in repeat clicking [6]. Prior victimization by online scammers may also predict repeat clicking behavior [6].

Personality factors. The persistent nature of repeat clicking suggests that personality factors may play a role in driving this behavior [2]. In fact, in the early twentieth century, researchers suggested that some individuals are more susceptible to accidents than other individuals in part due to personality traits [12]. Interestingly, this higher susceptibility to accidents appear to also follow a Pareto distribution [13]. As a result, some suggested that an "accident prone" personality type might exist, although this hypothesis was later discredited [14]. The more likely explanation is that a combination of relevant personality traits and individual differences, such as LOC, collectively influence accident proneness [14]. An internally oriented LOC implies that the individual believes that they can direct life events and steer their life direction. An externally oriented LOC implies that the individual believes that they are powerless to affect change and that events will happen as they are meant to, regardless of their own level of effort. Some researchers have speculated a relationship between an externally oriented LOC and increased accident proneness [14]; several studies support this relationship [16–22].

While there does appear to be a relationship between LOC and accident proneness, studies investigating the relationship between LOC and security behaviors have had mixed results. One study found no relationship between LOC and likelihood of clicking the hyperlink in a phishing email [23]; however, this was measured through a self-report survey, which are not always good proxies for actual behavior [24]. Another study found that individuals who demonstrated a more externally oriented LOC had weaker engagement with information security policies in the workplace [25], while another found that an internally oriented LOC indicated an increased cyber risk perception strongly related to reduced engagement in cyber misbehaviors [26]. Finally, another study found a positive correlation between internally oriented LOC in males and higher susceptibility to online investment scams [27]. A qualitative study using one-on-one semi-structured interviews with repeat clickers and protective stewards (users who repeatedly report potentially malicious emails without falling prey to them), indicated that repeat clickers reported a more internally oriented LOC than the protective stewards [6]. These research studies on repeat clicking suggest that individual differences are in part, if not as a whole, driving these behaviors.

Anyone is susceptible to phishing under the right conditions [1], and to be successfully "phished" once or twice may simply be bad luck. A study by Canham et al. [5] intentionally integrated immediate feedback by presenting recipients with copies of the phishing emails that they had just fallen prey to, with highlighted cues indicating what the recipient could have used to identify that phishing email. This feedback was provided every time a recipient failed a simulation [5]. To be successfully phished eight or more times indicates that the user is not improving from training or prior experience, consistent with other research findings [4], and their actions may be driven in large part by their individual differences.

Contextual Factors and Social Engineering. In addition to a main effect of individual traits, the stability and persistence of these behaviors may also be driven by an interaction with contextual factors or social engineering tactics. Contextual factors refer to situational circumstances that are beyond the immediate control of an email recipient such as world events (a disaster often provides a pretext for cybercriminals to use in emails) or work role (employees who are in constant contact with the public are more exposed). Social engineering tactics refer to the methods employed by cybercriminals in deceiving email recipients into engaging with their phishing emails.

1.3 Research Questions

This study investigated whether the persistent aspect of repeat clicking behavior is either being driven entirely as a main effect of individual characteristics or is driven by an interaction between individual traits and social engineering tactics or contextual effects. Most phishing research treats susceptibility as a binary construct without consideration for potential degrees of susceptibility, thus relying on one-time exposures to simulated phishing emails [2]. As such, there is a gap in prior research in understanding the underlying factors for a key segment of the susceptible population, the repeat clickers. This study explored the influential factors for occasional versus repeated human susceptibility to phishing emails by focusing on the differences between repeat clickers (RC), one-time clickers (1C), and zero-clickers (ZC)[1]. Our study was guided by three research questions:

- RQ1: Are there detectable individual differences between the RC, 1C, and ZC groups, in ways that are discoverable through psychometric assessments?
- RQ2: Will RC exhibit similar clicking patterns as the other groups (1C, ZC) in response to different types of phishing emails? For example, will RC uniformly click every link which lands in the email inbox, or will they click in a similar pattern to the other groups?
- RQ3: How will contextual effects impact RC click-rates compare to the other groups?

In social engineering, higher sophistication attacks are less likely to be identified by individuals as potentially malicious, and therefore are more likely to succeed. A challenge posed in investigating RQ2 was how to quantify or control for the difficulty of human detection of phishing emails. The NIST Phish Scale described in the next section was determined to be the best use for this evaluation metric.

---

[1] 1C and ZC were chosen to reduce confusion between the number 0 and the capital O.

1.4 Human Phishing Detection Difficulty Using the NIST Phish Scale

The NIST Phish Scale was developed to address the challenge of developing a human phishing detection metric that accounts for user behavior. The Phish Scale integrates two dimensions of email difficulty (see Fig. 1): the number of observable cues which might alert a user that the email is a phish, and the alignment of the message premise with the recipient's user context (e.g., work role, expectations). By accounting for both a phishing email's characteristics (cues) and context (premise alignment), the Phish Scale helps to provide richer insight into human detection difficulty of phishing emails.

Message Cues. Cybercriminals who send malicious emails have different goals than those who send legitimate messages and may contain "cues" in the email that alert the receiver to its potential maliciousness. Examples of such cues include mismatched hyperlinks, oddly worded phrases, and incorrect logos [9]. When the number of cues that an email contains increases, the likelihood that a potential victim will become suspicious correspondingly increases, thus lowering the difficulty of human detection. The Phish Scale currently includes five types of message cues: Error—relating to spelling and grammar errors and inconsistencies contained in the message; Technical indicator—pertaining to email addresses, hyperlinks, and attachments; Visual Presentation indicator—relating to branding, logos, design, and formatting; Language and Content—such as a generic greeting and lack of signer details, use of time pressure, and threatening language; and Common Tactic—use of humanitarian appeals, too good to be true offers, time-limited offers, and poses as a friend, colleague, or authority figure [33].

Premise Alignment. Studies analyzing simulated phishing email campaigns reveal that user context contributes significantly to susceptibility to phishing emails [9]. When a phishing email is highly congruent with a user's context (e.g., work role, job tasks, personal interests), that user is more likely to ignore signs that the email is potentially malicious and instead focus on the task-relevant information that is associated with their work role [9]. While contextual knowledge endogenously drives our visual attention toward certain aspects of an email, our attention may also be exogenously "captured" by features contained within the email [34]. This suggests that when an email is less relevant to a user's context, they will be more likely to visually process the message from a data-driven perspective and therefore be more sensitive to cues that the email is malicious.

The Phish Scale method outlines four elements of a phishing email that are related to user context: the email premise 1) mimics a workplace process or practice; 2) has work-place relevance; 3) aligns with other situations or events, including external to the workplace; and 4) engenders concerns over consequences for NOT clicking. A fifth element considers whether the user has been the subject of targeted training, specific warnings, or other exposure [35]. The more the phishing email's premise aligns with the context of the user, the harder it is for the user to detect the email as a phish.

Measuring Human Detection Difficulty Using the NIST Phish Scale. The Phish Scale measures the human detection difficulty of a phishing email by considering both the number of cues and the message's premise alignment [36]. The greater the number of observable cues and the more an email's message is mismatched to its recipient, the less difficult that phishing email is for the recipient to detect. On the other end of the spectrum, the fewer number of cues and the more closely the phishing email corresponds with the user's context, the more difficult that phish is to detect. These two components are measured for an email, and categorized according to the procedure outlined in prior publications [35]. The categories for each component are combined to create an overall phishing email human detection difficulty metric (illustrated in Fig. 1).

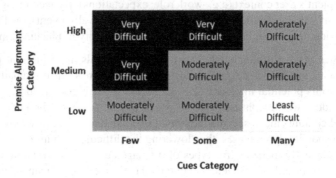

Fig. 1. The NIST Phish Scale (NPS).

The NIST Phish Scale was used as an evaluation metric in this study because it provides a holistic and integrated approach for measuring human phishing detection difficulty [33].

2 Methods

We conducted a study which utilized multiple simulated phishing campaigns run over the course of several weeks. In this study, we examined or controlled for all three potentially contributing factors (individual differences, social engineering tactics, and contextual factors). We examined individual level traits by collecting demographic, personality, and email security knowledge prior to sending simulated phishing emails. We examine the impact of social engineering tactics by rating each email using the NIST Phish Scale. Finally, we control for contextual factors by counter-balancing each simulated phishing email with an email sent explicitly by the research team, thus controlling for events (such as the outbreak of a pandemic) which might impact overall email response rates.

2.1 Participants

After the study protocol was reviewed and approved by the university human subjects review board, 120 undergraduate students were recruited to participate. These students were enrolled in a university undergraduate psychology course and participating in the psychology department's research subject pool. Three participants requested to be withdrawn from the study, leaving a total of 117 research participants whose data were analyzed. No explanation was provided for the request to have data removed. None of the participants received any formal phishing or security awareness training as part of this study.

2.2 Study Protocol

The study was conducted in two parts: Part I Online Questionnaires and Part II Phishing Email Campaigns. In Part I, informed consent was obtained prior to the start of any research procedures. In the consent form, subjects were informed that they were to be sent additional emails, but they were not explicitly told that these were phishing simulations. Subjects were asked to complete a series of questionnaires to collect their demographic data and their individual differences. These questionnaires queried participants about their gender, age, year in school, anxiety about internet usage, knowledge of phishing emails, confidence in detecting phishing emails, and whether they had previously been the victim of online fraud. After completing these questionnaires, participants were asked to provide their first name and university email address. Finally, they were reminded that the researchers would be contacting them via email in the upcoming weeks. The first part of the study took approximately 50 min including consent.

In Part II of the study, all participants were sent a total of eight emails, four phishing emails (*Phishing Email*) and four survey invitation emails (*Survey Invitation*). The latter was intended to act as a control to obtain click-rate baselines. The number of email campaigns was selected due to time constraints of fitting the study within the academic semester. During each email campaign, participants were randomly split into two equal groups without their knowledge. One group received a simulated phishing email, while the other group received an invitation to complete a study related survey. Group assignments rotated with each subsequent campaign. This design provided a counterbalanced control for contextual factors which might influence click-rates. The order of the *Phishing Emails* was also counterbalanced using a Latin Squares technique [37].

All emails included the participant's first name to create a feeling of personalization. If a participant clicked the embedded link in an email (*Phishing Emails* and *Survey Invitation*) the link directed them to complete a short survey asking about situational factors such as device usage (did they read the email on a mobile device, laptop, or desktop), amount of sleep obtained in the previous night, stress level, workload, consideration of consequences for clicking the link, and consequences for not clicking the link. The linked surveys were identical between the simulated *Phishing Emails* and *Survey Invitation* except for the first line which informed participants that this was a simulated phishing exercise as part of the research study (if participant had clicked the link in a *Phishing Email*), or alternatively the first line thanked them for completing the survey (if the participant had clicked the link in the *Survey Invitation*). This procedure is consistent with phishing simulation training programs commonly used by organizations around the world [11, 38–40].

Approximately two weeks after participants completed the Part I questionnaires, they were sent the first in a series of eight emails (four phishing and four study survey emails). The *Survey Invitation* emails were sent to obtain baseline click-rates and psychological states of the participants. These emails were intended to control for contextual factors and unexpected events which may have influenced click-rates for a particular campaign. All email campaigns were sent between March 16, 2020, and April 20, 2020, using the KnowBe4 phishing simulation platform. This study was conducted during the first few weeks following the university shutdown due to the COVID-19 pandemic, so having control emails (the *Survey Invitation* emails) to obtain baseline responses was critical to evaluating RQ3 because student response rates may have been influenced due to the shift to an online course format.

Research participants were not explicitly told that the intent of this study was to learn about phishing, nor told how many phishing simulations they were to be sent, until the debriefing at the conclusion of the study. The reason that participants were not explicitly informed of the true nature of this study is that prior research has demonstrated that when subjects are informed that they are participating in phishing research they do not behave in the same way that they naturally would, and that this adversely affects the research outcomes [24]. At the end of the study, all participants were asked to complete a final survey about their experiences and provided with a debriefing statement describing the phishing research objective.

2.3 Questionnaires

Since so little research has been conducted on the underlying factors of repeat click-ing, this study adopted an exploratory approach with regard to which individual differ-ences might contribute to this behavior. For this reason, the following assessments and questionnaires were administered[2]: Basic Demographics Questionnaire (developed for this study), Internet Anxiety Questionnaire (adapted from [41]), Online Behavior and Online Fraud Questionnaire (developed for this study), Phishing Knowledge Assessment (developed for this study), Phishing Detection Confidence (developed for this study), International Personality Item Pool (Neuroticism, Extraversion, and Openness (IPIP-NEO)-60 [28, 42], Need for Cognition [43], Curiosity [44], Tolerance for Ambiguity [45], Risk Taking [46], Risk Avoidance [47], Distrust [47], Locus of Control [48, 49].

2.4 Email Detection Difficulty

The four Phishing Emails were independently rated by two researchers familiar with the Phish Scale. During the assessment of scoring conflicts, a third researcher with knowl-edge of the target audience (student population) provided input towards the evaluation. A consensus was reached among all three parties, resulting in the difficulty ratings of 'very difficult' for three of the four Phishing Emails and 'moderately difficult' for one of the four Phishing Emails. The four Survey Invitation emails were identical.

The *Survey Invitation* email (presented in Fig. 2) informed participants that the email was part of the study they had volunteered for and asked for them to follow the link to complete a short survey.

The Lost ID Phishing Email (see Fig. 3) claimed that the sender had found the recipient's student ID and was attempting to confirm that the receiver was the same person as the ID. This email included an obscured image that appeared to be a thumbnail image of a student ID. To view the image, the participant needed to click on the image to view it. If the participant clicked on this image, the embedded link directed them to the study survey. This email had a very difficult human detection difficulty rating, with few cues and a medium premise alignment.

---

[2] A pre-print version of this manuscript is available which contains the full versions of all scales in the appendix.

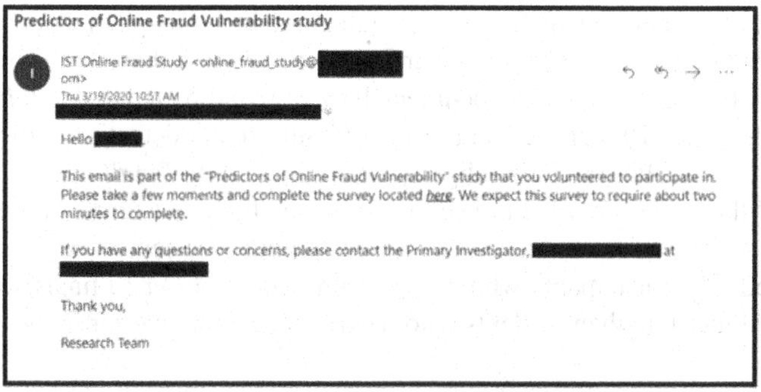

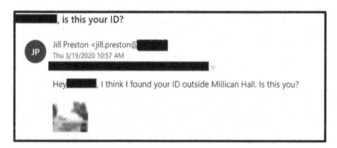

Fig. 2. The *Survey Invitation* Email (18.6% Response Rate across all groups)

Fig. 3. Lost ID *Phishing Email* (53.8% Click-Rate)

The Grade Change *Phishing Email* (see Fig. 4) claimed to notify the recipient that their grade had been changed. This email spoofed an online course management platform that was used by the university at the time of the study. A link was included in this email that claimed to take the participant to the course management site but in fact directed them to the *Phishing Email* survey landing page. The Grade Change email had a very difficult human detection difficulty rating, with some cues and a high premise alignment.

Fig. 4. Grade Change *Phishing Email* (54.7% Click-Rate)

The Final Exam *Phishing Email* (see Fig. 5) employed the pretext of being sent to the wrong recipient and implied that it was meant for someone with a similar name or email address as the participant. This email claimed to have a copy of an upcoming final exam for a teaching assistant to review and advised "do not share with students." If a participant clicked on the attached document, they were redirected to the *Phishing Email* survey landing page. This email had a very difficult human detection difficulty rating, with some cues and a high premise alignment. This *Phishing Email* was sent during the last month of the semester, which raised its premise alignment score. However, not all participants received this email at the exact same point in the semester. No order effects were observed; the participants who received this email closer to finals week did not respond at a higher rate than students who received the email earlier in the month.

Fig. 5. Final Exam *Phishing Email* (29.1% Click-Rate)

The final *Phishing Email* (see Fig. 6), Free iClicker, had a premise of a student no longer needing an iClicker (a wireless response device used by students in some classes). This email was created with the assistance of undergraduate research assistants who advised that this pretext would garner much interest since students are required to purchase iClickers for several classes as transient course requirements, and finding a device being offered for a low price or free (as described in this phishing email) would be perceived as highly desirable. If a participant clicked the embedded hyperlink, it directed them to the *Phishing Email* survey landing page. The iClicker email had a moderately difficult human detection difficulty rating, with some cues and a medium premise alignment.

Fig. 6. Free iClicker *Phishing Email* (5.1% Click-Rate)

2.5 Data Analysis

Findings from the initial survey were analyzed using a one-way analysis of variance (ANOVA) with the response group (ZC, 1C, or RC) as the comparative factor. Differences in the click-rates of the phishing email templates, and any potential order effects, were analyzed using a chi-square test with the control emails as the baseline response comparison.

3 Results

Due to the limited number of phishing emails which were sent, for the purposes of this analysis, repeat clickers are defined as someone who clicked on two or more hyperlinks within the simulated phishing emails. In this study, 27 (23.1%) subjects did not click on any of the phishing hyperlinks (ZC), 32 (27.4%) clicked on exactly one phishing hyperlink (1C), and 58 (49.6%) clicked on two or more phishing hyperlinks and thus met the definition of being a repeat clicker (RC) in this study.

3.1 Individual Differences, RQ1

Demographics. None of these assessments differed significantly between the groups. Surprisingly, there were no significant differences between the 1C and RC groups on any of the Knowledge Assessment questions, which included the self-assessed level of confidence to detect phishing emails.

Internet Usage. As measured by the online behavior questionnaire, the RC group spent less time (on a weekly basis) working online (M = 1.64), than the 1C (M = 7.06), or the ZC (M = 7.12) groups did; $F (2, 113) = 4.972$, $p < .01$, $\eta^2 = 0.81$. A Tukey post-hoc test confirmed this difference was between RC and the other groups ($p < .05$), rather than between the 1C and ZC. The questionnaire specified doing *paid* work as a different question from doing *schoolwork* online, meaning that the only significant difference was observed for paid time online. There were no differences between the groups in the total amount of time spent online, weekly time spent on any of the other online activities, nor internet anxiety. There was a difference in the number of times each group checked email throughout the day $F (2, 95) = 4.965$, $p < .01$, $\eta^2 = 0.095$, with the RC group checking more often (M = 4.04), than the 1C (M = 3.59), or ZC (3.17), with this separation being accounted for by the difference between the ZC and RC groups ($p < .01$).

Big 5 Personality. There were no differences found between the groups on any of the Big 5 Personality dimensions.

Locus of Control. There was a significant difference, $F (2, 114) = 2.536$, $p < .05$, $\eta^2 = 0.71$, between the groups on Locus of Control, with the RC group mean (M = 2.93), the 1C group (M = 3.325), and the ZC group (M = 3.379). This indicates that RC group was more internally oriented in their Locus of Control than were the other two groups. A Tukey post-hoc test did not indicate a significant difference at the 0.05 level between the RC and 1C groups ($p = .058$), but significance was observed between the RC and ZC groups ($p = .037$). No significant difference was observed between the between the 1C and ZC groups ($p = .960$).

Other Individual Differences. There was a difference in the Need for Cognition between the groups, F (2, 114) = 3.382, p < .05, η^2 = 0.056, with the ZC and 1C groups reporting a higher need than the RC group. There were no differences between the groups on the other questionnaires (Curiosity, Tolerance for Ambiguity, Risk Taking, Risk Avoidance, Distrust).

3.2 Social Engineering Tactics, RQ2

As depicted in Figs. 7 and 8, three of the *Phishing Emails* received higher click-rates than the mean response rate to the *Survey Invitation* emails (for the 1C and RC groups). The mean click-rate of 20.6% across these two groups is depicted as the dashed line in Fig. 7); the four simulated phishing emails received click-rates of 53.8% (Lost ID), 54.7% (Grade Change), 29.1% (Final Exam), and 5.1% (Free iClicker). It should be noted that while the order that the phishing emails were sent was counter balanced, Fig. 8 depicting Survey Invitation emails follows the order of receipt and response.

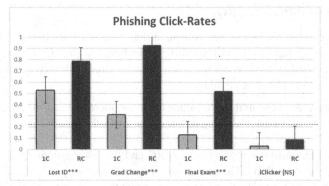

Fig. 7. Click-Rates for Each Phishing Email for Each Clicker Group (1C and RC)[3]

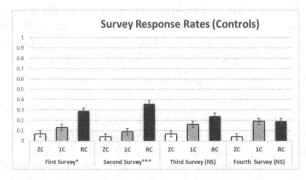

Fig. 8. Response Rates for Each Survey Invitation Email for Each Group (ZC, 1C, and RC)

---

[3] * Indicates p < .05, ** p < .01, and *** p < .001.

A matched comparison of the click-rates for each *Phishing Email* against the click-rate for each respective corresponding *Survey Invitation* email is listed in Table 1. The click-rates for the Lost ID and Grade Change *Phishing Emails* were significantly greater than the controls; the Final Exam *Phishing Email* was not statistically significant, and there was no difference between the Free iClicker *Phishing Emails* and the control.

Table 1. Chi-squared comparison of phishing emails to control emails.

Phishing Email	χ^2	p-value
Lost ID	9.42	.002
Grade Change	5.82	.016
Final Exam	2.88	.089
Free iClicker	0.001	.977

3.3 Contextual Factors, RQ3

As described previously, the *Survey Invitation* emails were sent to obtain baseline click-rates as a means of comparison with the phishing emails, controlling for unexpected events that may have influenced click-rates for a particular email campaign. Although the response rates for the *Survey Invitation* emails decreased over time (as depicted in Fig. 8), there were no differences between any of the email campaigns (the batch of emails including both phishing and control) over time, indicating that there were no influential circumstances impacting the overall likelihood of engaging with emails.

4 Discussion

4.1 Individual Differences, RQ1

The first research question in this study asked whether detectable differences exist between the RC group compared to the 1C and ZC groups. Differences were found in both the orientation of LOC and in the Need for Cognition.

Previous work suggested that an internally oriented LOC might be associated with repeat clicking behavior [6]. The difference in LOC between the 1C and RC groups, but not the ZC and 1C groups suggests that this factor is differentially associated with repeat clicking behavior, rather than general phishing susceptibility (otherwise a difference would have been observed between ZC and 1C). This factor should be explored through more extensive research; if it replicates, a potential explanation may be that repeat clickers are more responsive to security awareness training than those with an externally oriented LOC, but that they need to be convinced of the efficacy of security practices. This finding is also consistent with other research findings [26, 27]. A potential direction for future research might be exploring whether certain LOC scale items are more predictive of repeat clicking than others.

An intriguing finding was that repeat clickers were lower in their Need for Cognition scores than the other groups. The need for cognition refers to the intrinsic desire for a person to comprehend and structure environmental information [43, 50]. Thus, this appears to be a reasonable factor influencing repeat clicking behavior. Little research has been conducted on the relationship between need for cognition and phishing susceptibility [50], with no studies looking at the relationship with repeat clicking that the authors are aware of.

4.2 Social Engineering Tactics, RQ2

The second research question asked whether the RC group would exhibit similar clicking patterns as the other groups in response to different social engineering tactics (as measure by the Phish Scale). The rank ordering of Phishing Email click-rates for the RC group did not follow the same pattern as the 1C group. The rank order for the 1C click-rate was Lost ID, Grade Change, Final Exam, and iClicker. The RC group had a similar order, with Grade Change having a higher click-rate than Lost ID. The response rates for the surveys declined over time for the RC group, as they did for the other groups; however, these were significantly higher for the first two survey emails sent, and then without significant difference for the last two. Interestingly, the ZC group had a consistently lower survey response rate than the other groups. This suggests that perhaps they (like the RC group) are engaging with email habitually, which is consistent with other research [4]. These findings suggest that an interaction between social engineering tactics and repeat clicking may be occurring.

4.3 Contextual Factors, RQ3

Our final research question focused on the contextual effects of external circumstances that influence repeat clicking behavior. It is likely that the low click-rates for the Free iClicker email were driven by current events, since all email campaigns were sent between March 16, 2020, and April 20, 2020, during the first few weeks following the university shutdown due to the COVID-19 pandemic. When this *Phishing Email* was developed (pre-pandemic) the student research assistants advised that iClicker devices were highly sought after by students. When the university shutdown due to the COVID-19 pandemic, all classes were taught exclusively online, thus greatly reducing the value of iClickers, which were not used in online courses. This drastically reduced the appeal of these phishing emails for the target population. While this did not directly address RQ3, the severely low click-rates for the iClicker email does demonstrate the effect for susceptibility to specific messages sent within matched contexts, further warranting the relevance of the Phish Scale as an effective evaluation metric.

4.4 The NIST Phish Scale and Training Implications

At the time of this study, the Phish Scale was a novel method which had not yet been tested on a population outside of the U.S. Government; it was developed and tested based on data from a single U.S. Federal Government agency [35]. Although not the larger purpose of this study, tangentially, we sought to contribute to the ongoing testing of the Phish Scale by applying the Phish Scale in a university environment. The overall click-rates corresponded with the Phish Scale ratings, suggesting that it effectively predicted human phishing email detection difficulty outside of the development context.

While the study presented in this paper represents a smaller sample of emails than the original study [33], its results set the stage for further exploration into the differences between human phishing detection in professional and non-professional target audiences. It may be that since students and professional employees approach email from different contexts, the differences in their environment and tasks lead to diverging email behaviors. These populations may also be driven by diverse psychological motives. Phishing susceptibility factors could have important training implications as they demonstrate that organizations may need their security awareness training to account for a user's role and how it influences context.

Premise Alignment Impact on Overall Click-Rates. Robert Cialdini discusses 'magnetizers' of attention, the self-relevant, the unfinished, and the mysterious [51] which may have played a role in the click-rates for the various *Phishing Emails* in this study. The Lost ID email utilized all three magnetizers. Self-relevance was established by the email's claim of having the recipient's identification card and the message was ad-dressed to participants personally. The email was unfinished because it included the embedded image of an identification card which was obscured to the degree that the receiver could identify it as a student ID card, but not to the degree that they could resolve whether it was their ID card. Finally, it created a mystery. In fact, several participants reported that they had they currently possessed their student ID but wanted to know whose ID card had been found.

Applying these same magnetizers to the Grade Change *Phishing Email*, we observe a similar pattern in that it was self-relevant (it was a participant's grade that was claimed to have been changed), unfinished (the participant needed to click the link to read the complete message), and mysterious (the participant was not informed why the grade was being changed). Consistent with the Phish Scale difficulty ratings, these two emails received substantially higher click-rates than the other phishing emails (both over 50%), suggesting that user context, or an email's premise alignment, does play a significant role in likelihood of clicking. This is further supported when we consider that the Final Exam *Phishing Email* was not self-relevant unless the student happened to be in the class it purported to be from, not mysterious because it told the receiver exactly what the attachment contained, but it was unfinished since the receiver simply need to open the attachment to obtain the contents. The iClicker was neither mysterious, unfinished, nor self-relevant (due to the COVID-19 shutdown of in-person classes). Both the Final Exam and iClicker emails garnered substantially fewer clicks, further supporting the potential influence of attentional magnetizers and the influence of context on phishing email engagement.

High Click-Rates Might Be Helpful? Security departments often rely on phishing simulation click-rates (failures) as a singular metric of human security performance. Click-rates alone do not factor in user context and are absent of the detection difficulty of the emails being sent. Rather than focusing solely on click-rates and reducing them to zero, considering the users in an organization together with the difficulty they experience in identifying phishing emails may reduce vulnerabilities to highly sophisticated phishing emails in the wild. Additionally, considering user context in phishing awareness training programs can provide qualitative information on the topics or pretexts users might be more susceptible to (premise alignment). This information is key to understanding user behaviors in detecting phishing emails, potentially enhancing the training return on investment of phishing simulations.

Not widely discussed are the potential benefits of failing simulated phishing campaigns. Over 100 years of learning research demonstrates that receiving feedback on actions taken (both succeeding and failing) is mandatory for effective learning to occur [52]. The key for individuals to improve is to not continuously fail for the same reasons or at the same level of difficulty. Vygotsky discussed a zone of proximal development which represents the gap between what an individual is currently capable of, and what an individual is (currently) incapable of achieving [53]. It is critical to guide performers through this zone of proximal development to ensure that they do not become overwhelmed in the learning process. It is this process of guiding through the zone where a tailored approach to helping educate repeat clickers might be most effective.

5 Conclusion

This study represents a potentially paradigm shifting perspective on phishing susceptibility in that our findings suggest that differences exist between occasional and repeated victims of phishing email scams. This has significant implications for protecting users online and defending the human attack surface within organizations. Additional work should also seek to understand the underlying and contributing factors for these differences. While this work focused on the impact of individual differences on repeat clicking, future studies should also explore role-based influences on this behavior. One challenge here is that to study this phenomenon requires a long-term engagement with the study population. This challenge withstanding, significant benefits potentially exist for those companies or agencies which uncover the mystery behind repeat clickers.

6 Disclaimer

Any mention of commercial products or companies is for information only and does not imply recommendation or endorsement by the National Institute of Standards and Technology, nor does it imply that the products are necessarily the best available for the purpose.

Acknowledgements. The authors wish to thank Dr. Ben D. Sawyer, Dr. Erica Castilho Grao, Dr. Clay Posey, Michael Constantino, and Delainey Strickland for their assistance in collecting and analyzing the data for this study.

This research was conducted with the support of the National Institute of Standards and Technology (NIST) under Financial Assistance Award Number: 60NANB19D123. The views and conclusions contained in this document are those of the author and should not be interpreted as representing the official policies, either expressed or implied, of NIST or the U.S. Government.

References

1. Hadnagy, C.: Social Engineering: The Science of Human Hacking, 1st ed. Wiley (2018). https://doi.org/10.1002/9781119433729
2. Canham, M., Fiore, S.M., Constantino, M., Caulkins, B., Reinerman-Jones, L.: The Enduring Mystery of the Repeat Clickers (2019)
3. Verizon. 2023 Data Breach Investigations Report (DBIR). Verizon Enterprise Solutions. https://www.verizon.com/business/resources/reports/2023-data-breach-investigations-report-dbir.pdf. Accessed 19 Jun 2023
4. Caputo, D.D., Pfleeger, S.L., Freeman, J.D., Johnson, M.E.: Going spear phishing: exploring embedded training and awareness. IEEE Secur. Priv. 12(1), 28–38 (2013). https://doi.org/10.1109/MSP.2013.106
5. Canham, M., Posey, C., Strickland, D., Constantino, M.: Phishing for long tails: examining organizational repeat clickers and protective stewards. SAGE Open 11(1), 215824402199065 (2021). https://doi.org/10.1177/2158244021990656
6. Canham, M.: Repeat Clicking: A Lack of Awareness Is Not the Problem. PsyArXiv, preprint (2023). https://doi.org/10.31234/osf.io/36eqn
7. Li, W., Lee, J., Purl, J., Greitzer, F., Yousefi, B., Laskey, K.: Experimental Investigation of Demographic Factors Related to Phishing Susceptibility (2020). https://doi.org/10.24251/HICSS.2020.274
8. Lain, D., Kostiainen, K., Čapkun, S.: Phishing in Organizations: Findings from a Large-Scale and Long-Term Study. In: 2022 IEEE Symposium on Security and Privacy (SP), pp. 842–859 (2022). https://doi.org/10.1109/SP46214.2022.9833766
9. Greene, K., Steves, M., Theofanos, M., Kostick, J.: User context: an explanatory variable in phishing susceptibility. In: Proceedings 2018 Workshop on Usable Security, San Diego, CA: Internet Society (2018). https://doi.org/10.14722/usec.2018.23016
10. Elevate Security. High Risk Users and Where to Find Them (2023)
11. PhishMe. Enterprise Phishing Susceptibility Report (2015). https://cofense.com/wp-content/uploads/2017/10/PhishMe_EnterprisePhishingSusceptibilityReport_2015_Final.pdf
12. Vernon, H.M.: An investigation of the factors concerned in the causation of industrial accidents. J. Manag. Hist. 1(2), 65–78 (1918)
13. Hogan, R.: The accident-prone personality. People Strategy 39(1), 20–24 (2016)
14. Hansen, C.P.: Personality characteristics of the accident involved employee. J. Bus. Psychol. 2(4), 346–365 (1988)
15. Rotter, J.B.: Rotter's Internal-External Control Scale. Psychological Monographs: General and Applied (1966)
16. Bridge, R.G.: "Internal-external control and seat-belt use", presented at the Western Psychological Association. American Psychological Association, San Francisco (1971)
17. Hoyt, M.F.: Internal-external control and beliefs about automobile travel. J. Res. Pers. 7, 288–293 (1973)
18. Denning, D.L.: Correlates of employee safety performance. In: Presented at the Southeastern I/O Psychology Association Meeting, Atlanta, Georgia (1983)
19. Wichman, H., Ball, J.: Locus of control, self-serving biases, and attitudes towards safety in general aviation pilots. Aviat. Space Environ. Med. 54(6), 507–510 (1983)
20. Jones, J.W.: The Safety Locus of Control Scale. St. Paul, MN: The St. Paul Companies (1984)
21. Jones, J.W., Wuebker, L.: Development and validation of the Safety Locus of Control (SLC) scale. Percept. Mot. Skills 61, 151–161 (1985)
22. Mayer, R.E., Treat, J.R.: Psychological, social, and cognitive characteristics of high-risk drivers: a pilot study. Accid. Anal. Prev. 9, 1–8 (1977)

23. Ayaburi, E., Andoh-Baidoo, F.K.: Understanding phishing susceptibility: an integrated model of cue-utilization and habits. In: ICIS 2019 Proceedings (2019). https://aisel.aisnet.org/icis2019/cyber_security_privacy_ethics_IS/cyber_security_privacy/43

24. Parsons, K., McCormac, A., Pattinson, M., Butavicius, M., Jerram, C.: The design of phishing studies: Challenges for researchers. Comput. Secur. **52**, 194–206 (2015). https://doi.org/10.1016/j.cose.2015.02.008

25. Hadlington, L., Popovac, M., Janicke, H., Yevseyeva, I., Jones, K.: Exploring the role of work identity and work locus of control in information security awareness. Comput. Secur. **81**, 41–48 (2018)

26. Johnson, K.: Better Safe than Sorry: The Relationship between Locus of Control, Perception of Risk, and Cyber Misbehaviors – ProQuest. In: Doctoral dissertation, University of South Florida (2018). https://www.proquest.com/openview/42ccd20fc5e2b6403ece12dff9686055/1?pq-origsite=gscholar&cbl=18750. Accessed 30 Dec 2023

27. Whitty, M.T.: Is there a scam for everyone? Psychologically profiling cyberscam victims. Eur. J. Crim. Policy Res. **26**(3), 399–409 (2020). https://doi.org/10.1007/s10610-020-09458-z

28. McCrae, R.R., Costa, P.T.: Validation of the five-factor model of personality across instruments and observers. J. Pers. Soc. Psychol. **52**(1), 81–90 (1987). https://doi.org/10.1037/0022-3514.52.1.81

29. Lawson, P., Zielinska, O., Pearson, C., Mayhorn, C.B.: Interaction of personality and persuasion tactics in email phishing attacks. Proc. Hum. Factors Ergon. Soc. Ann. Meet. **61**(1), 1331–1333 (2017). https://doi.org/10.1177/1541931213601815

30. Pattinson, M., Jerram, C., Parsons, K., McCormac, A., Butavicius, M.: Why do some people manage phishing e-mails better than others? Inf. Manag. Comput. Secur. **20**(1), 18–28 (2012). https://doi.org/10.1108/09685221211219173

31. Sudzina, F., Pavlicek, A.: Propensity to click on suspicious links: impact of gender, of age, and of personality traits. In: Digital Transformation – From Connecting Things to Transforming Our Lives, University of Maribor Press, pp. 593–601 (2017). https://doi.org/10.18690/978-961-286-043-1.41

32. Workman, M.: Wisecrackers: A theory-grounded investigation of phishing and pretext social engineering threats to information security. J. Am. Soc. Inform. Sci. Technol. **59**(4), 662–674 (2008). https://doi.org/10.1002/asi.20779

33. Steves, M.P. Greene, K.K., Theofanos, M.F.: A phish scale: rating human phishing message detection difficulty. In: Proceedings 2019 Workshop on Usable Security, San Diego, CA: Internet Society (2019). https://doi.org/10.14722/usec.2019.23028

34. Canham, M., Hegarty, M.: Effects of knowledge and display design on comprehension of complex graphics. Learn. Instr. **20**(2), 155–166 (2010). https://doi.org/10.1016/j.learninstruc.2009.02.014

35. Steves, M., Greene, K., Theofanos, M.: Categorizing human phishing difficulty: a Phish Scale. J. Cybersecurity **6**(1), 1–16 (2020). https://doi.org/10.1093/cybsec/tyaa009

36. Dawkins, S., Jacobs, J.: NIST Phish Scale User Guide. National Institute of Standards and Technology, Gaithersburg, MD, NIST TN 2276 (2023). https://doi.org/10.6028/NIST.TN.2276

37. Shah, K.R., Sinha, B.K.: 4 Row-Column Designs. Theory of Optimal Designs. In: Lecture Notes in Statistics, no. 54. Springer-Verlag (1989). https://doi.org/10.1007/978-1-4612-3662-7

38. Carella, A., Kotsoev, M., Truta, T.M.: Impact of security awareness training on phishing click-through rates. In: 2017 IEEE International Conference on Big Data (Big Data), pp. 4458–4466 (2017). https://doi.org/10.1109/BigData.2017.8258485

39. Halevi, T., Memon, N., Nov, O.: Spear-phishing in the wild: a real-world study of personality, phishing self-efficacy and vulnerability to spear-phishing attacks. In: Social Science Research Network, Rochester, NY, SSRN Scholarly Paper ID 2544742 (2015). https://doi.org/10.2139/ssrn.2544742

40. Moody, G.D., Galletta, D.F., Dunn, B.K.: Which phish get caught? An exploratory study of individuals' susceptibility to phishing. Eur. J. Inf. Syst. **26**(6), 564–584 (2017). https://doi.org/10.1057/s41303-017-0058-x

41. Joiner, R., Brosnan, M., Duffield, J., Gavin, J., Maras, P.: The relationship between Internet identification, Internet anxiety and Internet use. Comput. Hum. Behav. **23**(3), 1408–1420 (2007). https://doi.org/10.1016/j.chb.2005.03.002

42. Maples-Keller, J.L., Williamson, R.L., Sleep, C.E., Carter, N.T., Campbell, W.K., Miller, J.D.: Using item response theory to develop a 60-item representation of the NEO PI–R using the international personality item pool: development of the IPIP–NEO–60. J. Pers. Assess. **101**(1), 4–15 (2019). https://doi.org/10.1080/00223891.2017.1381968

43. Cacioppo, J.T., Petty, R.E.: The need for cognition. J. Pers. Soc. Psychol. **42**(1), 116–131 (1982). https://doi.org/10.1037/0022-3514.42.1.116

44. Collins, R.P., Litman, J.A., Spielberger, C.D.: The measurement of perceptual curiosity. Personality Individ. Differ. **36**(5), 1127–1141 (2004). https://doi.org/10.1016/S0191-8869(03)00205-8

45. Herman, J.L., Stevens, M.J., Bird, A., Mendenhall, M., Oddou, G.: The tolerance for ambiguity scale: towards a more refined measure for international management research. Int. J. Intercult. Relat. **34**(1), 58–65 (2010). https://doi.org/10.1016/j.ijintrel.2009.09.004

46. Nicholson, N., Soane, E., Fenton-O'Creevy, M., Willman, P.: Personality and domain-specific risk taking. J. Risk Res. **8**(2), 157–176 (2005). https://doi.org/10.1080/1366987032000123856

47. Tellegen, A.: Multidimensional Personality Questionnaire-276 (MPQ-276) Test Booklet, 1st ed., vol. 1. University of Minnesota Press, Minneapolis (1995)

48. Levenson, H.: Differentiating among internality, powerful others, and chance. In: Research with the Locus of Control Construct, Lefcourt, H.M., Ed., Academic Press, pp. 1–15 (1981)

49. Oregon Research Institute. Locus of Control, Single Construct Scoring Keys, International Personality Item Pool (2022). https://ipip.ori.org/newSingleConstructsKey.htm

50. (Robert) Luo, X., Zhang, W., Burd, S., Seazzu, A.: Investigating phishing victimization with the Heuristic–Systematic Model: A theoretical framework and an exploration. Comput. Secur. **38**, 28–38 (2013). https://doi.org/10.1016/j.cose.2012.12.003

51. Cialdini, R.B.: Pre-Suasion: A Revolutionary Way to Influence and Persuade, Reprint edition. Simon & Schuster, New York (2016)

52. Mayer, R.E., Alexander, P.A.: Handbook of Research on Learning and Instruction. Taylor & Francis, Florence (2016)

53. Vygotsky, L.S., Cole, M.: Mind in Society: Development of Higher Psychological Processes. Harvard University Press, Cambridge (1978)

Impostor Syndrome in Final Year Computer Science Students: An Eye Tracking and Biometrics Study

Alyssia Chen[ID], Carol Wong, Katy Tarrit, and Anthony Peruma[✉][ID]

University of Hawai'i at Mānoa, Honolulu, Hawai'i, USA
{abc8,carolw8,katytm7,peruma}@hawaii.edu

Abstract. Imposter syndrome is a psychological phenomenon that affects individuals who doubt their skills and abilities, despite possessing the necessary competencies. This can lead to a lack of confidence and poor performance. While research has explored the impacts of imposter syndrome on students and professionals in various fields, there is limited knowledge on how it affects code comprehension in software engineering. In this exploratory study, we investigate the prevalence of imposter syndrome among final-year undergraduate computer science students and its effects on their code comprehension cognition using an eye tracker and heart rate monitor. Key findings demonstrate that students identifying as male exhibit lower imposter syndrome levels when analyzing code, and higher imposter syndrome is associated with increased time reviewing a code snippet and a lower likelihood of solving it correctly. This study provides initial data on this topic and establishes a foundation for further research to support student academic success and improve developer productivity and mental well-being.

Keywords: Cognitive Load and Performance · Eye Tracking · Biometrics · Heart Rate · Impostor Syndrome · Code Comprehension · Program Comprehension · Computer Science · Undergraduate Students

1 Introduction

Impostor syndrome, also known as impostor phenomenon, fraud syndrome, perceived fraudulence, or impostor experience, is a psychological phenomenon characterized by persistent self-doubt of intellect, skills, or accomplishments and feelings of fraudulence or inadequacy despite evidence of one's competence and accomplishments [5,6]. It is thought to affect high-achieving individuals across various domains, including higher education and high-skill professions [4,19]. Although there have been studies examining how women and minority groups cope with imposter syndrome [10], and how other variables are correlated such as self-esteem [11], and self-efficacy [14], there is limited research on the connection between impostor syndrome and undergraduate computer science students.

© The Author(s), under exclusive license to Springer Nature Switzerland AG 2024
D. D. Schmorrow and C. M. Fidopiastis (Eds.): HCII 2024, LNAI 14694, pp. 22–41, 2024.
https://doi.org/10.1007/978-3-031-61569-6_2

As undergraduate students progress through their computer science degree, they not only acquire new skills but also refine existing ones, ultimately becoming proficient in designing and implementing software systems. By the time they reach the end of their academic journey, these students possess the qualifications necessary to begin their careers in the tech industry. It is natural to assume that at this stage, these students are confident in their skills and feel well-prepared for professional success. However, previous research indicates that students enrolled in STEM programs, including those related to computer science, often experience feelings of inadequacy, potentially impacting their confidence in their skills [15]. As such, this study aims to examine the prevalence and relationship of impostor syndrome with code comprehension performance in fourth-year computer science students through an augmented cognition approach.

1.1 Goal and Research Questions

Code comprehension is an essential activity in software development and maintenance. Source code conveys the system's behavior, through identifier names [13], which developers rely on to understand the code they are working on to fix defects or incorporate feature changes [21]. As computer science students prepare to enter the workforce, feelings of self-doubt and insecurity associated with impostor syndrome can undermine their ability to comprehend codebases, thereby negatively impacting their confidence and job performance. Therefore, this study aims to understand how impostor syndrome impacts code comprehension. We envision our study laying the foundation for future research in this area while also providing initial insights to improve computer science education and support students as they transition to professional roles. To this extent, we aim to answer the following research questions (RQs):

RQ 1: To what extent are final-year undergraduate computer science students confident in their program comprehension skills? This research question intends to examine the level of impostor syndrome exhibited by computer science students who are about to graduate. The research question assesses the demographic factors closely associated with impostor syndrome.

RQ 2: How does impostor syndrome affect cognitive processes involved in comprehending code? This research question aims to better understand cognitive processes involved in comprehending code, and how impostor syndrome can affect these processes. This is achieved by tracking eye movements, monitoring heart rates, and taking other measurements, such as the confidence of participants, time taken to complete a code question, and how often participants answered the coding question correctly.

1.2 Contribution

The main contributions from this work are as follows:

- We provide preliminary yet promising findings on the extent to which impostor syndrome affects the code comprehension cognition of experienced undergraduate students.
- This study establishes groundwork for further research exploring interventions against impostor syndrome.
- We make our dataset publicly accessible for replication/extension purposes.

1.3 Paper Structure

The rest of this paper is organized as follows: Section 2 presents a review of related work on imposter syndrome in software engineering. Section 3 describes the methodology used for this study. Section 4 provides answers to both research questions and reports on the results of the proposed experiments. Section 5 discusses the potential threats to the validity of the study. Finally, Sect. 6 concludes by summarizing the findings and suggesting potential directions for future work.

2 Related Work

In this section, we report on related work in this area. While there exist studies that examine imposter syndrome in students and industry professionals, we limit our focus to the literature that addresses imposter syndrome among students who are either taking a computing course or studying a computing subject/topic, as well as software engineering professionals.

In a survey with 200 undergraduate computer science students, Rosenstein et al. [15] show that 57% of the surveyed students exhibited frequent feelings of the Impostor Phenomenon. The authors also highlight that women experienced these feelings more frequently (71%) compared to men (52%). Heels and Devlin [8] examine the roles chosen by female students in a large software engineering team project and report that despite strong academic backgrounds, female students tend to opt for less technical roles than male students. The authors recommend exploring how unconscious bias or imposter syndrome affects female students. Interviews with 16 Digital Technologies teachers from primary and secondary schools by Varoy et al. [20] show that female students experience imposter syndrome more than male students and feel they are not making as much progress as male students, even when they are doing better work. The teachers note that male students tend to loudly proclaim their achievements, while female students work more quietly and cooperatively. This led the female students to underestimate their own abilities and progress. In a study on coding bootcamps, Thayer and Ko [17] found that imposter syndrome can act as an informal boundary to entering the software industry and persist even after gaining experience and employment. Additionally, participants in coding bootcamps can also experience imposter syndrome, similar to those in the software industry.

A survey by Ginter [7] of 104 software engineers shows that individuals exhibiting feelings of imposter syndrome usually had insecure attachment styles, particularly anxiety and avoidance. The study also found that anxious attachment styles in individuals with imposter syndrome were linked to higher levels of depression and anxiety. In a study that surveyed 94 women employed at a global technology company, Trinkenreich et al. [18] note that imposter syndrome was a challenge women faced in software development teams and could lead to them leaving the organization. In an online survey of 134 Finnish women, Hyrynsalmi and Hyrynsalmi [9] reports that women are motivated to transition to the software industry but encounter challenges such as a lack of career counseling, uncertainty about the required education, and issues related to self-esteem and imposter syndrome.

3   Study Design

In this section, we provide details about the design of this study. At a high level, the study consisted of participants reviewing a set of code snippets and answering questions through online questionnaires. While reading code snippets, participants' eye movements and heart rates were monitored. We will elaborate on these activities below. The experiment took place in a private room without any windows, where only the participant and one investigator (i.e., an author) were present. A 24-inch monitor was used to display code snippets and questionnaires. The investigator used a secondary monitor, mouse, and keyboard to manage the experiment. After the calibration stage and before starting the experiment, each participant went through a trial run. This allowed to check if the eye tracker and biometric devices were functioning adequately but also to make sure participants understood and got familiar with the task. A couple trial code snippets were then displayed during this process and have not been included in the results. This study was approved by the Institutional Review Board of our institute and all participants provided consent prior to participating. The high-resolution images of the code snippets, survey questionnaire, and participant data are available at: [1].

3.1   Survey Design

As part of our study, we used three types of online questionnaires - a demographic pre-questionnaire, a code snippet questionnaire, and an impostor syndrome post-questionnaire. To construct and host these questionnaires, we leveraged Qualtrics. All participants answered survey questions using the same workstation that was connected to the eye tracker and biometrics device. Below, we have provided a brief description of each questionnaire.

Prior to code comprehension activities and questions, participants completed a pre-questionnaire capturing their demographics. All questions were required and are shown in Table 1.

During the coding analysis task, participants were presented with five individual code snippets, each accompanied by one single-choice question. The question

Table 1. Pre-Questionnaire capturing demographic details.

No.	Question	Type
1	What best describes your gender?	Single-Choice
2	What best describes your ethnicity?	Multi-Choice
3	What is your current academic year?	Single-Choice
4	What is your primary field of study/major?	Single-Choice
5	Are you a first generation college student?	Single-Choice
6	Do you have an immediate family member who has worked or is working in the software industry? (this includes internships)	Single-Choice
7	How many years of experience in the software industry do you have? (this includes internships)	Single-Choice
8	How many years of Java programming experience do you have?	Single-Choice
9	What is your preferred programming language?	Single-Choice
10	Do you have a software engineering-related job lined up post-graduation?	Single-Choice
11	How would you rate your overall experience with your programming education?	Single-Choice

required participants to either identify the correct output of the code or identify the number of the line where the code was causing a logical, runtime, or compile-time error. Participants only had five minutes to read each code snippet and answer the associated question. To reduce the possibility of participants guessing the answer, each question included an "I don't know" option. Section 4 provides screenshots of each code snippet, along with their associated question and multiple options for answer. Right after participants provided an answer to the question related to a specific code snippet, they were asked to provide feedback on the confidence-level for the answer they selected. After completing code snippets' comprehension activities, participants were asked to fill out a post-questionnaire to assess the extent of their imposter syndrome. For this study, Clance IP Scale questions [5] were customized to focus only on source code analysis and troubleshooting[1]. Those questions can be found in Table 2. All participants were required to answer all questions in this questionnaire.

3.2 Code Snippets

In this study, each participant was required to review five code snippets and answer their associated question. Code snippets were in the Java programming language as it is widely used in multiple courses at the University, and all students are familiar with this programming language. Code snippets covered concepts such as data structures, recursion, sorting, and string analysis, which are taught in undergraduate-level courses and are usually asked during job interviews in industry. Table 3 provides a summary of code snippets. The code snippets and their associated question are shown in Sect. 4.

---

[1] From The Impostor Phenomenon: When Success Makes You Feel Like A Fake (pp. 20–22), by P.R. Clance, 1985, Toronto: Bantam Books. Copyright 1985 by Pauline Rose Clance. Reprinted by permission. Do not reproduce without permission from Pauline Rose Clance, drpaulinerose@comcast.net.

Table 2. Post-Questionnaire containing the customized Clance IP Scale questions that focus on source code analysis and troubleshooting.

No.	Question	Type
1	I have often succeeded in programming tasks, even though I was afraid that I would not do well before I started working on it.	Single-Choice
2	I can give the impression that I'm more competent in my programming skills than I really am.	Single-Choice
3	I tend to avoid programming tasks and have a sense of dread when others assess my programming work.	Single-Choice
4	When people praise me for my code analysis and troubleshooting abilities, I'm afraid I won't be able to live up to their expectations of me in the future.	Single-Choice
5	I sometimes think my success in code analysis and troubleshooting is due to external factors (i.e., environmental or people) rather than due to my skills.	Single-Choice
6	I'm afraid people important to me may find out that I'm not as capable at programming as they think I am.	Single-Choice
7	I tend to remember the incidents in which I have not done my best in programming more than those times I have done my best.	Single-Choice
8	I rarely do a programming task as well as I'd like to do it.	Single-Choice
9	Sometimes I feel or believe that my success in analyzing and troubleshooting code has been the result of some kind of accident.	Single-Choice
10	It's hard for me to accept compliments or praise about my programming skills or accomplishments	Single-Choice
11	At times, I feel my success in code analysis and troubleshooting has been due to some kind of luck.	Single-Choice
12	I'm disappointed at times in my code analysis and troubleshooting accomplishments and think I should have accomplished much more.	Single-Choice
13	Sometimes I'm afraid others will discover how much code analysis and troubleshooting knowledge or ability I really lack.	Single-Choice
14	I'm often afraid that I may fail at a new code analysis and troubleshooting assignment or undertaking, even though I generally do well at what I attempt.	Single-Choice
15	When I've succeeded at programming and received recognition for my accomplishments, I have doubts that I can keep repeating that success.	Single-Choice
16	If I receive a great deal of praise and recognition for my code analysis and troubleshooting accomplishments, I tend to discount the importance of what I've done.	Single-Choice
17	I often compare my code analysis and troubleshooting abilities to those around me and think they may be more intelligent than I am.	Single-Choice
18	I often worry about not succeeding with a programming task, even though others around me have considerable confidence that I will do well.	Single-Choice
19	If I'm going to gain recognition for my code analysis and troubleshooting skills, I hesitate to tell others until it is an accomplished fact.	Single-Choice
20	I feel bad and discouraged if I'm not"the best" or at least "very special" in code analysis and troubleshooting situations that involve achievement.	Single-Choice

Table 3. Description of the five code snippets utilized in this study.

Id	Description	Task
1	This code snippet involves array size manipulation within a loop that will cause a runtime issue. Unlike the error in the other code snippets, participants were not explicitly informed that an error exists in the code.	Determine the output
2	This is an implementation of the bubble sort algorithm. However, there is an error in the condition used in the loop, which will lead to the list being sorted incorrectly. The method's name is called 'bubbleSort', so the participant is aware of the intended behavior of the code.	Identify the number of the line where the error occurs
3	This is a recursive function that prints a sequence of digits. There are no errors in the code.	Determine the output
4	This code snippet accepts a provided string and prints the length of the last word in the provided string. The names of the identifiers in the code do not indicate the code's behavior. There are no errors in this code.	Determine the output
5	This code checks if a given string is a palindrome. The implementation contains an error in the calculation that results in a runtime error.	Identify the number of the line where the error occurs

3.3   Eye Tracker and Biometric Device

Eye movements and physiological samples such as heart rate were recorded respectively using the Gazepoint GP3 HD Eye Tracker and the Biometrics device. These devices are research-grade and are commonly used for academic as well as medical research [2,3]. The eye tracker has a sampling rate of 150 Hz to reduce the chance of loss of tracking and a 0.5–1.0°C of visual angle accuracy. During the experiment, participants sat on a chair facing a computer monitor where code snippets and surveys were presented to them. Prior to the experiment, the camera was calibrated using the Gazepoint Control software. Participants were asked to make saccades to nine targets presented on the screen for calibration purposes. Those nine targets were presented at the top, at the middle and at the bottom of the screen going from the left through the middle to the right of the screen. The heart rate was measured using a finger sensor module. The Gazepoint Analysis software was utilized to manage the experiment, including starting/stopping the eye tracker and the creation of areas of interest (i.e., AOIs).

3.4   Data Preprocessing

Once data collection was completed, data for analysis was prepared using Python. The temporal gaze point data (a single gaze point represents where a user looked and when in milliseconds) from Gazepoint was first cleaned by removing durations of time where: (1) the code was not on the screen due to latency from Qualtrics when displaying the survey question, (2) the time between code snippets, and (3) the participant was looking away from the screen and was not focused on the code snippet. The times for (1) and (3) were determined manually by two investigators watching the video recordings with precision up to three decimal places. The cutoff time for (2) was automated by trimming the data up to when the participant submitted their answer for a code snippet question.

The following aggregate measures were calculated for each participant: average heart rate, total time spent on a snippet, and most looked at AOI (specifically, only AOIs containing code were analyzed for this study; answer choices below each code snippet were not considered). Duration spent in each AOI was determined by summing the differences in time between the first instance when a gaze point was identified to be within an AOI and the first instance when the participant moved to a different AOI. All durations for the AOIs were then normalized by the number of words, excluding non-alphanumeric characters (as described in Sharafi et al.[16]).

Other calculations for the data included determining levels of imposter syndrome (detailed in RQ1 of Sect. 4) and determining the correctness of answers (a binary true/false if the answer was correct) for each code snippet which were determined by two investigators. Additionally, recoding of ordinal variables to be numerical were coded starting from the number zero and non-codeable responses were designated as NaN.

3.5   Participants

In this study, fifteen final-year undergraduate students enrolled in the Computer Science program at the Information and Computer Sciences Department of the University of Hawai'i at Mānoa were recruited. These participants were not given any monetary compensation or extra credit for participating in the study; participation was voluntary.

Out of the fifteen participants who took the survey, nine of them identified as male, five as female, and one as non-binary/third gender. Moreover among the participant pool, ten identified themselves as Asian only, one as White/Caucasian, one as Black/African American, and the remaining three participants identified with two or more ethnicities.

In terms of Java programming experience, eight participants indicated they had one to two years of experience, four participants mentioned they had three to five years of experience, and three participants reported they had less than one year of experience. Additionally, six participants had between one to two years of industry experience, five participants had less than a year of industry experience, two participants had three to five years of industry experience, and the remaining two participants had no prior industry experience. Table 4 provides a breakdown of participants' demographics.

3.6   Pilot Study

We followed the best practice of conducting a pilot study to identify any flaws in our methodology. For this purpose, we recruited four students to participate in a pilot study, who were not included in the actual study. All data collected during the pilot study were discarded after its completion. During the pilot run, we identified certain survey questions that needed to be reworded to improve clarity as well as code snippets that required consistent formatting. We also made improvements to the positioning of the eye tracker and the participant's

Table 4. Demographic details of the participants in the study.

Participant ID	Gender	Ethnicity	Years of Exp. in Software Industry	Years of Exp. in Java
1	Male	White or Caucasian	1–2 years	1–2 years
2	Female	Asian	1–2 years	1–2 years
3	Female	Asian, White or Caucasian	1–2 years	3–5 years
4	Male	Asian	None	3–5 years
5	Male	Asian	>1 year	3–5 years
6	Female	Asian	1–2 years	1–2 years
7	Female	Asian	3–5 years	3–5 years
8	Non-binary / third gender	Asian	>1 year	>1 year
9	Male	Black or African American	None	1–2 years
10	Male	Asian	1–2 years	>1 year
11	Female	Asian, Native Hawaiian	1–2 years	1–2 years
12	Male	Asian	>1 year	1–2 years
13	Male	Asian	3–5 years	1–2 years
14	Male	Asian	>1 year	>1 year
15	Male	American Indian or Alaska Native, Asian, White or Caucasian	>1 year	1–2 years

chair. Furthermore, the pilot study helped us construct a script/instructions to follow when conducting the actual study.

4 Results

In this section, we report the study's results by answering our RQs.

4.1 RQ 1: To what extent are final-year undergraduate computer science students confident in their program comprehension skills?

Based on the Clance Imposter Phenomenon (IP) Scale [5], participants were sorted into four Imposter Phenomenon Characteristics (IPC) categories: Few IPC for those who demonstrated few imposter syndrome characteristics, Moderate IPC for those with moderate characteristics, Frequent IPC, and Intense IPC, with each corresponding to the severity level of IP. These levels correspond to how frequently and seriously IP interferes with a person's life.

Table 5. Range of values associated with each IPC level

IPC Level	Scores
Few	> 40
Moderate	41–60
Frequent	61–80
Intense	< 80

Once participants filled out the post-questionnaire based on a version of the Clance IP Scale adapted to the task, their score was calculated as follows: Each question had a range of multiple-choice answers, which were "not at all true," "rarely," "sometimes," "often," and "very true." Each answer mapped to a numerical value from 1 to 5, respectively. These values are then tallied to create an aggregate score for each participant and used to classify each participant into one of the four IPC groups. The range of values associated with each IPC category can be found in Table 5.

Of the fifteen participants, three had Few IPC, five had Moderate IPC, five had Frequent IPC, and two had Intense IPC. Of the three participants with Few IPCs, all three identified themselves as male. In the Moderate and Frequent IPC groups, each comprising five individuals, two participants identified themselves as female and three as male. Amongst the two participants with Intense IPC, one identified as female and the other one as non-binary/third gender.

A t-test to compare the IPC scores between males and females (the participant who responded "non-binary" was omitted) found that the nine males (M = 50.56, SD = 12.32) compared to the five females (M = 68.80, SD = 12.28) scored significantly lower on the modified Clance IP scale, $t(12) = -2.658$, $p = .021$. Therefore, females were associated with higher levels of the imposter phenomenon, particularly in relation to source code analysis and troubleshooting.

One-way ANOVA tests were additionally conducted to compare how IPC scores were related to software industry experience and Java experience. Findings show that there is no significant difference in IPC scores so there is no relationship between these variables ($p > .05$ for both).

Summary for RQ1. We found that female students had higher characteristics of imposter syndrome. The number of years of experience in the software industry or the tested programming language did not seem to correlate to the level of characteristics of imposter syndrome.

4.2 RQ 2: How Does Imposter Syndrome Affect the Cognitive Processes Involved in Comprehending Code?

To answer this research question, we examine the eye tracking and biometrics results of participants comprehending each code snippet in the study. Below, for each code snippet, we discuss the average heart rate, Areas of Interest (AOI) metrics, time spent by participants on the snippet, the percentage of correct answers, and the extent to which participants are confident with their answers. Additionally, Fig. 1 displays all five code snippets that were included in our study, along with their corresponding question.

AOIs are regions of a stimulus from which quantitative metrics can be derived [16]. Each AOI contains its own set of metrics, e.g., the average time participants took to look at a specific AOI. Each line of code, excluding those solely comprising of curly braces, was designated an AOI. Each stimulus had an average of 13.4 AOIs. As mentioned in Sect. 3, each AOI was normalized by the number of words it contained on its line in order to allow fair comparison between AOIs (words were characterized as sequences of alphanumeric characters that are separated by spaces after excluding non-alphanumeric characters).

The AOIs were then grouped into one of ten different categories, depending on the functionality of the line of code. These categories are as follows: else statement, for loop, if statement, import statement, method call, method declaration,

1. What is the correct output:

```
1   import java.util.ArrayList;
2   public static void main(String[] args) {
3       List<Integer> list = new ArrayList<>();
4       list.add(1);
5       list.add(2);
6       list.add(3);
7       for (Integer item : list) {
8           if (item.equals(1)) {
9               list.remove(item);
10          }
11      }
12      for (int i = 0; i < list.size(); i++) {
13          int curr = list.get(i);
14          System.out.print(curr);
15      }
16  }
```

○ Output:_____   ○ Null

○ Compile/Runtime error   ○ I don't know

2. If there's an error, which line number contains it?

```
1   static void bubbleSort(int[] arr) {
2       int n = arr.length;
3       int temp = 0;
4       for(int i = 0; i < n; i++){
5           for(int j = 1; j < i; j++){
6               if(arr[j-1] > arr[j]){
7                   temp = arr[j-1];
8                   arr[j-1] = arr[j];
9                   arr[j] = temp;
10              }
11          }
12      }
13  }
```

○ Line Number: _____   ○ I don't know

○ There is no error

3. What is the correct output:

```
1   public static void emptyVase(int flowersInVase) {
2       if (flowersInVase > 0) {
3           emptyVase(flowersInVase - 1);
4           System.out.print(flowersInVase);
5       }
6   }
7
8   public static void main (String[] argos){
9       emptyVase(7);
10  }
```

○ Output:_____   ○ Null

○ Compile/Runtime error   ○ I don't know

4. What is the correct output:

```
1   public int function(String input) {
2       int length = 0;
3       for (int i = input.length() - 1; i >= 0; i--) {
4           if (s.charAt(i) != ' ') {
5               length++;
6           } else {
7               if (length > 0)
8                   return length;
9           }
10      }
11      return length;
12  }
13
14  public static void main(String[] args) {
15      System.out.println(function("Hello World"));
16  }
```

○ Output:_____   ○ Null

○ Compile/Runtime error   ○ I don't know

5. If there's an error, which line number contains it?

```
1   public boolean palindromeChecker (String str) {
2       String reversedStr = "";
3       int length = str.length();
4       for (int i = (length - 1); i >=0; --i) {
5           reversedStr = reversedStr - str.charAt(i);
6       }
7       str = str.toLowerCase();
8       reversedStr = reversedStr.toLowerCase();
9       if (str.equals(reversed_str)) {
10          return true;
11      } else {
12          return false;
13      }
14  }
```

○ Line Number: _____   ○ I don't know

○ There is no error

Fig. 1. The five code snippets that were part of our study along with their associated question and answer choices.

recursive method call, return statement, variable assignment, and variable declaration. An example of a method declaration is "public static void main(String[] args) {", while an example of a method call is "list.add(1)."

Code Snippet 1 - Array Size Manipulation

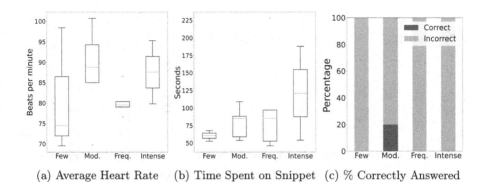

(a) Average Heart Rate   (b) Time Spent on Snippet   (c) % Correctly Answered

Fig. 2. Biometrics and Other Measures Averaged per IPC Group for Snippet 1
Average heart rate and time spent was further averaged within each IPC grouping (Few, Moderate, Frequent, and Intense IPC). The percentage of participants who scored correctly in each IPC grouping is displayed in the last figure.

It was found that for Code Snippet 1, only one participant from the Moderate IPC group answered the problem correctly (see Fig. 2c). The lowest median for the average heart rate occurred in the Few IPC group, whereas the highest median average heart rate occurred in the Moderate IPC group (see Fig. 2a). The amount of time participants took before submitting an answer was the lowest for those in the Few IPC group and the highest in the Intense IPC group (see Fig. 2b).

The lines of code that participants spent the longest duration on were import statements for Few IPC, Moderate IPC, and Frequent IPC (for each row in Table 6, the percentage was highest for these three IPC groups). Those in the Intense IPC spent the longest duration on if statements (23.87%). For all but those in Frequent IPC, the least amount of time was spent on method declarations.

Table 6. Duration spent on a Code Category in Snippet 1

	For Loop	If Stmt	Import Stmt	Method Call	Method Decl	Var Decl	Multiple
Few IPC	16.18% (0.46)	18.28% (0.52)	21.93% (0.62)	21.29% (0.6)	10.71% (0.3)	11.14% (0.32)	0.47% (0.01)
Moderate IPC	17.17% (0.8)	12.7% (0.59)	25.17% (1.17)	18.25% (0.85)	11.62% (0.54)	14.51% (0.67)	0.58% (0.03)
Frequent IPC	17.76% (0.91)	10.93% (0.56)	30.31% (1.56)	16.01% (0.82)	12.66% (0.65)	12.07% (0.62)	0.24% (0.01)
Intense IPC	20.63% (1.18)	23.87% (1.36)	14.71% (0.84)	17.65% (1.01)	9.67% (0.55)	11.26% (0.64)	2.21% (0.13)

Row percentages for each IPC are shown in each cell with red highlights denoting largest percentage and green highlights denoting smallest (ignoring the Multiple category). The duration normalized by number of words are in parenthesis.

Code Snippet 2 - Bubble Sort

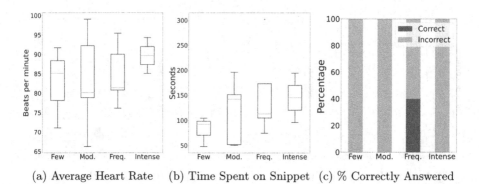

(a) Average Heart Rate   (b) Time Spent on Snippet   (c) % Correctly Answered

Fig. 3. Biometrics and Other Measures Averaged per IPC Group for Snippet 2

Average heart rate and time spent was further averaged within each IPC grouping (Few, Moderate, Frequent, and Intense IPC). The percentage of participants who scored correctly in each IPC grouping is displayed in the last figure.

As shown in Fig. 3, only two participants from the Frequent IPC group answered the problem correctly. The average heart rate was the lowest in the Moderate IPC group and Highest in the intense IPC group. Participants in the Few IPC group spent the least amount of time and those in the Intense IPC group spent the most.

Referring to Table 7, those from the Few IPC, Moderate IPC, and Frequent IPC spent the least amount of time on the if statements, while those in the Intense IPC group spent the least amount of time on variable assignments. Besides the Moderate IPC group, every group spent the most time on method declarations.

Table 7. Duration spent on a Code Category in Snippet 2

	For Loop	If Stmt	Method Decl	Var Asgmt	Var Decl
Few IPC	14.09% (0.66)	8.33% (0.39)	39.24% (1.84)	11.82% (0.55)	26.52% (1.24)
Moderate IPC	16.45% (1.01)	13.05% (0.8)	24.17% (1.48)	25.87% (1.59)	20.46% (1.26)
Frequent IPC	19.54% (1.69)	10.92% (0.95)	36.96% (3.2)	12.79% (1.1)	19.89% (1.72)
Intense IPC	17.95% (1.01)	13.02% (0.73)	36.51% (2.06)	12.7% (0.72)	19.74% (1.11)

Code Snippet 3 - Recursion

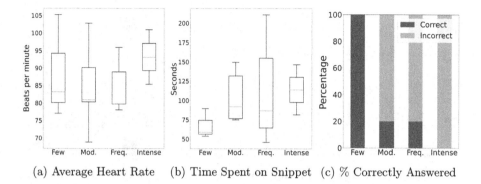

(a) Average Heart Rate   (b) Time Spent on Snippet   (c) % Correctly Answered

Fig. 4. Biometrics and Other Measures Averaged per IPC Group for Snippet 3

Average heart rate and time spent was further averaged within each IPC grouping (Few, Moderate, Frequent, and Intense IPC). The percentage of participants who scored correctly in each IPC grouping is displayed in the last figure.

For Code Snippet 3, all of the participants in the Few IPC group answered the problem correctly, whereas no participants from the Intense IPC group answered correctly (Fig. 4). One participant from the Moderate and Frequent IPC groups answered correctly. The lowest median average heart rate was from the Frequent IPC group, and the highest median was from the Intense IPC group. Participants from the Intense IPC group spent the longest amount of time on the snippet compared to those in the Few IPC group, who spent the shortest.

This snippet had less consistent results across the IPC groupings as can be seen in Table 8. However, it can seen that those in the Few IPC group spent the most time on if-statements and the least amount of time on recursive calls, whereas those in the Intense IPC group spent most of their time on method declarations and the least amount of time on if-statements.

Table 8. Duration spent on a Code Category in Snippet 3

	If Stmt	Method Call	Method Decl	Recursive Call
Few IPC	31.25% (1.08)	22.73% (0.79)	30.88% (1.07)	15.14% (0.52)
Moderate IPC	28.7% (2.39)	15.21% (1.27)	14.06% (1.17)	42.03% (3.5)
Frequent IPC	24.38% (2.13)	33.73% (2.95)	21.83% (1.91)	20.06% (1.75)
Intense IPC	8.06% (0.6)	34.43% (2.58)	34.54% (2.59)	22.96% (1.72)

Code Snippet 4 - String Analysis

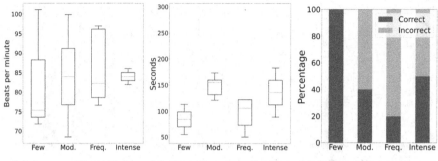

(a) Average Heart Rate   (b) Time Spent on Snippet   (c) % Correctly Answered

Fig. 5. Biometrics and Other Measures Averaged per IPC Group for Snippet 4

Average heart rate and time spent was further averaged within each IPC grouping (Few, Moderate, Frequent, and Intense IPC). The percentage of participants who scored correctly in each IPC grouping is displayed in the last figure.

Referring to Fig. 5, seven participants answered this question correctly, including all three from Few IPC, three between Moderate and Frequent IPC, and one from Intense IPC. The median average heart rate was similar between Moderate, Frequent, and Intense IPC, but those in the Few IPC group had the lowest average heart rate. For time spent on the snippet, participants with Intense IPC had the longest average duration; participants with Few IPC had the shortest average duration.

As seen in Table 9, participants with Few, Moderate, and Frequent IPC spent the longest duration on variable assignments. For code categories with the shortest duration, there was no consistency among the four IPC groups.

Table 9. Duration spent on a Code Category in Snippet 4

	Else Stmt	For Loop	If Stmt	Method Call	Method Decl	Return Stmt	Var Asgmt	Var Decl	Multiple
Few IPC	3.16% (0.26)	7.95% (0.65)	8.74% (0.72)	9.61% (0.79)	19.49% (1.6)	17.82% (1.46)	23.97% (1.97)	7.7% (0.63)	1.56% (0.13)
Moderate IPC	11.28% (1.83)	10.19% (1.66)	9.96% (1.62)	11.15% (1.81)	11.59% (1.88)	9.78% (1.59)	20.56% (3.34)	9.7% (1.58)	5.76% (0.94)
Frequent IPC	14.72% (2.29)	4.6% (0.72)	9.42% (1.47)	9% (1.4)	12.65% (1.97)	10.71% (1.67)	25.78% (4.02)	10.58% (1.65)	2.54% (0.4)
Intense IPC	15.12% (1.52)	7.69% (0.78)	5.32% (0.54)	7.72% (0.78)	24.46% (2.47)	8.23% (0.83)	12.54% (1.26)	15.35% (1.55)	3.57% (0.36)

Code Snippet 5 - Palindrome

For Code Snippet 5, eight participants answered correctly, again including all three from Few IPC, one from Moderate IPC, and four from Frequent IPC (See Fig. 6). No participant from the intense IPC group answered correctly. Those in the few IPC group had the lowest average heart rate, whereas those in the

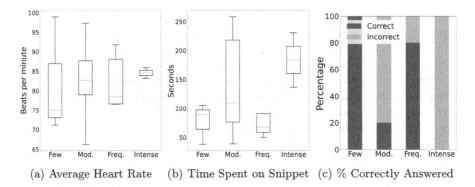

(a) Average Heart Rate   (b) Time Spent on Snippet   (c) % Correctly Answered

Fig. 6. Biometrics and Other Measures Averaged per IPC Group for Snippet 5

Average heart rate and time spent was further averaged within each IPC grouping (Few, Moderate, Frequent, and Intense IPC). The percentage of participants who scored correctly in each IPC grouping is displayed in the last figure.

intense IPC had the highest. Similar to the other snippets, participants with Few IPC spent the least amount of time on the snippet, whereas those with Intense IPC spent the most amount of time.

Referring to Table 10 all four IPC groupings spent the most time looking at method declarations. Those with Few and Moderate IPC spent the least amount of time on return statements, whereas those with Frequent and Intense IPC spent the least amount of time on if statements.

Table 10. Duration spent on a Code Category in Snippet 5

	Else Stmt	For Loop	If Stmt	Method Decl	Return Stmt	Var Asgmt	Var Decl
Few IPC	5.5% (0.33)	12.38% (0.75)	6.02% (0.37)	44.68% (2.72)	5.4% (0.33)	7.73% (0.47)	18.28% (1.11)
Moderate IPC	14.16% (1.81)	10.32% (1.32)	11.6% (1.48)	25.57% (3.26)	9.03% (1.15)	14.81% (1.89)	14.51% (1.85)
Frequent IPC	10.19% (0.74)	6.34% (0.46)	6.34% (0.46)	37.46% (2.74)	7.27% (0.53)	8.99% (0.66)	23.41% (1.71)
Intense IPC	20.88% (2.89)	3.94% (0.54)	1.67% (0.23)	40.36% (5.58)	9.97% (1.38)	7.14% (0.99)	16.04% (2.22)

Overall Analysis. When averaging time across all 5 code snippets and for each imposter syndrome level, there appears to be a trend where the median of the time spent increases as participants score higher on Clance IP Scale (Fig. 7b). When averaging how many times participants in each IPC group answered questions correctly across all code snippets, there was a downward trend (Fig. 7c). To measure the extent of the relationship between these variables, we conducted a Pearson correlation test. The Pearson correlation test yielded statistically significant (i.e., p-value < 0.05) correlation coefficients of 0.52, equating to a moderate positive correlation between IPC score and time spent on a snippet and −0.52, equating to a moderate negative correlation between IPC score and average correctness. While in Fig. 7a, there appears to be a positive trend between average heart rate and IPC, it was not statistically significant. Similarly, while there seems to be a pattern of those with high IPC being less confident in their answers in 7d, no significant results were found.

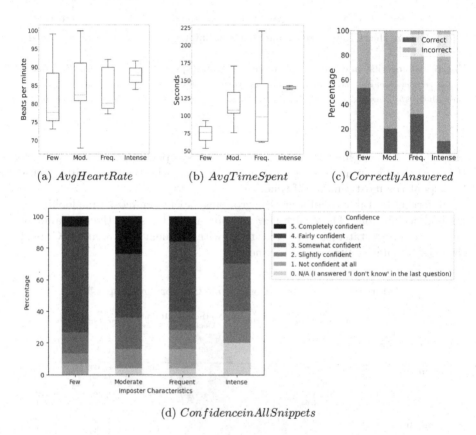

(a) *AvgHeartRate*   (b) *AvgTimeSpent*   (c) *CorrectlyAnswered*

(d) *ConfidenceinAllSnippets*

Fig. 7. Combined Results

To gain a deeper insight into overall how participants of varying IPC scores read code, a Pearson Correlation 2-tailed test was conducted to compare average normalized durations for each AOI code category (e.g., else-statement, for-loop). The test yielded a statistically significant (i.e., p-value < 0.05) correlation coefficient: 0.56 for the IPC score and Method Calls, equating to a positive moderate correlation, and 0.52 for the IPC score and Method Declarations. This could indicate that those with higher IPC scores tend to spend more time looking at code associated with these two categories.

Summary for RQ2. Students with higher characteristics of imposter syndrome were associated with spending longer on snippets and were less likely to answer the question related to each code snippet correctly. Across all code snippets, those with higher characteristics of imposter syndrome were more likely to look at the Method Call and Method Declaration code categories.

5   Threats to Validity

Although our study sample size is small and limited to a single institute, it remains valuable as an initial exploratory study providing a foundation for further research. Furthermore, research shows that program comprehension studies using an eye tracker have an average of 18.08 participants with a standard deviation of 9.90 [12]. Likewise, due to the small sample size, the small gender and race/ethnicity distribution in our participants' pool may not be representative of the general population. The number and type of code snippets used in this study in order to evaluate comprehension threaten the study's validity, as they may not represent real-world codebases that students will encounter in their careers. However, these code snippets represent basic programming concepts that students learn when preparing for their degree and are commonly asked in entry-level software engineering industry interviews.

The validity of our study may also be threatened by the limitations of the Gazepoint GP3 HD Eye Tracker and Biometrics Kit. However, these are research-grade devices that have been previously utilized in scientific publications [2,3]. Overall, while our study has some inherent limitations as an initial investigation, it establishes a valuable foundation for further research on this topic. Finally, as the experiment was conducted in a controlled lab environment, it may not fully reflect real-world software development situations and, therefore, could impact the validity of our results. However, the controlled setting helped us focus on the effects of imposter syndrome on code comprehension. Moreover, we followed established guidelines to set up our eye-tracking experiment [16].

6   Conclusion and Future Work

Imposter syndrome is a psychological barrier that can negatively affect the performance of students and professionals. While research on imposter syndrome in software engineering does exist, little is known about how it affects code comprehension cognition. In this exploratory study, we examine the level of imposter syndrome final-year undergraduate computer science students exhibit when comprehending code. We further measure the cognitive impact using an eye tracker and heart rate monitor. Our findings show that: (1) students identifying as males show lower levels of imposter syndrome, (2) higher levels of imposter syndrome are associated with increased duration of time spent on a snippet and lower chances of solving the problem correctly, and (3) those with higher imposter syndrome levels are more likely to look at method declarations and method calls.

While limited in scope, our study establishes a foundation for further research on imposter syndrome and its effects on core software engineering competencies.

Our future work involves working with industry professionals in a similar study to understand how imposter syndrome affects computer science professionals in their day-to-day work, including its impact on mental health.

Acknowledgments. We thank students who took the time to participate in our study.

Data Availability Statement. The high-resolution images of the code snippets, survey questionnaires, and participant data are available at: [1].

References

1. https://zenodo.org/doi/10.5281/zenodo.10656486
2. Eye-tracking technology for academic research | gazepoint. https://www.gazept.com/academic-research/?v=7516fd43adaa
3. Publications & citations | gazepoint. https://www.gazept.com/meet-the-team/publications/?v=7516fd43adaa
4. Chakraverty, D.: Faculty experiences of the impostor phenomenon in STEM fields. CBE Life Sci. Educ. **21**(4), ar84 (2022)
5. Clance, P.R.: Clance impostor phenomenon scale. Pers. Individ. Diff. (1985)
6. Clance, Pauline Rose Imes, S.A.: The imposter phenomenon in high achieving women: dynamics and therapeutic intervention. Psychother. Theor. Res. Pract. **15**(3) (1978). https://doi.org/10.1037/h0086006, https://doi.org/10.1037/h0086006
7. Ginter, A.N.: Imposter phenomenon, insecure attachment style, and mental health in software engineers: an examination of the moderating effect of self esteem. Ph.D. thesis, Alliant International University (2023)
8. Heels, L., Devlin, M.: Investigating the role choice of female students in a software engineering team project. In: Proceedings of the 3rd Conference on Computing Education Practice. CEP 2019, Association for Computing Machinery, New York, NY, USA (2019). https://doi.org/10.1145/3294016.3294028
9. Hyrynsalmi, S., Hyrynsalmi, S.: What motivates adult age women to make a career change to the software industry? In: 2019 IEEE International Conference on Engineering, Technology and Innovation (ICE/ITMC), pp. 1–8 (2019). https://doi.org/10.1109/ICE.2019.8792630
10. Maji, S.: "They Overestimate Me All the Time:" exploring imposter phenomenon among indian female software engineers. metamorphosis. J. Manag. Res. **20**(2), 55–64 (2021). https://doi.org/10.1177/09726225211033699, http://journals.sagepub.com/doi/10.1177/09726225211033699
11. Naser, M.J., Hasan, N.E., Zainaldeen, M.H., Zaidi, A., Mohamed, Y.M.A.M.H., Fredericks, S.: Impostor phenomenon and its relationship to self-esteem among students at an international medical college in the middle east: a cross sectional study. Front. Med. **9**, 850434 (2022). https://doi.org/10.3389/fmed.2022.850434, https://www.frontiersin.org/articles/10.3389/fmed.2022.850434/full
12. Obaidellah, U., Al Haek, M., Cheng, P.C.H.: A survey on the usage of eye-tracking in computer programming. ACM Comput. Surv. **51**(1) (2018). https://doi.org/10.1145/3145904

13. Peruma, A., Mkaouer, M.W., Decker, M.J., Newman, C.D.: An empirical investigation of how and why developers rename identifiers. In: Proceedings of the 2nd International Workshop on Refactoring, pp. 26–33. IWoR 2018, Association for Computing Machinery, New York, NY, USA (2018). https://doi.org/10.1145/3242163.3242169

14. Pákozdy, C., Askew, J., Dyer, J., Gately, P., Martin, L., Mavor, K.I., Brown, G.R.: The imposter phenomenon and its relationship with self-efficacy, perfectionism and happiness in university students. Curr. Psychol. (2023). https://doi.org/10.1007/s12144-023-04672-4

15. Rosenstein, A., Raghu, A., Porter, L.: Identifying the prevalence of the impostor phenomenon among computer science students. In: Proceedings of the 51st ACM Technical Symposium on Computer Science Education, pp. 30–36. SIGCSE 2020, Association for Computing Machinery, New York, NY, USA (2020). https://doi.org/10.1145/3328778.3366815

16. Sharafi, Z., Sharif, B., Guéhéneuc, Y.G., Begel, A., Bednarik, R., Crosby, M.: A practical guide on conducting eye tracking studies in software engineering. Empir. Softw. Eng. **25**, 3128–3174 (2020)

17. Thayer, K., Ko, A.J.: Barriers faced by coding Bootcamp students. In: Proceedings of the 2017 ACM Conference on International Computing Education Research, pp. 245–253. ICER 2017, Association for Computing Machinery, New York, NY, USA (2017). https://doi.org/10.1145/3105726.3106176

18. Trinkenreich, B., Britto, R., Gerosa, M.A., Steinmacher, I.: An empirical investigation on the challenges faced by women in the software industry: a case study. In: Proceedings of the 2022 ACM/IEEE 44th International Conference on Software Engineering: Software Engineering in Society, pp. 24–35. ICSE-SEIS '22, Association for Computing Machinery, New York, NY, USA (2022). https://doi.org/10.1145/3510458.3513018

19. Trinkenreich, B., Wiese, I., Sarma, A., Gerosa, M., Steinmacher, I.: Women's participation in open source software: A survey of the literature. ACM Trans. Softw. Eng. Methodol. **31**(4) (2022). https://doi.org/10.1145/3510460

20. Varoy, E., Luxton-Reilly, A., Lee, K., Giacaman, N.: Understanding the gender gap in digital technologies education. In: Proceedings of the 25th Australasian Computing Education Conference, pp. 69–76. ACE 2023, Association for Computing Machinery, New York, NY, USA (2023). https://doi.org/10.1145/3576123.3576131

21. Von Mayrhauser, A., Vans, A.M.: Program comprehension during software maintenance and evolution. Computer **28**(8), 44–55 (1995). https://doi.org/10.1109/2.402076

Can Neurofeedback Training Decrease Cognitive Bias? An Exploratory Analysis

Eddy J. Davelaar[(⊠)] [iD]

Birkbeck, University of London, London WC1E 7HX, UK
e.davelaar@bbk.ac.uk

Abstract. Cognitive biases are ubiquitous and finding ways to mitigate them has been an ongoing challenge. Here, we explore the possibility that brain training or neurofeedback could alter a particular bias that presents itself in a card selection task. Specifically, we address the win-stay/lose-shift strategy in the Iowa Gambling Task. Data was analyzed from a large neurofeedback study in which participants were trained to enhance the spectral power in the theta band (4–8 Hz) over 10 sessions. An active control group was included whose members were trained to enhance their sensorimotor rhythm (12–15 Hz). We show that theta power did increase over the sessions and that strategy use was modulated as a consequence. However, the impact was on the P(shift|loss), but not on P(stay|win) or P(WSLS). This was independent of the training group. The results are discussed in terms of different temporal scales associated with neural modulation of P(shift|loss) and P(stay|win). Suggestions for further research are provided in light of challenges during the running of the study.

Keywords: Neurofeedback · Cognitive Bias · Win-Stay/Lose-Shift · Iowa Gambling Task

1 Introduction

In psychology, and in particular the branch focusing on behavior economics, cognitive biases have played a large role in understanding how the human cognitive system operates. The general assumption is that there exists an ideal observer that has infinite cognitive capacity and makes rational decisions. In studies, participants' behavior patterns are then compared against the choices of an ideal observer (or rational agent) and deviations from the ideal are referred to as biases. Understanding the origins of these biases sheds light on how to avoid them and on how people navigate a complex world with places multiple demands on our decision-making capacity. Surprisingly, many of the biases are a consequence of limitations in mental capacity or an overreliance on prior information retrieved from memory. These biases are ubiquitous and might in part be understood as behavioral manifestations of the Law of Effect, which states that behaviors that lead to preferred consequences are more likely to re-occur and that behaviors that had undesirable consequences are less likely to re-occur. Thus, faster good decisions that used prior information will lead to a greater reliance on prior information in the future.

© The Author(s), under exclusive license to Springer Nature Switzerland AG 2024
D. D. Schmorrow and C. M. Fidopiastis (Eds.): HCII 2024, LNAI 14694, pp. 42–51, 2024.
https://doi.org/10.1007/978-3-031-61569-6_3

Depending on the situation, cognitive biases might be desirable, such as to shorten deliberation time. By and large, cognitive biases are discussed in terms of being detrimental, irrational, and in need of being countered. For example, the sunk-cost bias relates to repeating a behavior, which had a negative outcome in the past in the hope that the outcome this time will be positive. Such situations can be very complex, such as repeatedly deploying military personnel to a losing battlefront, or contracting the same company that provided faulty equipment, or buying additional shares in a market after incurring a loss on earlier trades. Of interest is the study by Hafenbrack, et al. [1] who showed that a mindful personality trait is correlated with a lower likelihood of succumbing to the sunk-cost bias. In their study, they found that people with a mindful personality trait were more likely to make choices based on the information at hand and were less influenced by preceding decisions and consequences. In other words, being or becoming mindful may lead people to avoid succumbing to the sunk-cost bias. Is it possible to apply brain training to counter cognitive bias?

When people go into a meditative state, the temporal dynamics of the brain activation changes, as measured objectively using electroencephalography (EEG). When this happens, the frontal part of the brain shows more theta waves [2], which is a relatively slow brain oscillation (4–8 Hz) that is commonly associated with stage 2 sleep. Cognitively, it is thought that theta waves represent a state of idling, which in the context of decision making could mean not making use of any prior information. This sets up the hypothesis that when people put themselves into a theta-dominated brain state, their cognitive biases related to usage of prior information should diminish. To test this hypothesis, we analyzed data from a neurofeedback study in which people were trained to voluntarily enhance their frontal theta activation. The cognitive bias under consideration is a strategy called win-stay/lose-shift strategy that is observable in task such as the Iowa Gambling Task [3]. To date, no neurofeedback investigation into biases have been reported in the literature. We consider the results reported here as exploratory, preliminary, and encouraging, providing a foundation for much-needed further investigation.

1.1 The Iowa Gambling Task and the Win-Stay/Lose-Shift Strategy

The Iowa Gambling Task (IGT) is a card selection task that requires participants to learn which particular deck of cards leads to maximal gain [3]. In the task, participants are presented with four decks of cards, with all cards faced down. On the face of each card is a number that indicates how many points the participant will gain or lose when it is selected. The aim is to accumulate as many points as possible by selecting a total of 100 cards across all decks. Decks C and D contain cards that would lead to a long-term gain and selecting predominantly from decks A and B would lead to a long-term loss. In addition, decks B and D contain cards leading to infrequent large losses, while A and C have equal frequency of gains and losses. The perfect choice is to draw cards only from decks C or D. Actual performance results show that participants first explore the decks and stick with deck D due to the high frequency of winning cards.

Various patterns have been observed in the sequence of card draws. Here, we focus on the Win-Stay/Lose-Shift (WSLS) strategy. The WSLS strategy refers to a sequential pattern of choices where when a positive card is drawn, the person is more likely to draw from the same deck again (win-stay), whereas after a negative card, the person is more likely to choose a different deck (lose-shift). It shares with the sunk-cost bias the influence of the memory of the preceding decision and consequence. The WSLS strategy explains why people shift their responses away from deck C after encountering a negative card, even though the deck has a long-term gain.

Several computational models of the IGT have been developed to understand and account for the entire sequence of card draws (see e.g., [4–6] for recent work). These models contain a common component, which is that each card deck has a value that is equal for all decks at first and over the course of the task differentiates with the better decks accumulating a higher value. The key part in models of the IGT is given in Eq. 1, which states that the value of deck i at time t + 1 is an updating function of the consequence C of selecting a card from deck i at time t. This consequence can be positive or negative.

$$V^i(t + 1) = V^i(t) + C^i(t) \tag{1}$$

Although the precise model details differ from this equation, the influence is the same. That is, the equation shows that when the four decks have similar values, large consequences can change the value rankings of the decks. This would solidify the first ranking position of a winning deck and lower the ranking of a losing deck. Thus, all models using Eq. 1 will have a mechanism through which the WSLS-strategy can be observed, albeit only in the beginning of the sequence of draws. In order to account for WSLS patterns throughout the task, Worthy, Hawthorne and Otto [7] proposed a model that explicitly implemented the strategy using a parameter for P(stay|win) and P(shift|loss). They found that data from half of their participant sample were fitted best with their WSLS model compared to other existing models. Of interest here is that the P(shift|loss) parameter (.89) was more than double the P(stay|win) parameter (.41), instead of equal. The differentiation between win-stay and lose-shift behavior has a neural correlate with modulation of increased frontal negativity following win trials in a block of trials where losses are heavy [8].

In summary, the IGT is a task that promotes a strategy that involves prior decision outcomes influencing current decisions. Modelling and neuroscientific work reveals that the two components of the WSLS-strategy might be dissociable.

1.2 Birkbeck EEG Neurofeedback and Neurophenomenology (BENN) Study

The current exploratory analyses use data from the Birkbeck EEG Neurofeedback and Neurophenomenology (BENN) study that investigated the impact of EEG neurofeedback training protocols on cognitive performance and subjective experiences. The study ran from June 2014 to July 2015 and was an early attempt to obtain detailed data on the impact of brain training on cognitive performance and subjective experience, using a mixed-methods approach. Two training protocols were chosen and were used as active control conditions for each other. The first was upregulation of theta (4–8 Hz) at the frontal (Fz) electrode. The second protocol was upregulation of the sensorimotor rhythm (SMR, 12–15Hz) at the right-central (C4) electrode. The choice of these protocols was based on the reading of the literature indicating differential outcomes with these, which are probably due to the differences in frequency (slow vs fast) and location (frontal vs central). An active control design was chosen, as other control conditions, such as wait-list control, non-training ("placebo"), or non-neurofeedback activity, were inappropriate given the qualitative arm of the study.

The qualitative part of the BENN study involved interviewing trainees after each of four training sessions and also after the very first introductory training session in which frontal alpha (Fz, 8–12 Hz) was upregulated. After the sessions that were not followed by an interview, the trainees completed a diary. The interviews and diaries asked the participants to relive the preceding training session and report their experiences. In an earlier publication [9], we have shown that this neurophenomenological methodology provided insight into the experiences of people who were able to upregulate their frontal alpha within a five minutes training session and those who did not. This led to a follow up study in which the phenomenological narratives were converted into guiding instructions to facilitate neurofeedback training success.

Before and after the entire training period of ten sessions, participants completed a battery of cognitive tests. These were a simple and complex response time (RT) task, the Stroop task, a Stroop task combined with a NoGo condition, the Balloon Analogue Risk-Taking test, and the IGT. All tests were computerized. The rationale for choosing these tasks was that they needed to have a sizeable theoretical literature that included multiple computational models of the cognitive performance. This was important to avoid choosing tasks where there is no consensus on what they measure. As an added bonus it means that the best fitting parameters of the computational models could be used in the statistical analyses to shed light on the mechanisms by which neurofeedback training exerts its impact on cognitive performance (see [10] for an example focusing on the RT and Stroop tasks).

The BENN study produced a wealth of data and explorations are still ongoing to produce further hypotheses that are then followed up in dedicated optimally designed studies. The study also provided insights into administrative and funding challenges when conducting this type of research and into the provision and quality of available hardware and software for neurofeedback research. The current analysis is inspired by a comment made at a public engagement event about whether brain training could be used to counter cognitive bias. The summary of the methodological details reported next are focused on the variables of interest and therefore omits the qualitative arm of the study and the tasks other than the IGT.

2 Methods

2.1 Participants

A total of 39 participants started the study (25 in the theta group, 14 in the SMR group). The unequal group sizes were due to scheduling issues, which meant that we ran out of time and funding. Out of 39, 25 participants (16 in the theta group, 10 in the SMR group) completed the study. Reasons for the 33% loss of participants are "loss of interest", no shows, "scheduled holidays", and "too busy a life to commit to multiple training sessions".

2.2 Design

The study conformed to a mixed factorial design with training group as the between-subject factor and test session (pre-/post-training) as within-subject factor. EEG frequency power and cognitive task performance were used as outcome variables. A correlational design was also used when assessing the association between the EEG data and cognitive task performance.

2.3 Materials and Procedure

The Iowa Gambling Task was computerized using E-prime software (version 2.0.10.242) and run on a desktop PC running Windows 7 operating system. Participants were seated at a distance of approximately 50 cm from the monitor and received written instructions on the screen, which were reinforced by the experimenter. In the task, participants would see the back of four playing cards with the digits 1, 2, 3, and 4 underneath each card. They were instructed that each card would have a number that would either increase or decrease their running total. In order to strengthen the subjective impact of a loss, no startup amount was provided. This necessarily means that a total score less than zero is possible. Participants were instructed to draw 100 cards in such way to maximize the cumulative total. The structure of the payoff scheme is shown in Fig. 1, which differs from the one used by Bechara et al. [3].

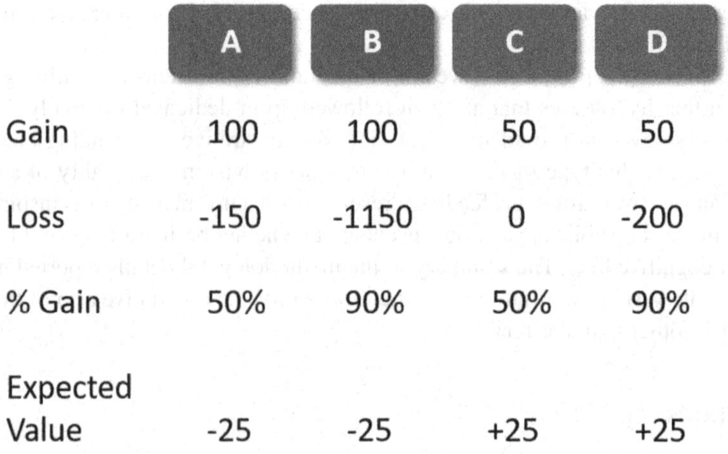

	A	B	C	D
Gain	100	100	50	50
Loss	-150	-1150	0	-200
% Gain	50%	90%	50%	90%
Expected Value	-25	-25	+25	+25

Fig. 1. Payoff scheme used for the Iowa Gambling Task. Each (virtual) deck of cards has cards with values under gain or loss and the given frequency. The expected value for each deck indicates that decks C and D are the normative advantageous decks.

The neurofeedback training sessions were scheduled for 2 to 3 times per week and included five blocks of five minutes each. An electrode was attached using conductive gel at location Fz or C4 based on the group allocation. The left and right mastoid were used as reference and ground, respectively. The sampling rate of the EEG neurofeedback software was 256 Hz and the impedance was kept below 10 kΩ. Of the five blocks, the first block was a resting-state block during which the participant would sit quietly with eyes open. The recording from this first block was used to set a threshold for the training blocks in that session. During the second, third, and fourth blocks, which were the training blocks, participants would see their EEG timeseries scrolling from right to left and a yellow bar extending or contracting vertically based on the power of the assigned EEG frequency band. Whenever, the power remained above the threshold for 250 ms, a counter would increase by one and the sound of a bell would come over the speakers. The fifth and final block was designed to be a block during which participants would try to increase the power in the target frequency band, but without receiving feedback. However, this proved too difficult and some participants invariably treated this block as a resting-state block in some sessions. Hence, these blocks were excluded from any analysis.

2.4 Data Integrity

Loss of data occurred during two iterations of software updates, which resulted in overwriting of earlier saved data files and corrupting the data log file. Although the EEG recordings were backed up every two weeks, data from the first half of November 2014 was unrecoverable, affecting data from both groups and the SMR group in particular. As a result, not all first and final sessions were available. Therefore, the resting block from the earliest and the latest available sessions were used. For the Theta group, there were 13 blocks from session 1, 3 blocks from session 2, 15 blocks from session 10 and 1 block from session 8. For the SMR group, there were 8 blocks from session 1, 1 block from session 2, 1 block from session 3, 8 blocks from session 10, 1 block from session 8, and 1 block from session 4. The loss of data from the SMR training sessions meant that there were too few remaining participants from whom to estimate full learning curves (over the 10 sessions) for comparison against the theta training group. In addition, only from 10 participants in the theta-training group full learning curves could be created.

2.5 Data Processing

The IGT data consisted of a sequence of 100 card selections per participant. These were processed to create the following outcome variables: total accumulated points, P(stay|win), P(shift|loss), and P(WSLS).

The neurofeedback software provided amplitudes of theta and SMR for each session-block. However, due to the proprietary nature of the software algorithms, no details on the data processing is available. Therefore, in addition to conducting the analyses with the provided amplitudes, we also processed the raw data separately. For this, all EEG recordings were divided into windows of 2 s with a 50% overlap. Windows that were associated with more than 1% signal failure or that contained eye blinks or other muscle artefacts were excluded from data processing. The remaining windows were mean-centered, windowed using a hamming window, and subjected to spectral decomposition between 0 and 40 Hz in steps of 0.5 Hz. The relative spectral power in the SMR (12–15 Hz) and theta (4–8 Hz) bands were extracted for each window and averaged for each participant. Available values per participant were the mean relative theta and SMR power for the resting-state blocks of the first and final sessions, the associated mean amplitudes, and, for some from the theta-training group, the mean amplitudes of the training blocks.

2.6 Data Analysis Strategy

The data was analyzed in two steps. In the first step, the IGT and neural data were subjected to a 2 × 2 mixed ANOVA. Due to the exploratory nature, no adjustment of multiple comparisons was made. In the second step, the difference in resting-state frequency power from the first to the final session was correlated with the difference in the IG-variable. In a final analysis, the slope of the regression function fitted to learning curves of the theta-training participants were used as predictors of the change in IGT-variable (see [11] for a similar approach in the context of frontal alpha and Stroop performance).

3 Results

3.1 Iowa Gambling Task Performance

Table 1 shows the overall behavioral results. It is immediately clear that this version of the gambling task was challenging and that participants made net losses. In fact, from the 26 participants, only 9 managed to obtain a net gain. However, at the group level the total points were not significantly different from zero. The P(stay|win) were not significantly different from chance (= 0.5), but were lower than P(shift|loss), which were all significantly above chance (as indicated in Table 1). This is consistent with Worthy et al.'s [7] modelling work showing that P(shift|loss) > P(stay|win). Although only the P(WSLS) in the SMR group after training was above chance, when the data of both training groups were pooled together for the pre-training test session, the overall results were marginally significant above chance, $t(25) = 1.91, p = .067$, suggesting that the small sample size masked the small effects. This is also the explanation behind the lack of any significant effect in the 2 x 2 mixed ANOVAs conducted for these four variables.

Table 1. Results for the Iowa Gambling Task (means and standard deviations)

	Theta training group (N = 16)		SMR training group (N = 10)	
IGT-variable	Before training	After training	Before training	After training
Total points	−675 (2233)	−121.88 (2022)	−1215 (2346)	−895 (2075)
P(stay|win)	.54 (.21)	.44 (.28)	.53 (.26)	.61 (.19)
P(shift|loss)	.72 (.26)**	.77 (.26)***	.78 (.25)**	.72 (.28)*
P(WSLS)	.56 (.17)	.49 (.23)	.57 (.21)	.62 (.16)*

*** p < .001, ** p < .01, * p < .05 compared to chance (= .50).

3.2 EEG Profiles

Table 2 summarizes the means and standard deviations of the EEG variables. The 2 x 2 mixed ANOVAs revealed a marginal effect of time on the theta amplitude, $F(1, 24) = 3.20$, $p = .086$, $MSe = 0.562$, partial $\eta^2 = .12$, which was due to a increase from the first to the last session. Although the SMR group had lower numerical scores, the group difference was not significant ($p = .101$). For the SMR amplitude, there was a significant effect of time, $F(1, 24) = 5.54$, $p = .027$, $MSe = 0.121$, partial $\eta^2 = .19$, and a marginal group difference, $F(1, 24) = 3.76$, $p = .064$, $MSe = 0.222$, partial $\eta^2 = .14$. All other unreported main effects and interactions were not significant. As mentioned above, the computation of the amplitudes is unknown and hence relative scores were computed to control for any systematic differences related to signal quality across groups and sessions. The relative theta and the relative SMR power did not reveal any significant patterns. Given that the expectation is that participants in the theta training group would enhance their relative theta power, a paired t-test was conducted. As expected, relative theta power did increase in the theta training group, $t(15) = 2.26$, $p = .039$, but the relative SMR power also increased, albeit marginally, $t(15) = 2.08$, $p = .055$. In the SMR group, neither of the relative frequency powers reached significance, which means that despite the training sessions they did not manage to increase their resting-state SMR frequency.

Table 2. Results for EEG variables (means and standard deviations)

Resting-state EEG variable	Theta training group (N = 16)		SMR training group (N = 10)	
	Before training	After training	Before training	After training
Theta amplitude	3.60 (0.87)	3.89 (1.28)	2.74 (1.49)	3.21 (1.39)
SMR amplitude	1.29 (0.21)	1.45 (0.55)	0.96 (0.47)	1.26 (0.32)
Relative theta power	.0196 (.0027)[a]	.0215 (.0029)[a]	.0195 (.0043)	.0199 (.0031)
Relative SMR power	.0084 (.0011)	.0095 (.0026)	.0088 (.0021)	.0089 (.0017)

[a] significant difference

3.3 Covariation Between EEG Frequency Band Power and IGT-Variables

The preceding results sections may imply that there is no association between change in brain activation and change in cognitive performance. However, group level differences across time are statistically independent from brain-behavior associations at the individual level. Hence, the next analyses focused on covariation of changes in brain measures and cognitive measures. To do this, differences between post- and pre-training test sessions were calculated for all four IGT and all four EEG variables. These were then correlated, separately for each training group and in combination. As the total sample size is low for correlational analyses, almost all correlations were non-significant, although not necessarily small. However, two meaningful correlations were obtained.

First, the change in relative theta power correlated with the change in P(shift|loss), $r(26)$ = $.37$, $p < .05$. Second, the linear slope of the learning curve for the 10 participants in the theta-training group also correlated with the change in P(shift|loss), $r(10) = .64$, $p < .05$. None of the other correlations reached significance.

4 Discussion

In this analysis, we sought to find evidence pertaining whether training in increasing theta brain wave would have an impact on the WSLS-strategy observable in the IGT. Although hampered by diminished statistical power, the results show that increases in theta power is associated with increases in P(shift|loss). Therefore, although the answer to the question whether theta neurofeedback training can counter the win-stay/lose-shift strategy is negative, based on the current data, we did find that one component (lose-shift) is enhanced.

These results support the findings by Forder and Dyson [8] who observed a neural dissociation between win-stay and lose-shift behavior. In particular, they noted a contextual modulation of feedback related negativity over frontal brain electrodes for win trials, but not for loss (or draw) trials in a Rock-Paper-Scissors task. The current findings complement this picture when assuming that neural modulation of win-stay and lose-shift behaviour occur at different timescales, with the former on shorter timescales scales than the latter.

The lack of a training effect in the SMR group could be due to several factors. First and foremost, it may require more than 10 sessions to observe significant results within participants. In addition, the protocol only used the SMR signal for the feedback. In other work [12], we combined upregulation of SMR frequency with suppression of theta rhythm (to counter sleepiness during training) and suppression of upper beta (to counter strategy of muscle clamping). After 15 training sessions, we observed significant increases in resting-state SMR. Thus, only using the SMR signal for feedback might not be the best training strategy. The other, more statistical reason, could be that the number of participants in the training group and the proportion of those participants that are particularly able to be trained. These insights will inform better research designs that looks at SMR neurofeedback.

There are a number of limitations to the current analyses. First of all, the design was not optimized to investigate changes in WSLS-strategy use. To do this, the sequence of gains and losses could be adjusted to clearly identify the strategy used. In addition, at least one task could be added that promotes the usage of the WSLS-strategy. An obvious candidate is Rock-Paper-Scissors. The second limitation is the sensitivity to the neurofeedback research design to software malfunction, participant drop-out rate, and time availability. This greatly impacted data acquisition and the final available sample size and therefore statistical power. One approach to mitigate these issues is to conduct a multi-site neurofeedback study, where the risk is spread and larger sample sizes can be obtained within the same time frame, even with a similar dropout rate. A final limitation is that the EEG was not recorded during the IGT. Although not strictly a limitation of this study, having the EEG recording during the IGT could identify whether those participants who increased their theta power exhibit different in-task EEG dynamics than those who did not increase (or even decreased) their resting-state theta power.

These limitations aside, the current results are considered to be at pilot level and should encourage further investigation using dedicated research designs. Here, we have shown encouraging results suggesting that brain training could in principle modulate cognitive biases. This opens up a wide range of possibilities and research questions to be explored further.

Acknowledgments. The author acknowledges the work by the BENN data collection team, Soma Almasi, Joe Barnby, Emily Hickson, Natasha Maia, and Christian Ramtale. The BENN study was funded by a Wellcome/Birkbeck ISSF Mid-Career Award ref 204790/z/16/z and a School of Science Research Grant to Eddy Davelaar and Virginia Eatough.

Disclosure of Interests. The author has no competing interests to declare that are relevant to the content of this article.

References

1. Hafenbrack, A.C., Kinias, Z., Barsade, S.G.: Debiasing the mind through meditation: mindfulness and the sunk-cost bias. Psychol. Sci. **25**(2), 369–376 (2014)
2. Ivanovski, B., Malhi, G.S.: The psychological and neurophysiological concomitants of mindfulness forms of meditation. Acta Neuropsychiatry **19**(2), 76–91 (2007)
3. Bechara, A., Damasio, A.R., Damasio, H., Anderson, S.W.: Insensitivity to future consequences following damage to human prefrontal cortex. Cognition **50**(1–3), 7–15 (1994)
4. Haines, N., Vassileva, J., Ahn, W.Y.: The outcome-representation learning model: a novel reinforcement learning model of the Iowa gambling task. Cogn. Sci. **42**(8), 2534–2561 (2018)
5. Ligneul, R.: Sequential exploration in the Iowa gambling task: validation of a new computational model in a large dataset of young and old healthy participants. PLoS Comput. Biol. **15**(6), e1006989 (2019)
6. Steingroever, H., Wetzels, R., Wagenmakers, E.-J.: A comparison of reinforcement learning models for the Iowa Gambling Task using parameter space partitioning. J. Prob. Solv. **5**(2), 1–32 (2013)
7. Worthy, D.A., Hawthorne, M.J., Otto, A.R.: Heterogeneity of strategy use in the Iowa gambling task: a comparison of win-stay/lose-shift and reinforcement learning models. Psychon. Bull. Rev. **20**(2), 364–371 (2013)
8. Forder, L., Dyson, B.J.: Behavioural and neural modulation of win-stay but not lose-shift strategies as a function of outcome value in Rock, Paper Scissors. Sci. Rep. **6**, 33809 (2016)
9. Davelaar, E.J., Barnby, J.M., Almasi, S., Eatough, V.: Differential subjective experiences in learners and non-learners in frontal alpha neurofeedback: piloting a mixed-method approach. Front. Hum. Neurosci. **12**, 402 (2018)
10. Davelaar, E.J.: Testing the specificity of EEG neurofeedback training on first- and second-order measures of attention. In: Schmorrow, D.D., Fidopiastis, C.M. (eds.) AC 2017. LNCS (LNAI), vol. 10284, pp. 19–27. Springer, Cham (2017). https://doi.org/10.1007/978-3-319-58628-1_2
11. Berger, A.M., Davelaar, E.J.: Frontal alpha oscillations and attentional control: a virtual reality neurofeedback study. Neuroscience **378**, 189–197 (2018)
12. Davelaar, E.J., Jilek, J.: Sensorimotor rhythm is associated with reinforcement learning and cognitive impulsivity: a neurofeedback study. Curr. Neurobiol. **11**(2), 27–36 (2020)

Deciphering Emotional Responses to Music: A Fusion of Psychophysiological Data Analysis and LSTM Predictive Modeling

Maheep Mahat$^{(\boxtimes)}$ and Denis Gracanin

Virginia Tech, Blacksburg, VA 24060, USA
{maheepmahat,gracanin}@vt.edu

Abstract. This paper presents a comprehensive study on the utilization of the "Emotion in Motion" database, the world's largest repository of psychophysiological data elicited by musical stimuli. Our work is centered around three key endeavors. First, we developed an interactive online platform to visualize and engage with the database, providing a user-friendly interface for researchers and enthusiasts alike to explore the intricate relationships between music and physiological responses. This platform stands as a significant contribution to the field, offering novel ways to interact with and interpret the complex data. Second, we conducted an in-depth correlation analysis of the physiological signals using Dynamic Time Warping within the database. By categorizing the data into two main genres of music — classical and modern — and further subdividing them into three age-specific groups, we gleaned valuable insights into how different demographics respond to varied musical styles. This segmentation illuminated the nuanced interplay between age, music genre, and physiological reactions, contributing to a deeper understanding of music's emotional impact. Finally, we developed a predictive model using Long Short-Term Memory (LSTM) networks, capable of processing Electrodermal Activity (EDA) and Pulse Oximetry (POX) signals. Our model adopts a sequence-to-vector prediction approach, effectively forecasting seven distinct emotional attributes in response to musical stimuli. This LSTM-based model represents a significant advancement in predictive analytics for music-induced emotions, showcasing the potential of machine learning in deciphering complex human responses to art. Our work not only provides novel tools and insights for analyzing psychophysiological data but also opens new avenues for understanding the emotional power of music across different demographics, ultimately bridging gaps between music psychology, physiology, and computational analysis.

Keywords: Psychophysiology · Electrodermal Activity · Pulse Oximetry · LSTM · DTW

© The Author(s), under exclusive license to Springer Nature Switzerland AG 2024
D. D. Schmorrow and C. M. Fidopiastis (Eds.): HCII 2024, LNAI 14694, pp. 52–67, 2024.
https://doi.org/10.1007/978-3-031-61569-6_4

1 Introduction

The intricate relationship between music and its emotional impact on listeners has long captivated researchers across various disciplines. This intersection of music psychology, physiology, and computational analysis offers profound insights into the human emotional experience. The "Emotion in Motion" database, renowned as the world's largest repository of psychophysiological responses to musical stimuli, provides an unprecedented opportunity to explore this domain [1,2]. Our research harnesses this extensive dataset to unravel the complex dynamics of emotional responses elicited by music, leveraging advanced analytical and machine learning techniques.

The primary objective of our study is threefold. Firstly, we aim to democratize access to this rich dataset by creating an interactive online platform. This platform is designed not only for researchers in the field but also for a broader audience interested in the study of music-induced emotions. It facilitates an intuitive exploration of the data, enabling users to visualize and interact with the diverse array of physiological signals recorded in response to musical pieces.

Secondly, we delve into the dataset to conduct a comprehensive correlation analysis. By categorizing the physiological signals based on musical genres—classical and modern—and further stratifying them across three distinct age groups, we seek to uncover patterns and correlations that may illuminate how demographic factors influence emotional responses to different types of music. This analysis is pivotal in understanding the subjective nature of musical perception and its physiological manifestations.

Lastly, at the forefront of our study is the development of a predictive model using Long Short-Term Memory (LSTM) networks. This model is tailored to process two key physiological signals: Electrodermal Activity (EDA) and Pulse Oximetry (POX). Employing a sequence-to-vector prediction approach, the model is designed to predict a spectrum of seven emotional attributes in response to music. This innovative application of LSTM in the realm of music psychology represents a significant leap in predictive analytics, offering a nuanced understanding of the emotional effects of music.

Through this multifaceted approach, our research not only contributes valuable tools and analyses to the field of music-induced emotion study but also underscores the potential of integrating machine learning with psychophysiological data. As we explore these emotional undercurrents, we shed light on the universal yet deeply personal experience of music, opening pathways for future interdisciplinary research in this fascinating area.

2 Literature Review

The study of psychophysiology in response to music, particularly focusing on EAD and POX, presents a unique area of research. Boucsein's book on EDA [3] is a comprehensive source that covers its role in psychophysiology, offering a deep dive into its biological aspects and practical applications. Complementing this,

Figner and Murphy [4] discuss the use of skin conductance, a key component of EDA, in judgment and decision-making re-search. Tobin [5] provides essential knowledge on POX, particularly its importance in intensive care monitoring, contributing to our understanding of physiological monitoring.

The emotional impact of music is an area rich with research. Juslin and Västfjäll examine the various emotional responses triggered by music and the processes behind them, highlighting the complexity of this interaction [6]. Similarly, the work of Tomic and Janata on temporal patterns in music [7] offers insights into the importance of rhythm and its psychological effects. In terms of computational analysis, the use of Hidden Markov Models in music mood classification by Eghbalzadeh et al. [8] and Müller's examination of dynamic time warping [9], showcase the application of these techniques in understanding music's influence on emotions.

Research by Salimpoor et al. sheds light on the physiological basis of musical experiences, particularly the role of dopamine in emotional experiences related to music [10]. Hodges further expands on this by discussing various psychophysiological measures used in the context of musical emotion [12]. The foundational work by Cacioppo et al. [13] provides a broad overview of psychophysiology, setting the groundwork for understanding these measurements. The challenges in recording and visualizing psychophysiological data are discussed by Stern et al. [13] and Fairclough [14], emphasizing the complexities involved in interpreting such data.

Visualization techniques, important for understanding psychophysiological data, are explored in various studies. Keil et al. offer guidelines for data visualization in electroencephalography and magnetoencephalography [15], while Francois and Miall present 3D visualization techniques for functional data [16].

The practical application of these visualization techniques in gaming research is highlighted by Kivikangas et al. [17], and Mandryk and Atkins demonstrate their use in continuous emotion modeling [18]. Finally, looking at future trends, Healey and Picard discuss the application of physiological sensors in real-world settings, pointing towards the growing importance of wearable technology and data visualization in psychophysiological research [20].

3 Methodology

Our methodology encompasses a multifaceted approach to understanding the emotional impact of music through psychophysiological data. Initially, we established an interactive platform for the "Emotion in Motion" database, enabling effective visualization and interaction with extensive psychophysiological data, including EDA and POX signals. This platform not only facilitated access to detailed participant data but also provided a synchronized view of EDA and POX responses with audio stimuli, allowing for a simulated real-time analysis of participants' emotional responses.

Building upon this foundation, we employed Dynamic Time Warping (DTW) for a thorough correlation analysis, categorizing musical pieces into classical and modern genres and further dividing listener responses by age groups. This stratification resulted in detailed heatmaps, elucidating patterns across different demographics.

Finally, we developed an LSTM predictive model, intricately designed to process combined EDA and POX sequences. This model, through its complex architecture comprising multiple LSTM layers and a dense output layer, was trained to predict emotional attributes from physiological responses, providing a deep understanding of the interplay between music, emotion, and physiological change.

3.1 Emotion in Motion Platform

The foundation of our research methodology involved the development of a specialized platform for visualizing the "Emotion in Motion" database. This platform was designed to facilitate access to participant data, allowing for an in-depth exploration of their physiological responses to musical stimuli.

A key feature of this platform is its ability to provide a coordinated multiple-view display, integrating both EDA and POX responses. This integration is synchronized meticulously with the audio tracks, enabling a simulated real-time feed-back mechanism. Such a setup offers a dynamic and comprehensive view of the participants' reactions, capturing the nuances of their psychophysiological responses as they experience different pieces of music.

By leveraging this platform, we were able to not only observe but also quantitatively analyze the intricate interplay between the emotional impacts of music and corresponding physiological changes. This innovative approach to data visualization and interaction stands as a cornerstone of our methodology, paving the way for a more nuanced understanding of the relationship between music and its emotional and physiological effects on listeners.

3.2 Physiological Responses Analysis

T-Test Analysis on Rating Based Emotion Responses for People with and Without Hearing Impairment: Each individual was asked to rate their feeling for 7 different emotions on a scale of 1 to 5. To examine the impact of hearing impairments on individuals' emotional and experiential responses to music, we conducted a series of Independent Samples T-tests. Our objective was to compare the ratings across seven different attributes—activity, engagement, familiarity, tension, positivity, power, and like/dislike—between two distinct groups: individuals with hearing impairments and those without.

Our initial dataset comprised responses from a collection of trials, each associated with multiple media items and corresponding ratings for the aforementioned attributes. To ensure a balanced comparison, we first identified the top 10 most popular media items within the dataset based on their frequency of occurrence in the specified experiment. This step ensured that our analysis focused on media items with sufficient data coverage across trials.

Given the potential for missing or incomplete ratings within the trials, we implemented a preprocessing step to handle such instances. Specifically, for trials where the ratings for a particular media item were not provided, we replaced the missing values with zeros. This approach allowed us to maintain consistency in the dataset, ensuring that each trial contributed equally to the subsequent analysis without introducing bias from incomplete data.

We segregated the trials into two groups based on the presence of hearing impairments, as reported in the trial responses. This segregation resulted in two distinct sets of data for comparison: one representing ratings from individuals with hearing impairments (215 trials) and another from individuals without hearing impairments. To balance the groups for statistical comparison, we randomly selected 215 trials from the larger group of individuals without hearing impairments, matching the sample size of the group with impairments.

For each of the seven attributes, we conducted an Independent Samples T-test to compare the mean ratings between the two groups. The T-statistic was computed to measure the difference in means relative to the variability observed within the groups, while the P-value was used to assess the statistical significance of the observed differences. A P-value threshold of 0.05 was predetermined to denote statistical significance (Table 1).

The analysis yielded the following results:

Table 1. Result of T-test analysis

Emotions	T-statistic	P value %
Activity	0.872	0.384
Engagement	−1.019	0.309
Familiarity	1.140	0.255
Positivity	−0.375	0.708
Power	1.290	0.198
Tension	0.575	0.566
Likeness	−0.118	0.906

Activity, Engagement, Positivity, Like/Dislike: The negative T-statistics for "activity", "engagement", "positivity", and "like and dislike" suggest that the mean ratings for these attributes are lower in the group with hearing impairments compared to the group without, but none of these differences are statistically significant (P-values are all well above 0.05). Familiarity, Power: Conversely, the positive T-statistics for "familiarity" and "power" suggest higher mean ratings in the group with hearing impairments compared to those without. Again, these differences are not statistically significant, as indicated by P-values above 0.05.

Familiarity, Power: Conversely, the positive T-statistics for "familiarity" and "power" suggest higher mean ratings in the group with hearing impairments compared to those without. Again, these differences are not statistically significant, as indicated by P-values above 0.05.

Tension: "Tension" has a positive T-statistic, suggesting a slightly higher mean rating among the group with impairments, but the difference is not statistically significant (P-value = 0.566).

None of the attributes exhibited statistically significant differences between the groups, as all P-values exceeded the 0.05 threshold. This suggests that within the scope of our dataset and analysis, hearing impairments do not significantly affect how individuals rate their experience across the tested music attributes. It is important to note that the lack of statistical significance does not imply an absence of differences but rather indicates that any potential differences were not detectable with the employed statistical tests under the study conditions.

T-Test Analysis of EDA Signals for People with and Without Hearing Impairment: Continuing our analysis, Our investigation sought to examine physiological responses through Electrodermal Activity (EDA) signals among individuals with and without hearing impairments. To facilitate a balanced comparison, we selected a sample size of 150 individuals for each group, ensuring an equal representation of participants with and without hearing impairments. This sample size was determined to provide sufficient statistical power for detecting meaningful differences between the groups while maintaining manageability for detailed signal analysis.

The EDA signals were acquired under controlled environmental conditions to minimize external influences on physiological responses. Following data collection, a series of preprocessing steps were applied to each signal to ensure consistency and comparability across the participant pool. These preprocessing steps included:

Noise Filtering: Application of low-pass filters to remove high-frequency noise, which is not relevant to the EDA responses of interest.

Normalization: Adjustment of signal amplitude across participants to a common scale, accounting for individual variations in baseline skin conductance levels.

Length Standardization: To facilitate direct comparison of signals across all participants, each EDA signal was standardized to a uniform length. This was achieved through truncation of longer signals and padding of shorter signals with zeros, ensuring that all processed signals contained an identical number of data points, conducive to aggregate analysis. These preprocessing efforts aimed to refine the EDA signals into a format amenable to feature extraction and subsequent statistical analysis, laying a foundation for rigorous comparison of physiological responses between individuals with and without hearing impairments.

From the preprocessed EDA signals, we extracted key features representing the physiological responses of interest. These features included the frequency and amplitude of Skin Conductance Responses (SCRs), reflective of autonomic arousal in response to stimuli. Each EDA signal was analyzed to identify SCR events, with the mean SCR amplitude and frequency calculated for each participant.

To assess the impact of hearing impairment on autonomic arousal, we conducted independent samples T-tests comparing the mean SCR amplitude and frequency between groups (individuals with versus without hearing impairments). The analysis aimed to determine if hearing impairment was associated with significant differences in physiological responses to stimuli.

The T-test comparing the mean SCR amplitude yielded a T-statistic of 0.9587219179851065 and a P-value of 0.33847603147970595. Similarly, the comparison of SCR frequency produced analogous statistical values, indicating the comparative analysis's outcome. The statistical analysis revealed no significant differences in the EDA signal features between individuals with and without hearing impairments. The T-statistic values indicated a minimal difference in mean SCR amplitude and frequency between the two groups, while the P-values (above the conventional alpha level of 0.05) suggested that these differences were not statistically significant.

Our findings suggest that, within the scope of the analyzed EDA signal features, hearing impairment does not significantly affect the physiological responses measured through EDA. This outcome contributes to our understanding of the autonomic nervous system's response to stimuli in populations with sensory impairments, indicating that the presence of hearing impairment may not substantially alter the physiological markers of arousal and emotional engagement as captured by EDA.

Dynamic Time Warping for Physiological Signal Responses Analysis: A pivotal aspect of our research methodology was the implementation of Dynamic Time Warping (DTW) for the analysis of physiological responses. Initially, we applied DTW to analyze the EDA signals, comparing them against each other to identify patterns and correlations. A similar approach was adopted for POX signals, allowing us to delve into the intricate dynamics of these physiological responses.

The crux of the DTW algorithm lies in the construction and computation of a cost matrix, which encapsulates the distance between each pair of elements from two sequences being compared. Let's consider two sequences $X = x_1, x_2, ..., x_m$ and $Y = y_1, y_2, ..., y_n$, where m and n represent their respective lengths. The cost matrix D is initialized with dimensions $(m + 1) \times (n + 1)$, and all elements are set to infinity, except for $D[0][0]$, which is initialized to 0. This matrix will store the cumulative distances between points across both sequences.

The core of the DTW algorithm involves iteratively filling this matrix. For each element $D[i][j]$, the algorithm calculates the distance between (x_i, y_j), typically using a measure such as the Euclidean distance. This distance is then added to the minimum of the three adjacent elements $(D[i-1][j], D[i][j-1]$, and $D[i-1][j-1])$ in the cost matrix, corresponding to the operations of insertion, deletion, and match, respectively. This process is succinctly captured in the following Python code snippet:

```
for i in range (1, m+1):
    for j in range (1, n+1):
        cost = distance (x_i, y_j)
        D[i][j] = cost + min(D[i-1] [j], D[i][j-1],   D[i-1][j-1])
```

Here, `distance (x_i, y_j)` computes the chosen distance metric between the elements (x_i, y_j). The cumulative minimum cost at each matrix cell ultimately leads to the total cost of aligning the two sequences, found at $D[m][n]$.

To deepen our analysis, we segmented the audio signals into two distinct categories: classical music and modern music. This classification was crucial in understanding how different genres of music elicited varying physiological responses. Furthermore, we divided the participants into three age groups — 20 to 30, 30 to 50, and 50 to 80 years-to explore age-related variations in response to these musical categories. For each age range and music genre, we performed DTW, leading to a comprehensive set of analyses across six distinct groupings for each signal type.

This systematic approach yielded a total of 12 different results, visualized as heatmaps: EDA for classical music (Fig. 1), EDA for modern music (Fig. 2), POX for classical music (Fig. 3), and POX for modern music (Fig. 4). These heatmaps provided a clear, intuitive representation of the correlations within each group, offering insights into how age and music genre influenced the EDA and POX signals. In addition to these 12 results, we also generated two additional heatmaps by applying DTW to compare EDA signals with each other and POX signals with each other.

The heatmaps served as a visual guide to under-standing the complex relationships between the physiological responses and the musical stimuli, considering both the type of music and the age of the listener. This comprehensive approach allowed us to uncover nuanced patterns and trends in the data, providing a deeper understanding of the psychophysiological impact of music across different demographics and genres.

3.3   Model to Predict Emotional Attributes

Building upon the foundation of our methodology, we developed an LSTM predictive model with a carefully structured architecture to analyze and predict emotional responses based on physiological data (EDA and POX signals). The model was designed to process sequences of combined EDA and POX data, mapping these to predictions about emotional states as induced by musical stimuli.

The LSTM model's efficacy in handling sequential data stems from its unique gating mechanisms, governed by several key equations. Each LSTM unit comprises three gates: the input gate i (Eq. 1), the forget gate f (Eq. 2), and the output gate o (Eq. 3), alongside a cell state C (Eq. 4) that holds the memory for hidden state update h (Eq. 5).

$$i_t = \sigma(W_i \cdot [h_{t-1}, x_t] + b_i) \tag{1}$$

$$f_t = \sigma(W_f \cdot [h_{t-1}, x_t] + b_f) \tag{2}$$

$$o_t = \sigma(W_o \cdot [h_{t-1}, x_t] + b_o) \tag{3}$$

$$\tilde{C}_t = \tanh(W_C \cdot [h_{t-1}, x_t] + b_C) \qquad C_t = f_t * C_{t-1} + i_t * \tilde{C}_t \tag{4}$$

$$h_t = o_t * \tanh(C_t) \tag{5}$$

σ represents the sigmoid activation function, tanh is the hyperbolic tangent activation function, W and b denote the weights and biases of the respective gates, (h_{t-1}) is the previous hidden state, x_t is the current input, and $*$ denotes element-wise multiplication. These equations collectively enable the LSTM to regulate the flow of information, making selective decisions about what to retain or discard over time, which is crucial for learning from long and complex sequences.

Model Architecture and Layers. The model was instantiated using Keras' Sequential API, a linear stack of layers that allows for the easy building of deep learning models. The first layer in our model is an LSTM layer with 150 units. This number of units was chosen to ensure sufficient model complexity to capture the nuances in the data without causing overfitting. The input shape for this layer was set to $(2200, 2)$, reflecting our data's structure with 2200 time steps and two features per time step (one for EDA, one for POX). The *return sequences* parameter was set to *True*, enabling the layer to return the full sequence of outputs for each input sequence, a necessary configuration for sequence-to-sequence learning.

A second LSTM layer, also with 150 units, was added. This layer, with *return sequences* set to *False*, returns only the last output in the output sequence. This setup helps in reducing the dimensionality of the output and prepares it for the final dense layer.

The model's output layer is a Dense layer with 7 units, corresponding to the seven emotional attributes we aim to predict. Each unit in this layer provides a prediction for one of the emotional attributes, giving us a multi-dimensional output that encapsulates the predicted emotional state based on the input physiological data.

Compilation and Training. The model was compiled using the *adam* optimizer. Adam is an adaptive learning rate optimizer that has proven effective in various deep learning applications. It is particularly well-suited for datasets with noisy and sparse gradients. For the loss function, Mean Squared Error was employed, aligning with our goal of predicting continuous variables (ratings of emotional attributes). This loss function computes the mean of the squares of the differences between predicted and actual values, making it suitable for regression tasks.

The training process involved feeding the combined EDA and POX sequences and the corresponding emotional ratings into the model. We set the number of epochs to 150 and the batch size to 32. The choice of 150 epochs was based on the observation of the loss value. We observed that the loss value did not change noticeably after 150 epochs and so we concluded it was sufficient for the model to converge without over-fitting. A validation split of 20 percent was used during training to monitor the model's performance on unseen data, ensuring generalizability and preventing overfitting.

Model Evaluation. Post-training, the model's performance was evaluated using a separate test dataset. The loss on this test dataset was computed to assess the model's predictive accuracy on new, unseen data. This evaluation step is crucial to understand the model's practical applicability and its ability to generalize beyond the training data.

The outcome of the LSTM model is a set of predictions for the seven emotional attributes, based on the input physiological data sequences. These predictions represent the model's understanding and mapping of complex physiological signals to specific emotional states, offering a novel approach to deciphering the emotional impact of music through machine learning. This model, with its intricate architecture and careful training, stands as a significant contribution to the field, demonstrating the potential of deep learning in understanding and predicting human emotional responses.

4   Evaluation and Results

In our sequence analysis, we utilized DTW to investigate relationships within our dataset, focusing on two music categories: classical and modern. For each category, we conducted DTW analysis on three age ranges—20 to 30, 30 to 50, and 50 to 80 years for both EDA and POX signals. For each age range, we had a sample space of 50 for EDA and 25 for POX signals. The sample space for both classical and modern music were 10 songs. This led to twelve DTW heatmaps per music type, each visualizing the physiological response patterns across different age groups. These heatmaps effectively demonstrated the variance in responses to music genres across demographics, showcasing DTW's utility in elucidating complex physiological data patterns.

The analysis of the distance matrix reveals distinct patterns in how physiological responses vary with musical genres.

Age 20 to 30 (EDA): In Fig. 1, we can observe from the image on left that for age group of 20 to 30, when listening to classical music, there seems to be very high similarity between the EDA signals of the participants.

Age 30 to 50 (EDA): In Fig. 1, we can observe from the image on the center that for the age range of 30 to 50, when listening to classical music, there seems to be somewhat less similarity between the EDA signals but overall, the signals seem to be mostly similar to each other.

Age 50 to 80 (EDA): In Fig. 1, we can observe from the image on the right that for the age range of 50 to 80, when listening to classical music, there seems to be very high similarity between the EDA signals of the participants.

Age 20 to 30 (EDA): In Fig. 2, we can observe from the image on left that for age group of 20 to 30, when listening to modern music, there seems to be somewhat dissimilarity between the EDA signals in comparison to when this group listened to classical music.

Age 30 to 50 (EDA): In Fig. 2, we can observe from the image on the center that for the age range of 30 to 50, when listening to modern music, there seems to be somewhat less similarity between the EDA signals and in comparison to when they listened to classical music, their EDA signal responses seem to be similar overall.

Age 50 to 80 (EDA): In Fig. 2, we can observe from the image on the right that for the age range of 50 to 80, when listening to modern music, there seems to be quite a bit of dissimilarity between the EDA signals of the participants. In comparison to classical music, there seems to be quite a difference.

Age 20 to 30 (POX): In Fig. 4, we can observe from the image on left that for age group of 20 to 30, when listening to classical music, there seems to be very noticeable dissimilarity between the POX signals as well as very noticeable similarity for some signals. In comparison to listening to modern music, this age group seems to have pox signals that resonate with with each other better.

Age 30 to 50 (POX): In Fig. 4, we can observe from the image on the center that for age group of 30 to 50, when listening to classical music, there seems to be slightly less similarity between the POX signals in comparison to the age group of 20 to 30. In comparison to signals when listening to modern music, there seems to be less resonance between the POX signals.

Age 50 to 80 (POX): In Fig. 4, we can observe from the image on the right that for age group of 50 to 80, when listening to classical music, there seems to be more dissimilarity between the responses in comparison to when listening to modern music for this age group but overall, there is no distinct indication of anything discernible. This result seems to be in line with the other age groups when listening to classical music.

Age 20 to 30 (POX): In Fig. 4, we can observe from the image on left that for age group of 20 to 30, when listening to modern music, there seems to be very noticeable dissimilarity between the POX signals.

Age 30 to 50 (POX): In Fig. 4, we can observe from the image on the center that for age group of 30 to 50, when listening to modern music, there seems to be less dissimilarity between the POX signals in comparison to the age range of 20 to 30.

Age 50 to 80 (POX): In Fig. 4, we can observe from the image on the center that for age group of 50 to 80, when listening to modern music, there seems to be more similarity between the POX signals for this age group in comparison to the age range of 20 to 30 and 30 to 50.

From the heatmaps generated for classical and modern music for participants of three distinct age groups, we can observe that there seems to be noticable difference between the participant's EDA signals when listening to classical music vs when listening to modern music for the age group of 20 to 30 and 50 to 80.

Unlike EDA signals, the POX signals do not demonstrate any clear differentiation between classical and modern music as well as between the age groups. This observation leads to an intriguing conclusion: EDA signals appear to be more reflective and sensitive to variations in musical genres and age groups in comparison to POX signals. This difference in response patterns underscores the potential of EDA signals as more effective indicators for distinguishing between different types of musical experiences for different age groups.

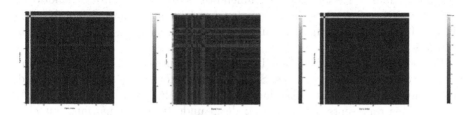

Fig. 1. Distance matrix of EDA signals for the classical music: **Left:** age 20 to 30. **Middle:** age 30 to 50. **Right:** age 50 to 80.

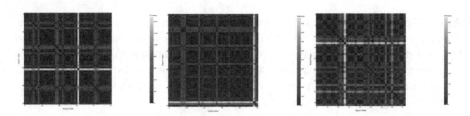

Fig. 2. Distance matrix of EDA signals for the modern music: **Left:** age 20 to 30. **Middle:** age 30 to 50. **Right:** age 50 to 80.

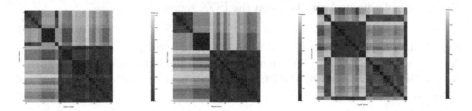

Fig. 3. Distance matrix of POX signals for the classical music: **Left:** age 20 to 30. **Middle:** age 30 to 50. **Right:** age 50 to 80.

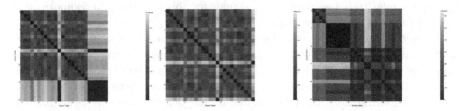

Fig. 4. Distance matrix of POX signals for the modern music: **Left:** age 20 to 30. **Middle:** age 30 to 50. **Right:** age 50 to 80.

In our study, the developed model demonstrates a proficient capability to predict seven distinct emotional states that individuals are likely to experience while listening to music. Recognizing the inherently subjective nature of emotions, where definitive accuracy is challenging, our model's performance is notably significant. It marks a substantial advancement in comprehending human emotional responses to music.

Furthermore, this achievement has promising implications for the development of recommendation systems. Such systems, informed by our model, could analyze user inputs to tailor selections more closely aligned with individual preferences. This represents not only a stride in understanding emotions but also in enhancing user experience through personalized content curation based on emotional responses (Table 2).

Table 2. Accuracy obtained from LSTM for each emotion

Emotions	Accuracy %
Activity	82.05
Engagement	73.6
Familiarity	84
Chills + Thrills + Shivers	89
Positivity	80.06
Tension	87.6
Likeness	72.5

5   Conclusion

This study represents a stride in the field of psychophysiology and its intersection with music. By harnessing the extensive data from the "Emotion in Motion" database, we have developed an interactive platform that allows for an in-depth exploration and visualization of psychophysiological responses to musical stimuli. Our application of DTW to analyze EDA and POX signals across different musical genres and age groups has yielded insightful findings. Particularly, we observed that EDA signals more distinctly differentiate between classical and modern music genres compared to POX signals, suggesting a higher sensitivity of EDA in reflecting emotional responses to different types of music and for different age groups.

Furthermore, the implementation of a LSTM predictive model has been an important part of our research. This model's ability to predict seven different emotional states from physiological data showcases the potential of machine learning in decoding complex human emotions. The implications of this are twofold: first, it enhances our understanding of the nuanced relationship between music and its emotional impact on listeners; second, it paves the way for developing sophisticated recommendation systems that can personalize content based on an individual's emotional responses.

Our research highlights the intricate connections between music, emotion, and physiological responses. It indicates new avenues for future investigations into how music can evoke a spectrum of emotions and how these can be quantified and utilized in practical applications. The convergence of psychophysiological data analysis and machine learning, as demonstrated in this study, sets a precedent for further interdisciplinary research that can expand our understanding of the human emotional experience.

Acknowledgments. This work was supported in part by Virginia Tech Institute for Creativity, Arts, and Technology.

Disclosure of Interests. The authors have no competing interests to declare that are relevant to the content of this article.

References

1. Bortz, B., Jaimovich, J., Knapp, R.B.: Emotion in motion: a reimagined framework for biomusical/emotional interaction. In: Proceedings of the International Conference on New Interfaces for Musical Expression (NIME 2015), pp. 44–49 (2015)
2. Tasooji, R., Gracanin, D., Knapp, R.B.: Exploring the impact of labeling on psychophysiological data analysis. In: Proceedings of the EmotionAware 2022 Workshop, the 20th International Conference on Pervasive Computing and Communications (PerCom 2022), pp. 371–376 (2022)
3. Boucsein, W.: Electrodermal activity. In: Springer Science & Business Media, New York (2012). https://doi.org/10.1007/978-1-4614-1126-0
4. Figner, B., Murphy, R.O.: Using skin conductance in judgment and decision making research. In: A Handbook of Process Tracing Methods for Decision Research, pp. 163–184 (2011)
5. Tobin, M.J.: Principles and Practice of Intensive Care Monitoring. McGraw-Hill (1990)
6. Juslin, P.N., Västfjäll, D.: Emotional responses to music: the need to consider underlying mechanisms. Behav. Brain Sci. **31**(5), 559–575 (2008)
7. Tomic, S.T., Janata, P.: Beyond the beat: modeling metric structure in music and performance. J. Acoust. Soc. Am. **124**(6), 4024–4041 (2008)
8. Eghbal-zadeh, H., Schedl, M., Widmer, G., Haunschmid, E.: Hidden Markov models for mood classification in music. In: Proceedings of the 16th International Society for Music Information Retrieval Conference (2015)
9. Müller, M.: Dynamic time warping. Inform. Retrieval Music Motion, 69–84 (2007)
10. Salimpoor, V.N., Benovoy, M., Larcher, K., Dagher, A., Zatorre, R.J.: Anatomically distinct dopamine release during anticipation and experience of peak emotion to music. Nat. Neurosci. **14**(2), 257–262 (2011)
11. Hodges, D.A.: Psychophysiological measures. In: Handbook of music and emotion: Theory, research, applications, pp. 279–311 (2010)
12. Cacioppo, J.T., Tassinary, L.G., Berntson, G.: Handbook of psychophysiology. Cambridge University Press (2007)
13. Stern, R.M., Ray, W.J., Quigley,K.S.: Psychophysiological Recording. Oxford University Press (2001)
14. Fairclough, S. H.: Fundamentals of physiological computing. Interact. Comput. **21**(1-2), 133–145 (2009)
15. Keil, A., et al.: Committee report: publication guidelines and recommendations for studies using electroencephalography and magnetoencephalography. Psychophysiology **51**(1), 1–21 (2014)
16. Francois, C., Miall, R.C.: An Interactive 3D visualization tool for time series of functional maps. In: VIIP, p. 6 (1996)
17. Kivikangas, J.M., et al.: Review on psychophysiological methods in game research. In: Proceedings of 1st Nordic DiGRA (2011)
18. Mandryk, R.L., Atkins, M.S.: A fuzzy physiological approach for continuously modeling emotion during interaction with play technologies. Int. J. Hum.-Comput. Stud. **65**(4), 329–347 (2007)
19. Mahat, M.: Prediction and prevention of addiction to social media using machine learning. In: Swain, D., Pattnaik, P.K., Athawale, T. (eds.) Machine Learning and Information Processing. AISC, vol. 1311, pp. 319–329. Springer, Singapore (2021). https://doi.org/10.1007/978-981-33-4859-2_31

20. Healey, J., Picard, R.W.: Detecting stress during real-world driving tasks using physiological sensors. In: IEEE Transactions on Intelligent Transportation Systems
21. Mahat, M.: Detecting cyberbullying across multiple social media platforms using deep learning. In: 2021 International Conference on Advance Computing and Innovative Technologies in Engineering (ICACITE), Greater Noida, India, pp. 299–301 (2021)
22. Rajgure, Sumit, Mahat, Maheep, Mekhe, Yash, Lade, Sangita: Reconstructing obfuscated human faces with conditional adversarial network. In: Swain, Debabala, Pattnaik, Prasant Kumar, Gupta, Pradeep K.. (eds.) Machine Learning and Information Processing. AISC, vol. 1101, pp. 95–104. Springer, Singapore (2020). https://doi.org/10.1007/978-981-15-1884-3_9

The Influence of Educational and Entertainment Videos on Children's Frontal EEG Activity: A Case Study

Bruna Martins[1] and Ana Rita Teixeira[1,2,3(✉)]

[1] Polytechnic of Coimbra, Coimbra Education School, Coimbra, Portugal
ateixeira@ua.pt
[2] Institute of Electronic Engineering, Telecommunications of
Aveiro (IEETA, UA), Aveiro, Portugal
[3] Center for Research and Innovation in Education (InED), School of Education,
Polytechnic Institute of Porto, Porto, Portugal

Abstract. The frontal regions of the brain are crucial for cognitive functions such as decision-making and emotional regulation. Understanding how these regions respond to different visual stimuli is essential for advancing our understanding of childhood cognitive development, especially in human interaction. The study of brain wave patterns, such as the P100 wave, in children provides valuable insights into cognitive processes and the brain development of the younger population, particularly when investigating frontal channels. The P100 wave plays a crucial role in visual processing and attention allocation in children.

In this study, a cohort of 20 nine-year-old children, including 8 girls and 12 boys, was recruited. The experiment involved presenting 14 videos on a computer for 15 s, interspersed with periods of a neutral screen. The primary objective was to assess the influence of these videos on brain wave activity. Initially, surveys were administered to parents and then to the children to understand habits, preferences, and academic performance. Subsequently, Muse device data were correlated with survey information. Studies indicate that alpha band activity is linked to visual processing and attention maintenance, while theta band activity is associated with memory consolidation and increased cognitive engagement, especially in human interaction. The research highlights significant disparities in brain responses between entertainment and educational videos, emphasizing the positive impact of engaging content and interactive experiences on the activation of frontal regions. Additionally, the analysis of the P100 component revealed a greater prominence in response to entertainment videos compared to educational ones.

Keywords: Children · P100 · alpha · theta · muse · EEG

1   Introduction

Technology has been one of the most significant and fascinating evolutions throughout history, profoundly impacting society. Since ancient times, humans have created tools with the aim of making their lives easier and achieving new goals. In contemporary times,

© The Author(s), under exclusive license to Springer Nature Switzerland AG 2024
D. D. Schmorrow and C. M. Fidopiastis (Eds.): HCII 2024, LNAI 14694, pp. 68–76, 2024.
https://doi.org/10.1007/978-3-031-61569-6_5

technology has become one of the fastest innovations, influencing everything from how we live to how we interact.

Society increasingly relies on technology for almost every aspect of daily life. This dependence has grown, encompassing the need for technology in performing daily tasks, decision-making, communication, and ultimately integrating into what is known as modern society. YouTube has emerged as a platform that not only provides entertainment but also serves as a learning tool, holding considerable importance in the lives of children. This platform offers a wide variety of videos, essentially becoming a pastime for children. We are aware that currently approximately one-third of internet users are under the age of 18. This sample demonstrates that the internet is increasingly being utilized by children without adult supervision. Children are acquiring the capability to master various tools available to them, leading to a significant transformation in the way they engage and interact within society [1].

However, despite being a source of entertainment for children, the developmental impact of YouTube is a subject of debate. There are opposing opinions, with some arguing against the platform's benefits and others supporting its positive contributions. While many advocate for the educational and creative benefits of using this platform, there are also concerns about the negative impacts of excessive screen time. The primary objective of this project is to understand the impact of YouTube on children's development, considering the diverse content of videos and comprehending children's reactions through observation and the assistance of the Muse 2 device. The aim is to decode the extent to which YouTube is impactful on the nervous system of children. This research will delve into both the positive and negative aspects of children's exposure to YouTube, considering educational, creative, and potential detrimental effects. The frontal regions of the brain hold a pivotal role in facilitating higher-order cognitive functions, including decision-making and emotional regulation [2]. Understanding how these cerebral areas respond to a diverse range of visual stimuli is of paramount importance for advancing our comprehension of infant cognitive development, particularly in the context of human interaction [3]. Moreover, the study of brainwave patterns, particularly the P100 wave, in children has opened up intriguing avenues for understanding the cognitive processes and developmental aspects of the young brain [4]. The P100 wave, an early visual event-related potential (ERP) component, is known for its role in visual processing and attention allocation. When it comes to children, investigating the P100 wave within the frontal channels offers valuable insights into their cognitive development and information processing [5].

Utilizing EEG Muse technology [6], we performed an extensive analysis of brain activity patterns within the alpha and theta frequency bands before, during, and after children's exposure to specific video content and human interaction scenarios. Additionally, we scrutinized the amplitude and latency of the P100 wave. This comprehensive investigation revealed noteworthy changes in frequency spectra and P100 wave characteristics within the frontal regions, highlighting distinct cerebral responses when comparing entertaining and educational video materials, as well as the impact of human interaction.

2   Methodology and Procedure

In this study, a cohort of 17 children, comprising 8 females and 12 males, all aged 9 years, were recruited. The experimental protocol involved the presentation of 14 distinct videos, each displayed on a PC screen for 8 s, interspersed with periods of a neutral screen. The primary aim of this research is to assess the influence of these videos on brain wave activity. Initially, a survey was administered to both parents and teachers, as well as the children themselves, in order to comprehensively characterize the children's habits, preferences, and academic performance. Subsequently, the data collected from the Muse device was correlated with the information gathered from these surveys.

2.1   Procedure

The research progressed through the following stages:

a) Conducting a questionnaire survey with the teacher and the parents
b) Collecting data by observing a video with the assistance of the Muse 2 device.
c) Administering a questionnaire survey to the students.

2.2   Protocol

The experimental protocol involved the presentation of 14 distinct videos, each displayed on a PC screen for 15 s, interspersed with periods of a neutral screen during 2 s. The videos comprised both entertaining (1) and informative (2) content, as showed in Fig. 1.

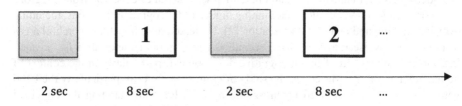

Fig. 1. Experimental Protocol

In Table 1 is described the videos id (#), the time (in sec) and the type of the video (Pause, Entertaining and Informative).

3   Results and Discussion

The teacher questionnaire survey aims to assess the overall school performance across different subjects. The results provide an overview of the students' academic achievements, encompassing various assessments and overall educational activities, Fig. 2. School performance is gauged through factors such as grades, test scores, class participation, and other assessments reflecting the students' comprehension and mastery of the taught material. The data indicates that, on a global scale, the class exhibits high performance across all subjects, with a notable emphasis on environmental studies. Portuguese and Math demonstrate similar levels of achievement.

Table 1. Videos Information: id (#), time/sec) and type of videos (pause, entertaining, informative)

#	Time	Type	#	Time	Type
1	2 seg	Pause	16	15 seg	Informative
2	15 seg	Entertaining	17	2 seg	Pause
3	2 seg	Pause	18	15 seg	Entertaining
4	15 seg	Informative	19	2 seg	Pause
5	2 seg	Pause	20	15 seg	Informative
6	15 seg	Entertaining	21	2 seg	Pause
7	2 seg	Pause	22	15 seg	Entertaining
8	15 seg	Informative	23	2 seg	Pausa
9	2 seg	Pause	24	15 seg	Informative
10	15 seg	Entertaining	25	2 seg	Pause
11	2 seg	Pause	26	15 seg	Entertaining
12	15 seg	Informative	27	2 seg	Pause
13	2 seg	Pause	28	15 seg	Informative
14	15 seg	Entertaining	29	2 seg	Pause
15	2 seg	Pause			

Note that the choice of entertaining videos was influenced by the children's preferences, while the selection of informative videos was made in collaboration with both teacher feedback and the preferences expressed by the children

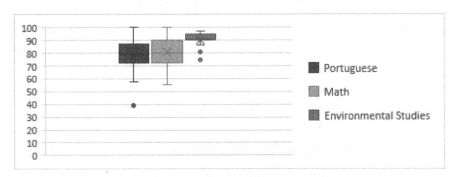

Fig. 2. School Performance in %

The parents are also participating in this study to better understand the habits of their children using the internet. Over a period of two months, the children were supervised. The questions we are interested in knowing from the parents are:

Q1 - How often does your child use the internet at home?
Q2 - How many hours does your child spend on the internet per day?
Q3 - How much time, on average does your child dedicate to watching videos on YouTube?

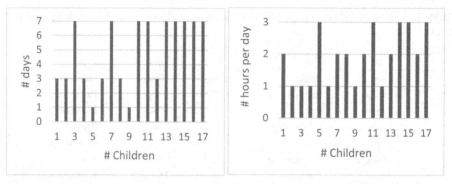

Fig. 3. Number of days per week and the average number of hours per day that each child engages in internet activities

Analysis of Fig. 3 reveals a consistent pattern in the internet usage habits of children, signaling their daily access and an average duration of over one hour spent on online activities. Notably, Fig. 4 highlights a distinct focus on YouTube, with an average daily usage of approximately 1.6 h. This observation emphasizes the widespread adoption of internet usage among children, highlighting a daily routine of online involvement. The substantial time allocation to YouTube implies a significant preference for video content consumption, underscoring the platform's popularity within this demographic. In order to delve into the content and attention levels during video consumption, an analysis of alpha and theta waves' power energy was conducted as part of the experimental protocol.

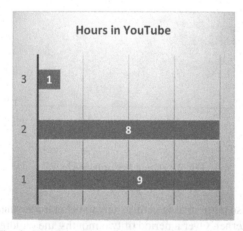

Fig. 4. Number of hours in the YouTube 1h, 2h and 3h

Analyzing data from the Muse device, we assessed both theta and alpha activity across all videos. Segregating them into categories—entertaining videos (1), informative videos (2), and breaks (3)—the results indicate a significant elevation in average theta wave activity for entertaining videos (1), followed by informative videos (2), and, lastly, during breaks (3), as shown in Fig. 5. This underscores the participants' greater focus and attention towards entertaining. This pattern suggests that children exhibit heightened cognitive engagement, attention, and focus during entertaining videos on YouTube. The higher theta wave activity during informative videos indicates a considerable level of cognitive involvement, albeit to a lesser extent than during entertainment. The lowest theta wave activity observed during breaks suggests a relaxation or disengagement phase.

Understanding the neurological responses to different content categories on YouTube provides valuable insights into the preferences and attention levels of children. Such findings can contribute to the development of content strategies that align with the cognitive capacities and interests of the target audience, fostering a more informed approach to digital content creation for this demographic.

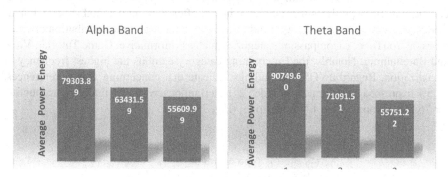

Fig. 5. Average Power Energy considering Alpha and Theta bands

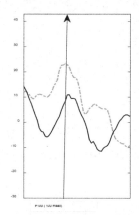

Fig. 6. P100 wave considering the mean of entertainment videos and the mean of informative videos

The analysis of P100 was conducted, revealing notable differences in amplitude between entertainment and informative videos, Fig. 6. Specifically, the P100 amplitude was found to be higher in response to entertainment videos compared to informative ones. This elevated P100 amplitude suggests heightened neural engagement or attention during the early processing stages, potentially attributed to the visually stimulating or attention-grabbing nature of entertainment content as opposed to informative content.

The T-test analysis was conducted, and the results demonstrate a statistically significant difference between entertainment videos and informative ones (p = 0.00145).

Following the test, all children are required to respond to a questionnaire, addressing the following inquiries:

- Q1 - Are you currently utilizing the internet?
- Q2 - Do you access the internet at home?
- Q3 - When you are online, do your parents generally remain nearby?
- Q4 - What do you enjoy watching the most on YouTube?"
- Q5 - Which video did you like the most?

After conducting a thorough analysis of the results, it was observed that every child, constituting 100%, utilizes the internet at home, often without parental supervision, as evidenced by responses to Q1, Q2, and Q3. Figure 6 illustrates the distribution of video types on YouTube, encompassing categories such as Informative, Game Tutorial, Vlog, and Entertaining. Notably, the Entertaining category exhibits the highest frequency of visualization. Regarding Q5, the findings indicate that concerning video preferences, 23.5% expressed a preference for video 2 (Entertaining), while the majority, accounting for 76.5%, favored video 1 (Informative) (Fig. 7).

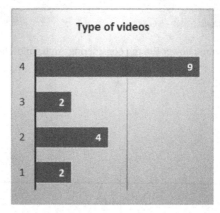

Fig. 7. Type of videos visualized in YouTube (left graph), where 1 - informative; 2- Game Tutorial; 3-Vlog and 4 - Entertaining

Taking into account all the presented results, there is a significant correlation between the P100, power energy in theta and alpha bands, and the type of video content (specifically, entertaining videos). This information contributes to a better understanding of how visual processing and cognitive states may be influenced by different types of video content a correlation analysis was conducted to enhance the understanding of the obtained findings.

4 Conclusions and Further Work

Our findings suggest that alpha band activity may be intricately linked to the processing of visual information and the maintenance of sustained attention, while the theta band could be associated with memory consolidation and heightened cognitive engagement, especially when coupled with human interaction [7, 8]. Moreover, our study illuminated substantial disparities in cerebral responses between entertaining and educational videos, underlining the positive impact of entertaining content and interactive experiences in stimulating the activation of frontal regions. Furthermore, the P100 component was analyzed in response to each video individually, revealing that it is more prominent in response to entertainment videos in comparison to educational ones. The observed differences in P100 amplitude between entertainment and informative videos suggest variations in early neural processing. Further research and a detailed exploration of the specific characteristics of the videos and the experimental design can provide deeper insights into the cognitive and emotional processes involved.

The implications of comprehending these precise cerebral reactions, within the context of human interaction, are profound for the realms of childhood education and entertainment [9]. Our results underscore the pivotal role of engaging and entertaining content, as well as meaningful human interaction, in fostering cognitive engagement and facilitating learning in children. Additionally, they offer invaluable insights for the development of more efficacious and captivating educational materials and interactive learning experiences. In sum, this study significantly contributes to the burgeoning field of infant cognitive development neuroscience, providing pathways to optimize educational and entertainment experiences tailored to children's needs, preferences, and the enriching influence of human interaction.

References

1. Livingstone, S., Davidson, J., Bryce, J., Batool, S., Haughton, C., Nandi, A.: Children's online activities, risks and safety: a literature review by the UKCCIS evidence group. In: UKCCIS Evidence Group Literature Review. LSE Consulting, London, UK (2017)
2. Katahira, K., Yamazaki, Y., Yamaoka, C., Ozaki, H., Nakagawa, S., Nagata, N.: EEG correlates of the flow state: a combination of increased frontal theta and moderate frontocentral alpha rhythm in the mental arithmetic task. Front. Psychol. **9**, 300 (2018). https://doi.org/10.3389/fpsyg.2018.00300
3. Luu, P., Tucker, D.M., Makeig, S.: Frontal midline theta and the error-related negativity: neurophysiological mechanisms of action regulation. Clin. Neurophysiol. **115**(8), 1821–1835 (2004). https://doi.org/10.1016/j.clinph.2004.03.031
4. Lee, P.-L., Hsieh, J.-C., Wu, C.-H., Shyu, K.-K., Wu, Y.-T.: Brain computer interface using flash onset and offset visual evoked potentials. Clin. Neurophysiol. **119**(3), 605–616 (2008). https://doi.org/10.1016/j.clinph.2007.11.013
5. Teixeira, A., Rodrigues, I., Gomes, A., Rodríguez, G.: P100 ERP as a tool to identifying problem solving. In: Rocha, A., Adeli, H., Dzemyda, G., Moreira, F. (eds.) Information Systems and Technologies. WorldCIST 2022. LNNS, vol. 469. Springer, Cham (2022). https://doi.org/10.1007/978-3-031-04819-7_58
6. Krigolson, O.E., Williams, C.C., Norton, A., Hassall, C.D., Colino, F.L.: Choosing MUSE: validation of a low-cost, portable EEG system for ERP research. Front Neurosci. **11**, 109 (2017). https://doi.org/10.3389/FNINS.2017.00109/BIBTEX

7. Klimesch, W.: Alpha-band oscillations, attention, and controlled access to stored information. Trends Cogn. Sci. **16**(12), 606–617 (2012). https://doi.org/10.1016/J.TICS.2012.10.007

8. Shtoots, L., Dagan, T., Levine, J., Rothstein, A., Shati, L., Levy, D.A.: The effects of theta EEG neurofeedback on the consolidation of spatial memory. Clin. EEG Neurosci. **52**(5), 338–344 (2021). https://doi.org/10.1177/1550059420973107

9. Oggiano, M.: Neurophysiology of Emotions. Neurophysiology - Networks, Plasticity, Pathophysiology and Behavior (2022).https://doi.org/10.5772/INTECHOPEN.106043

A Comparative Study of High and Low Performing Students' Visual Effort and Attention When Identifying Syntax Errors

Caren A. Pacol[1,2]([✉]) [iD], Maria Mercedes T. Rodrigo[1] [iD],
and Christine Lourrine S. Tablatin[2] [iD]

[1] Ateneo de Manila University, Quezon City, Metro Manila, Philippines
ambat_caren@yahoo.com
[2] Pangasinan State University, Urdaneta, Pangasinan, Philippines

Abstract. Debugging is an important skill to learn for novice programmers and since compiler error messages are instrumental to the debugging process, investigating how novice programmers read and process these messages has become a subject of interest among computer science education researchers. Prior studies were valuable because they identified differences in the visual attention patterns of high and low performers and of experts and novices. They were, however, subject to certain limitations. In this study, we attempted to bridge these gaps by continuing the study of Rodrigo and Tablatin [18] and Tablatin and Rodrigo [21]. Using the methodology detailed in Rodrigo & Tablatin [18], we investigated how student programmers process literal and non-literal syntax errors embedded in Java and C++ programs. The analysis of eye tracking data collected from participants of two schools revealed a variation in visual effort and attention patterns of high and low performers. We conclude that low performance is not always associated with low visual attention. The novice programmer code comprehension errors may be rooted in other causes such as tracing and debugging strategies that students use, cognitive skills, individual preference of learning and programming experience. These factors are out of scope for this paper but may be the subject of future work.

Keywords: Eye-tracking · Compiler Error Messages · Error Lines · Syntax Errors · Visual Attention · Visual Effort

1 Introduction

Novice programmers rely on compiler error messages to assist them in identifying and rectifying errors within their programs during the debugging process. However, students often struggle with understanding these compiler error messages and consequently find it difficult to debug their programs. Students reported that such errors are frustrating and have described them as "barriers to progress" [3]. Further, students have difficulty locating and repairing syntax errors using only the typically terse error messages provided by the average compiler [7, 19]. McCall and Kolling [14] noted in their study that Java error messages, are confusing from the novices' point of view due to the following

© The Author(s), under exclusive license to Springer Nature Switzerland AG 2024
D. D. Schmorrow and C. M. Fidopiastis (Eds.): HCII 2024, LNAI 14694, pp. 77–94, 2024.
https://doi.org/10.1007/978-3-031-61569-6_6

observations: (1) a single error may, in different context, produce different diagnostic messages and (2) the same diagnostic message may be produced by entirely different and distinct errors.

Programming errors can be categorized into two broad groups: language specification errors and program specification errors. Language specification errors arise when the program fails to meet the requirements and rules of the programming language, making them detectable by the compiler or interpreter. When a properly structured program deviates from its specified correctness criteria, it contains program specification errors or sometimes called logic errors [2]. This paper focused on language specification errors which are often also known as compiler errors or syntax errors. When the compiler or interpreter detects a language specification error, it sends feedback to the programmer through error messages, and these can be either literal or non-literal error messages. Literal syntax error messages are compiler-reported errors that exactly correspond to the actual error. For instance, in Java, if the error 'semicolon (;)' expected were literal, it means that a semicolon is missing and that adding a semi-colon to the line indicated will solve the problem. Non-literal syntax error messages are those that do not accurately correspond to the real error [8]. If the error 'semicolon (;)' expected were non-literal, this would mean that adding a semi-colon to the line indicated would not solve the problem because the error that caused the message was located somewhere else.

Because debugging is an important skill to learn and since compiler error messages are instrumental to the debugging process, investigating how novice programmers read and process these messages has become a subject of interest among computer science education researchers. Researchers have employed a number of methods to study how novice programmers debug code. These include qualitative studies by Whalley, Settle and Luxton-Reilly [26], Javier [9], Yen, Wu, and Lin [27] and eye tracking by Lin et al. [12]. Whalley et al. [26] conducted qualitative analysis and observed that comprehension, evidence-based activities, and workflow practices contribute to novice debugging success. Javier [9] conducted qualitative interview, document reviews and observation to understand information technology life-long learners who were subjected to a hands-on experience, program tracing and interviews. He found novice programmers' difficulties in program structures, debugging, code comprehension and code navigation. Yen, Wu, and Lin [27] undertook a qualitative investigation that aimed to categorize difficulty levels associated with various types of errors among novice and expert programmers. The participants were requested to vocalize their thought processes during debugging activities, specifically focusing on syntax, semantic, and logic errors encountered while utilizing a compiler. The findings indicated that novice programmers often encounter confusion during the debugging of semantic errors, leading them to engage in backward inference. The study documented key metrics such as debugging time, completion time, and the frequency of debugging behaviors [27]. Lin et al. [12] asserted that, to minimize cognitive load during debugging and observe students' insights without requiring verbalization of their actions, they opted for the utilization of eye-tracking methodology over the think-aloud protocol.

In this study, we used eye tracking to collect quantitative data about how novice programmers read and act upon compiler error messages. Eye tracking is a technique that provides a direct measure of the visual attention of a programmer while performing a program comprehension task [6]. Several studies have employed eye tracking to quantify the cognitive effort and processing required in comprehending computer code. Jessup [10] and colleagues conducted a pilot study to examine group differences in code comprehension abilities and perceptions of experts and novice computer programmers. They found that experts had more fixations than novices implying that experts were devoting more attention to tasks and employing greater cognitive skills compared to novices.

In 2018, Villamor et al examined the eye movement patterns of participants within pairs as they traced and debugged segments of code. They conducted a dual eye-tracking study, capturing their fixations and calculating gaze-related metrics for these individuals. The findings indicate that individuals categorized as more successful tend to initially familiarize themselves with the program, exhibit heightened focus on the lines with the errors and demonstrate a higher level of task engagement [24]. In a series of programming tasks, Turner, and colleagues [23] investigated how different programming languages influenced the performance of developers. To quantify visual effort, the researchers documented four eye tracking metrics: (1) the number of fixations and (2) the duration for the entire program, as well as (3) the fixation count and (4) duration specifically on the defective lines within the programs. Each of these metrics was expected to increase with the visual effort expended by the participants. The authors' analysis revealed no significant differences in any of the metrics, except for a higher number of fixations on the buggy lines of the Python programs compared to the C++ programs [23]. Tablatin and Rodrigo [21] studied the difference in visual attention of students while finding syntax errors in C++ using fixation count and fixation duration metrics. They found that high performing students had significantly higher visual attention on error lines than the low performing students.

Prior studies were valuable because they identified differences in the visual attention patterns of high and low performers and of experts and novices. They were, however, subject to certain limitations. Jessup et al. [10] and Turner [23] did not include analysis of programmers' interaction with compiler error messages. There was no uniformity in the type of errors inserted in the code as they could be syntactic or semantic in Villamor et al. [24]. The number of errors per program also varied. The font size could be small which may lead to ambiguity when interpreting fixation locations. Whether an error was literal or non-literal was not taken into account in the study of Tablatin and Rodrigo [21]. We therefore attempt to bridge these gaps by continuing the study of Rodrigo and Tablatin [18] and Tablatin and Rodrigo [21]. Using the methodology detailed in Rodrigo & Tablatin [18], we investigate how student programmers process literal and non-literal syntax errors embedded in Java and C++ programs. Through this study, we hope to contribute new knowledge about how student programmers read and process these types of errors using different programming languages. Our research questions include:

1. How does visual attention to compiler error messages for literal syntax errors differ between high-performing and low-performing novice programmers?
2. How does visual attention to compiler error messages for non-literal syntax errors differ between high-performing and low-performing novice programmers?

3. How does visual attention to error lines for literal syntax errors differ between high-performing and low-performing novice programmers?
4. How does visual attention to error lines for non-literal syntax errors differ between high-performing and low-performing novice programmers?
5. How does student visual attention to compiler error messages differ with their visual attention to error lines for literal syntax errors?
6. How does student visual attention to compiler error messages differ with their visual attention to error lines for non-literal syntax errors?
7. How does student visual effort on the error lines differ when locating literal vs. non-literal syntax errors?

Note that error lines refer to the line(s) in the code containing the error(s). We referred to the number of fixations and fixation durations on an area of interest (AOI) as visual effort. We termed the amount of fixations directed towards an AOI, relative to the total amount of fixations on the entire stimuli as visual attention.

2 Method

2.1 Participants

Students in their college level who had completed at least one programming course participated in this study. A total of 63 participants were recruited, 31 from School A in Metro Manila and 32 from School B in Pangasinan. The actual number of samples included in the analysis varied because data of some students had to be excluded. The details of the final numbers will be given below.

2.2 Stimuli

Characteristics of the Stimuli. The stimuli characteristics presented in Tablatin and Rodrigo [21] were the same in this study. However, two sets of stimuli were used. The two sets of stimuli had the same problem descriptions, problem sequences, and problem solutions. The first set of stimuli was written in Java while the second was written in C++. The Java stimuli were used in the eye tracking experiment with respondents from School A while the C++ stimuli were used with respondents from School B.

Code Complexity and Criteria. The complexity of the code and criteria presented in Tablatin and Rodrigo [21] were also the same in this study.

2.3 Experimental Setup and Procedure

The experimental setup and procedures described in the studies of Rodrigo and Tablatin [18] and Tablatin and Rodrigo [21] was also used in this study.

2.4 Comprehension Task and Evaluation

The primary task for the participants was to locate program errors. There was no need for the participants to correct the errors. The evaluation of participant performance was based on the accuracy of their responses.

2.5 Sources of Data

There were three sources of data in this study: eye tracking metrics, video recordings and slide viewer data. The eye tracking data were collected and saved in an individual CSV file composed of information regarding the fixation timestamp, the location of fixations, fixation durations, blinking counts, pupil dilations, and separate values for the left and right eye movements. Figure 1 shows an example of eye tracking data exported as a file from the Gazepoint Analysis software. In this study, the fixation timestamp, location of fixations, and fixation durations were extracted from these eye tracking data. Fixation timestamp represents the duration in seconds that has passed since the most recent system initialization or calibration. It is registered after the image transmission from the camera to the computer. The location of fixations is represented by the FPOGX, FPOGY, and the X- and Y-coordinates of the fixation POG, as a fraction of the screen size. The fixation POG data provides the user's point-of-gaze as determined by the internal fixation filter. The fixation durations FPOGD is the duration of the fixation POG in seconds [16].

The slide viewer data logged the action type, timestamp, slide number, and locations of marked areas in each of the slides. The action type represents a press on one of the Next, Previous, and Reset buttons or a mark on the selected error in a program line. The timestamp is the start time in seconds when the action took place. The slide identifies the slide numbers that were visited. Note that only positive numbered slides were marked with X and Y points since these are the slides containing the program solutions. Figure 2 shows a screenshot of the sample slide viewer data. The odd numbered slides are the problem descriptions. The X and Y columns represent the location in the slides that were marked by the user. The eye tracking and slide viewer data were used to generate segmented data for each participant. The segmentation refers to the process of separating the fixation data that were captured per slide. This was done to perform statistical analysis of data on fixations of participants in each problem.

Video data of each participant's fixation map and answers in the test were generated and exported. The video data was used to review the participant fixations and test responses. The responses of the students in each problem were evaluated, giving 1 point for every correctly identified syntax error. We grouped students' data into high and low performing based on their total scores in Problem 2 and Problem 4 (literal syntax error problems). We did the same on their total scores in Problem 1, Problem 3 and Problem 5 (non-literal syntax error problems). The scores of all participants in literal syntax error problems were averaged. If the total score of the respondent is greater than or equivalent to the average score of all students, the participant was classified as high performing. Otherwise, the participant was classified as low performing. The same method was employed on non-literal syntax error problems.

2.6 Data Pre-processing

Participants' eye movements, including the timestamp of fixation occurrences, the x and y coordinates indicating fixation locations, and the duration of each fixation were saved on a CSV file. The Areas of Interest (AOIs) of the five programs were drawn using the OGAMA Areas of Interest module [25] to obtain AOI coordinates.

In this study, the compiler error message and the line in the code containing the error (error line) were marked as AOIs. The AOI coordinates obtained from OGAMA are provided with respect to the screen resolution settings used during AOI definition. To align the fixation locations with the program codes, we transformed the eye tracking data by scaling the x and y coordinates. Specifically, the x coordinates were multiplied by 1366 and the y coordinates were multiplied by 768. This adjustment was made to ensure that the coordinates matched the program code layout used during the experiment, which was designed for a screen resolution of 1366×768. In addition, the fixation durations were recorded in terms of seconds by the eye tracker and were converted into milliseconds by multiplying the duration with 1000 [21]. These processes were done for the eye tracking data of the participants to determine their visual effort and attention in finding the literal and non-literal syntax errors.

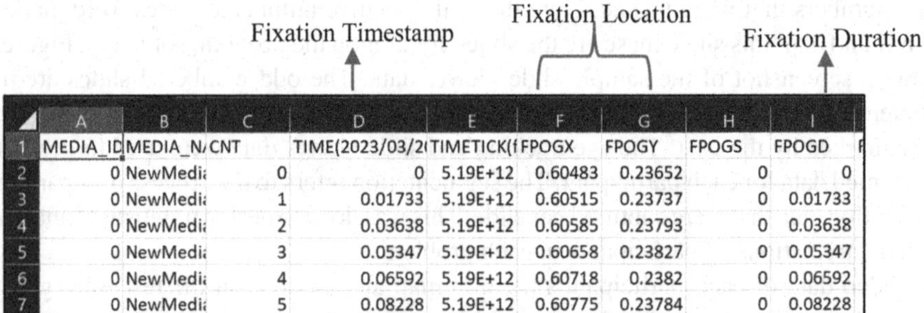

Fixation Timestamp   Fixation Location   Fixation Duration

	A	B	C	D	E	F	G	H	I
1	MEDIA_ID	MEDIA_N/	CNT	TIME(2023/03/2(	TIMETICK(f	FPOGX	FPOGY	FPOGS	FPOGD
2	0	NewMedi;	0	0	5.19E+12	0.60483	0.23652	0	0
3	0	NewMedi;	1	0.01733	5.19E+12	0.60515	0.23737	0	0.01733
4	0	NewMedi;	2	0.03638	5.19E+12	0.60585	0.23793	0	0.03638
5	0	NewMedi;	3	0.05347	5.19E+12	0.60658	0.23827	0	0.05347
6	0	NewMedi;	4	0.06592	5.19E+12	0.60718	0.2382	0	0.06592
7	0	NewMedi;	5	0.08228	5.19E+12	0.60775	0.23784	0	0.08228
8	0	NewMedi;	6	0.10107	5.19E+12	0.60833	0.23745	0	0.10108
9	0	NewMedi;	7	0.11816	5.19E+12	0.60861	0.23737	0	0.11816
10	0	NewMedi;	8	0.13379	5.19E+12	0.60911	0.23687	0	0.13379
11	0	NewMedi;	9	0.14795	5.19E+12	0.6096	0.23641	0	0.14795
12	0	NewMedi;	10	0.16504	5.19E+12	0.61016	0.23555	0	0.16504
13	0	NewMedi;	11	0.18066	5.19E+12	0.61057	0.23525	0	0.18066
14	0	NewMedi;	12	0.19727	5.19E+12	0.61098	0.23495	0	0.19727
15	0	NewMedi;	13	0.21362	5.19E+12	0.61176	0.23482	0	0.21362
16	0	NewMedi;	14	0.22998	5.19E+12	0.61199	0.23487	0	0.22998
17	0	NewMedi;	15	0.24634	5.19E+12	0.61223	0.23494	0	0.24634
18	0	NewMedi;	16	0.26294	5.19E+12	0.61287	0.23487	0	0.26294

Fig. 1. Screenshot of Eye tracking Data saved as CSV file

2.7 Eye-Tracking Metrics

We included two eye-tracking metrics that are commonly collected when participants read computer code: fixation count (FC) and fixation duration (FD). Additionally, we calculated the time to first fixation, proportional fixation count, and proportional fixation

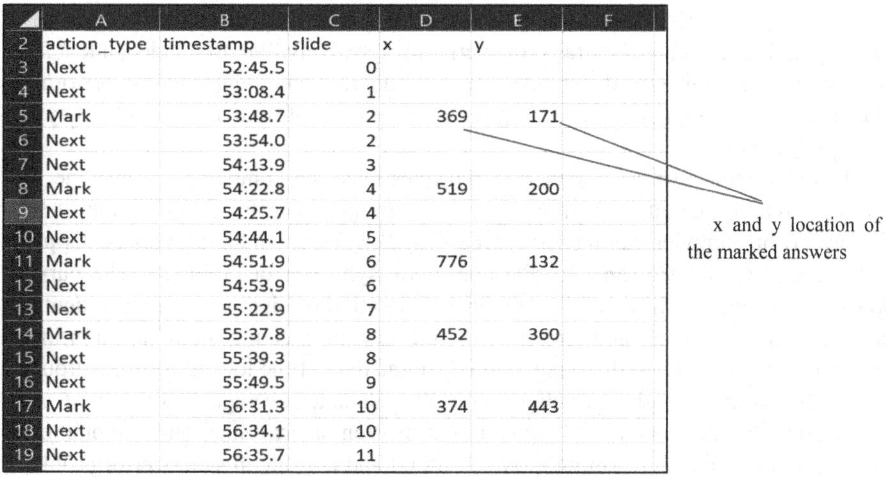

	A	B	C	D	E	F
2	action_type	timestamp	slide	x	y	
3	Next	52:45.5	0			
4	Next	53:08.4	1			
5	Mark	53:48.7	2	369	171	
6	Next	53:54.0	2			
7	Next	54:13.9	3			
8	Mark	54:22.8	4	519	200	
9	Next	54:25.7	4			
10	Next	54:44.1	5			
11	Mark	54:51.9	6	776	132	
12	Next	54:53.9	6			
13	Next	55:22.9	7			
14	Mark	55:37.8	8	452	360	
15	Next	55:39.3	8			
16	Next	55:49.5	9			
17	Mark	56:31.3	10	374	443	
18	Next	56:34.1	10			
19	Next	56:35.7	11			

x and y location of the marked answers

Fig. 2. Screenshot of Slide Viewer Data saved as CSV file

durations to measure the visual attention on two areas of interest in each program namely, the compiler error message and the error line. We used fixation count and fixation duration to measure visual effort of participants on the areas of interest. The definitions of each of the metrics is as follows:

Fixation Count. Fixation count (FC) was defined as the number of fixations made within the pixel range of code for each participant and for each of the five programs.

Fixation Duration. Fixation duration (FD) was computed separately for each participant and for each of the five programs by computing the fixation duration in milliseconds of each fixation spent within the pixel range of the stimuli.

Proportional Fixation Count. Proportional fixation count (PFC) was calculated by dividing the fixation count on an area of interest (AOI) by the total number of fixations on the entire slide during test duration on each problem.

Proportional Fixation Duration. Proportional fixation duration (PFD) was calculated by dividing the fixation duration on an area of interest (AOI) by the total fixation durations on the entire slide during the test duration on each problem.

Time to First Fixation. Time from the beginning of a program slide displayed on screen until the participant fixates on a given AOI which in this case are the error line and the compiler error message.

2.8 Data Analysis

To answer the first to fourth research questions, we calculated the average proportional fixation count, average proportional fixation duration and average time to first fixation on error lines and compiler error messages in the literal and non-literal syntax error problems. The purpose was to determine the difference in the visual attention given by high and low performing students on error lines and compiler error messages when identifying literal and non-literal syntax errors respectively. We used independent samples t-test to determine the difference in the visual attention of high and low performing students on the compiler error messages and error lines of both and non-literal syntax error problems.

To answer the fifth and sixth research questions, we compared the average proportional fixation count as well as the average proportional fixation duration of high performers on compiler literal error messages and error lines in literal syntax error problems. Then, we did the same for the non-literal syntax error problems. The purpose was to determine the differences in the visual attention of high performing students on compiler error messages and error lines when they are locating literal and non-literal syntax errors. We applied the same methods to the data of the low performing group.

To answer the seventh research question, we calculated average fixation count, average fixation duration and average time to first fixation on error lines and compiler error messages of the high performing group on literal and non-literal syntax error problems respectively. This was to determine the difference in the visual effort exerted by the students when they identify literal syntax errors versus when they identify non-literal syntax errors. The same methods were employed on the data of the low performing group. We used the independent samples t-test in the statistical tests to answer the first to fourth research questions. A paired samples t-test was used to answer the fifth to seventh research questions.

3 Results

Data of 12 participants obtained from School A and 6 participants obtained from School B were discarded due to lack of fixations recorded and/or frequent head movements resulting in inaccurate recording of fixations. Thus, the data included in the analysis were from 19 students from School A and 26 students from School B. The grouping based on performance resulted in 15 high performers and 4 low performers in School A, and 18 high performers and 8 low performers in School B, specifically for addressing literal syntax errors. Meanwhile, 12 students were high performing and 7 were low performing in School A whereas in School B, 16 students were high performing while 10 were low performing in non-literal syntax error problems.

Comparison of Visual Attention to Compiler Error Messages of High and Low Performing Novice Programmers.

3.1 Compiler Error Messages for a Literal Syntax Error

School A. To determine if there was difference in the visual attention of high and low performing students on compiler error messages, we analyzed the average proportional fixation count, average proportional fixation duration and average time to first fixation. Results revealed that the average proportional fixation count, average proportional fixation duration, and average time to first fixation on compiler error messages did not significantly differ between high and low performers.

School B. The same fixation metrics used to analyze the data of School A were used to analyze the data of School B. We also found that the visual attention of high and low performers did not differ in terms of the average proportional fixation count, average proportional fixation duration, and average time to first fixation on compiler error messages of literal syntax error problems.

These results imply that the visual attention on the compiler error messages of literal syntax error problems is the same regardless of the student performance and school.

3.2 Compiler Error Messages for a Non-literal Syntax Error

School A. We found no significant differences between groups in terms of average proportional fixation count, average proportional fixation duration, and average time to first fixation on compiler error messages.

School B. Results show that high performers had significantly greater average proportional fixation count ($M = 0.15$, $SD = 0.08$) than low performers ($M = 0.08$, $SD = 0.09$), $t(24) = -2.17$, $p = 0.040$. However, we found no significant differences between high and low performers on average proportional fixation duration and average time to first fixation on compiler error messages in non-literal syntax error problems. Figure 3 illustrates the visual summary of distribution and skewness of the average proportional fixation count on compiler error messages. The data shows a higher median proportional fixation count among high-performing students when compared to their low-performing counterparts. The findings imply that high performers exerted more visual attention on the compiler error messages of non-literal syntax error problems compared to the low performers.

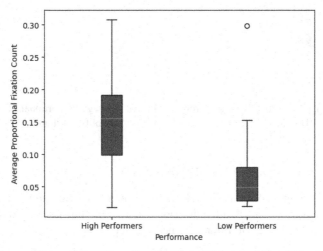

Fig. 3. Average Proportional FC on Compiler Error Messages (School B) – Non-literal

Comparison of Visual Attention to Error Lines of High and Low Performing Novice Programmers

3.3   Error Lines with a Literal Syntax Error

School A. To determine if visual attention to error lines differ between high-performing and low-performing novice programmers, we analyzed the average proportional fixation count, average proportional fixation duration, and average time to first fixation on the error lines of literal syntax error problems. Similar to the result of the visual attention to compiler error messages on literal and non-literal syntax error problems, we also found no significant differences between these two groups.

School B. The result of the analysis revealed that the average proportional fixation count of high performers on error lines was significantly greater ($M = 0.10$, $SD = 0.05$) than low performers ($M = 0.04$, $SD = 0.01$), $t(21.78) = -4.68$, $p < 0.001$. Similarly, high performers had significantly greater average proportional fixation duration ($M = 0.10$, $SD = 0.06$) than low performers ($M = 0.04$, $SD = 0.02$), $t(21.13) = -4.16$, $p < 0.001$. However, we found no significant differences between the groups in terms of the average time to first fixation. Figures 4 and 5 show the distribution and skewness of average proportional fixation count and average proportional fixation duration on error lines. High performers had significantly higher median average proportional fixation count and average proportional fixation duration than low performers. The results imply that high performers had more visual attention on the error lines of literal syntax error problems compared to the low performers.

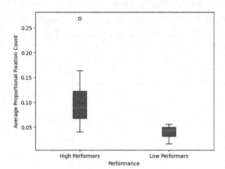

Fig. 4. Average Proportional FC on Error Lines (School B) – Literal

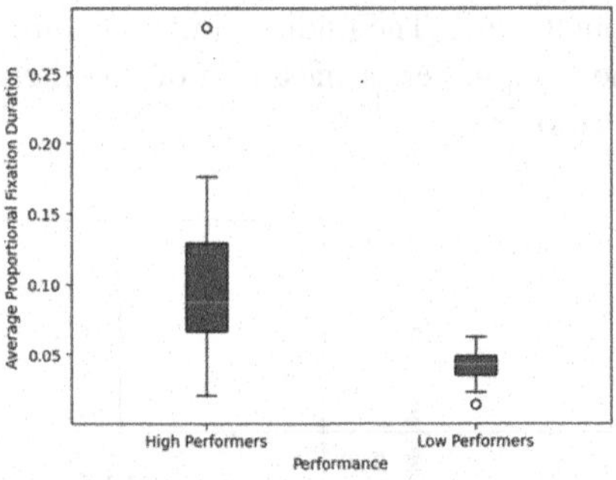

Fig. 5. Average Proportional FD on Error Lines (School B) – Literal

3.4   Error Lines with a Non-literal Syntax Error

School A. We compared the high and low performers' average proportional fixation count, average proportional fixation duration and average time to first fixation on error lines but found no significant differences between the groups.

School B. The analysis of the visual attention to error lines of non-literal syntax error problems revealed that high performers had greater average proportional fixation counts on error lines ($M = 0.06$, $SD = 0.04$) than low performers ($M = 0.03$, $SD = 0.01$), $t(19.23) = -3.18$, $p < 0.01$. Additionally, high performers had greater average proportional fixation durations on error lines ($M = 0.07$, $SD = 0.05$) than low performers ($M = $

0.03, $SD = 0.01$), $t(17.65) = -3.01$, $p < 0.01$. The average time to first fixation of high performers on the error lines was not significantly different from that of low performers. Figures 6 and 7 present a visual overview depicting the distribution and skewness of the average proportional fixation count and average proportional fixation duration on the error lines for both groups. The visual representation indicates a positive skewness in both datasets, revealing that high-performing students exhibit more dispersed data, a higher median average proportional fixation count, and higher median average proportional fixation duration in comparison to their low-performing counterparts.

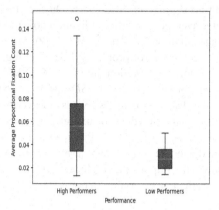 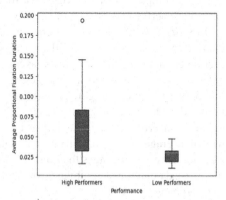

Fig. 6. Average Proportional FC on Error Lines (School B) – Non-literal

Fig. 7. Average Proportional FD on Error Lines (School B) – Non-literal

Based on the School B dataset, we observed that high performers exerted more visual attention to the error lines of non-literal syntax error problems as indicated by greater average proportional fixation count and average proportional fixation duration. This finding supports the findings of Chandrika & Amudha [6] and Sharif et al. [20] that experts tend to concentrate more on areas where the errors are located while novices read the code more broadly. The greater number of fixations on an AOI indicates its importance [4]. Hence, high performers were observed to have more fixations on the error lines.

Comparison of Student Visual Attention to Compiler Error Messages vs. Error Lines

3.5 Literal Syntax Error

For both Schools A and B, we compared high performers' visual attention on error lines versus their visual attention on compiler error messages and found no significant differences in terms of average proportional fixation count and average proportional fixation duration. When we performed the same analysis with the data from low performers, we also found no significant differences.

3.6 Non-literal Syntax Error

School A. School A's high and low performers exerted as much visual attention on error lines and on compiler error messages. Average proportional fixation count on error lines versus compiler error messages and average proportional fixation durations on error lines versus compiler error messages were not significantly different.

School B. For non-literal syntax error problems, low performers exerted the same visual effort on error lines and compiler error messages. When comparing low performers' average proportional fixation counts and average proportional fixation durations on error lines and compiler error messages, we found no significant differences. On the other hand, high performers had significantly greater average proportional fixation count ($M = 0.15$, $SD = 0.08$) on compiler error messages than on error lines ($M = 0.06$, $SD = 0.04$), $t(15) = -4.120$, $p = 0.001$ in non-literal syntax error problems. Likewise, high performers had significantly greater average proportional fixation duration ($M = 0.15$, $SD = 0.08$) on compiler error messages than on error lines ($M = 0.07$, $SD = 0.05$), $t(15) = -3.331$, $p = 0.005$. Figures 8 and 9 show the distribution and skewness of average proportional fixation count and average proportional fixation duration of high performers on compiler error messages and error lines. High performers had significantly higher median average proportional fixation count and average proportional fixation duration on compiler error messages than on error lines. This implies that high performers paid more visual attention to compiler error messages than on error lines in non-literal syntax error problems.

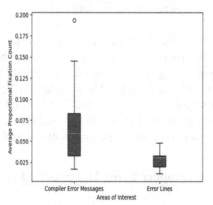
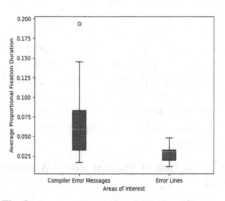

Fig. 8. Average Proportional FC Compiler Error Messages vs. Error Lines (School B) – Non-literal

Fig. 9. Average Proportional FD Compiler Error Messages vs. Error Lines (School B)– Non-literal

Comparison of Visual Effort of Novice Programmers on Error Lines when Locating Literal vs. when they are Locating Non-literal Syntax Errors. To determine if visual effort of students differ when locating literal versus non-literal syntax errors, we compared the average time to first fixation, average fixation count and average fixation duration on error lines of samples in literal and non-literal syntax error problems.

3.7 Literal vs. Non-literal Syntax Errors

School A. Low performers had significantly greater average fixation count on error lines in non-literal syntax error problems ($M = 12.14$, $SD = 8.22$) than in literal syntax error problems ($M = 5.64$, $SD = 4.41$), $t(6) = -2.782$, $p = 0.032$. However, low performers exert about the same visual effort in terms of the average fixation duration and average time to first fixation when locating literal and non-literal syntax errors. When we compared high performers' average fixation counts, average fixation durations, and average time to first fixation when they located literal and non-literal syntax errors, we found no significant differences. Figure 10 presents a visual overview illustrating the distribution and skewness of the average fixation count on the error lines of literal and non-literal syntax error problems for the low performing group. This shows that low-performing students exhibit a higher median average fixation count on error lines in non-literal syntax error problems than in literal syntax error problems.

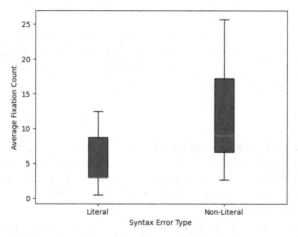

Fig. 10. Average FC on Error Lines Literal vs. Non-Literal (School A – Low Performers)

School B. We compared high-performing students' visual effort on error lines when errors were literal versus when errors were non-literal. Their average fixation counts, and average fixation durations were not significantly different. The same finding was true for the low-performing students. However, low performers showed significantly longer average time to first fixation on error lines of non-literal syntax error problems ($M = 23.97$, $SD = 15.88$) than in literal syntax error problems ($M = 12.48$, $SD = 8.21$), $t(9) = -2.389$, $p = 0.041$. Meanwhile, though it was only approaching significance, high performers also had longer average time to first fixation on error lines of non-literal syntax error problems ($M = 17.07$, $SD = 10.69$) than in literal syntax error problems ($M = 10.37$, $SD = 11.16$), $t(15) = -2.013$, $p = 0.062$. Figures 11 and 12 show the distribution and skewness of the average time to first fixation on the error lines of literal and non-literal syntax error problems for the high and low performing groups. This shows that for both high and low-performing students they exhibited longer median average time to first fixation on error lines of non-literal syntax error problems than in literal syntax error problems. This implies that for both groups it took longer for the students to notice the error lines in non-literal than in literal syntax error problems.

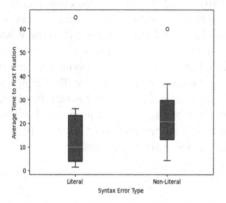

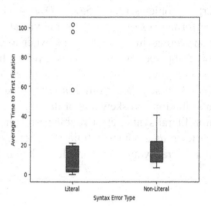

Fig. 11. Average TTFF on Error Lines Literal vs. Non-Literal (School B – Low Performers)

Fig. 12. Average TTFF on Error Lines Literal vs. Non-Literal(School B – High Performers)

4   Discussion

This study is the third in a series of publications concerned with the ways in which novice programmers read and act upon compiler error messages. The overarching goal of these studies is to determine the extent to which novices process compiler error messages and to draw implications on the benefits, if any, of efforts that researchers invest in designing better and better messages.

The first publication by Rodrigo and Tablatin [18] discussed the data collection methodology that this study used. The goal of the publication was to address some of the limitations of prior work such as, there was no uniformity in the type of errors inserted in the code as they could be syntactic or semantic. The number of errors per program also varied. The font size could be small which may lead to ambiguity when interpreting fixation locations. The second publication [21] was a first analysis of the data collected using the methods described in Rodrigo & Tablatin [18]. They found that high performing students had significantly higher visual attention on error lines than the low performing students. A limitation of the study was that whether an error was literal or non-literal was not taken into account. This report addresses this limitation by examining the visual effort and attention patterns of novice programmers on AOIs such as compiler error messages and error lines considering in the analysis whether a syntax error was literal or non-literal.

The analysis conducted on eye tracking data obtained from participants of School A and School B answered the research questions.

1. How does visual attention to compiler error messages for literal syntax errors differ between high-performing and low-performing novice programmers?

High and low performers from School A and School B did not differ in terms of visual attention exerted on compiler error messages when identifying literal syntax error.

2. How does visual attention to compiler error messages for non-literal syntax errors differ between high-performing and low-performing novice programmers?

   High and low performers from School A did not differ in terms of visual attention exerted on compiler error messages. Meanwhile, findings in the School B dataset indicated that high performers exerted more visual attention towards the compiler error messages than low performers in non-literal syntax error problems. Prior work by Bylinski [4] claimed that fixation counts are an indicator of the relative importance of an AOI with more fixations implying higher importance. High performers in this group fixated more on compiler messages, implying that they gave more importance to these messages than low performers did.

3. How does visual attention to error lines for literal syntax errors differ between high-performing and low-performing novice programmers?

   High and low performers from School A did not differ on visual attention exerted on error lines when identifying literal syntax error. On the other hand, high performers from School B had significantly greater visual attention on error lines as compared to the low performers.

4. How does visual attention to error lines for non-literal syntax errors differ between high-performing and low-performing novice programmers?

   In the case of non-literal syntax errors, high and low performers from School A did not differ on visual attention given on error lines. Meanwhile, findings in the School B dataset indicated that high performers gave more visual attention towards the error lines than low performers in non-literal syntax error problems. The visual inclinations of high performers may be correlated with the cognitive style theory known as field-independent (FI), which characterizes individuals who usually embrace an analytical processing approach, concentrating on pertinent details [17]. Conversely, the visual patterns exhibited by low performers might be connected to a field-dependent (FD) cognitive style. Individuals with an FD cognitive style typically utilize a holistic processing method for visual information, potentially facing difficulties in pinpointing relevant details within complex visual stimuli [21].

5. How does student visual attention to compiler error messages differ with their visual attention to error lines for literal syntax errors?

   High performing students invested the same amount of visual attention on compiler error messages and error lines. Similarly, low performing students invested the same amount of effort on both areas of interest.

6. How does student visual attention to compiler error messages differ with their visual attention to error lines for non-literal syntax errors?

   In School A, high performers' visual attention on compiler error messages and error lines did not differ significantly. This was also true of low performers. In School B, high performers gave more attention to compiler error messages than on error lines in non-literal syntax error problems. The visual behavior of high performers may be an indication that they were trying to comprehend the compiler error messages to locate the non-literal syntax errors. This implies that paying more attention to the compiler error messages is a strategy employed by high performers in School B to locate non-literal syntax errors.

7. How does student visual effort on the error lines differ when locating literal vs. non-literal syntax errors?

The findings in School A dataset indicate that low performers exerted more visual effort on error lines when locating non-literal than when locating literal syntax errors. Meanwhile, the syntax error type did not have an effect on the visual effort of high performers on error lines.

In the case of the School B dataset, both low and high-performing students took longer time to notice the error lines in non-literal than in literal syntax error problems. However, in terms of average fixation count and average fixation duration the syntax error type did not have an effect on the visual effort of both high and low performers on error lines.

5 Conclusion

The analysis of eye tracking data collected from participants of two schools revealed a variation in visual effort and attention patterns of high and low performers. It was found in this study that the visual attention of high and low performing students on compiler error messages and error lines can be influenced by the error type injected in the program. The dataset from School B showed that high performing students gave more visual attention towards the compiler error messages and error lines in non-literal syntax error problems. In many of the other comparisons, particularly between groups from School A, we found no significant differences.

From these findings, we glean the following insights. We may conclude that low performance is not always associated with low visual attention. There were cases in the study where high and low performers did not differ significantly on visual attention metrics. The novice programmer code comprehension errors, therefore, may be rooted in other causes such as tracing and debugging strategies that students use [5], cognitive skills, individual preference of learning [15] and programming experience [11]. These factors are out of scope for this paper but may be the subject of future work.

It is interesting to observe that the high and low performers in School A hardly varied while the high and low performers in School B did. This may imply greater homogeneity in School A and more diversity in School B. A homogeneous group is composed of students who have common traits, such as proficiency, age, or gender. A diverse or heterogeneous group is composed of mixed students with varying characteristics [13]. A homogeneous group in a program comprehension and bug finding task may be described as composed of student programmers who have the same orientation, personality, proficiency, etc. Students in School A probably had more shared characteristics which could have been the reason why visual patterns of high and low performers hardly varied. The high or low performance of students might be attributed to a difference in one or more factors, such as those identified in the second paragraph of this section. Students in School B probably had more differences in characteristics which caused the variation in the visual patterns of high and low performers.

A limitation of this study is that the analysis focused on fixations which capture eye gaze positions but not sequences. Similar to the approach of Tablatin and Rodrigo [21], we have investigated the participants' fixations on compiler error messages and error lines, but we have incorporated the types of errors injected in each of the programs.

Examining the entire scanpath as a cohesive entity to identify patterns in code reading, rather than assessing individual eye movement attributes in isolation, has become crucial for making definitive conclusions about the nature and understanding of cognitive processes [1, 22]. While fixation data helps us quantify student attention, examining the methodologies employed by experts or high-achieving students during comprehension tasks, such as debugging, will enable us to identify effective strategies that can be explicitly imparted to enhance the code reading and comprehension skills of students.

References

1. Andrzejewska, M., et al.: Eye-tracking verification of the strategy used to analyse algorithms expressed in a flowchart and pseudocode. Interact. Learn. Environ. **24**(8), 1981–1995 (2016)
2. Becker, B.A., et al.: Compiler error messages considered unhelpful: the landscape of text-based programming error message research. In: Proceedings of the Working Group Reports on Innovation and Technology in Computer Science Education, pp. 177–210 (2019)
3. Becker, B.A.: An effective approach to enhancing compiler error messages. In: Proceedings of the 47th ACM Technical Symposium on Computing Science Education (SIGCSE '16). ACM, New York, NY, USA, pp. 126–131 (2016)
4. Bylinskii, Z., Borkin, M.A., Kim, N.W., Pfisher, H., Oliva, A.: Eye fixation metrics for large-scale evaluation and comparison of information visualizations. In: Burch, M., Chuang, L., Fisher, B., Schmidt, A., Weiskopf, D. (eds.) Eye Tracking and Visualization, pp. 235–255, Springer, Cham (2015)
5. Castro, L.M.C., Cifuentes, J.P.Q., Kumar, A.: Preference for debugging strategies and debugging tools and their relationship with course achievement: preliminary results of a study involving novice programmers. In: 2023 Annual Conference & Exposition. Baltimore Convention Center (2023)
6. Chandrika. K.R., Amudha, J.: An eye tracking study to understand the visual perception behavior while source code comprehension. Int. J. Control Theor. Appl. **10**(19), 169–175 (2017). International Science Press
7. Denny, P., Luxton-Reilly, A., Tempero, E., Hendrickx, J.: Understanding the syntax barrier for novices. In: Proceedings of the 16th Annual Joint Conference on Innovation and Technology in Computer Science Education (ITiCSE '11). ACM, New York, NY, USA, pp. 208–212 (2011)
8. Dy, T., Rodrigo, M.M.: A detector for non-literal java errors. In: Koli Calling '10, Koli, Finland (2010). ACM
9. Javier, B.S.: Understanding their voices from within: difficulties and code comprehension of life-long novice programmers. Int. J. Arts Sci. Educ. **1**(1), 53–76 (2021). ISSN: 1234–5678
10. Jessup, S., Willis, S., Alarcon, G.M.: Using eye-tracking data to compare differences in code comprehension and code perceptions between expert and novice programmers. In: Proceedings of the 54th Hawaii International Conference on System Sciences 2021 (2021)
11. Ko, A.J., Uttl, B.: Individual differences in program comprehension strategies in unfamiliar programming systems. In: Proceedings of the 11th IEEE International Workshop on Program Comprehension (IWPC'03) (2003)
12. Lin, Y.T., Wu, C.C., Hou, T.Y., Lin, Y.C., Yang, F.Y., Chang, C.H.: Tracking Students' cognitive processes during program debugging—an eye-movement approach. IEEE Trans. Educ. **59**(3), 175–186 (2016)
13. Llego, M.A.: Student Learning Groups: Homogeneous or Heterogeneous. TeacherPH (2022). Retrieved December 5, 2023. https://www.teacherph.com/student-learning-groups-homogeneous-heterogeneous/

14. McCall, D., Kölling, M.: A new look at novice programmer errors. ACM Trans. Comput. Educ. **19**(4), 1–30 (2019). https://doi.org/10.1145/3335814
15. Nazeri, S., Suliman, A.: Factors influencing the teaching and learning of programming. Indian J. Sci. Technol. **11**(4), 1–6 (2018). https://doi.org/10.17485/ijst/2018/v11i4/121087
16. OPEN GAZE API BY GAZEPOINT (2013). Retrieved from https://www.gazept.com/dl/Gazepoint_API_v2.0.pdf on October 31, 2023
17. Raptis, G.E., Katsini, K., Belk, M., Fidas, C., Samaras, G., Avouris, N.: Using eye gaze data and visual activities to infer human cognitive styles: method and feasibility studies. In: Proceedings of the 25th Conference on User Modeling, Adaptation and Personalization (UMAP '17). (Bratislava Slovakia, 2017), ACM, New York, NY, USA, pp. 164–173 (2017)
18. Rodrigo, M., Tablatin, C.L.S.: How do programming students read and act upon compiler error messages?". In: Augmented Cognition: 17th International Conference, AC 2023, Held as Part of the 25th HCI International Conference, HCII 2023, Copenhagen, Denmark, July 23–28, 2023, Proceedings July 2023, pp. 153–168 (2023).
19. Schorsch, T.: CAP: an automated self-assessment tool to check pascal programs for syntax, logic and style errors. In: Proceedings of the Twenty-sixth SIGCSE Technical Symposium on Computer Science Education (SIGCSE '95). ACM, New York, NY, USA, pp. 168–172 (1995)
20. Sharif, B., Falcone, M., Maletic, J.I.: An eye-tracking study on the role of scan time in finding source code defects. In: Proceedings of the Symposium on Eye Tracking Research and Applications (ETRA'12), ACM, pp. 381–384 (2012)
21. Tablatin, C.L.S., Rodrigo, M.: Visual attention patterns in processing compiler error messages. In: Proceedings of the 31st International Conference on Computers in Education. Asia-Pacific Society for Computers in Education (2023)
22. Tablatin, C.L.S., Rodrigo, M.: Identifying code reading strategies in debugging using STA with a tolerance algorithm. APSIPA Trans. Sig. Inf. Process. **2022**(11), e6 (2022)
23. Turner, R., Falcone, M., Sharif, B., Lazar, A.: An eye-tracking study assessing the comprehension of C++ and Python source code. In: Proceedings of the Symposium on Eye Tracking Research & Applications, ACM, New York, ETRA '14, pp. 231–234 (2014)
24. Villamor, M., Rodrigo, M., Mercedes, T.: Characterizing individual gaze patterns of pair programming participants. In: Proceedings of the 26th International Conference on Computers in Education (ICCE 2018), APSCE, Taiwan, 2018, pp. 193–198 (2018)
25. Vosskühler, A.: OGAMA description (for Version 2.5). Berlin, Germany: Freie Universität Berlin, Fachbereich Physik (2009). Retrieved April 23, 2023 from http://www.ogama.net/sites/default/files/pdf/OGAMA-DescriptionV25.pdf
26. Whalley, J., Settle, A., Luxton-Reilly, A.: A think-aloud study of novice debugging. ACM Trans. Comput. Educ. **23**(2), 1–38 (2023). Article No.: 28, https://doi.org/10.1145/3589004
27. Yen, C.Z., Wu, P.H., Lin, C.F.: Analysis of experts' and novices' thinking process in program debugging. In: Engaging Learners Through Emerging Technologies, pp. 122–134 (2012)

Mapping Signaling Mechanisms in Neurotoxic Injury from Sparsely Sampled Data Using a Constraint Satisfaction Framework

Jeffery Page[1], Kimberly A. Kelly[2], Lindsay T. Michalovicz[2], James P. O'Callahghan[2], Shichen Shen[3], Xiaoyu Zhu[3], Jun Qu[3], Jonathan Boyd[4], and Gordon Broderick[1(✉)]

[1] Center for Clinical Systems Biology, Rochester General Hospital, Rochester, NY, USA
`gordonbroderick55@gmail.com`
[2] Centers for Disease Control and Prevention, NIOSH, Morgantown, WV, USA
[3] Department of Pharmaceutical Sciences, University at Buffalo, Buffalo, NY, USA
[4] Department of Orthopaedic Surgery, Virginia Commonwealth University School of Medicine, Richmond, VA, USA

Abstract. Gulf War Illness (GWI) is a poorly understood exposure-induced neuroinflammatory disorder where complexity and the high cost of animal exposure studies has led to fragmented and sparse data sets incompatible with conventional data mining. We propose a numerical approach for generating hypotheses from sparse data to describe dysregulation of phosphoproteomic signaling in GWI brain. In an established animal model, hippocampus, and prefrontal cortex (PFC) samples were collected in mice exposed to corticosterone (CORT) to mimic high physiological stress, sarin surrogate diisopropyl fluorophosphate (DFP), CORT and DFP (CORT + DFP), as well as controls. IonStar liquid chromatography/ mass spectrometry (LC/MS) profiling produced a network of 93 undirected interactions (Pearson correlation Bonferroni < 1%) linking 12 hippocampal and 5 PFC phosphoproteins. With only one pre-treatment resting state and one post-treatment transient observation, conventional rate models were infeasible. Instead, a simple discrete state transition logic was applied to each network node requiring baseline be a steady state from which the network could evolve through the transient 6-h post-treatment state. Solving this as a Constraint Satisfaction (SAT) problem produced 3 competing network models where DFP directly targeted phosphorylated subspecies of sodium channel protein type 1 subunit alpha (Scn1a), protein kinase C gamma (Prkcg), sacsin molecular chaperone (Sacs), in PFC and R3H domain containing 2 (R3hdm2) in hippocampus potentiated by corticosteroids. In simulation-based searches for intervention targets inhibition of Prkcg was disproportionately represented in rescuing the model-predicted persistent illness state, though companion targets were also necessary. Results such as these suggest that a dynamically constrained model-informed design can be highly useful in the initial phases of investigation into complex poorly understood illness where detailed data is largely unavailable.

Keywords: Neurotoxic insult · animal model · network regulatory dynamics

© The Author(s), under exclusive license to Springer Nature Switzerland AG 2024
D. D. Schmorrow and C. M. Fidopiastis (Eds.): HCII 2024, LNAI 14694, pp. 95–110, 2024.
https://doi.org/10.1007/978-3-031-61569-6_7

1   Introduction

Gulf War Illness (GWI) is a complex neuroinflammatory disorder affecting 1 of 3 Veterans of the 1990–91 Gulf War. Among the symptoms of GWI are those associated with sickness behavior (e.g. headache, fatigue, gastrointestinal distress, and neuropathic pain), suggestive of underlying neuroinflammation potentially from low-level neurotoxic exposure potentiated by in-theatre stress [1–3]. In developing a rodent model of GWI, we have shown that the exposure of mice to the stress hormone, corticosterone (CORT), at levels associated with high physiological stress, in combination with diisopropyl fluorophosphate (DFP), as a nerve agent mimic, results in marked neuroinflammation [3]. Moreover, this initial exposure to DFP can induce a "priming" of the neuroinflammatory response that persists for months in a mouse (equivalent to years in a human), consistent with the protracted sickness behavior phenotype exhibited by ill Veterans over the 26 years since their returning from theater [4–6]. Despite these important observations, the underlying molecular mechanisms of illness remain poorly understood. The complexity of the persistent GWI pathology itself coupled with the high cost of comprehensive proteomic profiling in brain tissue of exposed animals has led to fragmented and sparse data sets that are generally incompatible with conventional data mining.

The initial biological response to diverse chemical/biochemical insults is primarily coordinated by cellular signal transduction networks, which typically follow a fundamental framework: the phosphorylation/dephosphorylation cycle mediated by protein kinases and phosphatases [7–9]. Our prior work has shown that increased phosphorylation of signal transducer and activator of transcription 3 (STAT3), which activates this transcription factor, serves as a key downstream effector of proinflammatory mediators from various neurotoxic exposures [10] including CORT and DFP treatment in our GWI mouse model [1]. Indeed, exposure to these insults perturb a much broader dynamic and highly integrated network of signaling pathways responsible for normal biological function and maintenance, inducing inflammation that can progress to a chronic condition as a result of overcompensation and dysregulation [11–13]. Accordingly, an experimental approach that casts a much wider net on key phosphoproteins that mediate signal transduction through various stress and inflammatory pathways is desperately needed to elucidate the regulatory response mechanisms that support not only the onset but most importantly the dynamically stable persistence of GWI symptomatology long after insult. Only once we have identified these regulatory drivers will it be possible to identify targets that may be amenable to modulation by already available kinase/substrate inhibitors and modulators [14]. Unfortunately, mapping regulatory feedback dynamics typically requires well-sampled time course experiments making them more accessible to in vitro experimentation due to the excessive expense often associated with repeated in vivo experimentation.

Here, we demonstrate a constraint satisfaction framework where we leverage sparse experimental observations by casting individual phosphoproteins in the context of a broader regulatory network and where we apply specific hypotheses regarding the system's dynamic behavior that we expect to be true in the vicinity of these observations. Applying these additional constraints of regulatory stability to only 3 transient post-exposure observations and one pre-treatment baseline resulted in a small number of competing models that consistently inferred phosphoproteomic profiles characteristic of stable persistent illness as well as corresponding sets of actionable targets.

2 Methods

2.1 A Small Set of Animal Experiments

All procedures were performed within protocols approved by the Centers for Disease Control and Prevention-Morgantown Institutional Animal Care and Use Committee and the US Army Medical Research and Materiel Command Animal Care and Use Review Office, and the animal facility was certified by AAALAC International. Upon arrival, mice were individually housed in a temperature- (21 ± 1 °C) and humidity-controlled ($50\% \pm 10$) colony room that was maintained under filtered positive-pressure ventilation and a 12 h light (0600 EDT)/12 h dark cycle (1800 EDT) and acclimated for one week prior to the commencement of experimental procedures. Mice were given ad libitum access to food (Harlan 7913 irradiated NIH-31 modified 6% rodent chow) and sterile water. In this work, we used our acute exposure model [3] where adult male ($N = 30$, 8–12 weeks, ~ 30 g) C57BL/6 mice (Jackson Laboratory) were selectively administered the stress hormone CORT (200 mg/L in 0.6% EtOH), or not, in drinking water for 7 days then exposed to the sarin surrogate DFP by an intraperitoneal injection (4 mg/kg) or saline control (0.9%) on day 8. These mice were chosen as young adult males constituted the majority of deployed troops in the 1991 GW. Baseline control (saline, $N = 12$), CORT ($N = 6$), DFP ($N = 6$), and CORT + DFP ($N = 6$) exposed mice were sacrificed by focused wave microwave irradiation at 6 h post-exposure for all phosphoprotein analyses. Brains were removed and dissected free-hand into multiple regions, including the prefrontal cortex (PFC) and hippocampus, and immediately frozen on dry-ice and stored at -80 °C. We have chosen to examine these brain areas as they showed a significant neuroinflammatory response to these exposures in previous studies [1, 3].

2.2 Phosphoproteomic Profiling of Hippocampus and PFC

Samples were analyzed in triplicate using the IonStar liquid chromatography/ mass spectrometry (LC/MS) platform. Prior to analysis samples were pooled among like-treated animals to increase sample quantity and protein concentrations in each of the pooled samples measured in duplicate. The IonStar pipeline consists of two major components: i) an experimental procedure for robust sample preparation and enabling consistent, sensitive and reliable data acquisition for many biological replicates [15–17]; and ii) a data processing pipeline with optimal alignment, sensitive feature detection and stringent quality control [18–21]. IonStar supports very broad-spectrum profiling, routinely exceeding 6000 protein groups with ≥ 2 peptide/protein in human cell/tissue samples. It also displays excellent reproducibility for low-abundance protein quantification with $< 0.2\%$ missing data, across ~ 6 orders of magnitudes in abundance. Cells were lysated by a pressurized cell in a detergent-cocktail buffer (0.5% sodium deoxycholate, 2% SDS, 2% IGEPAL® CA-630 and protease/phosphatase inhibitor cocktail), followed by a surfactant-aided/precipitation-on-pellet-digestion (SOD) method to achieve quantitative and efficient recovery of peptides, including these from hydrophobic membrane proteins [15–17, 22]. To achieve in-depth profiling and accurate peptide ion-current quantification, digests were separated on a 100-cm-long column with 2-μm-particles by an ultra-high-pressure chromatographic setup. An Orbitrap LUMOS ultra-high-field and high-resolution mass spectrometer was then used to acquire quantitative ion-current signal and for protein identification. Individual data files were searched against the Swiss-Prot human protein database using MSGF + package leading to the quantifiable detection of 10,894 phosphorylation modifications to over 2,800 master protein species.

Phosphoprotein species of interest were those with technical replicates significantly different from saline in at least one treatment (i.e. CORT, DFP or CORT + DFP) at an adjusted t-test p-value corresponding to a Bonferroni correction > 1% and expressed with a Ln2 transformed fold change (FC) > 2 (Fig. 1). Calculations were performed using the Python functions *scipy.stats.ttest_ind* in the SciPy v1.11.4 library.

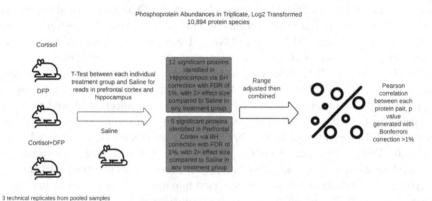

Fig. 1. Stringent identification of phosphoprotein species emerging in response to challenge with CORT, DFP alone and CORT + DFP in C57bl/6J male mice (Jackson Labs) at a Bonferroni Correction <1% and a signal to noise ratio >2. Putative interactions were inferred from simple Pearson correlation of Ln2 transformed, range-adjusted abundance values with a Bonferroni correction >1%.

2.3   Identification of a Phosphoproteomic Regulatory Network in Brain

A first putative undirected interaction network was inferred using simple Pearson correlation as a reasonable measure of association between significantly responsive phosphoprotein species given the low number of abundance values, namely triplicate measures at each of 4 conditions. Significance of the coefficient of determination R^2 was based on the F statistic from the underlying linear regression computed using the *sklearn.linear_model.LinearRegression* function in the Python scikit-learn library. Raw p-values for these pairwise associations were once again corrected for multiple comparison using a Bonferroni correction with a cut off threshold of 1%. Significant undirected associations were then translated into pairs of putative opposing *directed* interactions. Of these, only those candidates directed regulatory interactions that supported a flow of information through the network consistent with experimental observations and postulated network dynamics were retained as explained below.

Information flow through this putative directed network was modeled by applying a simple discrete decisional logic to each node originally proposed by Thomas [23] and further refined by Mendoza and Xenarios [24]. Each phosphoprotein-phosphoprotein regulatory interaction was defined by a direction, (i.e. source to target), as well as its action on a downstream target (i.e. inactivating or activating). The activation level of each phosphoprotein node was described as one of three discrete qualitative states, namely Low (0), Nominal (1), or High (2). An increase or decrease in the activation level of any given node was dictated by the states and actions of its upstream neighbors. The competing actions of upstream neighbors activated to levels above their respective perception thresholds were aggregated using a simple piece-wise linear function weighing the actions of weak inactivators against those of strong activators, and vice versa. Based on this combinatorial context-specific process an increase or decrease in the activation of each node is proposed as an update in the next iteration [25] (Fig. 2).

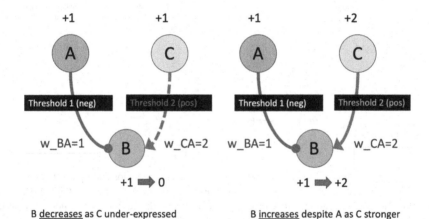

B decreases as C under-expressed   B increases despite A as C stronger

Fig. 2. Simple state transition logic directing the flow of information through the network. In this parameter space, each network node carries a baseline activation term and every regulatory interaction is characterized by a perception threshold and a strength of action weight.

Here, the direction (source-target) and mode of action (positive activating or negative inactivating) for each network interaction as well as logic parameters describing signal transmission thresholds and decisional weights dictating each node's state transition [26, 27] were defined as free variables and plausible values determined by solving a Constraint Satisfaction (SAT) problem [28] (Fig. 3). The expression or activation profiles observed served as both hard and soft constraints that must be met by any acceptable solution parameter set. In addition, constraints were imposed that dictate the expected dynamic behavior in the vicinity of each observation. Specifically, with respect to the observed phosphoprotein activation values at baseline (saline), we require not only that these values be recovered exactly, but also that this observed baseline state be explained by the model as a dynamically stable resting state. In other words, not only must the observed baseline state be recovered exactly, but the next predicted state must also be identical to the current state in the absence of an external perturbation i.e. it must be explained as a steady state. These are both defined as hard constraints. In contrast, as we do not know a priori the state transition time step we establish as soft constraints the 6-hrs post-exposure phosphoprotein activation profiles to be transient observations that the most suitable network models should explain as closely as possible (Manhattan distance) in their response following each exposure. This parameter search problem was encoded using the open-source Constraint Programming and Modeling in Python (CPMpy) library in Python [29]. Solutions were generated by invoking the CP-SAT solver [30] within the Google OR-Tools optimization toolbox [31]. CP-SAT applies lazy clause generation, a hybrid approach which combines the strengths of finite domain propagation in Constraint Programming (CP) with the efficiency of Boolean Satisfiability (SAT) solvers.

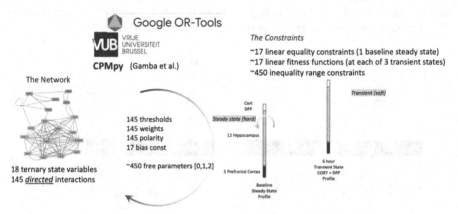

Fig. 3. Inferring a directed regulatory network structure and behavior from phosphoproteomic data collected in mice at baseline and at 6 h post- exposure to CORT, DFP or CORT + DFP by using this data to validate regulatory programs where the predicted dynamic responses include those observed. In essence the data is used to define a series of constraints and model parameters used as free variables in a large Constraint Satisfaction (SAT) problem.

2.4 Mapping Regulatory Traps and Escape Trajectories

As mentioned above, we used a discrete decisional logic to manage the signal propagation through the phosphoproteomic regulatory network and direct its evolution from one state to the next. At any given iteration, each of the network nodes is assessed for incoming signals activated above their respective perception thresholds. Based on the specific combination of active upstream mediators and their mode of action (activator or inactivator), the state of a downstream node is directed to either remain unchanged, increase, or decrease in the next iteration. Depending on the specific network update scheme, this predicted state change is applied to a single random node (asynchronous update) or to all eligible nodes simultaneously (synchronous update). Here, we used a synchronous update of all node states to improve computational efficiency and because we are primarily interested in stable persistent behaviors. Using this framework, simulations of phosphoprotein signaling under different conditions were conducted as part of a multi-objective optimization problem directed at identifying the smallest sets of target phosphoproteins that if manipulated concurrently in a specific manner (i.e. activated or inactivated) would render the persistent illness attractor unstable and trigger a reset of phosphoprotein signaling to one ensuring a normal resting state.

Such phosphoprotein Minimal Intervention Sets (MIS) were identified by stating and solving a computationally efficient Answer Set Programming (ASP) problem [32] where idealized manipulations of network targets were iteratively assessed. As reported in previous work by our group [33], this optimization consisted of concurrently minimizing the number of target phosphoprotein nodes being manipulated, the final distance to the target state achieved by the intervention (calculated using the L1-norm), and the number of state transitions required (efficiency) to reach this treatment stabilized state. This multi-objective optimization problem was encoded in MiniZinc [34] using an in-house parser and solved with the greedy solver Chuffed [35].

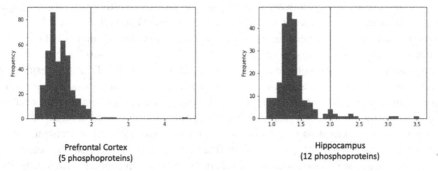

Fig. 4. Number of phosphoprotein species expressed significantly (Bonferroni $< 1\%$) in the hippocampus and PFC with effect size $Ln2(FC) > 2$ at 6 h pots-exposure.

3   Results

3.1   Plausible Regulatory Response Networks

We selected as nodes in the regulatory network those candidate phosphoprotein species where changes in abundance were both significant in the context of technical replication at a Bonferroni correction $< 1\%$ and important in terms of affect size with a $Ln2(FC) > 2$ (Fig. 4). We found 12 such proteins in the hippocampus and 5 in the PFC. Together with 3 insult external perturbation nodes, this resulted in a network of 20 nodes interconnected by 93 undirected associations (Pearson R^2 significant at Bonferroni correction $< 1\%$) (Fig. 5). Interestingly, the brain phosphoproteome targets in the PFC directly associated with the compound CORT + DFP insult consisted of the union of those targets affected by the agents CORT and DFP applied individually, suggesting a straightforward additive insult to the PFC. The 4 phosphoproteins targeted directly consisted of modifications to the master proteins Scn1, Prkcg, and Sacs in the PFC and R3hdm2 in the hippocampus.

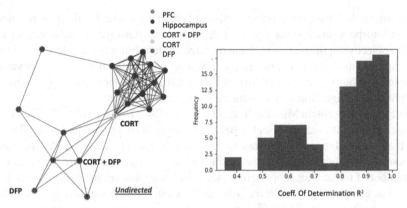

Fig. 5. An initial undirected association network linking 17 phosphoprotein and 3 exogenous insult nodes through 93 undirected associations.

As we are interested in the network response dynamics resulting from the propagation of the neurotoxic insult through the network, we translated all undirected associations between phosphoproteins into pairs of oppositely directed regulatory actions. The actions of exogenous agents were assumed to be unidirectional into the phosphoproteomic network. Focusing on the compounded actions of CORT + DFP, this resulted in a network of 18 nodes linked by 145 directed interactions. The corresponding parameter space consists of 17 bias terms for each of the phosphoprotein nodes and for each of the 145 directed interactions (network edges) a perception threshold, a mode of action (positive or target activation vs negative or target inactivation) as well as decisional logic weight resulting in over 450 parameters or free variables. The corresponding search for parameter values was formulated as a Constraint Satisfaction problem defined by 450 constraints on the range for each parameter, as well as 17 linear equality constraints describing the network steady state at baseline and another 17 linear inequality constraints setting an upper bound on departure from the 6-h transient response state for each of the 3 insults. Overall, the parameter search was subject to 520 constraints on 452 free variables.

Applying a lazy clause generation CP-SAT solver to this problem produced only 3 plausible solution sets where the network architecture and regulatory state transition logic could explain the baseline (saline) profile in 17 phosphoproteins as a stable steady state from which the network response to each insult evolved at 6 h to within 5% deviation (Manhattan distance) of the observed transient phosphoprotein signature (Fig. 6). In all 3 models, the direction of regulatory actions selected in the solution set supported the propagation of the neurotoxic insult through the PFC into the hippocampus. Moreover, 12 of 145 directed edges were unanimously retained across solution sets, with another 68 retained in 2 of the 3 network models (Fig. 7).

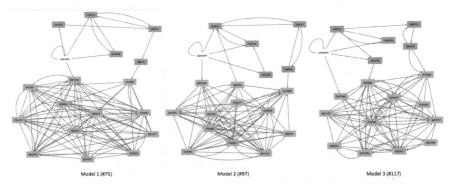

Model 1 (#75) Model 2 (#97) Model 3 (#117)

Fig. 6. Parameters sets identified by solving the Constraint Satisfaction (SAT) problem of Fig. 3, define 3 competing network models with < 5% deviation (Manhattan distance) from transient 6-h profile. In all 3 models information transferred to hippocampus (green nodes) from the prefrontal cortex (grey nodes), 12 of 145 directed edges unanimously retained across all 3 models, and 68 of 145 are retained in 2 of 3 solution sets (red is inactivating, green is activating). (Color figure online)

3.2 Predicting Persistent Illness as a Regulatory Trap

Here, we explore the idea that the persistence of chronic or very slowly evolving illness may at least in part result from an alternative homeostatic regulatory drive or coincide with a pathologic regulatory trap. To identify the regulatory traps or persistent illness conditions supported by each of the 3 candidate models above, we formulated another Constraint Satisfaction problem. This time the network structure and state transition regulatory parameters remained fixed, but we added a constraint whereby we required the regulatory network model in question to describe unknown stationary point attractors, or phosphoprotein profiles at which the next predicted network state would remain unchanged i.e. a steady state. Solving this problem for each of the 3 candidate network models identified 4 such stable point attractors or potential illness regulatory traps, one for each of models 1 and 2, and 2 for model 3. We then conducted simulations where each model was initialized with the phosphoproteomic profiles observed at 6 h following each insult to confirm which attractors would likely lie on the response path.

Of the 2 attractors supported by model 3 only one emerged as a natural endpoint following the observed responses to insult. The alternative attractor for model 3 was therefore removed from further analysis. Attractors predicted by models 1 and 2 both captured the eventual progression of insult to a persistent state (Table 1). At these candidate profiles for persistent illness, 8 of the 17 phosphoprotein species are unanimously predicted to be at their lowest activation level. Indeed, at the attractor predicted by model 2 as a persistent outcome of CORT + DFP exposure, only 2 phosphoprotein species are activated above the minimum level, namely modifications to master proteins Prkcg (P63318) and Sacs (Q9JLC8). Both are predicted to be persistently activated in the PFC at their highest level. Modifications to Srrm2 (Q8BTI8) in the PFC and Pcyt1a (P49586) in the hippocampus were also predicted to be activated in persistent states supported by models 1 and 3, offering additional potential biomarkers of chronic GWI.

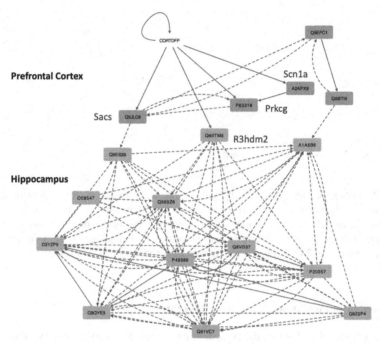

Fig. 7. Consensus network aggregating the 3 candidate networks showing unanimously retained directed interactions as solid lines and where red indicates inactivation and green activation of a downstream target. The combined insult of CORT and DFP directly upregulates 4 phosphoproteins, namely Scn1a, Prkcg, and Sacs in the PFC and R3hdm2 in the hippocampus. (Color figure online)

3.3 Predicted Rescue Strategies

In order to identify strategies for manipulating the phosphoproteome in a way that would promote an escape from the stable illness profiles described in Table 1, we formulated and solved a simulation-based Answer Set Programming (ASP) optimization problem for each model network, individually. In this approach, the model network was initialized at the corresponding predicted persistent illness attractor and sets of phosphoproteins were selected from a pool of allowable targets, and their exogenous up or downregulation were exhaustively evaluated in terms of their ability to deliver the network to the baseline normal steady state over a user-specified horizon. Here, we allowed all 17 network nodes to be selected as a target and assessed the proximity to the desired normal steady state produced by each candidate manipulation after 50 time steps. We found 59 solution sets that displaced the network state from illness to within a Manhattan distance of 20 (or ~ 59% deviation) from the desired normal resting state; namely, 16 candidate manipulations to targets in model 1, 22 manipulations to targets in model 2, and 21 manipulations to targets in the phosphoproteome network of model 3 (Fig. 8). No single target solution set was identified with all solutions requiring the manipulation of at least 4 targets and only 8 solutions delivered the network back to a lasting baseline steady state (Manhattan distance of 0).

Table 1. Activation states in 17 network phosphoproteins at predicted long-term the persistent illness state where Low = 0, Nominal = 1, High = 2

	Master Protein	Model 1	Model 2	Model 3
Hippocampus	Q9QYE3	0	0	0
	Q9ES28	2	0	0
	O08547	0	0	0
	P20357	1	0	0
	Q91VC7	0	0	0
	Q80TM6	1	0	0
	P49586	1	0	2
	Q8VD37	0	0	0
	D3YZP9	0	0	0
	Q569Z6	0	0	0
	A1A5B6	1	0	0
	Q9Z0P4	0	0	0
PFC	P63318	0	2	0
	Q8BTI8	1	0	2
	A2APX8	0	0	2
	Q9EPC1	0	0	0
	Q9JLC8	0	2	0

Of these minimal sets, concurrent downregulation of 5, 6, 7 and 8 phosphoprotein targets in model 2 delivered the network exactly to the desired baseline self-sustaining stable resting state eliminating the need for continued treatment. The smallest set of 5 targets involved the inhibition of phosphorylated forms of Parva (Q9EPC1), Sacs (Q9JLC8), and Prkcg (P63318) in the PFC, along with inhibition of Palm (Q9Z0P4) and R3hdm2 (Q80TM6) in the hippocampus. Likewise, concurrent downregulation of 4, 5, 8 and 10 targets in model 3 exactly restored the network to the baseline steady state. The smallest of these sets consisted in the inhibition of Srrm2 (Q8BTI8) and Prkcg (P63318) in the PFC jointly with the inhibition of SGIP1 (Q8VD37) and Map2 (P20357) in the hippocampus. Importantly, all larger solution sets predicted to produce a full lasting recovery were supersets of these minimal solutions for each model, respectively.

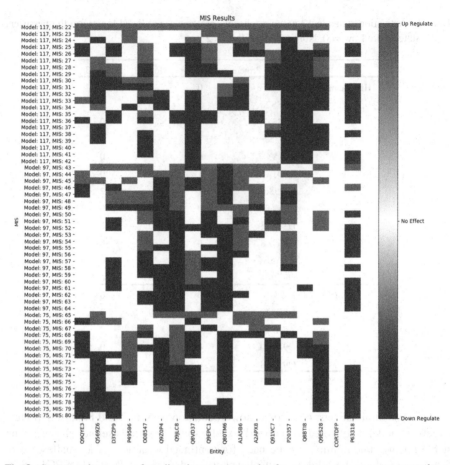

Fig. 8. Summary heat map of predicted escape strategies for concurrent exogenous up or down regulation of network phosphoprotein targets that would destabilize the persistent illness state (attractor) in favor of a return to stable baseline activation levels.

Looking across all intervention solutions in all 3 models, we used a simple desirability score to rank the participation of individual phosphoproteins being inhibited in those intervention sets most effective at restoring the stale baseline phosphoprotein signature (Fig. 9). This desirability score counted only those instances where a phosphoprotein target was selected for inhibition in an intervention set and weighed this instance by the squared reduction in Manhattan distance d to the desired target state delivered by that intervention (i.e. [Max. d − intervention residual d) / Max $d]^2$). Based on this score, inhibition of three phosphoproteins appeared especially appealing, namely Prkcg (P63318) in the PFC, as well as SGIP1 (Q8VD37) and R3hdm2 (Q80TM6) in the hippocampus. These targets were consistently selected for inhibition in those intervention sets selected to be the most successful.

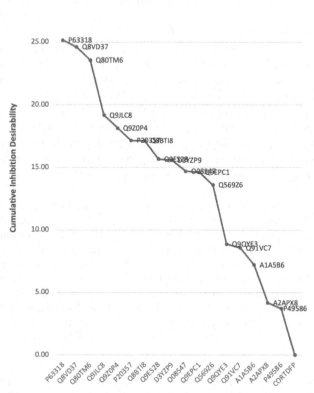

Fig. 9. Ranking of individual phosphoproteins selected as intervention targets based on the frequency each is selected to be inhibited in an intervention set weighted by the squared reduction in distance from the target state of baseline activation levels. Higher scores correspond to targets selected for inhibition in a greater number of more effective intervention sets.

4 Discussion

Here, we demonstrated a formal analytical framework whereby we augmented the use of very sparse experimental data by including and validating hypotheses regarding the expected dynamic regulatory behavior of the biological system. In the case study presented here, we have applied this approach to an early investigation of protein phosphorylation patterns in a brain induced model of Gulf War Illness. Though representing sizable resources and complex experimental procedures, the resulting data set remained small by data modeling standards. Applying this data to the validation of putative phosphoprotein regulatory network models, we identified three such models capable of explaining experimental observations and predicting plausible phosphorylation signatures for the onset and persistence of chronic illness. Moreover, using these same models and illness signatures in a simulation-based optimization scheme pointed to the inhibition of specific targets for the rescue and recovery of baseline phosphoprotein signaling. One of the more prominent targets was protein kinase C gamma (PKCγ), Prkcg (P63318). PKC isoforms and inhibitors have gained attention in the study and treatment of several neurological illnesses, including Alzheimer's disease, ataxia, stroke, amyotrophic lateral sclerosis, and psychological disorders [36, 37].

Early results such as these are not meant to be definitive but rather offer potential avenues of study based on a systematic analysis of sparse but important new experimental data. While powerful when used appropriately, the amount and type of data needed to adequately support conventional data mining can make these methods challenging to deploy in the early stages of data collection or in small pilot studies. Here, we propose reversing the problem from one of model creation to one of model selection. By using whatever data available to validate a candidate regulatory network model rather than assemble said model de novo, the proposed approach provides an opportunity to gain early insight and perhaps even inform ongoing research studies.

Acknowledgments. This work was supported by Rochester Regional Health in conjunction with Elsevier BV (Amsterdam) under a collaborative research sponsorship (Broderick, PI), the US Department of Defense through Congressionally Directed Medical Research Programs (CDMRP) award GW170081 (Boyd, O'Callaghan, Kelly, Broderick, Qu) award, and Intramural funding from the Centers for Disease Control and Prevention - National Institute for Occupational Safety and Health (O'Callaghan, Kelly, Michalovicz). Pathway Studio (© 2020), Elsevier Text Mining, Elsevier Knowledge Graph and EmBio are trademarks of Elsevier Limited. Copyright Elsevier Limited except certain content provided by third parties. We wish to acknowledge the excellent technical support of Brenda K. Billig, Christopher M. Felton, and Ali A. Yilmaz.

Mandatory Disclosure. The opinions and assertions contained herein are the private views of the authors and are not to be construed as official or as reflecting the views of the US Department of Veterans Affairs, the US Department of Defense, Rochester Regional Health, or Elsevier BV. The findings and conclusions in this report are those of the authors and do not necessarily represent the official position of the National Institute for Occupational Safety and Health, Centers for Disease Control and Prevention. This work was supported by the Assistant Secretary of Defense for Health Affairs through the Gulf War Illness Research Program. Opinions, interpretations, conclusions, and recommendations are those of the author and are not necessarily endorsed by the Department of Defense.

Disclosure of Interests. The authors have no competing interests to declare that are relevant to the content of this article.

References

1. Locker, A.R., Michalovicz, L.T., Kelly, K.A., Miller, J.V., Miller, D.B., O'Callaghan, J.P.: Corticosterone primes the neuroinflammatory response to Gulf War Illness-relevant organophosphates independently of acetylcholinesterase inhibition. J. Neurochem. **142**(3), 444–455 (2017)
2. Michalovicz, L.T., Kelly, K.A., Sullivan, K., O'Callaghan, J.P.: Acetylcholinesterase inhibitor exposures as an initiating factor in the development of Gulf War Illness, a chronic neuroimmune disorder in deployed veterans. Neuropharmacology **171**, 108073 (2020)

3. O'Callaghan, J.P., Kelly, K.A., Locker, A.R., Miller, D.B., Lasley, S.M.: Corticosterone primes the neuroinflammatory response to DFP in mice: potential animal model of Gulf War illness. J. Neurochem. **133**(5), 708–721 (2015)
4. Carrera Arias, F.J., et al.: Modeling neuroimmune interactions in human subjects and animal models to predict subtype-specific multidrug treatments for Gulf War illness. Int. J. Mol. Sci. **22**(16), 8546 (2021)
5. Michalovicz, L.T., Kelly, K.A., Miller, D.B., Sullivan, K., O'Callaghan, J.P.: The β-adrenergic receptor blocker and anti-inflammatory drug propranolol mitigates brain cytokine expression in a long-term model of Gulf War illness. Life Sci. **285**, 119962 (2021)
6. White, R.F., et al.: Recent research on Gulf War illness and other health problems in veterans of the 1991 Gulf War: effects of toxicant exposures during deployment. Cortex **74**, 449–475 (2016)
7. Kholodenko, B.N.: Cell-signalling dynamics in time and space. Nat. Rev. Mol. Cell Biol. **7**(3), 165–176 (2006)
8. Newman, R.H., et al.: Construction of human activity-based phosphorylation networks. Mol. Syst. Biol. **9**, 655 (2013)
9. Boyd, J.W., Neubig, R.R. (eds.): Cellular Signal Transduction in Toxicology and Pharmacology: Data Collection, Analysis, and Interpretation. John Wiley & Sons, New York (2019)
10. O'Callaghan, J.P., Kelly, K.A., VanGilder, R.L., Sofroniew, M.V., Miller, D.B.: Early activation of STAT3 regulates reactive astrogliosis induced by diverse forms of neurotoxicity. PLoS ONE **9**(7), e102003 (2014)
11. Kholodenko, B.N., Hancock, J.F., Kolch, W.: Signalling ballet in space and time. Nat. Rev. Mol. Cell Biol. **11**(6), 414–426 (2010)
12. von Kriegsheim, A., et al.: Cell fate decisions are specified by the dynamic ERK interactome. Nat. Cell Biol. **11**(12), 1458–1464 (2009)
13. Vrana, J.A., Currie, H.N., Han, A.A., Boyd, J.: Forecasting cell death dose-response from early signal transduction responses in vitro. Toxicol. Sci. **140**(2), 338–351 (2014)
14. Vrana, J.A., Boggs, N., Currie, H.N., Boyd, J.: Amelioration of an undesired action of deguelin. Toxicon **74**, 83–91 (2013)
15. Duan, X., et al.: A straightforward and highly efficient precipitation/on-pellet digestion procedure coupled with a long gradient nano-LC separation and Orbitrap mass spectrometry for label-free expression profiling of the swine heart mitochondrial proteome. J. Proteome Res. **8**(6), 2838–2850 (2009)
16. An, B., Zhang, M., Johnson, R.W., Qu, J.: Surfactant-aided precipitation/on-pellet-digestion (SOD) procedure provides robust and rapid sample preparation for reproducible, accurate and sensitive LC/MS quantification of therapeutic protein in plasma and tissues. Anal. Chem. **87**(7), 4023–4029 (2015)
17. Nouri-Nigjeh, E., et al.: Highly multiplexed and reproducible ion-current-based strategy for large-scale quantitative proteomics and the application to protein expression dynamics induced by methylprednisolone in 60 rats. Anal. Chem. **86**(16), 8149–8157 (2014)
18. Tu, C., et al.: Large-scale, ion-current-based proteomics investigation of bronchoalveolar lavage fluid in chronic obstructive pulmonary disease patients. J. Proteome Res. **13**(2), 627–639 (2014)
19. Shen, X., Hu, Q., Li, J., Wang, J., Qu, J.: Experimental null method to guide the development of technical procedures and to control false-positive discovery in quantitative proteomics. J. Proteome Res. **14**(10), 4147–4157 (2015)
20. Tu, C., et al.: Ion-current-based proteomic profiling of the retina in a rat model of Smith-Lemli-Opitz syndrome. Mol. Cell. Proteomics **12**(12), 3583–3598 (2013)

21. Tu, C., Li, J., Sheng, Q., Zhang, M., Qu, J.: Systematic assessment of survey scan and MS2-based abundance strategies for label-free quantitative proteomics using high-resolution MS data. J. Proteome Res. **13**(4), 2069–2079 (2014)

22. Shen, S., et al.: Ion-current-based temporal proteomic profiling of Influenza-a-virus-infected mouse lungs revealed underlying mechanisms of altered integrity of the lung microvascular barrier. J. Proteome Res. **15**(2), 540–553 (2016)

23. Thomas, R.: Regulatory networks seen as asynchronous automata: a logical description. J. Theor. Biol. **153**, 1–23 (1991)

24. Mendoza, L., Xenarios, I.: A method for the generation of standardized qualitative dynamical systems of regulatory networks. Theor. Biol. Med. Model. **3**(1), 1–18 (2006)

25. Sedghamiz, H., Morris, M., Craddock, T.J.A., Whitley, D., Broderick, G.: High-fidelity discrete modeling of the HPA axis: a study of regulatory plasticity in biology. BMC Syst. Biol. **12**(1), 76 (2018)

26. Sedghamiz, H., Chen, W., Rice, M., Whitley, D., Broderick G.: Selecting optimal models based on efficiency and robustness in multi-valued biological networks. In: 2017 IEEE 17th International Conference on Bioinformatics and Bioengineering (BIBE), pp. 200–205. IEEE, New York (2017)

27. Sedghamiz, H., Morris, M., Craddock, T.J.A., Whitley, D., Broderick, G.: Bio-modelchecker: using bounded constraint satisfaction to seamlessly integrate observed behavior with prior knowledge of biological networks. Front. Bioeng. Biotechnol. **7**, 48 (2019)

28. Barták, R.: Constraint programming: in pursuit of the Holy Grail. Theor. Comput. Sci. **17**(12), 555–564 (1999)

29. Guns, T.: Increasing modeling language convenience with a universal n-dimensional array, CPpy as python- embedded example. In: The 18th workshop on Constraint Modelling and Reformulation (ModRef 2019). University of Connecticut, Stamford (2019)

30. Navara, M., Petrík, M.: Generators of fuzzy logical operations. In: Nguyen, H.T., Kreinovich, V. (eds.) Algebraic Techniques and Their Use in Describing and Processing Uncertainty. SCI, vol. 878, pp. 89–112. Springer, Cham (2020). https://doi.org/10.1007/978-3-030-38565-1_8

31. Cuvelier, T., Didier, F., Furnon, V., Gay, S., Mohajeri, S., Perron, L.: OR-tools' vehicle routing solver: a generic constraint-programming solver with heuristic search for routing problems. In: 24e congrès annuel de la société française de recherche opérationnelle et d'aide à la décision (2023)

32. Guziolowski, C., et al.: Exhaustively characterizing feasible logic models of a signaling network using Answer Set Programming. Bioinformatics **29**(18), 2320–2326 (2013)

33. Sedghamiz, H., Morris, M., Whitley, D, Craddock, T.J.A., Pichichero, M., Broderick, G.: Computation of robust minimal intervention sets in multi-valued biological regulatory networks. Front. Physiol. **10**, 241 (2019)

34. Nethercote, N., Stuckey, P.J., Becket, R., Brand, S., Duck, G.J., Tack, G.: MiniZinc: Towards a standard CP modelling language. In: Bessière, C. (ed.) CP 2007. LNCS, vol. 4741, pp. 529–543. Springer, Heidelberg (2007). https://doi.org/10.1007/978-3-540-74970-7_38

35. Chu, G., Garcia De La Banda, M., Mears, C., Stuckey, P. J.: Symmetries, almost symmetries, and lazy clause generation. Constraints **19**, 434–462 (2014)

36. Battaini, F.: Protein kinase C isoforms as therapeutic targets in nervous system disease states. Pharmacol. Res. **44**(5), 353–361 (2001)

37. Lordén, G., Newton, A.C.: Conventional protein kinase C in the brain: repurposing cancer drugs for neurodegenerative treatment? Neuronal Signaling, **5**(4), NS20210036 (2021)

An Integrative Assessment
of Cognitive-Motor Processes Underlying
Mental Workload and Performance Under
Varying Levels of Controllability

Kyle F. Pietro[1]([✉]), Hyuk Oh[1,3], Justin A. Blanco[4], Jessica M. Mohler[5],
Walter R. Bixby[6], Rodolphe J. Gentili[1,3], Roberto Celi[2],
and Bradley D. Hatfield[1,3]

[1] Department of Kinesiology, Human Performance Biopsychology Laboratory,
University of Maryland, College Park, College Park, MD, USA
kpietro@umd.edu
[2] Department of Aerospace Engineering, University of Maryland, College Park,
College Park, MD, USA
[3] Neuroscience and Cognitive Science Program, University of Maryland,
College Park, College Park, MD, USA
[4] Department of Electrical and Computer Engineering,
United States Naval Academy, Annapolis, MD, USA
[5] Midshipmen Development Center, United States Naval Academy,
Annapolis, MD, USA
[6] Physical Education Department, United States Naval Academy,
Annapolis, MD, USA

Abstract. A study of mental workload is essential to understanding
the intrinsic limitations of the human information processing system
and the resultant cognitive-motor behavior, the results of which hold
great importance for any discipline connected to human operators in the
context of safety-critical behavior. Mental workload and the quality of
cognitive-motor performance are known to be impacted by task demand.
However, one feature of task demand far less understood is the controllability of a system (e.g., the responsiveness of a flight platform and its
handling qualities). In the realm of Human-Machine Interface, the assessment of system controllability has typically been conducted through subjective measurements, such as the Cooper-Harper Rating Scale (CHR)
[9], Bedford Workload Scale (BWS) [43], or the NASA Task Load Index
(NASA-TLX) [21]. A fundamental element of the decision-making process for handling qualities associated with operator workload includes the
reporting of the control compensation required to overcome deficiencies
and errors that could impact and inhibit the successful completion of a
task. However, subjective ratings suffer reduced sensitivity to dynamic
changes in operator workload, and are solely dependent on subjective
estimates of effort to control compensation within a system, despite such
wide usage in the field. Conversely, objective metrics, such as power spectra derived from the electroencephalogram (EEG) paired with behavioral

© The Author(s), under exclusive license to Springer Nature Switzerland AG 2024
D. D. Schmorrow and C. M. Fidopiastis (Eds.): HCII 2024, LNAI 14694, pp. 111–129, 2024.
https://doi.org/10.1007/978-3-031-61569-6_8

performance measures exist as an attractive alternative. Thus, the purpose of the present study was to assess brain dynamics explicitly related to mental workload and subjective ratings as reported during compensatory tracking tasks of varying complexity while also challenged with progressively increasing levels of difficulty.

Keywords: Mental Workload · Handling Qualities · EEG · Subjective Rating Scales · Objective Biomarkers · Compensatory Tracking Tasks · McRuer's Crossover Model

1   Introduction

Mental and physical workload are often referred to as analogous to one another in that they each are comprised of two components: stress (task demand) and strain (related impact on the individual) [49]. While this comparison is extremely simplistic, it offers an attractive approach to empirically explain mental workload, which is otherwise a complex multidimensional construct [18,49]. As such, the joint organization of mental processes functioning in concert with coordinated motor processes is characterized as psychomotor behavior. Psychomotor behavior is indicated by the level of work output relative to the mental and physical effort required to execute a task. Essentially, psychomotor behavior can be broken into two separate branches: mental workload and attentional reserve, where mental workload represents the amount of mental and physical effort required to complete a task, and attentional reserve is simply "what is left over" [39,40]. There is empirical evidence that the two constructs are inversely related [24].

Hatfield and Hillman [22] have coined the term "Psychomotor Efficiency", which postulates that an individual can refine their neural network to become more efficient, which is a hallmark of expert or high-level performance. Higher efficiency of psychomotor behavior is indicative of an adaptive state, which suggests that the magnitude of effort required for a task is inversely related to attentional reserve; that is, decreased effort is associated with elevated reserve [24]. Notably, increased availability of attentional reserve, resulting from mental and physical work reduction, allows the operator to respond to sudden increases in task demand, in addition to unexpected or surprise stimuli and events. However, a suboptimal response, resulting from scarcity of attentional reserve, could result in operator error and even catastrophic consequences. Therefore, optimized efficiency of operator behavior is desirable as it contributes to safe and reliable manipulation of the system within a broad range of conditions.

While high-level performers should be able to overcome increased levels of challenge (e.g., poor system controllability) by relying on well-learned skills, there is evidence that increasing levels of task load have the ability to regress an individual away from automaticity, resulting in decreased efficiency. An attenuation in performance is dependent on whether the operator is able to regulate their state such that adverse effects of increased arousal and workload do not interfere with task execution [13]. However, in such cases, the maintenance of performance comes at a cost (e.g., increased cognitive effort resulting in decreased efficiency). In some cases, an operator's effectiveness may be preserved due to heightened activation, but efficiency must be sacrificed. In the short term, this may appear as acceptable given that the primary objective is accomplished, but over longer periods of time, reduced efficiency may appear as increased stress, fatigue, overload, or perhaps a catastrophic consequence.

Historically, mental workload has been assessed within three main classifications: physiological, subjective, and task-performance-based measures. While physiological measures have the benefit of being objective, they do not always occur in the same time scale, nor do they always occur as what might be predicted (i.e., increased stress and/or demand can lead to reduced mental workload [12,29]). On the other hand, subjective measures, while considering the individual's perception, can often be biased by the experience of the individual on the task as well as on the measure, itself. Task-performance-based measurements can offer some insight into understanding an individual's workload, but failing in a task can increase perceptions of workload [17], and also suffers from many of the same limitations as subjective measures. While each measurement modality has its own strengths and weaknesses, ultimately the sensitivity of each measurement type can vary based on the workload experienced by the operator [46]. Thus, the optimal method for measuring mental workload is to employ a combination of techniques while considering the characteristics of the task, participant, and context of the measurement environment [31].

The electroencephalogram (EEG) provides an objective biomarker characterized by excellent temporal resolution to gain insight into the electrical activity of the cerebral cortex, which is an index of arousal and workload. Specifically, the desynchronization of broadband alpha activity (α) reflects a state of high excitability, whereas synchronized alpha activity reflects a state of inhibition or comparatively low excitability [30]. Therefore, for a given task, the measurement of regional alpha activity can provide a metric for brain regions that are relatively inhibited during the processing of a task. Conversely, activity in the theta band (θ), particularly over the frontal midline, plays an important integrational role in task engagement, working memory, and emotional arousal [33,44]. Theta band power increases when experiencing difficult, attention-demanding tasks that require sustained concentration [15,16]. When a challenging condition is compared to a resting condition, EEG alpha desynchronizes and EEG theta synchronizes [30]. As such, some studies have utilized the $\frac{\theta}{\alpha}$ ratio as an objective biomarker to index mental workload [4,16,23,24,26].

While previous research has utilized objective and subjective metrics to examine mental workload and system controllability, few studies have employed an integrative approach. Furthermore, even fewer studies have examined brain dynamics associated with varying levels of system controllability. Therefore, the purpose of this study was to examine how objective brain dynamics and subjective workload ratings will respond to a series of specific compensatory tracking tasks when task demand and system controllability are manipulated. It was hypothesized that subjective ratings of workload (BWS, NASA-TLX) and the objective biomarker of workload, $\frac{\theta}{\alpha}$ ratio, would increase, whereas behavioral performance would decrease, in response to increasing task demand and levels of difficulty.

2   Methods

This study followed a 2 (Condition: Single-axis vs. Multi-axis) x 3 (Level of Difficulty (HQR): Level 1 (low), Level 2 (medium), Level 3 (high)) repeated-measures design. Order of Condition and HQR were counterbalanced across all participants. The primary dependent variables of interest include subjective ratings (BWS, NASA-TLX), EEG $\frac{\theta}{\alpha}$ ratio, and quality of behavioral performance.

A total of eight healthy, right-handed participants (3 Females), were recruited via email and consented according to best clinical research practices under approved United States Naval Academy and University of Maryland, College Park IRB consent processes. Hand dominance was evaluated according to the Edinburgh Handedness Inventory [42]. Before any testing began, participants were provided with a thorough explanation of the purpose, design, protocol, and risks of participation of the study. Fleet pilots affiliated with the United States Naval Academy were the primary participant pool for this study, however one United States Air Force Aviator also participated.

2.1   Description of Task

The task employed in this experiment is a highly idealized version of pitch and roll control of an aircraft in a turbulent atmosphere, and is based on the display shown in Fig. 1, which consists of a green line representative of the horizon, and a magenta shape (the "bowtie") representative of the aircraft, e.g., the aircraft dashboard. There are two versions of the task: (i) a single-axis, and (ii) a multi-axis, each employed as 'conditions' in the present study.

In the single-axis (or "pitch") version, the green horizon line moves vertically on the screen with a "Sum-of-Sines" (SoS) motion. The SoS allows the generation of a deterministic signal with precisely defined spectral characteristics, but which appears to the participant as completely random. The SoS command signal in the task is driven by an automated command signal generated by a custom coded simulation environment (MATLAB r2022b, The MathWorks Inc.). Participants control the vertical motion of the bowtie using a joystick, and were asked to track the green line by keeping the green dot inside the magenta circle of the bowtie. This is an idealized version of the task of maintaining the pitch attitude of an aircraft in the presence of turbulence. The transfer function from joystick fore-aft longitudinal displacement δ_{lon} to vertical motion z of the bowtie is essentially of the type $\ddot{z} + M_q \dot{z} = M_\delta \delta_{lon}$, and the breakpoint frequency M_q is changed to obtain tasks with three levels of difficulty (low, medium, high). Decreasing M_q progressively changes the nature of the frequency response from $1/s$ to $1/s^2$, and increases the difficulty of the task because the participant needs to remove and reverse the sign of the input before the desired vertical displacement has been achieved. All transfer functions were stable.

The multi-axis (or "pitch-roll") version of the task consists of the single-axis version and, additionally, the green horizon line can rotate by an angle ϕ, with it own SoS motion. The participants must also control the rotational motion of the bowtie using the joystick, and were asked to also track the green line by keeping it inside the wedge shaped portions of the bowtie. The multi-axis task is an idealized version of the task of maintaining pitch and roll attitude of an aircraft in the presence of turbulence. The transfer function from joystick right-left lateral displacement δ_{lat} to angular motion ϕ of the bowtie is essentially of the type $\ddot{\phi} + L_p\dot{\phi} = L_\delta\delta_{lat}$, and the breakpoint frequency L_p is again changed to obtain tasks with three levels of difficulty (low, medium, high). Decreasing L_p progressively has the same consequences as decreasing M_q for the single-axis task. The SoS input begins with 10 s of non-scoring time (i.e., 0 to 10 s) that includes a 5 s initial linear ramp up in amplitude. This is followed by 60 s of scoring time (i.e., 10 to 70 s) and a 5 s cool down period (i.e., 70 to 75 s) where the amplitude is ramped back to zero (see Fig. 2b). Thus, each task lasted 75 s and was followed by post-scenario questionnaires. However, the window of interest for this experiment consisted of the 60 s scoring time window.

Although the experiment employs an idealized version of an aircraft piloting task, no specific piloting training was required. These are compensatory tracking tasks[1] based on the seminal task devised by McRuer et al. [38]. This task was executed to quantify the "attentional demand" and the "excess control capacity", where the attentional demand and the excess control capacity are negatively related.

"Desired" and "Adequate" performance levels were defined for the pitch and the roll portions of the tasks, see Table 1. Participants were asked to aggressively track the displayed green line representing the command signal, and to keep errors within the specified tolerances in Table 1. Participants were reminded that for pitch, desired performance was to keep the green dot within the inner circle, while adequate performance was to keep it within the magenta circle. Desired performance for roll was to keep the green line within the inner most wedge shape, and adequate performance is to keep it within the magenta wedge shape.

2.2   Procedure

All data collection occurred in a laboratory space at the United States Naval Academy. Participants were sized and fitted with a stretchable fabric cap in which electrodes recorded electrical brain activity via 64 electrodes housed within a stretchable lycra cap (actiCAP slim, actiCHamp, BrainProducts, GmbH), sampled at 2500 Hz and referenced to site FCz with a common ground. Electrode placement followed the international 10–10 system [5].

Participants were seated comfortably at a distance of 65 cm in front of a 47 cm x 29 cm computer monitor. Participants controlled all input to the system via a HOTAS WARTHOG^{TM} (Thrustmaster®, France) joystick controller. To simulate a more realistic experience, the joystick was attached to an adjustable height extension apparatus, below the computer monitor (see Fig. 2a). Following

---

[1] In the literature, the task of the present paper, where both the target line and the operator-controlled line are displayed, is sometimes defined as "tracking task", as opposed to a "compensatory task" where only the error between the two lines is displayed [38].

equipment set up, participants completed two, two-minute reference conditions, which consisted of sitting passively (i) with their eyes closed, and (ii) while viewing the bowtie display (Fig. 1). Finally, the participants were oriented to the subjective metrics of interest, and the objectives of the task were described to the participant. Participants were allowed to ask questions for clarification on these questionnaires, and the descriptions of each were provided to the participant if they needed to refer back to this information while completing each questionnaire. Participants then completed three "practice" trials of the task related to the assigned counterbalanced order of condition (i.e., Single-axis or Multi-axis).

(a)   (b)

Fig. 1. Bowtie heads-up display (magenta polygon) which participants controlled during the compensatory tracking tasks **(a)** Single-axis Condition, **(b)** Multi-axis Condition [32, 37]

Following three practice trials, participants were provided an opportunity to ask any questions about the task and the objective was repeated. Participants completed a total of six SoS compensatory tracking tasks which followed a counterbalanced combination of three levels of task difficulty, nested within two conditions ((i) Single-axis (Pitch), (ii) Multi-axis (Pitch-Roll)). The levels of difficulty (HQR) are indicated as "Level 1", "Level 2", and "Level 3" Cooper-Harper Ratings[2] (CHR): these are rigorous terms that have specific regulatory meanings that will not be discussed here for reasons of space. For the purpose of this paper, it is sufficient to replace them with "Low", "Medium", and "High" difficulty, respectively.

Both desired and adequate levels of performance can be calculated after task completion based upon the scoring period, and an overall performance assessment can be provided (see Table 1 for experiment criteria). This result, paired with the combined usage of objective and subjective metrics, can provide not only measures related to handling qualities and mental workload, but also when exactly the operator may have felt their highest (or lowest) level of workload to make their decision for the subjective rating.

---

[2] The parameters of the joystick transfer functions were selected to yield Level 1, 2, and 3 CHR according to ADS-33 [1], but the actual ratings were not determined because not all participants were properly trained in issuing them.

Table 1. Performance standards for task objectives

	Desired	Adequate
Pitch: At least $x\%$ of the scoring time within pitch attitude error tolerance:	50% $\pm 1°$	75% $\pm 2°$
Roll: At least $x\%$ of the scoring time within roll attitude error tolerance:	50% $\pm 5°$	75% $\pm 10°$

Both objective and subjective metrics were used in this study. As an objective biomarker of mental workload, the theta/alpha ratio ($\frac{\theta}{\alpha}$) was computed as the mean theta power spectral density of all frontal EEG channels divided by the mean alpha power spectral density of all parietal EEG channels.

The subjective ratings utilized for this experiment were the Bedford Workload Scale (BWS) [43] and the NASA Task Load Index (NASA-TLX) [21] overall measure of workload. The BWS is a modification of the CHR, designed to measure an operator's spare mental capacity. The TLX is a well known multidimensional assessment which divides workload into six subscales, which can be weighted and combined to serve as an overall workload metric. The degree to which each of the six factors within the NASA-TLX contribute to the workload of the specific task to be evaluated is determined by the participants' responses to pair-wise comparisons among the six factors [20]. There are 15 possible pairwise comparisons of the six scales, where each comparison is presented to the participant on a flash card. Participants are asked to circle the scale title that represents the more important contributor to workload for the specific task being performed in the experiment [20]. The ratings of factors deemed most important in creating the workload of a task are given more weight in computing the overall workload score. Participants were allowed to ask questions for clarification on these questionnaires, and the descriptions of each were provided to the participant if they needed to refer back to this information while completing each questionnaire.

3   Signal Processing

EEG data pre-processing was conducted using BrainVision Analyzer (v.2.1, BrainProducts, Gmbh), MATLAB R2023b (The MathWorks Inc.), and EEGLAB v.2022.1 [11]. EEG data were inspected for bad channels in BrainVision Analyzer and, when necessary, bad channels were replaced with spherically interpolated channels. Raw EEG data was first re-referenced to a common-average of all EEG channels, and then high-pass filtered with a zero-phase shift Infinite Impulse Response Butterworth filter. The EEG data were then subjected to a biased extended Infomax Independent Component Analysis (ICA) to correct for ocular artifact in BranVision Analyzer. The EEG data were then exported for further processing in MATLAB.

EEG data were subjected to a custom elliptic infinite impulse response (IIR) band-pass filter from 1 to 30 Hz. EEG data were then downsampled to 256 Hz and subjected to the extended Infomax ICA. Independent components (ICs) determined to be unrelated to the task-relevant EEG signal were removed using the Multiple Artifact Rejection Algorithm (MARA) plugin in EEGLAB [48]. A current source density (CSD) transformation was applied to these denoised EEG data using the CSD Toolbox, (version 1.1) [27, 28]. EEG data were baseline corrected using the mean of the one-second period prior to the beginning of the scoring period. Power spectral densities were computed for each 60 s trial using Welch's method [47] utilizing a periodic hamming window of 4 s with 50% overlap and the number of fast Fourier transform (FFT) points of 5000. Power spectra were approximated by applying the trapezoidal rule to each EEG frequency band, including delta (1–4 Hz), theta (4–8 Hz), broadband alpha (8–13 Hz), and broadband beta (13–30 Hz).

3.1   Performance Scoring Criteria

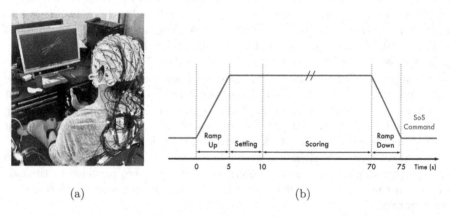

(a)   (b)

Fig. 2. (a) Experimental setup; Participant completing Multi-axis Condition while psychophysiological signals are recorded. **(b)** Visual representation for SoS timeline, blue line represents the SoS amplitude which follows a short (5 s) ramp up, then held constant, and ramped down (5 s).

Participants' performance scoring was computed for the middle 60 s of each trial according to their adherence to the performance standards criteria (see Fig. 2b, and Table 1). A constraint was placed on the performance data where pitch and/or roll are invalidated if either of the axes did not meet the performance standards listed in Table 1. Performance was scored for 60 s, using a sliding 5 s window, with 50% overlap. Finally, overall mean scores for desired, adequate, and inadequate were generated for each participant and each trial.

3.2   Statistical Analysis

Statistics were calculated in RStudio (version 2023.06.1+524, RStudio, Boston, MA). The independent variables include Condition and Level of Difficulty (HQR). The dependent variables were subjective ratings (BWS, NASA-TLX), EEG $\frac{\theta}{\alpha}$ ratio, and behavioral performance. Each dependent variable was subjected to separate 2 (Condition: Single-axis vs. Multi-axis) x 3 (HQR: Level 1, Level 2, Level 3) completely within-subjects repeated-measures ANOVAs to examine main and interactive effects for workload and HQR. A significance criterion of $\alpha = 0.05$ was utilized for all tests. P-values were adjusted for multiple comparisons using the False Discovery Rate. Effect sizes are reported where appropriate [8]. Significant relationships are reported as : *p<.05; **p<.01; ***p<.001. For all figures below, HQR represents the Handling Qualities Levels manipulation, and vertical error bars represent standard error of the mean (Fig. 3).

4   Results

4.1   Bedford Workload Scale

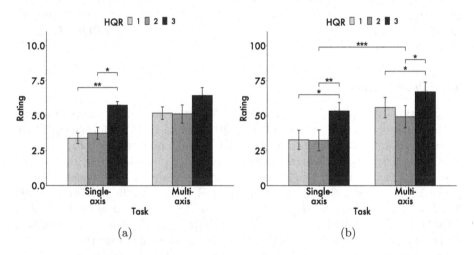

Fig. 3. (a) Mean BWS rating by Condition and HQR **(b)** Mean weighted NASA-TLX overall workload rating by Condition and HQR

A repeated measures ANOVA was performed to compare effects of Single-axis and Multi-axis Conditions as well as HQR on BWS ratings. There was no significant main effect for Condition ($F_{(1,7)} = 6.08, p = .06$). There was a significant main effect for HQR ($F_{(2,14)} = 13.86, p < .01$). Pairwise comparisons for the Single-axis Condition revealed that the mean BWS rating was significantly different in HQR 1 ($M = 3.38 \pm 0.38$) vs. HQR 3 ($M = 5.75 \pm 0.3$) HQR ($t_{(7)} = -5.65, p < .01, d = -2.0$), and in HQR 2 ($M = 3.75 \pm 0.42$) vs. HQR 3 ($M = 5.75 \pm 0.3$) HQR ($t_{(7)} = -3.39, p < .05, d = -1.20$).

4.2   NASA-TLX Overall Workload

A repeated measures ANOVA was performed to compare effects of Single-axis and Multi-axis Conditions as well as HQR on NASA-TLX overall workload ratings. There was a significant main effect for Condition ($F_{(1,7)} = 15.84, p < .01$). There was a significant main effect for HQR ($F_{(2,14)} = 23.83, p < .001$). Pairwise comparisons for the Single-axis Condition revealed that the mean NASA-TLX Overall workload rating was significantly different in HQR 1 ($M = 32.89 \pm 6.84$) vs. HQR 3 ($M = 53.3 \pm 6.1$) HQR ($t_{(7)} = -3.63, p < .05, d = -1.28$), and in HQR 2 ($M = 32.3 \pm 7.6$) vs. HQR 3 ($M = 53.3 \pm 6.1$) HQR ($t_{(7)} = -5.97, p < .01, d = -2.11$). Pairwise comparisons for the Multi-axis Condition revealed that the mean NASA-TLX Overall workload rating was significantly different in HQR 1 ($M = 55.8 \pm 7.3$) vs. HQR 3 ($M = 67.1 \pm 6.91$) HQR ($t_{(7)} = -4.0, p < .05, d = -1.41$), and in HQR 2 ($M = 49.25 \pm 7.95$) vs. HQR 3 ($M = 67.1 \pm 6.91$) HQR ($t_{(7)} = -3.70, p < .05, d = -1.31$) (Fig. 3b).

4.3 $\frac{\theta}{\alpha}$ Ratio

A repeated measures ANOVA was performed to compare effects of Single-axis and Multi-axis Conditions as well as HQR on EEG $\frac{\theta}{\alpha}$ ratio. There were no significant main effects for Condition ($F_{(1,7)} = 1.50, p > .05$), nor HQR ($F_{(2,14)} = 1.01, p > .05$) (Fig. 4).

4.4   Performance

Single-axis. A repeated measures ANOVA was performed to compare effects of the Single-axis Condition as well as HQR on participant performance. There were significant main effects for HQR for desired performance ($F_{(1.1,7.73)} = 27.83, p < .001$), and adequate performance ($F_{(2,14)} = 24.65, p < .001$). Pairwise comparisons for the Single-axis Condition revealed that the mean desired performance was significantly different in HQR 1 ($M = 65.65 \pm 5.75$) vs. HQR 3 ($M = 36.1 \pm 3.3$) HQR ($t_{(7)} = 5.12, p < .01, d = 1.81$), and in HQR 2 ($M = 64.86 \pm 5.02$) vs. HQR 3 ($M = 36.1 \pm 3.3$) HQR ($t_{(7)} = 5.74, p < .01, d = 2.03$). Pairwise comparisons for the Single-axis Condition revealed that the mean adequate performance was significantly different in HQR 1 ($M = 89.7 \pm 5.25$) vs. HQR 3 ($M = 65.92 \pm 5.71$) HQR ($t_{(7)} = 4.9, p < .01, d = 1.73$), and in Level 2 ($M = 91.5 \pm 3.8$) vs. Level 3 ($M = 65.92 \pm 5.71$) HQR ($t_{(7)} = 5.5, p < .01, d = 1.93$) (Fig. 6).

Multi-axis. A repeated measures ANOVA was performed to compare effects of the Multi-axis Condition as well as HQR on participant performance. There were significant main effects for HQR for desired pitch performance ($F_{(1.1,7.8)} = 27.05, p < .01$), and desired roll performance ($F_{(2,14)} = 27.01, p < .001$). There were significant main effects for HQR for adequate pitch performance ($F_{(2,14)} = 24.12, p < .001$), and adequate roll performance ($F_{(1.18,8.3)} = 10.1, p < 0.01$).

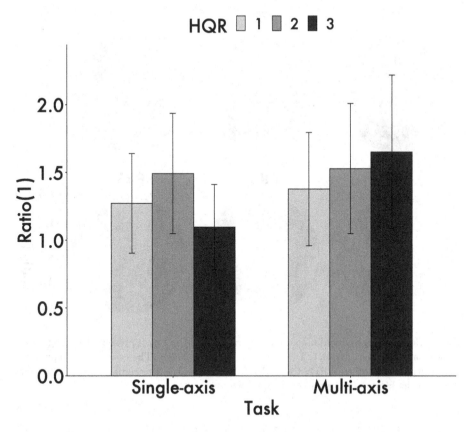

Fig. 4. Mean $\frac{\theta}{\alpha}$ ratio by Condition and HQR

Pairwise comparisons for the Multi-axis Condition revealed that the mean desired pitch performance was significantly different in HQR 1 ($M = 45.94 \pm 8.11$) vs. HQR 3 ($M = 24.65 \pm 5$) HQR ($t_{(7)} = 4.91, p < .01, d = 1.73$), and in HQR 2 ($M = 47.84 \pm 8.11$) vs. HQR 3 ($M = 24.65 \pm 5$) HQR ($t_{(7)} = 5.7, p < .01, d = 2.02$). Pairwise comparisons for the Multi-axis Condition revealed that the mean desired roll performance was significantly different in HQR 1 ($M = 50.1 \pm 7.6$) vs. HQR 3 ($M = 29.67 \pm 6.32$) HQR ($t_{(7)} = 5.81, p < .001, d = 2.05$), and in HQR 2 ($M = 53.72 \pm 7.52$) vs. HQR 3 ($M = 29.67 \pm 6.32$) HQR ($t_{(7)} = 5.9, p < .001, d = 2.07$).

Pairwise comparisons for the Multi-axis Condition revealed that the mean adequate pitch performance was significantly different in HQR 1 ($M = 71.21 \pm 10.16$) vs. HQR 3 ($M = 48.03 \pm 9.12$) HQR ($t_{(7)} = 4.81, p < .01, d = 1.70$), and in HQR 2 ($M = 73.1 \pm 9.7$) vs. HQR 3 ($M = 48.03 \pm 9.12$) HQR ($t_{(7)} = 5.4, p < .01, d = 1.91$). Pairwise comparisons for the Multi-axis Condition revealed that the mean adequate roll performance was significantly different in HQR 1 ($M = 72.21 \pm 8.21$) vs. HQR 3 ($M = 54.62 \pm 10.3$) HQR ($t_{(7)} = 4.50, p < .01, d =$

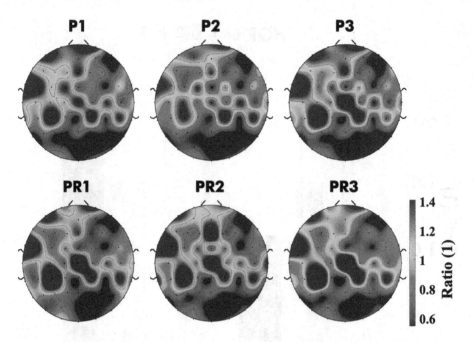

Fig. 5. Scalp topographical maps of the $\frac{\theta}{\alpha}$ ratio. The top row represents the Single-axis Condition (P=pitch), HQR 1, 2, 3, left to right, respectively. The bottom row represents the Multi-axis Condition (PR=Pitch-Roll), HQR 1, 2, 3, left to right, respectively. Plots represent looking down upon the scalp, nose forward.

1.59), and in HQR 2 ($M = 75.67 \pm 7.3$) vs. HQR 3 ($M = 54.62 \pm 10.3$) HQR ($t_{(7)} = 3.22, p < .05, d = 1.14$).

Brain-Performance Relationships. An exploratory analysis was conducted using cross-correlation to examine the synchronous activity between the brain and behavioral performance measured within the bowtie. Some significant relationships appeared such that within the Single-axis Condition, the synchronous activity between the brain and performance markedly decreased from HQR 1 to HQR 3 (Fig. 7a). Additional cross-correlations revealed several regional wavelet power spectra significantly involved in behavioral performance. In the Single-axis Condition, beta activity in the superior and inferior parietal lobule, as well as alpha activity in the superior temporal gyrus were identified. For the pitch component of the Multi-axis Condition, delta activity in both the middle and inferior temporal gyrus, and superior parietal lobule were identified. For the roll component of the Multi-axis Condition, theta and beta activity in the superior frontal gyrus, and beta activity in the cuneus were identified.

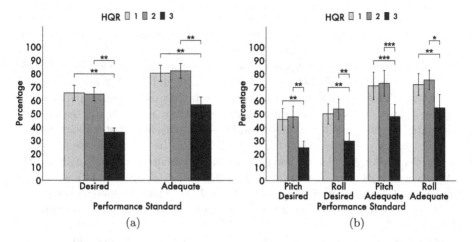

Fig. 6. (a) Mean Single-axis performance for desired and adequate tolerances and HQR **(b)** Mean Multi-axis performance for desired and adequate tolerances and HQR; The Y-axis, percentage, represents the scoring percentage that participants met based on Table 1.

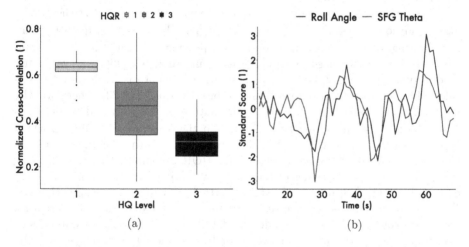

Fig. 7. (a) Normalized cross-correlations between brain activity and behavioral performance. Boxplot edges represent the 25th, 50th, and 75th percentiles for HQR 1, 2, 3, left to right, respectively, in the Single-axis Condition. **(b)** Standardized scoring for a single participant between Multi-axis (roll angle) behavioral performance and theta activity at the superior frontal gyrus (SFG).

5 Discussion

This experiment employed McRuer et al.'s seminal task [38] to examine how objective brain dynamics and subjective workload ratings respond to a series of specific compensatory tracking tasks when task demand and system controllability were manipulated. As expected, subjective ratings of workload are sensitive to changes in handling qualities[3]. Participants reported experiencing higher levels of workload on the BWS between HQR 1 and 3, and HQR 2 and 3, in the Single-axis Condition. Participants reported experiencing higher levels of workload on the NASA-TLX between HQR 1 and 3, and HQR 2 and 3, in both Conditions. This result is understandable given that participants' performance significantly decreased in the same negative pattern for both the desired and adequate tolerances. While the $\frac{\theta}{\alpha}$ ratio failed to achieve statistical significance, this variable is visibly trending higher by HQR for the Multi-axis Condition.

Participants were able to perceive changes in mental workload utilizing the BWS, when HQR were manipulated. The effect sizes of the contrasts within the Single-axis Condition were large (i.e., $d \leq -1.20$) which indicates that participants perceived much higher levels of workload in HQR level 3, compared to HQR 1 and 2.

As expected, participants rated the NASA-TLX overall workload as significantly higher for HQR 3 compared to HQR 1 and 2, for both Conditions. The effect sizes of these contrasts were large (i.e., $d \leq -1.28$) which indicates that participants perceived markedly higher workload for HQR 3 compared to HQR 1 and 2, for both Conditions.

The result for the $\frac{\theta}{\alpha}$ ratio was opposite of what was expected for the Single-axis Condition such that the $\frac{\theta}{\alpha}$ ratio was higher when handling qualities were less challenging. This result is at odds with previous findings that the $\frac{\theta}{\alpha}$ ratio has been shown to increase with task demand and challenge [26]. However, many studies typically employ more complex, multicomponent tasks which differ considerably in processing demands from the present study [16,23]. Therefore, the usage of the $\frac{\theta}{\alpha}$ ratio may depend on the nature of the task and/or demand, given the trending increase of the $\frac{\theta}{\alpha}$ ratio in the Multi-axis Condition, which is in line with our hypotheses. Additionally, it is interesting for the Single-axis Condition that the $\frac{\theta}{\alpha}$ ratio was higher for HQR 2 compared to HQR 1 since this is not observed for either of the subjective ratings results. Similar to Hancock and Warm's [18] model of sustained attention, it may be possible that the $\frac{\theta}{\alpha}$ ratio loosely follows an inverted-U pattern as related to handling qualities levels. Moreover, this result is understandable since each trial was only 75 s in length, and the $\frac{\theta}{\alpha}$ ratio was computed for the middle 60 s scoring period. The result from the present study is likely to be different given a longer duration, paired with increased effort or arousal, such as in real flight. Future efforts will examine the $\frac{\theta}{\alpha}$ ratio undulations over time, to more closely probe the dynamic nature of workload.

While the theory-based approach for $\frac{\theta}{\alpha}$ ratio failed to achieve significance, it is possible to see some trends within the data driven results outlined in Fig. 5. Standardized difference scores were computed within Conditions, across HQR

---

[3] Recall that, for example, "Level 1 CHR" means that the parameters of the transfer function from joystick displacement to bowtie displacement correspond to Level 1 HQ in ADS-33 [1], and not that the CHR was explicitly assessed by the participant as being "Level 1".

for all electrodes to highlight some specific brain regions/structures that may be relevant in the detection of mental workload as related to varying HQR. For the Single-axis Condition, the $\frac{\theta}{\alpha}$ ratio computed at EEG electrodes AF7, FT7, T7, CP3, and Cz were significantly related to increasing levels of workload and HQR. AF7 and FT7 are located near the frontal eye fields and the middle temporal gyrus [34], which controls rapid eye movements related to the scanning of details within an image and high-level visual processing and perception of complex objects, respectively. This pattern of eye movements as related to the continuous visual-spatial reorientation of the bowtie could be analyzed in conjunction with eye-tracking, a well-known metric of workload. Additionally, CP3 is related to the inferior parietal lobule, which is related to the interpretation of sensory information processing and sensorimotor integration. For the Multi-axis Condition, Fz, FT7, CP3, P7, and P8, were significantly related to increasing levels of workload and HQR. This result is understandable given that Fz is located above the superior frontal gyrus [34], which has been suggested to be critical in the manipulation and monitoring of information as well as spatial working memory [10]. Additionally, P7 and P8 are functionally located over the inferior parietal lobule and supramarginal gyrus, which is implicated in the interpretation of tactile sensory information in addition to the perception of space and limb location.

As expected, behavioral performance decreased significantly in HQR 3, compared to HQR 1 and 2, for both Conditions. This finding was true for both the desired and adequate tolerances. The effect sizes of these contrasts were large (i.e., $d \geq 1.14$) which indicates that participants performed significantly worse in HQR 3, compared to levels 1 and 2, for both Conditions.

Related to Human-Computer Interaction, the synchronous activity between the brain and behavioral performance measured within the bowtie was analyzed using cross-correlation. Some significant relationships appeared such that regional wavelet power spectra in the superior and inferior parietal lobule in the beta band was significantly related to behavioral performance. This result is plausible since it has been demonstrated that beta oscillatory activity, related to directionally-specific connectivity, is involved in the coordination and facilitation of accurate upper limb movement [7]. Furthermore, the results related to delta activity in the middle and inferior temporal gyrus seems promising. While most research on delta activity has been collected during sleep, there is some evidence to suggest that delta is linked to motivation [33], and may modulate distant areas of the brain from the frontal lobes during attention demanding tasks [19]. Notably, theta and beta activity in the superior frontal gyrus, was highly related to the roll component of the Multi-axis Condition (Fig. 7b). This suggests that the addition of the roll component elicited increased task engagement in order to maintain performance. These results as related to beta activity warrant further investigation, since it has been suggested that beta activity may allow for more efficient processing of sensorimotor feedback required for monitoring current motor processes and recalibration of the sensorimotor system [2].

These findings highlight part of a programmatic approach to further understand the brain dynamics and subjective ratings associated with varying levels of handling qualities. The long-term goals of this work are to: (i) increase the safety and efficiency of human-operated machinery, (ii) investigate localized neural correlates of handling qualities such as within the inferior parietal lobule and the superior frontal gyrus, and (iii) further understand the relationship between mental workload and the decision-making process. Future work will further examine the delta and beta EEG power spectra as these have been implicated in brain activity related to motivational processes, cognitive processes related to attention, sensorimotor function, decision making, and efficient cognitive performance under conditions of mental effort [6, 14, 19, 33, 45]. Additional future work will include the prediction of subjective ratings related to brain states as well as examining neural correlates of decision making using time-frequency analyses. The results of this work can be extended to human-machine teaming for optimal design of a machine-teammate to reduce human-operator workload [36]. Moreover, we will implement knowledge-based machine learning approaches to estimate human-operator responses to dynamically changing task-load and stress [3, 25, 31, 35, 41]. Such an effort may be able to improve one's mental health and can aid in the reduction of mental workload during lengthy and stressful missions.

Acknowledgments. The authors would like to express their appreciation for the guidance and support provided by our grant technical monitor and point of contact, Matthew Rhinehart (Senior Engineer, NAWCAD), who was helpful in providing technical advice as well as setting up the parameters of the bowtie display and the joystick transfer functions, and colleagues at the U.S. Naval Academy, especially all volunteer participants. This study was supported by Naval Air Warfare Aircraft Division (NAWCAD), Sponsor Award Number: N00421-21-1-0003, Award Number: 304805-00001.

References

1. Anon.: Aeronautical design standard performance specification handling qualities requirements for military rotorcraft, ADS-33E. Technical report, Army Aviation and Missile Command, Redstone Arsenal, Alabama (2000)
2. Baker, S.N.: Oscillatory interactions between sensorimotor cortex and the periphery. Curr. Opin. Neurobiol. **17**(6), 649–655 (2007). https://doi.org/10.1016/j.conb.2008.01.007
3. Blanco, J.A., et al.: Quantifying cognitive workload in simulated flight using passive, dry EEG measurements. IEEE Trans. Cognitive Dev. Syst. **10**(2), 373–383 (2018). https://doi.org/10.1109/tcds.2016.2628702
4. Borghini, G., et al.: Avionic technology testing by using a cognitive neurometric index: a study with professional helicopter pilots. In: 37th Annual International Conference of the IEEE Engineering in Medicine and Biology Society (EMBC), pp. 6182–6185 (2015).https://doi.org/10.1109/EMBC.2015.7319804
5. Chatrian, G.E., Lettich, E., Nelson, P.L.: Ten percent electrode system for topographic studies of spontaneous and evoked EEG activities. Am. J. EEG Technol. **25**(2), 83–92 (1985). https://doi.org/10.1080/00029238.1985.11080163

6. Chen, X.J., Kwak, Y.: Contribution of the sensorimotor beta oscillations and the cortico-basal ganglia-thalamic circuitry during value-based decision making: a simultaneous EEG-fMRI investigation. NeuroImage **257**, 119300 (2022). https://doi.org/10.1016/j.neuroimage.2022.119300

7. Chung, J.W., Ofori, E., Misra, G., Hess, C.W., Vaillancourt, D.E.: Beta-band activity and connectivity in sensorimotor and parietal cortex are important for accurate motor performance. Neuroimage **144**, 164–173 (2017). https://doi.org/10.1016/j.neuroimage.2016.10.008

8. Cohen, J.: Statistical Power Analysis for the Behavioral Sciences. Routledge, 2nd edn. (1988https://doi.org/10.4324/9780203771587

9. Cooper, G.E., Harper, R.P.: The Use of Pilot Rating in the Evaluation of Aircraft Handling Qualities. National Aeronautics and Space Administration (1969)

10. Courtney, S.M., Ungerleider, L.G., Keil, K., Haxby, J.V.: Object and spatial visual working memory activate separate neural systems in human cortex. Cereb. Cortex **6**(1), 39–49 (1996). https://doi.org/10.1093/cercor/6.1.39

11. Delorme, A., Makeig, S.: EEGLAB: an open source toolbox for analysis of single-trial EEG dynamics including independent component analysis. J. Neurosci. Methods **134**(1), 9–21 (2004). https://doi.org/10.1016/j.jneumeth.2003.10.009

12. DiDomenico, A., Nussbaum, M.A.: Interactive effects of physical and mental workload on subjective workload assessment. Int. J. Ind. Ergon. **38**(11–12), 977–983 (2008)

13. Gaillard, A.W.: Comparing the concepts of mental load and stress. Ergonomics **36**(9), 991–1005 (1993). https://doi.org/10.1080/00140139308967972

14. Gentili, R.J., et al.: Brain biomarkers based assessment of cognitive workload in pilots under various task demands. IEEE (2014). https://doi.org/10.1109/embc.2014.6944961

15. Gevins, A.: High-resolution EEG mapping of cortical activation related to working memory: effects of task difficulty, type of processing, and practice. Cereb. Cortex **7**(4), 374–385 (1997). https://doi.org/10.1093/cercor/7.4.374

16. Gevins, A., Smith, M.E.: Neurophysiological measures of cognitive workload during human-computer interaction. Theor. Issues Ergon. Sci. **4**(1–2), 113–131 (2003). https://doi.org/10.1080/14639220210159717

17. Hancock, P.A.: The effect of performance failure and task demand on the perception of mental workload. Appl. Ergon. **20**(3), 197–205 (1989). https://doi.org/10.1016/0003-6870(89)90077-X

18. Hancock, P.A., Warm, J.S.: A dynamic model of stress and sustained attention. Hum. Factors **31**(5), 519–537 (1989). https://doi.org/10.1177/001872088903100503

19. Harmony, T.: The functional significance of delta oscillations in cognitive processing. Front. Integr. Neurosci. **7**, 83 (2013). https://doi.org/10.3389/fnint.2013.00083

20. Hart, S.G.: Nasa task load index (TLX) volume 1.0; paper and pencil package (1986)

21. Hart, S.G., Staveland, L.E.: Development of NASA-TLX (task load index): results of empirical and theoretical research. Adv. Psychol. **52**, 139–183 (1988).https://doi.org/10.1016/S0166-4115(08)62386-9

22. Hatfield, B.D., Hillman, C.H.: The psychophysiology of sport: a mechanistic understanding of the psychology of superior performance, 2nd edn., chap. 14, pp. 362–386. Wiley, New York (2001)

23. Hockey, G.R., Nickel, P., Roberts, A.C., Roberts, M.H.: Sensitivity of candidate markers of psychophysiological strain to cyclical changes in manual control load during simulated process control. Appl. Ergonomics **40**(6), 1011–8 (2009). ISSN 0003-6870, https://doi.org/10.1016/j.apergo.2009.04.008

24. Jaquess, K.J., et al.: Empirical evidence for the relationship between cognitive workload and attentional reserve. Int. J. Psychophysiol. **121**, 46–55 (2017). https://doi.org/10.1016/j.ijpsycho.2017.09.007

25. Johnson, M.K., Blanco, J.A., Gentili, R.J., Jaquess, K.J., Oh, H., Hatfield, B.D.: Probe-independent EEG assessment of mental workload in pilots. In: 2015 7th International IEEE/EMBS Conference on Neural Engineering (NER), pp. 581–584 (2015). https://doi.org/10.1109/NER.2015.7146689

26. Kamzanova, A.T., Kustubayeva, A.M., Matthews, G.: Use of EEG workload indices for diagnostic monitoring of vigilance decrement. Hum. Factors **56**(6), 1136–1149 (2014). https://doi.org/10.1177/0018720814526617

27. Kayser, J., Tenke, C.E.: Principal components analysis of Laplacian waveforms as a generic method for identifying ERP generator patterns: I. evaluation with auditory oddball tasks. Clin. Neurophysiol. **117**(2), 348–368 (2006). ISSN 1388-2457,https://doi.org/10.1016/j.clinph.2005.08.034

28. Kayser, J., Tenke, C.E.: Principal components analysis of Laplacian waveforms as a generic method for identifying ERP generator patterns: II. adequacy of low-density estimates. Clin. Neurophysiol. **117**(2), 369–380 (2006). ISSN 1388-245https://doi.org/10.1016/j.clinph.2005.08.033

29. King, R., Schaefer, A.: The emotional startle effect is disrupted by a concurrent working memory task. Psychophysiology **48**(2), 269–272 (2011). https://doi.org/10.1111/j.1469-8986.2010.01062.x

30. Klimesch, W., Sauseng, P., Hanslmayr, S.: EEG alpha oscillations: the inhibition-timing hypothesis. Brain Res. Rev. **53**(1), 63–88 (2007). https://doi.org/10.1016/j.brainresrev.2006.06.003

31. Klyde, D.H., Lampton, A.K., Mitchell, D.G., Berka, C., Rhinehart, M.: A new approach to aircraft handling qualities prediction (2021). https://doi.org/10.2514/6.2021-0178

32. Klyde, D.H., et al.: Piloted simulation evaluation of tracking mission task elements for the assessment of high-speed handling qualities. J. Am. Helicopter Soc. **65**(3), 1–23 (2020). https://doi.org/10.4050/jahs.65.032010

33. Knyazev, G.G.: Motivation, emotion, and their inhibitory control mirrored in brain oscillations. Neurosci. Biobehav. Rev. **31**(3), 377–395 (2007). https://doi.org/10.1016/j.neubiorev.2006.10.004

34. Koessler, L., et al.: Automated cortical projection of EEG sensors: anatomical correlation via the international 10–10 system. Neuroimage **46**(1), 64–72 (2009). https://doi.org/10.1016/j.neuroimage.2009.02.006

35. Lampton, A.K., Klyde, D.H., Musso, D., Mitchell, D., Rhinehart, M.: Further development of an approach to aircraft handling qualities prediction. In: AIAA SCITECH 2024 Forum (2024). https://doi.org/10.2514/6.2024-2479

36. Lu, C., et al.: Assessment of augmented operator's mental workload with visual assistive technology in simulated rotorcraft piloting tasks. In: Proceedings of the 77th Annual Forum, The Vertical Flight Society (2021). https://doi.org/10.4050/F-0077-2021-16742

37. McRuer, D.T., Krendel, E.S.: Mathematical models of human pilot behavior. Report, Advisory Group for Aerospace Research and Development. AGARDograph No. 188 (1974). https://apps.dtic.mil/sti/tr/pdf/AD0775905

38. McRuer, D.T., Myers, T.T., Thompson, P.M.: Literal singular-value-based flight control system design techniques. J. Guid. Control. Dyn. **12**(6), 913–919 (1989). https://doi.org/10.2514/3.20500

39. Miller, M.W., Groman, L.J., Rietschel, J.C., McDonald, C.G., Iso-Ahola, S.E., Hatfield, B.D.: The effects of team environment on attentional resource allocation and cognitive workload. Sport Exerc. Perform. Psychol. **2**(2), 77–89 (2013). https://doi.org/10.1037/a0030586

40. Miller, M.W., Rietschel, J.C., McDonald, C.G., Hatfield, B.D.: A novel approach to the physiological measurement of mental workload. Int. J. Psychophysiol. **80**(1), 75–8 (2011). https://doi.org/10.1016/j.ijpsycho.2011.02.003

41. Oh, H., et al.: A Composite Cognitive Workload Assessment System in Pilots Under Various Task Demands Using Ensemble Learning. In: Schmorrow, Dylan D., Fidopiastis, Cali M. (eds.) AC 2015. LNCS (LNAI), vol. 9183, pp. 91–100. Springer, Cham (2015). https://doi.org/10.1007/978-3-319-20816-9_10

42. Oldfield, R.: The assessment and analysis of handedness: the Edinburgh inventory. Neuropsychologia **9**(1), 97–113 (1971). https://doi.org/10.1016/0028-3932(71)90067-4

43. Roscoe, A.H., Ellis, G.A.: A subjective rating scale for assessing pilot workload in flight: a decade of practical use. Report, Royal Aerospace Establishment Farnborough (United Kingdom) (1990)

44. Sauseng, P., Griesmayr, B., Freunberger, R., Klimesch, W.: Control mechanisms in working memory: a possible function of EEG theta oscillations. Neurosci. Biobehav. Rev. **34**(7), 1015–1022 (2010). https://doi.org/10.1016/j.neubiorev.2009.12.006

45. Vogel, W., Broverman, D.M., Klaiber, E.L.: EEG and mental abilities. Electroencephalogr. Clin. Neurophysiol. **24**, 166–175 (1968). https://doi.org/10.1016/0013-4694(68)90122-3

46. de Waard, D.: The measurement of drivers' mental workload. Ph.D. thesis, University of Groningen (1996)

47. Welch, P.: The use of fast fourier transform for the estimation of power spectra: A method based on time averaging over short, modified periodograms. IEEE Trans. Audio Electroacoust. **15**(2), 70–73 (1967). https://doi.org/10.1109/tau.1967.1161901

48. Winkler, I., Haufe, S., Tangermann, M.: Automatic classification of artifactual ICA-components for artifact removal in EEG signals. Behav. Brain Funct. **7**(1), 30 (2011). https://doi.org/10.1186/1744-9081-7-30

49. Young, M.S., Brookhuis, K.A., Wickens, C.D., Hancock, P.A.: State of science: mental workload in ergonomics. Ergonomics **58**(1), 1–17 (2015). https://doi.org/10.1080/00140139.2014.956151

Advancing Cognitive Abilities
and Performance with Augmented Tools

Does Using ChatGPT Result in Human Cognitive Augmentation?

Ron Fulbright and Miranda Morrison[(✉)]

University of South Carolina Upstate, 800 University Way, Spartanburg, SC 29303, USA
fulbrigh@uscupstate.edu, morrisme@email.uscupstate.edu

Abstract. Human cognitive performance is enhanced by the use of tools. For example, a human can produce a much greater, and more accurate, volume of mathematical calculation in a unit of time using a calculator or a spreadsheet application on a computer. Such tools have taken over the burden of lower-level cognitive "grunt work" but the human still serves the role of the expert performing higher-level thinking and reasoning. Recently, however, unsupervised, deep, machine learning has produced cognitive systems able to outperform humans in several domains. When humans use these tools in a human/cog ensemble, the human's cognitive ability is augmented. In some cases, even non-experts can achieve, and even exceed, the performance of experts in a particular domain—synthetic expertise. A new cognitive system, ChatGPT, has burst onto the scene during the past year. This paper investigates human cognitive augmentation due to using Chat-GPT by presenting the results of two experiments comparing responses created using ChatGPT with results created not using ChatGPT. We find using ChatGPT does not always result in cognitive augmentation and does not yet replace human judgement, discernment, and evaluation in certain types of tasks. In fact, Chat-GPT was observed to result in misleading users resulting in negative cognitive augmentation.

Keywords: human cognitive augmentation · cognitive systems · human/cog ensembles

1 Introduction

Human performance of any kind is augmented by the use of tools. Physical performance is enhanced by using simple tools like hammers, shovels, and axes. Likewise, human cognitive performance is augmented by the use of tools able to process and transform information. For example, unaided, a human might take several minutes to add a column of numbers, and then the sum would need to be checked because of the possibility of error in the calculations. However, using a calculator or a computer spreadsheet, a human could produce a reliable sum in a fraction of a second. In fact, entry of the numbers becomes the limiting factor in terms of speed. Today, we commonly use software able to process words, images, video, and numbers to perform our volume of daily work. Such tools have taken over the burden of lower-level cognitive "grunt work." So far, though, the human still serves the role of the expert and performs the high-level thinking.

© The Author(s), under exclusive license to Springer Nature Switzerland AG 2024
D. D. Schmorrow and C. M. Fidopiastis (Eds.): HCII 2024, LNAI 14694, pp. 133–146, 2024.
https://doi.org/10.1007/978-3-031-61569-6_9

Recently, however, cognitive systems technology ("AIs") built using unsupervised, deep, machine learning techniques, has produced tools able to outperform humans in several domains formerly thought to be possible only as the result of high-level human cognitive processing. We call such systems "cogs." When humans use tools like these in a collaborative manner (a human/cog ensemble) human cognitive performance is enhanced—augmented. If a human's cognitive ability is augmented enough, even a non-expert can achieve, and even exceed, the performance of an expert in a particular domain, something called synthetic expertise. So far, though, such cognitive systems are narrow in their applicability. Even though they outperform humans, they are limited to just that domain.

Things are changing. Systems like the new Chat Generative Pre-Trained Transformer (ChatGPT), have gained much attention recently. ChatGPT is a large language model trained to predict the most probable next word in a sequence of words and is fine-tuned for conversational usage. ChatGPT mimics human-created text. Instead of being limited to a narrow domain, users can conduct extended textual dialogs with ChatGPT on practically any topic and most of the time, text generated by ChatGPT is indistinguishable from text produced by another human. Every day, millions of people use ChatGPT for assistance in learning, researching, getting advice, writing music, poetry, and prose, generating computer program code, and much more. A person using ChatGPT certainly fits our definition of a human/cog ensemble. Accordingly, the hypothesis explored in this paper is:

H1: In a human/cog ensemble consisting of a person using ChatGPT we should be able to observe, measure, and characterize human cognitive augmentation in the form of enhanced performance when performing a task.

To investigate the hypothesis, we designed two experiments to compare human cognitive performance with and without using ChatGPT. In one experiment we found a person using ChatGPT as a assistive tool was marginally better than a person not using ChatGPT but not enough for the result to be compelling. In the other experiment we found using ChatGPT had no effect on a person's ability to perform the task and even misled users resulting in negative cognitive augmentation.

2   Previous Work

2.1   Cognitive Systems

With recent advances in artificial intelligence (AI) and cognitive systems (cogs), we are at the beginning of a new era in human history in which humans will work in partnership with artificial entities capable of performing high-level cognition rivaling or surpassing human ability (Kelly & Hamm 2013; Wladawsky-Berger 2015; Gil, 2019; Fulbright 2016a; 2016b; 2020). Already, there are artificial systems and algorithms outperforming humans and achieving expert-level results.

For example, a deep-learning algorithm has learned to detect lung cancers better than human doctors (Sandoiu, 2019). The algorithm outperforms humans in recognizing problem areas reducing false positives by 11% and false negatives by 5%.

Google's convolutional neural network, Inception v4, outperformed a group of 58 human dermatologists using dermoscopic images and corresponding diagnoses of melanoma (Haenssle et al. 2018).

In the field of diabetic retinopathy, a study evaluated the diagnostic performance of a cognitive system for the automated detection of diabetic retinopathy (DR) and Diabetic Macular Edema (DME) (Abràmoff, et al. 2018). The cog exceeded all pre-specified superiority goals.

At the University of California San Francisco and the University of California Berkeley, an algorithm running on a convolutional neural network was better than experts at finding tiny brain hemorrhages in scans of patients' heads (Kurtzman, 2019). The cog was able to complete a diagnosis in only one second, something a human would take many minutes to do.

Cognitive systems are already better than humans at diagnosing childhood depression (Lavars 2019), predicting mortality (Wehner 2019), detecting valvular heart disease (Stevens, 2023), and assessing cancerous tumors (Towers-Clark 2019).

Not only are cognitive systems able to outperform humans in some domains, they are able to do things humans cannot. For example, the FIND FH machine learning model analyzed the clinical data of over 170 million people and discovered 1.3 million of them were previously undiagnosed as being likely to have familial hypercholesterolemia (Myers et al. 2019). Follow-on studies of the individual cases flagged by the cog have shown over 80% of the cases do in fact have a high enough clinical suspicion to warrant evaluation and treatment. This means on the order of 800,000 people could receive life-extending treatment who otherwise would not.

An algorithm named Word2Vec sifted through some 3.3 million abstracts and discovered associations previously unknown by human readers and predicted a new thermoelectric material four years before it was discovered (Tshitoyan, 2019; Gregory 2019).

2.2 Cognitive Augmentation

We can view data, information, knowledge, and wisdom (DIKW) as a hierarchy based on relative value (Ackoff 1989). Each level is of a higher value than the level below it partly because of the processing involved to produce the information stock at that level and partly due to the utility of the information stock at that level. Information is processed data, knowledge is processed information, etc. Processing at each level can be modeled as a cognitive process. Data, information, or knowledge, generically referred to as *information stock*, is input to the cognitive process. The cognitive process transforms the input and produces the higher-valued output. This transformation is accomplished by the expenditure of a certain amount of *cognitive work* (W) (Fulbright 2020).

In a human/cog ensemble, a collaborative team consisting of one or more humans and one or more cognitive systems), cognitive processing of the entire ensemble is a mixture of human cognitive processing (WH) and artificial cognitive processing (WC) ($W^* = WH + WC$) as depicted in Fig. 1 (Fulbright 2020; 2020a; Fulbright & Walters 2020).

A human working alone is able to achieve a certain amount of cognitive work. A human aided by a cognitive system is able to achieve a greater amount of cognitive work.

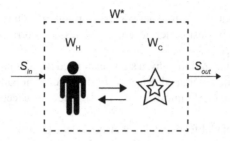

Fig. 1. A Human/Cog ensemble performing a cognitive process.

We call this increase in cognitive performance, cognitive augmentation (Fulbright 2017; 2020).

The amount of cognitive augmentation depends on how sophisticated the cognitive system, how much of the total cognitive work it performs, and how well the human collaborates with the cognitive system. Throughout history, humans have created ever-evolving technology to assist in cognitive processing. As these systems get more capable, especially now in the era of artificial intelligence and unsupervised deep machine learning, cognitive augmentation will increase rapidly.

Level 0:   No Augmentation
the human performs all
cognitive processing

Level 1:   Assistive Tools
e.g., abacus, calculators,
software, etc.

Level 2:   Low-Level Cognition
pattern recognition, classification, speech
human makes all high-
level decisions

Level 3:   High-Level Cognition
concept understanding,
critique
conversational natural
language

Level 4:   Creative Autonomy
human-inspired/unsuper-
vised synthesis

Level 5:   Artificial Intelligence
no human cognitive pro-
cessing

Fig. 2. Levels of Cognitive Augmentation.

Different Levels of Cognitive Augmentation have been defined ranging from no augmentation at all (all human thinking) to fully artificial intelligence (no human thinking) as shown in Fig. 2 (Fulbright 2020; 2020a; Fulbright & Walters 2020).

In previous work, we have conducted various experiments designed to measure and characterize cognitive augmentation. Fulbright (2017; 2018) discusses several kinds of metrics and proposes several metrics to employ when measuring cognitive augmentation. Fulbright (2019) calculates cognitive augmentation for a given task finding cognitive augmentation as high as 74% when people are provided different numbers of hints by a simulated cognitive system. Fulbright & McGaha (2023) shows how information of different types affects the level of cognitive augmentation when tasked with solving several different kinds of puzzles. In both of these studies, enhanced cognitive accuracy and cognitive precision were measured.

In all three of these studies assistive information supplied to the human was simulated and did not come from an actual cognitive system. However, ChatGPT represents a cognitive system, already used by millions, with which to conduct experiments in cognitive augmentation. There have been some notable studies comparing human performance to ChatGPT.

2.3 ChatGPT and Cognitive Augmentation

Li et al. (2023) compared the results of ChatGPT versus human performance on the Objective Structured Clinical Examination (OSCE) in obstetrics and gynecology. ChatGPT was asked to answer discussion questions in seven key disciplines within obstetrics and gynecology. ChatGPT outscored human test-takers in questions regarding postpartum management, urogynecology and pelvic floor problems, labor management, and post-operative care. ChatGPT did not outperform humans in early pregnancy care, core surgical skills, or gynecologic oncology. Li et al. (2023) theorized those question require multiple answers and higher-level reasoning.

Kung et al. (2023) found comparable results when administering the United States Medical Licensing Examination (USMLE) to ChatGPT. ChatGPT beat the passing score of 60% on most areas but narrowly failed to pass the multiple choice-question Sect. (59.1%) and the multiple-choice with forced justification Sect. (52.4%) on Step 2CK of the exam. Step 2CK is typically administered to students who have successfully completed their fourth year of medical school (Kung et al. 2023).

In taking the American Board of Neurological Surgery Self-Assessment Examination 1, Ali et al. (2023) found ChatGPT 3.5 achieved a score of 73.4% and GPT-4 achieved a score of 83.4% relative to the human average of 72.8%. Both versions of ChatGPT exceeded last year's passing threshold of 69%.

Liéven et al. (2023) determined GPT-3.5 performed higher than the needed passing score on questions taken from the USMLE and MedMCQA examinations, however, GPT-3.5 still underperformed on both examinations in comparison to humans.

Brin et al. (2023), determined GPT-4 to have performed 10.77% better than human test-takers on multiple-choice questions from the USMLE involving soft skills, such as empathy, leadership, emotional intelligence, and communication.

Similarly, Eloyseph et al. (2023) found ChatGPT to score 74.35% higher than males and 66.27% higher than females on the Levels of Emotional Awareness Scale (LEAS), a test measuring emotional intelligence in the form of open-ended questions that are evaluated by licensed psychologists. It is also worth noting ChatGPT took the LEAS evaluation twice: once in January and once in February. ChatGPT improved its LEAS score by 13% between the two exams.

Duong & Solomon (2023) compared the ability of ChatGPT to humans in answering multiple-choice questions about genetics. Humans answered questions with 1.61% greater accuracy overall, but ChatGPT performed 8.51% better than humans on questions that relied on memorization instead of critical thinking.

Jarou et al. (2023) administered multiple-choice questions from the American College of Emergency Physicians (ACEP) study guide. Human respondents scored 36.32% higher than GPT-3.5 and 19.5% higher than GPT-4; yet GPT-4 scored 33.71% higher than GPT-3.5.

Additionally, Katz et al. (2023) compared the performance of GPT-3.5 and GPT-4 with human respondents on the Uniform Bar Exam. GPT-4 performed 11.3% better than human test-takers, but GPT-3.5 could not exceed human performance in any of the subject areas tested on the exam.

Instead of situations in which ChatGPT replaces humans, this paper is interested in exploring how using ChatGPT enhances a user's cognitive ability as stated in the hypothesis, H1. Unfortunately, there have not yet been a lot of studies like this. Noy and Zhang (2023) assigned 444 professionals with tasks related to their respective profession, such as sensitive e-mails, press releases, and reports. After completing the initial task, the group was split in two. The control group was asked to repeat the task using LaTeX, a document preparation program, while the test group used ChatGPT to assist them with their second task. Those using ChatGPT reduced the time spent on the task by 35.16% and improved their score on the second task by 15.45%.

3   The Experiments

This paper presents the results of two experiments in which we asked students to perform a task and comparing their performance with that of an expert. Students were tasked with two different challenges, an innovation problem and an expert advice question. Students used ChatGPT 3.5 (circa November 2023, January 2024) in these experiments.

3.1   Innovation Challenge

For the innovation challenge, students were given the following problem statement: *When shooting skeet, fragments from the skeet fall on and cause harm to the grass field by preventing sunlight and water from reaching the grass. What changes can I make to protect the grass?*

This is the same problem statement used in a previous cognitive augmentation experiment described in Fulbright (2019). In that experiment, students were given hints in the form of innovative suggestions (called operators) and the results showed it was possible to affect the innovative solutions arrived at by the participants toward a desired goal— the preferred solution. In fact, results showed as much of a 74% increase in cognitive accuracy was achieved demonstrating significant cognitive augmentation.

Participants were asked to synthesize three innovative solutions to the problem. Any solution could not interfere with the sheet shooting activity, must be relatively easy and inexpensive to implement, and involve as little change to the current situation as possible. One-half of the participants were instructed to not use any Internet-based resource at all. The other half were instructed to use only ChatGPT.

This innovation problem was chosen because it is a problem used in teaching innovation at the university undergraduate level for over many years. As such, there is a long history of solutions, and patterns of solutions, to compare new results with. Because of this history, we know what type of solutions people give when not aided by any cognitive system or assistive information and we know what type of solutions are given by professional/expert innovators.

With respect to H1, our goal was to see if using ChatGPT altered the type of solutions. If H1 was verified in this experiment, we would expect to see the solutions trend toward the professional/expert type of solutions.

3.2 Retirement Decision

For the second experiment, participants were given detailed information about an imaginary college professor approaching retirement. Information provided included: age, profession (and pros and cons of the profession), salary, debt, medical situation, retirement savings, with the goals of being able to remain in the current home, travel at least twice per year after retirement, and not outliving their money.

Participants were asked if the person should retire early at 67 or wait until the age of 70. A person can go to a retirement planning expert and ask this question and receive a detailed response including an explanation of why it is better to retire at 67 or wait until 70. None of the participants, being university students, were experts in retirement planning. However, we asked each participant to provide a specific answer (either 67 or 70) and then also provide a justification to support the answer. In our judgement of the results, it did not matter which age was given as the answer. We focused on the level of detail in the justification. A detailed and specific justification, in our view, constituted an expert-level answer to the challenge.

One-half of the participants were instructed to use ChatGPT only, an no other Internet-based resource, and the other half was instructed to use any Internet-based resource except ChatGPT. With respect to H1, we expected to see an increase in the ability of participants to provide an expert-level answer due to using ChatGPT.

4 The Results

4.1 Innovation Challenge Results

For the innovation challenge, 13 students used ChatGPT and 13 students did not use ChatGPT to synthesize a total of $N = 96$ ideas to solve the skeet shooting innovation challenge. As we have seen in earlier studies using this problem statement, ideas fell into three broad categories: changing the field (**F**), changing the skeet (**T**), or ideas not solving the problem at all (**X**). Ideas involving the field fell into three different subcategories and ideas involving the skeet fell into two categories:

F^T   protecting the field with a tarp, net, or some other kind of covering

F^C   ways of cleaning the field or making picking up fragments easier

F^G   changing or replacing the grass on the field

T^B   replacing clay skeet with biodegradable material

T^C   changing the clay skeet to make cleanup more easier

X ideas addressing ideas other than the stated problem

Figure 4 shows the results for students not using ChatGPT. Overwhelmingly, most ideas (79.5%) involved changing the field in some way such as covering it with a tarp or net to prevent fragments from reaching the grass or various ways to clean the field after fragments have fallen onto the grass. The remainder (20.5%) of the ideas involved changing the clay skeet such as making the skeet out of biodegradable material or out of some material other than clay to facilitate easier cleanup. Field-related ideas outnumbered skeet-related ideas 3.8:1.

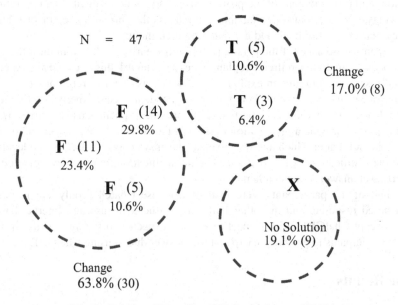

Fig. 3. Solutions Using ChatGPT for Assistance (47 ideas).

Figure 3 shows the results for students using ChatGPT. As in Fig. 4, ideas involving changing the field vastly outnumber ideas involving changing the skeet by almost exactly the same ratio 3.75:1. Therefore, we see no difference in the type of ideas generated as a result of using ChatGPT. Therefore, the hypothesis, H1, is refuted.

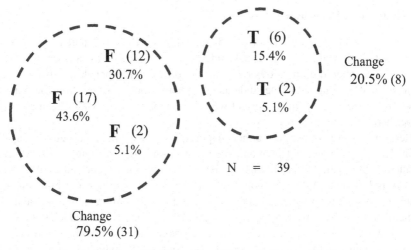

Fig. 4. Solutions Not Using ChatGPT for Assistance (39 ideas).

Interestingly, students using ChatGPT synthesized a number of ideas having no effect at all on the primary problem—littering of the grass by the fragments. Examining these ideas in detail shows these ideas were related to "educating shooters about the environmental impact" and "educating shooters about gun safety." These ideas can be explained when one analyzes the response from ChatGPT when given the problem statement as the prompt. ChatGPT is trained from articles and other content available on the Internet. Because the problem statement involves guns and shooting, ChatGPT responded with suggestions to educate shooters about gun safety because on the Internet, when one sees a document about guns and shooting, it is very likely to also include comments about safety. Even though the concepts of guns and safety are understandably related, the safety issue has nothing to do with solving the problem given in the problem statement—littering the grass field. ChatGPT however does not perform such in-depth analysis to realize this. ChatGPT's responses are driven by word association. Likewise, because the problem statement mentions littering and damaging grass, ChatGPT finds associations with environmental issues important and therefore responded to students suggesting education about the environment since this is found in millions of pages on the Internet when litter and harming grass is mentioned. While one could argue you might be able to talk a shooter out of shooting after they understand the harm to the grass, this is not likely to change the mind of the vast majority of shooters, so is not a practical solution. Interestingly, in this case, using of ChatGPT actually distracted students by misleading them to consider things having nothing to do with the problem. Therefore, one could argue using ChatGPT actually decreased cognitive ability—resulting in negative cognitive augmentation.

4.2 Retirement Decision Results

For the retirement decision challenge, 15 students used ChatGPT and 10 students did not use ChatGPT. The challenge asked students to provide a specific answer, whether or not the subject should retire at 67 or 70 and also provide an expert-level justification of that answer. We explained to the students how people could visit a retirement planning professional and receive guidance and we asked students to provide a similar-quality answer here.

Responses were judged to be either "expert quality" or "non-expert quality" as seen in Fig. 5. The difference between an expert and a non-expert response is in the details provided in the justification. To answer the question properly, one must calculate the monthly inflow and outflow of money. To do that, one has to find out how much per month social security payments would be and add to that withdrawals from savings to augment the monthly inflow. Once this is established, one has to calculate how long the subject's money would last. Very different answers are obtained if one retires at age 67 versus 70. In judging the responses, we did not consider which answer the student provided. It did not matter at what age the student decided the subject should retire. What we did look for, though, is did the student conduct and include the analysis needed to justify their response. Reponses including the analysis were deemed "expert" and the responses not including the analysis were deemed "non-expert."

Another characteristic of non-expert responses was "generic" information like "the person must consider how long their savings will last." While this is certainly is something a person needs to consider when planning retirement, one would not have to visit an expert to get this advice. Any friend, family member, or easy search on the Internet will produce a list of such things for one to consider. In fact, the first response from ChatGPT gives a list of 8–10 such generic issues to consider. So, a response simply containing generic information like this was considered "non-expert."

Figure 5 shows students not using ChatGPT provided expert-quality answers 40% of the time. Students using ChatGPT provided expert-quality answers 53% of the time. While this is an increase, it is not a definitive increase in our opinion. Of further note, is of the students using ChatGPT, there was only one more expert response than non-expert response. If ChatGPT provided demonstrable cognitive augmentation for this task, one would expect many more expert answers than non-expert answers from the group of students using ChatGPT.

Students not using ChatGPT were allowed to use any other Internet-based resource and reported the tool or information source they used. We observed all expert-quality answers from the non-ChatGPT group were provided by students who used a retirement calculator available on the Internet. We believe the students using a retirement calculator were cognitively augmented just like students using ChatGPT. In fact, the retirement calculator is an assistive tool designed specifically to help answer retirement planning questions whereas ChatGPT is not. Although we are not able to definitively conclude it in this study, we believe if non-ChatGPT students were not allowed to use a retirement calculator, the number of expert-quality answers would be much lower and students using ChatGPT would have performed much better.

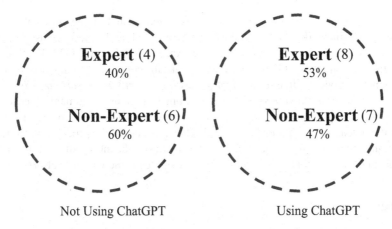

Fig. 5. Responses to the Retirement Decision Challenge (25 responses).

5   Conclusion

Our hypotheses, H1 was refuted in the innovation experiment and only moderately confirmed in the retirement decision experiment. In fact, in the innovation experiment, ChatGPT actually misled students to thinking about issues irrelevant to the problem statement, resulting in negative cognitive augmentation. Both experiments involved tasks requiring detailed analysis, high-level reasoning, and human judgment and were questions without a definite right and wrong answer. To this extent, we confirm the findings of Li et al. (2023), Liéven et al. (2023), Jarou et al. (2023), and Katz et al. (2023) who found ChatGPT outperformed humans on some types of questions but not those involving higher-level analysis.

Our results show using ChatGPT does not guarantee expert-level performance. None of the students participating in this study were experts at using ChatGPT. For some, this task was the first time they ever used ChatGPT. If students had more experience with ChatGPT, more expert-level results might be expected. Also, students who participated were not given detailed instructions on how to answer retirement questions nor how to think innovatively. If they had known more about the subject, it stands to reason more would have been able to provide expert-quality answers. This can be explored in future studies.

It is necessary to note, when designing these experiments, we found it quite difficult to determine tasks to give to students. We tested and discarded several tasks before deciding on the innovation and retirement challenges because we found ChatGPT was able to simply spit out a perfectly correct answer on the first prompt. Over time, we realized we could not ask students to perform any task involving just simple knowledge retrieval because ChatGPT does this quite well. To create a challenge tough enough, we realized the tasks needed to require cognitive processes involving *understanding, evaluation, appraisal, critique,* and *judgment* in order to exercise the students and ChatGPT more vigorously.

We recognize these types of cognitive processes represent the upper levels of Bloom's Taxonomy, a framework for categorizing educational goals and therefore classifying levels of cognitive processes (Bloom et. al., 1956; Anderson & Kratwohl, 2001). We expect future studies to show ChatGPT already able to take the cognitive "grunt work" of lower-level cognitive processes like *recall, defining, listing, classifying, describing, discussing, explaining, translating,* and *recognizing* away from the human in a human/cog ensemble. Any task involving these levels of cognitive processing will be done quicker and better by ChatGPT leaving the human to do the higher-level cognitive processing. Relieving the human of the cognitive "grunt work" will result in significant cognitive augmentation in the form of higher-quality, higher-value results in less time with less effort.

References

Abràmoff, M.D., Lavin, P.T., Birch, M., Shah, N., Folk, J.C.: . Pivotal trial of an autonomous AI-based diagnostic system for detection of diabetic retinopathy in primary care offices. Digital Med. **1**, 39 (2018). https://www.nature.com/articles/s41746-018-0040-6, (Accessed January 2024)

Ackoff, R.: From Data to Wisdom. J. Appli. Syst. Analy. **16** (1989). https://faculty.ung.edu/kmelton/Documents/DataWisdom.pdf (Accessed February 2023)

Ali, R., et al.: Performance of CHATGPT and GPT-4 on Neurosurgery Written Board Examinations. Neurosurgery (2023). https://doi.org/10.1227/neu.0000000000002632

Anderson, L.W., Krathwohl, D.R., Airasian, P.W., Cruik-shank, K.A., Mayer, R.E.: A taxonomy for learning, teaching, and assessing: a revision of Bloom's taxonomy of educational objectives, Pearson (2001)

Bloom, B.S., Engelhart, M.D., Furst, E.J., Hill, W.H., Krath-wohl, D.R.: Taxonomy of educational objectives: The classification of educational goals. Handbook I: Cognitive domain. New York: David McKay Company (1956)

Brin, D., et al.: Comparing ChatGPT and GPT-4 performance in USMLE soft skill assessments. Sci. Rep. **13**(1) (2023). https://doi.org/10.1038/s41598-023-43436-9

Duong, D., Solomon, B.D.: Analysis of large-language model versus human performance for genetics questions. Eur. J. Hum. Genet. (2023). https://doi.org/10.1038/s41431-023-01396-8

Elyoseph, Z., Hadar-Shoval, D., Asraf, K., Lvovsky, M.: ChatGPT outperforms humans in emotional awareness evaluations. Front. Psychol. **14** (2023). https://doi.org/10.3389/fpsyg.2023.1199058

Fulbright, R.: The Cogs Are Coming: The Cognitive Augmentation Revolution, Proceedings of the Association Supporting Computer Users in Education 2015 (49th, Myrtle Beach, SC) (2016a). https://eric.ed.gov/?q=cognitive+development+in+early+childhood&ff1=dtysince_2014&pg=1340&id=ED570900, (Accessed January 2024)

Fulbright, R.: How personal cognitive augmentation will lead to the democratization of expertise. Adv. Cognitive Syst. **4** (2016b). http://www.cogsys.org/posters/2016/poster-2016-3.pdf, (Acccessed January 2024)

Fulbright, R.: Cognitive augmentation metrics using representational information theory. In: Schmorrow D., Fidopiastis C. (eds.) Augmented Cognition. Enhancing Cognition and Behavior in Complex Human Environments, AC 2017. LNCS, vol. 10285. Springer, Cham (2017). https://doi.org/10.1007/978-3-319-58625-0_3

Fulbright, R.: On measuring cognition and cognitive augmentation, In: Yamamoto, S., Mori, H. (eds.) Human Interface and the Management of Information, HIMI 2018. LNCS, vol. 10905. Springer, Cham (2018). https://doi.org/10.1007/978-3-319-92046-7_41

Fulbright, R.: Calculating Cognitive Augmentation -A Case Study, In: Schmorrow, D., Fidopiastis, C. (eds.) Augmented Cognition, AC 2019. LNCS, vol. 11580. Springer, Cham (2019). https://doi.org/10.1007/978-3-030-22419-6_38

Fulbright, R.: Democratization of Expertise: How Cognitive Systems Will Revolutionize Your Life. CRC Press, Boca Raton (2020)

Fulbright, R.: The expertise level. In: Schmorrow D., Fidopiastis C. (eds.) Augmented Cognition. Human Cognition and Behavior. HCII 2020. LNCS, vol. 12197. Springer, Cham (2020a). https://doi.org/10.1007/978-3-030-50439-7_4

Fulbright, R., Walters, G.: Synthetic Expertise. In: Schmorrow D., Fidopiastis C. (eds.) Augmented Cognition. Human Cognition and Behavior. HCII 2020. LNCS, vol. 12197. Springer, Cham (2020). https://doi.org/10.1007/978-3-030-50439-7_3

Fulbright R. and McGaha, S.: The Effect of Information Type on Human Cognitive Augmentation. In: Schmorrow, D., Fidopiastis, C. (eds.), Augmented Cognition: HCII 2023, LNCS, vol. 14019, pp. 206- 220. Springer, Cham (2023). https://doi.org/10.1007/978-3-031-35017-7_14

Gil, D.: Cognitive systems and the future of expertise, YouTube video located at (2019) https://www.youtube.com/watch?v=0heqP8d6vtQ (Accessed February 2023)

Gregory, M.: AI Trained on Old Scientific Papers Makes Discoveries Humans Missed, Vice Internet page located at (2019). https://www.vice.com/en_in/article/neagpb/ai-trained-on-old (Accessed January 2024)

Haenssle, H.A., et al.: Man against machine: diagnostic performance of a deep learning convolutional neural network for dermoscopic melanoma recognition in comparison to 58 dermatologists. Annals Oncol. **29**(8), 1836–1842 (2018). https://academic.oup.com/annonc/article/29/8/1836/5004443, (Accessed November 2019)

Jarou, Z.J., Dakka, A., McGuire, D., Bunting, L.: ChatGPT versus human performance on emergency medicine board preparation questions. Ann. Emerg. Med. (2023). https://doi.org/10.1016/j.annemergmed.2023.08.010

Katz, D.M., Bommarito, M.J., Gao, S., Arredondo, P.: GPT-4 Passes the Bar Exam. SSRN Electron. J. (2023). https://doi.org/10.2139/ssrn.4389233

Kelly, J.E., Hamm, S.: Smart Machines: IBMs Watson and the Era of Cognitive Computing. Columbia Business School Publishing, Columbia University Press, New York, NY (2013)

Kung, T. H., et al.: Performance of ChatGPT on USMLE: potential for ai-assisted medical education using large language models. PLOS Digital Health 2(2) (2023). https://doi.org/10.1371/journal.pdig.0000198

Kurtzman, L.: AI Rivals Expert Radiologists at Detecting Brain Hemorrhages: Richly Annotated Training Data Vastly Improves Deep Learning Algorithm's Accuracy, UCSF News, University of California San Francisco (2019). https://www.ucsf.edu/news/2019/10/415681/ai-rivals-expert-radiologists-detecting-brain-hemorrhages, (Accessed January 2024)

Lavars, N.: Machine learning algorithm detects signals of child depression through speech, New Atlas, published May 7 (2019). https://newatlas.com/machine-learning-algorithm-depression/59573/ (Accessed February 2023)

Li, S. W., et al.: ChatGPT Outscored Human Candidates in a Virtual Objective Structured Clinical Examination in Obstetrics and Gynecology. Am. J. Obstetrics Gynecol. **229**(2) (2023). https://pubmed.ncbi.nlm.nih.gov/37088277/, (Accessed January 2024)

Liévin, V., Hother, C. E., and Winther, O.: Can Large Language Models Reason About Medical Questions? arXiv (2023). https://doi.org/10.48550/arXiv.2207.08143

Myers, K. D., et al.: Precision screening for familial hypercholesterolaemia: a machine learning study applied to electronic health encounter data. Lancet Digital Health (2019). https://www.thelancet.com/journals/landig/article/PIIS2589–7500(19)30150–5/fulltext , (Accessed January 2024)

Noy, S., Zhang, W.: Experimental evidence on the productivity effects of generative artificial intelligence. Science **381**(6654), 187–192 (2023). https://www.science.org/, https://doi.org/10.1126/science.adh2586, (Accessed January 2024)

[Stevens] Listen to your heart: AI tool detect heart diseases that doctors often miss, Stevens Institute of Technology media release (2023). https://www.stevens.edu/news/listen-to-your-heart-ai-tool-detects-cardiac-diseases-that-doctors-often#%20, (Accessed January 2024)

Sandoiu, A.: Artificial intelligence better than humans at spotting lung cancer. Medical News Today Newsletter, May 20 (2019). https://www.medicalnewstoday.com/articles/325223.php#1, (Aaccessed November 2019)

Tshitoyan, V., et al.: Unsupervised word embeddings capture latent knowledge from materials science literature Nature **571** (2019). https://www.nature.com/articles/s41586-019-1335-8, (Accessed January 2024)

Towers-Clark, C.: The Cutting-Edge of AI Cancer Detection, Forbes, published April 30 (2019). https://www.forbes.com/sites/charlestowersclark/2019/04/30/the-cutting-edge-of-ai-cancer-detection/#45235ee77336 last accessed February 2023

Wehner, M.: . AI is now better at predicting mortality than human doctors, New York Post, published May 14 (2019). https://nypost.com/2019/05/14/ai-isnow-better-at-predicting-mortality-than-humandoctors/?utm_campaign=partnerfeed&utm_medium=syndicated&utm_source=flipboard last accessed February 2023

Wladawsky-Berger, I.: The Era of Augmented Cognition, The Wall Street Journal: CIO Report Internet page located at (2015). http://blogs.wsj.com/cio/2013/06/28/the-era-of-augmented-cognition/ (Accessed February 2023)

Assessment of a Novel Virtual Environment for Examining Cognitive-Motor Processes During Execution of Action Sequences in a Human-Robot Teaming Context

Jayesh Jayashankar[1,2], Anna L. Packy[1,2], Arya Teymourlouei[3], Alexandra A. Shaver[1], Garrett E. Katz[4], James A. Reggia[2,5,6], James Purtilo[2(✉)], and Rodolphe J. Gentili[1,2,6(✉)]

[1] Department of Kinesiology, University of Maryland, College Park, MD, USA
rodolphe@umd.edu
[2] Neuroscience and Cognitive Science Program, University of Maryland, College Park, MD, USA
purtilo@umd.edu
[3] Department of Computer Science, University of Maryland, College Park, MD, USA
[4] Electrical Engineering and Computer Science, Syracuse University, Syracuse, NY, USA
[5] Institute for Advanced Computer Studies, University of Maryland, College Park, MD, USA
[6] Maryland Robotics Center, University of Maryland, College Park, MD, USA

Abstract. With the development of advanced AI and robotic systems, there is a growing interest in examining human-robot teaming. While the vast majority of human-robot studies has focused on technological developments, only a limited body of work has considered employing neurophysiological data and real-world activities to examine human cognitive-motor processes in such a teaming context. Although human-robot teaming can be examined using physical systems, virtual environments also offer numerous advantages such as versatility, scalability, and cost-effectiveness. Therefore, here we propose and assess a novel virtual environment (VTEAM) through which human cognitive-motor processes can be examined when individuals perform alone or with a robotic teammate, sequential tasks that have similar features to real-world activities. This new experimental platform allows synchronous behavioral and neurophysiological (EEG) data collection to provide a more comprehensive examination of human cognitive-motor behavior. VTEAM was evaluated by assessing its usability, as well as the resulting team performance and human perception of the workload and of the robotic teammate. The findings revealed appropriate levels of usability and workload when individuals operated VTEAM to complete two tasks alone or with the robotic teammate. When engaged, the robotic teammate - which individuals perceived as likeable, intelligent and safe - was able to improve task performance, suggesting that this platform can robustly assess human-robot teaming. Thus, this novel experimental platform appears to be appropriate for investigating human cognitive-motor processes when individuals perform and learn action sequences alone or collaboratively with a robotic teammate.

J. Jayashankar, A. L. Packy and A. Teymourlouei are co-first authors.

© The Author(s), under exclusive license to Springer Nature Switzerland AG 2024
D. D. Schmorrow and C. M. Fidopiastis (Eds.): HCII 2024, LNAI 14694, pp. 147–166, 2024.
https://doi.org/10.1007/978-3-031-61569-6_10

Keywords: Virtual environment · Action sequences · Human-robot team · Mental workload · Cognitive-motor performance · AI-based humanoid robots

1 Introduction

A large body of work has examined human cognitive-motor processes underlying task performance under varying conditions when individuals perform alone or in a teaming environment (e.g., [1–3]). In these past works, a more restricted effort has investigated the neural mechanisms underlying various constructs such as, but not limited to, mental workload, trust, emotion, stress or situational awareness when individuals perform various tasks (e.g., flight or monitoring tasks) while interacting with automation which aims to assist the user [4, 5]. However, while informative, these prior works did not necessarily focus on interactions and particularly on collaborations between human individuals and robotic systems having AI capabilities as is done here [4–6]. As far as we know, compared to robotic development, only a fairly limited effort has focused on the human cognitive-motor processes during human-robot interactions, and this body of work is even sparser when considering human-robot teaming contexts where individuals work with a robotic partner to collectively complete a task [6–8]. Specifically, only a restricted amount of human-robot teaming studies has examined human cognitive-motor processes in this context via brain dynamics (e.g., EEG, fNIRS) [6–9]. In addition, prior efforts did not necessarily assess action sequence tasks that can involve complex dependencies similar to real world activities (e.g., solving a puzzle, executing a complicated maintenance task). Such tasks are particularly interesting since they can be computationally demanding for both the AI-based robot and humans while being well suited for team execution [10–12]. Typically, these sequential tasks can require an elevated deployment of cognitive-motor resources in novices (e.g., planning; working memory; attention [13]) and an extensive amount of practice to be learned. They also can involve multiple degrees of freedom as well as a lot of hand-eye coordination [14]. Thus, it would be informative to examine human cognitive-motor processes when individuals team-up with a robotic partner to collaboratively execute sequential tasks while combining behavioral and neurophysiological analyses to provide a more comprehensive understanding of human behavior in such a social context. Such an approach not only informs human-robot teaming technology but also human behavior.

The examination of cognitive-motor processes during human-robot teaming can be conducted with physical robots which offer realistic environments. However, although having their own limitations, virtual platforms offer the advantage of being versatile, scalable, portable and applicable to situations that would be too complex, costly or unsafe with physical robots. In addition, they permit examining human-robot teaming while manipulating the team environment at will with various scenarios and applications (e.g., tele-operations, tele-autonomy). In some cases, these virtual platforms can serve as a preparatory step before using physical robots and thus can be considered not as a replacement but instead as a complementary approach to physical systems. While simulated environments for examining human-robot teaming are available, these various platforms do not necessarily involve a human executing sequential tasks (having tunable characteristics) with a humanoid robotic teammate that can be parametrized to manipulate the team environment while allowing synchronous collection of behavioral and neuroimaging data (e.g., [15–18]). Thus, as a first step, we describe here a novel virtual platform (virtualized teaming or VTEAM) that permits examination of behavioral and human neural processes when individuals execute and learn sequential cognitive-motor tasks alone or with a robotic teammate under various tasks and teaming conditions. The VTEAM platform currently allows one to i) generate various sequential tasks and scenarios that can be parametrized (e.g., varying the levels of cognitive-motor demands), ii) manipulate the team environment by having the human perform alone or with the robotic teammate while parametrizing the synthetic partner (e.g., number of turns, period of engagement/disengagement); and iii) collect both performance and neuroimaging (here electroencephalography or EEG) data in a synchronized fashion based on markers generated by specific events (e.g., task/scenario starts and ends, robotic teammate engagement/disengagement). In the following, the usability of this new virtual platform and more generally how it can affect human cognitive-motor behavior are investigated to ensure that no major design issues inducing experimental bias are detected. While an EEG event marker system will be used in VTEAM for subsequent human cognitive-motor studies, no EEG is collected in this current study because we are only testing the system's usability. Once validated, VTEAM could be employed to conduct human-robot teaming studies that incorporate various empirical manipulations (e.g., task demands, teaming environments). Thus, the aim of this work was to evaluate the usability of this new experimental platform and identify which characteristics are appropriately designed and which should be revised to be improved. Specifically, VTEAM's evaluation was conducted by examining the level of usability and workload and comparing these to available standards, and by assessing the performance obtained when individuals execute sequential tasks with and without a robotic teammate. It was hypothesized that if this novel platform is appropriate, the usability and workload levels perceived by humans when performing alone or with the robotic teammate sequential tasks should be beyond the industry standards. Conversely, if this platform has features which result in usability and mental workload that do not meet established standards, it could compromise the data integrity and thus should be revised to be enhanced.

2 Material and Methods

2.1 The Virtual Environment

General Presentation. The VTEAM system offers a flexible experimental platform including customizable tasks to examine the human cognitive-motor processes in participants executing sequential tasks. This virtual platform contains a dashboard and a task completion environment (see Fig. 1). The dashboard allows the administrative experimenter to parametrize the experimental tasks as well as the teaming environment (see details below). Once the administrator has selected and parametrized the task along with the teaming environment, participants perform through the 3D virtual environment the task alone or with a simulated humanoid robot (Baxter, Rethink robotics™) teammate placed in front of them. While various scenarios could be implemented in VTEAM, as of now two tasks of interest involving sequences of actions were designed. The first task is based on the sliding block puzzle-game RushHour™ (RH) [19] which consists of sliding blocks in a sequential manner on a grid to move one single specific block outside the board. The second task is a circuit breaker (CB) task which consists of maintaining an electrical panel where faulty fuses must be replaced (see Sect. 2.2 for details). The entire virtual environment, including both tasks, was implemented in C# using the Unity game engine.

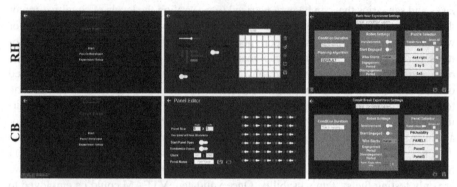

Fig. 1. Administrator's VTEAM interface for the RH (top row) and CB (bottom row) tasks. First column: main menu of the virtual environment for both the RH and CB tasks. Second column: developer dashboard for the administrator to create, validate and save different scenarios for each task. Third column: dashboard to create and load experimental conditions by selecting the scenarios and the presence/absence of the robot as well as its level of involvement.

The VTEAM experimental platform presented here is based and expands upon two previous virtual systems: the Simulator for Maryland Imitation Learning Environment (SMILE) [20, 21] and the Virtualized Learning (VLEARN) platform [22], both developed at the University of Maryland, College Park. SMILE was initially developed to provide a simulated environment where animated demonstrations of sequential tasks could be generated and then observed by a humanoid robot (Baxter, Rethink robotics™) that learns the sequences through imitation. The main idea behind SMILE was that the humanoid could successfully learn via imitating complex action sequences by focusing solely on object activities in the virtual environment without using information from the demonstrator's movements. More recently, VLEARN was developed by the SEAM lab at the University of Maryland, College Park to examine human cognitive-motor control and learning processes during execution of various sequential tasks without robotic teaming. The primary aim of developing VLEARN was to provide a portable web-based virtual environment where individuals can perform and practice remotely different tasks that involve action sequences of varying complexity. Prior works suggested that some tasks executed via this virtual environment produced usability, performance, mental workload and fatigue levels comparable to those observed with the corresponding physical system [22]. Although both SMILE and VLEARN are very useful for robotic imitation learning and examining human cognitive-motor performance, neither of them allows for examining human cognitive-motor processes when individuals collaborate with a humanoid robotic system that can be tuned in various manners to manipulate the human-robot team dynamics. Therefore, the novel virtual environment VTEAM presented here serves a different purpose than the VLEARN and SMILE platforms, by allowing one to assess cognitive motor-performance when individuals execute action sequences on a variety of tasks collaboratively with an AI-based humanoid robot having adaptive planning capabilities.

For both tasks the VTEAM interface allows for generating a scenario and its associated parameters. First, the experimenter dashboard allows the researcher to create a scenario for a given task. Specifically, for the RH task, the administrator can choose the size of a grid board. Once this is defined, the size of the blocks and their position on the board as well as the location of the exit gate can be selected thus providing one or more scenarios (or puzzles) to be solved. Then, the VTEAM platform automatically verifies the scenarios, checking whether they are solvable or not. If they are not solvable, they will have to be updated. Once a new solvable scenario is created it will be saved in the database using a specific name provided by the administrator. Similarly, for the CB task, the dashboard allows the administrator to create different electrical panel scenarios where its size and the faulty/functioning fuses indicated by red/green LEDs can be selected. Also, for further manipulation of task demands, the administrator can select the option of identifying each fuse with a specific number that must be matched with the appropriate action when participants perform the task. Once a new electrical panel scenario is created, an internal validation process checks all the logic related to the slots with faulty fuses, disallowing illegal moves and evaluating that the respective button presses are valid. Once a new scenario is validated it is saved in the database using a particular name selected by the administrator.

For both tasks, any scenarios that have been saved can then be subsequently selected to be loaded for an experimental study. If multiple scenarios are selected, they can be either presented in a specific or in a random order to the participants. Therefore, various scenarios with different levels of complexity can be created and stored to be then presented to the participants during the study. Once all the scenarios are completed, these keep cycling through until the end of the experimental session. Although the primary purpose of VTEAM is to examine cognitive-motor processes in a human-robot teaming context, it also allows for individuals to perform alone since this provides a control condition against which the teaming condition can be compared. Thus, for both tasks, the experimenter dashboard provides the possibility to select if individuals will perform the task alone or with the humanoid robot as well as the duration of the experimental condition. If the humanoid robot option is selected, the administrator can parametrize the robotic teammate as to which of the human or robotic teammate will start the task as well as to identify the task period(s) during which the robot will be engaged with the human. This latter option enables the robot to engage/disengage dynamically throughout multiple periods during the experiment. For example, in a condition set for ten minutes, ten scenarios (RH puzzles or CB electrical panels) could be selected, and the robotic teammate could be involved for five minutes and be disengaged for the remaining period. Once all the parameters have been selected, the saved experimental conditions are loaded to run the corresponding testing session. During data collection the virtual environment can record the action sequences completed by the participants and the robotic teammate while communicating with EEG systems allowing to collect data on human cortical dynamics, thus providing a more comprehensive cognitive-motor performance assessment (see Fig. 1).

The long-term goal of this platform is to allow the examination of the neural mechanisms underlying cognitive-motor performance and learning when individuals collaboratively complete various tasks with a robotic teammate having AI capabilities. Thus, the proposed environment enables i) smooth manipulation of the interactive elements for different tasks that individuals can execute alone or collaboratively with a robotic partner, ii) a robust action sequence planning system driving the robotic teammate execution when interacting with the user, iii) a flexible platform allowing a wide range of task, scenarios and teaming parametrization and iv) the capability to record each action of the sequences as well as interact with neuroimaging data (e.g., EEG) collection systems by generating multiple event-markers. This allows one to analyze performance and brain dynamics providing a more comprehensive assessment of the human cognitive motor processes.

Software Architecture. The proposed virtual platform was developed using Unity, a software system for building and deploying real-time gaming programs and rendered through WebGL. These programs are built in the language C# and incorporate substantial packages for graphics, plus a physics engine to offer realistic behaviors. Once parametrized, all the experimental settings (i.e., human alone or human-robot teaming) as well as scenarios (e.g., RH puzzle to solve, CB panel configuration) generated for both tasks are saved as XML files. The saved experimental settings and scenarios can be subsequently loaded from the folders they reside in, offering thus a testing database for implementing data collection (Fig. 2, bottom row). In VTEAM, the various task components are manipulated via simple computer mouse operations such as click, drag and drop.

When the robotic teammate is activated, the planning algorithm implemented through the Python programming language receives the current state of the task and then computes the action for the robot to execute. The Python script runs a breadth first search algorithm (BFS) which takes as input the current state of the task in a csv format and provides the next move in a format representative of the current state of the object to be acted upon and the new state of the object they should reside in.

VTEAM's login capabilities can record all the actions of the sequential task executed by the participants and the robotic teammate during data collection. These actions are then stored in a csv file for future analysis. Additionally, the appropriate interfaces were included such that EEG signals can be synchronized with the task activities for purposes of subsequent analysis. Specifically, each task embeds button presses to generate event markers that are sent out to another computer (in our case the EEG software was BrainVision Recorder, Brain Products GmbH) collecting EEG data which indicate the beginning and end of the task as well as completion of different scenarios. If the teaming environment has been activated, additional event markers are also generated when the robot engages/disengages during task completion (Fig. 2, top row). These EEG event markers allow one to mark the period covering the signals of interest for subsequent analysis of human cortical dynamics. Therefore, this feature enables VTEAM to synchronize task execution with collection of behavioral and cortical data allowing subsequent measurement of performance and cortical dynamics and enabling a combined examination of the

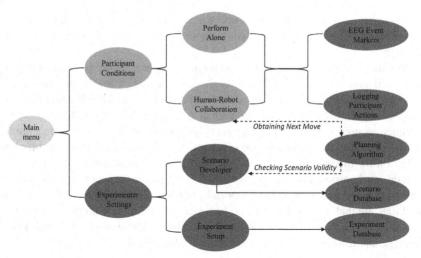

Fig. 2. High-level architecture employed to implement VTEAM. The red circles represent the experimenter dashboard, the green circles represent the participant conditions, and the blue circles refer to EEG event markers generation, logging of actions, planning algorithm and external storage of XML and csv files forming the scenario and experiment databases.

human cognitive-motor processes of interest. Since the primary aim of this current work is only to assess the usability of VTEAM without actually analyzing brain data, the EEG was not collected. However, this study revealed that VTEAM was able to successfully send all of the correct triggers to the EEG recoding system.

2.2 Experimental Evaluation

Participants. Fifteen healthy individuals participated (6 men; 9 women; age range 19 - 39 years). Participants did not report any neurological impairment nor use of medication that can affect the central nervous system. At the time they completed the study, participants were free of drug and alcohol use and had a normal or corrected-to-normal vision. Before the start of the study, all participants provided written informed consent which was approved by the University of Maryland, College Park Institutional Research Board.

Experimental Tasks. VTEAM was assessed by means of two tasks that can be executed by individuals alone and while teaming with the robotic partner. The first task was a modified version of the RH task which consists of moving a red block to an exit location by clearing other blocks obstructing its path [19, 23, 24] (for details see sections below). The second task was the CB maintenance task which consists of replacing faulty fuses in an electrical panel with new ones (for details see sections below). Although multiple reasons led us to consider both tasks in this work, two were particularly important. First, they can be computationally demanding for both the AI-based robot and humans since they involve dependency between task components requiring and engaging multiple cognitive processes (e.g., high-level planning, reasoning, decision-making) to generate the appropriate action sequences and solve the problem [10–12]. Second, both tasks are well suited to be executed by individuals alone or working collaboratively with a robotic teammate.

Individuals executed alone or with the robotic partner different scenarios of both the RH and CB tasks through VTEAM to evaluate its degree of usability. This was done by comparing the obtained usability scores to standard thresholds whenever these were available as well as by evaluating the human workload and team performance. While the sequences presented to the participants could have been chosen to induce significant cognitive demands, the scenarios used in this study did not involve excessive complexity. The reason for this is that the aim of this work was not to investigate the recruitment of neural mechanisms when individuals performed under varying demands but rather to investigate the usability of the proposed platform. Thus, a good level of usability would indicate that this platform would be suitable to examine human cognitive-motor processes when individuals collaborate with an AI-based humanoid robot with adaptive planning capabilities to complete both tasks introduced here.

Rush Hour Task. The first task, which is based on the RH puzzle-game, includes a horizontal board where several blue blocks of different lengths form a gridlock around a red block as well as an exit gate. This task aims to move sequentially the blue blocks with a minimum of moves and/or distance travelled to get the red block off the board through the exit gate (Fig. 3). The rules of the task were that all the blocks can solely be displaced along their longest edge without moving them off the board, jumping, and collisions. Also, a block that has been moved can be moved again later and the red block has to be moved out to the designated gates indicated as the exit point. The application was designed such that rule-breaking moves were not permitted. As previously mentioned, this work aimed to assess the usability of this novel virtual experimental platform rather than examining changes in the engagement of the neural resources in response to varying demand. Therefore, participants were required to solve various scenarios of the RH task employing a fairly limited number (i.e., 4–8) of blocks. A total of ten scenarios were presented to the participants. When a scenario was completed, a new one was loaded. This process was repeated over multiple iterations during the entire execution of the task which lasted for a total duration of five minutes.

Circuit Breaker Maintenance Task. The maintenance task required participants to replace faulty fuses by functioning ones in an electrical panel. The faulty fuses to be replaced were indicated by a red LED. The participants picked up and discarded the faulty fuse and then replaced it with a new functioning one. Once a functioning fuse was placed the LED turned green, the participant moved to the next faulty fuse (see Fig. 3). For the same reasons mentioned above, participants were required to complete six scenarios with a limited number of fuses (i.e., 2–8) to be replaced. Similar to the RH task, once all scenarios were successfully executed, the panels would cycle over the task completion which lasted for a total duration of five minutes.

Experimental Procedures. Participants were asked to execute both the RH and CB tasks alone as well as collaborating with the robotic teaming over a single testing session. The order of the tasks (RH, CB) and performance conditions of execution (alone, teaming with the robot) were counterbalanced. Before performing each task, participants went

Fig. 3. VTEAM interface for the participants. Execution of the RH and CB maintenance tasks when individuals performed alone (PA) and collaboratively with the humanoid robot (HRT). PA-RH: rush hour performed alone; HRT-RH: rush hour during human-robot teaming; PA-CB: circuit breaker performed alone; HRT-CB: circuit breaker during human-robot teaming.

through a two-minute familiarization period where they executed each task alone (i.e., without robotic teammate) to become accustomed to the goals and rules of the task as well as the control interface. This familiarization period combined with the execution of action sequences being not excessively complex ensured that the usability and the participant's cognitive-motor states were mainly linked to utilizing VTEAM and not to the recruitment of cognitive-motor processes (e.g., working memory; attention; high-level planning) resulting from demands due to overly challenging action sequences. During the familiarization stage, individuals practiced both tasks with scenarios (i.e., puzzles, panels) that were not presented to the participants during the testing session without the robotic teammate to ensure that no learning effect would bias the subsequent assessment of the experimental platform.

For both RH and CB tasks, participants had to perform multiple scenarios during a five-minute period either performing alone or collaboratively with the humanoid robot. When the robot was involved, participants had to alternate turns with the robot which would be indicated by a message stating, "Your Turn" and "Robot's Turn" on the top left corner of the screen (Fig. 3). For the RH task, when the environment was first loaded, the condition started when the participants pressed the red button on the bottom right of the screen to load the first scenario. Participants had to press the green button before making the first move for every puzzle (Fig. 3). This was employed to indicate the completion of human planning and moving towards executing the action sequences for the task. Once a scenario was solved a new one would be loaded after a two-second window resulting in participants completing multiple scenarios until the five-minute task duration elapsed. An exploratory analysis was also conducted with the RH task since in addition to the 3D view, a 2D view of the board displayed on the top right corner of the screen allowed participants to move the blocks in this 2D display with the same control as for the regular 3D view. Thus, participants were also required to solve puzzles with this 2D perspective for 2 min (not shown in Fig. 3).

Similarly, for the CB maintenance task, when one of the scenarios was loaded, participants could see the status of the panel on the bottom right portion of their screen. If the status of the panel indicated "Fail", the stop button needed to be pressed to begin replacing the defective fuses (indicated by a red LED) that had to be discarded into a trash can located on the left of the panel. To perform this action participants had to click on the defective item and then click on the trash can to discard it. Once this action was completed, a new fuse had to be selected from the set of non-defective fuses (also located on the left of the panel). To vary the conditions, some scenarios had fuses that were identified by a number which is mapped to the slot it needs to fit into. Once all the LEDs were green, the restart button on the right would be clicked and if the message displayed "Success", a new panel was loaded. Participants cycled through fixing multiple panels until the end of the five-minute task duration. For both the RH and CB tasks, appropriate EEG event markers were sent to BrainVision Recorder (Brain Products GmbH) to indicate the beginning and end of a scenario, a task and a change in the robot's engagement.

After each experimental condition of each task, individuals were asked to complete several questionnaires such as the Post-Study System Usability Questionnaire (PSSUQ) [25], System Usability Scale (SUS) [26], Subjective Mental Effort Questionnaire (SMEQ) [27], Single Ease Question (SEQ) [27] to determine the perceived usability of the proposed experimental platform. These surveys have been largely employed to reliably estimate the usability of various systems (e.g., software, websites, devices) even with relatively small sample sizes [26–28]. The PSSUQ consists of 16 questions recorded on a 7-point Likert Scale. The PSSUQ provides a total score (Overall), as well as the system usefulness (SysUse), information quality (InfoQual), and interface quality (IntQual) subcomponents, respectively [25]. This survey also has the advantage of providing standards for the Overall, SysUse, InfoQual and IntQual score dimensions [25]. Moreover, the SUS includes 10 questions where positive and negative statements about the system are alternated. The answers to the statement are collected by means of a 5-point Likert scale [29]. Like the PSSUQ, the SUS also has the advantage of providing a well-established industry standard value of 68 [30, 31]. The SMEQ included a single scale with 9 levels ranging from "Not at all hard to do" to "Tremendously hard to do" [27]. Finally, the SEQ is a single questionnaire survey which assesses the perceived difficulty of a user-performed task [27]. After task completion, participants also completed the well-established NASA Task Load Index (TLX) survey to assess the perceived workload during cognitive motor-performance [32, 33]. The NASA-TLX score was computed for the overall workload to enable direct comparison with standards previously reported in the literature [34]. In addition, participants completed the Godspeed survey [35] after they performed the tasks collaborating with the humanoid robot to indicate the characteristics of the robot they interacted with in terms of its anthropomorphism, animacy, likeability, perceived intelligence, and safety. Although secondary, here the perceived usefulness of the 2D perspective option for the RH task was assessed in an exploratory manner via a Visual Analog Scale (VAS) survey that participants had to complete including the three following questions "How often did you refer to the 2D grid display to plan your actions?"; "How helpful was the 2D grid display when forming strategies to solve the various puzzles?"; "How would you like the presence of a 2D display when solving tasks of this kind?").

Data Processing
Survey Data. The scores for the PSSUQ, SMEQ and SEQ were averaged across participants. For the PSSUQ this averaging process was conducted for all 16 questions to obtain the total score (Overall). The averaging of questions 1–6, questions 7–12, and questions 13–15, provided the scores for the system usefulness (SysUse), information quality (InfoQual), and interface quality (IntQual) subcomponents, respectively [25]. The raw SUS scores were normalized and then combined resulting in a single score

between 0–100 for each participant, task and performance condition [30, 31]. Similarly, each subscale of the NASA TLX scores was averaged, resulting in scores between 0–100 for each task and performance condition [32]. The VAS scores were also averaged across participants.

Performance Data. For each trial, task and condition of execution, the sequence deviation error (SDE) was computed to quantify the discrepancies between the number of moves and spaces utilized to execute an optimal *reference sequence* from that generated by the human or the human-robot team. Here the reference sequences were defined as the sequences using the minimum number of actions to complete each scenario of both tasks. The average SDE was computed for each participant, task, and conditions. An elevation of the SDE indicates a decrement of performance.

Statistical Analysis. The primary aim of this work was to assess the usability of VTEAM when individuals performed action sequence tasks with the humanoid robot. Thus, the surveys scores were interpreted based on specific ranges provided by the literature and whenever possible, by statistically comparing them to well-established standards. In particular, when individuals performed either alone or collaboratively with the humanoid robot both tasks, the scores obtained for the four subscales of the PSSUQ scores (Overall, SysUse, InfoQual, IntQual), the SUS and the five dimensions (ANT, ANI, LIK, INT, SAF) of the Godspeed were subjected to statistical analysis. Specifically, a series of one-sample t-tests or Wilcoxon signed-ranked tests (depending on whether the data were normally distributed or not) compared the mean scores obtained for these three surveys with their respective standard when individuals performed each task either alone or collaboratively with the humanoid robot. The standards for the Overall, SysUse, InfoQual and IntQual dimensions of the PSSUQ were 2.82, 2.80, 3.02 and 2.49, respectively [25]. For these four PSSUQ dimensions, scores smaller and greater than these threshold values represent above and below average usability [25, 30]. The standard for the SUS was the widely acknowledged industry threshold value of 68 which represents an average usability level (i.e., scores below and above this level indicate a system having a below and above average usability) [30, 31]. The SMEQ, SEQ and NASA TLX scores were qualitatively assessed by comparing their range to the corresponding scale and to available standards previously provided in the literature [27, 34]. Although no established standards for the Godspeed questionnaire are available from the literature, the same statistical approach was employed with the threshold being the midpoint of the five-point scale [35]. The same methodology was used for the VAS surveys for which the threshold was the midpoint of the scale. Also, the paired versions of the same tests were employed to compare the SDE obtained when individuals performed the task alone and with the robotic teammate. Finally, for each task, the same statistical analysis was employed for the SDE when individuals executed the task alone and with the robotic teammate to assess if the generated sequences were optimal or not (a SDE not different from zero would be optimal). For all the statistical analyses, the Cohen's d effect sizes were calculated and reported whenever appropriate. To account for multiple comparisons, the false discovery rate (Benjamini-Hochberg) correction was applied. For all statistical analyses the significance level was set to $p < 0.05$. All the statistical computations were executed in MATLAB™.

3 Results

3.1 Usability

A qualitative analysis suggested that the vast majority of the trials did not reveal any major technical issues (e.g., system crashed or frozen) during the entire time whether individuals executed the tasks either alone or with the robotic partner ($<0.005\%$).

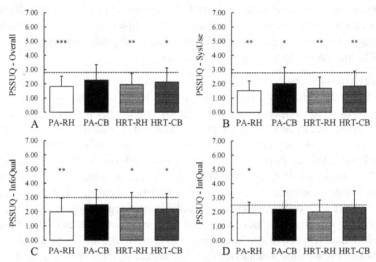

Fig. 4. Usability scores for the Overall (A), SysUse (B), InfoQual (C) and IntQual (D) dimensions of the PSSUQ survey when individuals execute the RH and CB tasks either alone or teaming with the humanoid robot. The dashed black line illustrates the thresholds usability levels (see text for further details). PA-RH: rush hour performed alone; PA-CB: circuit breaker performed alone; HRT-RH: rush hour during human-robot teaming; HRT-CB: circuit breaker during human-robot teaming. The stars represent the level of statistical significance when comparing the average score values for a given condition relative to the acceptability threshold. *: $p < 0.05$; **: $p < 0.01$; ***: $p < 0.001$.

For both tasks and conditions of execution the PSSUQ scores were either at or beyond the minimal usability threshold. Namely, the Overall PSSUQ scores were all smaller than the threshold value for all conditions (PA-RH: $t(14) = -5.412$, $p < 0.001$, $d = 1.321$; HRT-RH: $t(14) = -4.292$, $p = 0.001$, $d = 1.048$; HRT-CB: $t(14) = -2.731$, $p = 0.022$, $d = 0.667$) except when individuals performed alone the CB task (PA-CB: $t(14) = -2.029$, $p = 0.062$, $d = 0.495$) (see Fig. 4A). In addition, the SysUse PSSUQ score was significantly smaller than its threshold value for all conditions (PA-RH: $z = -3.333$, $p = 0.003$, $d = 0.860$; PA-CB: $t(14) = -2.659$, $p = 0.019$, $d = 0.649$; HRT-RH: $z = -3.161$, $p = 0.003$, $d = 0.816$; HRT-CB: $t(14) = -3.594$, $p = 0.004$, $d = 0.877$) (see Fig. 4B). Similarly, the scores of the InfoQual subscales were significantly smaller than the cut-off values for all conditions (PA-RH: $t(14) = -4.176$, $p = 0.004$, $d = 1.019$; HRT-RH: $t(14) = -2.743$, $p = 0.021$, $d = 0.970$; HRT-CB: $z = -2.503$, $p = 0.021$, $d = 0.646$) except when individuals execute alone the CB task (PA-CB: $t(14) = -1.917$, p

= 0.076, d = 0.468) (see Fig. 4C). Finally, the scores of the IntQual dimension were similar to the cut-off values for all conditions (HRT-RH: t(14) = -2.267, p = 0.079, d = 0.213; PA-CB: t(14) = 0.601, p = 0.558, d = 0.269; HRT-CB: z = -0.972, p = 0.442, d = 0.251) except when individuals performed alone the RH task (PA-RH: t(14) = -2.884, p = 0.048, d = 0.491) which was significantly smaller (see Fig. 4D).

The scores obtained with the SUS questionnaire revealed that for both tasks and condition of performance were significantly higher than the industry threshold (PA-RH: t(14) = 4.414, p = 0.001, d = 1.077; HRT-RH: t(14) = 4.487, p = 0.001, d = 1.095; HRT-CB: t(14) = 2.323, p = 0.048, d = 0.567) apart from when the CB task was executed by the individuals alone (PA-CB: z = 1.763, p = 0.078, d = 0.455) (see Fig. 5A). The average SMEQ score for both task and condition of execution were comprised between 0 and 10 which corresponds to lowest range of task difficulty level of the scale (PA-RH: 6.333 ± 7.188; PA-CB: 8.000 ± 12.649; HRT-RH: 7.000 ± 5.916; HRT-CB: 4.667 ± 5.164) (Fig. 5B). Similarly, the average SEQ scores all ranged between 6 and 7 which represents lowest level of task difficulty on this scale (PA-RH: 6.000 ± 1.840; PA-CB: 6.533 ± 0.516; HRT-RH: 6.467 ± 0.516; HRT-CB: 6.733 ± 0.458) (Fig. 5C). The exploratory analysis of the VAS survey examining the usefulness of the 2D display did not reveal any significant results (p > 0.345 for all comparisons).

3.2 Workload

The statistical analysis conducted on the composite NASA TLX score revealed that for both task and performance conditions the overall workload ranged from 16 to 18, which represents the 10% lowest workload percentile based on the examination of a database of publications citing the NASA-TLX using various tasks [34] (PA-RH: 16.000 ± 8.038; PA-CB: 17.300 ± 7.810; HRT-RH: 15.067 ± 6.429; HRT-CB: 16.600 ± 6.378) (Fig. 5D). Although these ranges are not available for each dimension of this survey the mental demand dimension which has been suggested as representative of the mental workload ranged from 15 to 19 which in this context is also low.

3.3 Human Performance Alone and Human-Robot Team Performance

The SDE was different from zero when individuals performed the RH task alone (t(14) = 6.762, p < 0.001, d = 1.651) or with their robotic partner (t(14) = 5.547, p < 0.001, d = 1.354). However, the same contrast was not significant when individuals executed alone (z = 2.023, p = 0.065, d = 0.522) or with the robot (z = 1.342, p > 0.170, d = 0.346) the CB task. Also, the SDE was smaller when individuals completed the RH task with their robotic partner compared to alone (t(14) = 4.498, p = 0.001, d = 1.418) whereas this was not observed for the CB task (z = 1.753, p = 0.096, d = 0.453) (Fig. 6).

3.4 Human Perception of the Humanoid Robotic Teammate

The statistical analysis revealed that the humans perceived their humanoid robotic teammate as having intelligence and safety levels above average when jointly executing either the RH task (INT: t(14) = 5.530, p < 0.001, d = 1.350; SAF: t(14) = 2.738, p = 0.020,

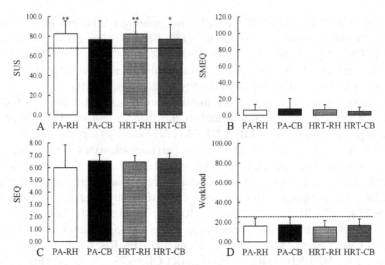

Fig. 5. Usability scores for the SUS (A), SMEQ (B), SEQ (C) and the NASA-TLX (overall workload) (D) surveys when individuals executed the RH and CB tasks either alone or together with the humanoid robot. The dashed black line illustrates the threshold usability level in panel A and the 10% lowest workload percentile, respectively (see text for details). See Fig. 4 for definition of abbreviations PA-RH; PA-CB; HRT-RH; PA-CB. The stars represent the level of statistical significance when comparing the average score value for a given condition relative to the threshold. *: $p < 0.05$; **: $p < 0.01$; ***: $p < 0.001$.

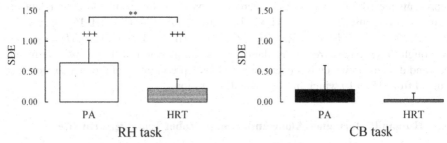

Fig. 6. Performance (SDE) when individuals executed alone (PA) or collectively with the robotic teammate (HRT) the RH and CB tasks. The stars (*) and crosses (+) represent the significance level for the PA vs. HRT contrast and the PA or HRT vs. standard contrast, respectively. *: $p < 0.05$; **: $p < 0.01$; ***: $p < 0.001$; +: $p < 0.05$; ++: $p < 0.01$; +++: $p < 0.001$.

$d = 0.667$) or the CB maintenance task (INT: $z = 3.097$, $p = 0.004$, $d = 0.800$; SAF: $z = 2.588$, $p = 0.014$, $d = 0.668$). In addition, the participants perceived their humanoid robotic teammate with a likability level above average when jointly executing the RH task (LIK: $t(14) = 2.458$, $p = 0.031$, $d = 0.600$) but was not different from the average for the CB maintenance task (LIK: $z = 1.622$, $p = 0.105$, $d = 0.419$). However, the perceived anthropomorphism and animacy were below average during completion of the RH (ANT: $t(14) = -5.493$, $p < 0.001$, $d = 1.341$; ANI: $t(14) = -3.606$, $p < 0.001$, d

= 0.880) and CB maintenance tasks (ANT: t(14) = -6.849, p < 0.001, d = 1.672; ANI: t(14) = -5.792, p < 0.001, d = 1.414) (Fig. 7).

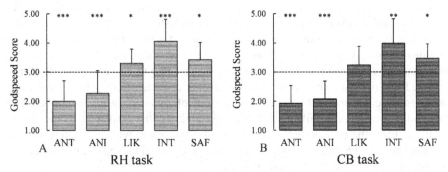

Fig. 7. Scores for the perceived anthropomorphism, animacy, likability, intelligence and safety dimension of the Godspeed survey when individuals executed the RH and CB tasks together with the humanoid robot. The dashed black line illustrates the mid-scale threshold levels for each dimension (see text for details). ANT: anthropomorphism; ANI: animacy, LIK: likability, INT: intelligence and SAF: safety. The stars represent the level of statistical significance when comparing the average score value for a given condition relative to the mid-scale threshold. *: p < 0.05; **: p < 0.01; ***: p < 0.001.

4   Discussion

The results revealed that, regardless of the surveys employed in this work, individuals who executed alone or with the robotic teammate the RH and CB tasks, consistently evaluated the platform's usability as meeting or exceeding the industry standards available from the literature. Similarly, based on thresholds taken from past literature, the perceived workload by individuals when executing both tasks alone and collaboratively with the robotic teammate was low. The performance for the RH task was greater when individuals collaborated with the robotic teammate relative to the condition where they performed alone (a tendency was also observed for the CB task). While performing alone or with their robotic partner, participants were able to generate optimal sequences for the CB task whereas they were sub-optimal for the RH task. After teaming, the perceived anthropomorphism and animacy of the humanoid robot was below average whereas the perception as being intelligent and safe was above the threshold for both tasks. The likeability was above and equal to average for the RH and CB task, respectively.

4.1   Usability and Workload When Individuals Perform Alone and with the Robotic Teammate

All of the dimensions of the PSSUQ, the SUS and the SEQ surveys robustly indicated that the usability of VTEAM when individuals executed both tasks either alone or with their robotic partner was similar to or beyond industry standards [25, 27, 30, 31]. In particular, for the PSSUQ, this was observed for the overall assessment but also for the system usefulness, information and interface quality. In addition, the level of perceived workload when the individuals perform both tasks alone and with the robot was observed as low [34]. This is consistent with the findings above which revealed that the usability level exceeded standards. Namely, it is coherent with the notion that executing action sequences (without excessive complexity) performed with VTEAM that has a good usability would likely result in a low workload level. Thus, taken together both the usability and workload levels observed here suggest that this virtual platform can be operated straightforwardly without adding a layer of challenge that could possibly result in biases and confounding factors during the study of human cognitive-motor behavior. In addition, when made available to the user, the option of the 2D display did not appear to affect much the user preferences. This is also consistent with the finding that the environment (which was 3D by default) had a good usability, suggesting that the 2D perspective option is not necessarily needed.

4.2 Effects of Robotic Teammate on Performance, Human Workload and Perception

When individuals executed collaboratively the RH task with the robotic teammate, the obtained performance was greater relative to that observed when participants performed the same task alone. Although, this was not the primary aim of this work, this very important finding suggests that VTEAM is sensitive enough to examine human-robot team dynamics even when performing action sequences of modest complexity. This is interesting, since future experimental work could employ graded complexity levels of action sequences and not just consider two very different level of demands as is often done in experimental work (e.g., [1, 33]). Although the same performance improvement was not as prominent as for the RH task, a tendency was observed for the CB task. Such a difference may be due to different degrees of task constraints. While the RH task has a few rules, the CB task has more constraints between the objects when they are manipulated due to causal relationships driven by the physics and the task rules (e.g., a fuse has to be removed before being replaced, the panel has to be open before accessing the fuses, the LED colors indicate the fuse status and only the faulty fuses have to be replaced). Thus, the completion of this task appears to be more structured and thus possibly less challenging than the RH task. Therefore, it is possible that the robotic teammate would have less effect on the performance of the CB maintenance task which is in essence more structured than the RH task. This is also consistent with the fact that sequences produced when the individuals performed alone the CB task were optimal (although a tendency of being suboptimal was observed) and that the engagement of the robotic partner further facilitated such optimal performance. Furthermore, contrary to the performance, the same comparison did not lead to any modulation of the perceived workload. This was expected, since as mentioned above, the sequences employed here were relatively easy to complete and generated a low workload. Thus, while the robotic teammate could still assist the users by improving their performance, these sequences were likely not complex enough to induce a great need of assistance and thus a change of workload. An exploratory analysis of the six dimensions of the NASA-TLX confirmed that for both tasks the engagement of the robot did not affect any of the subscale scores ($p > 0.05$, all comparisons considered).

The perception of the robotic teammate by the human varied according to different features considered. Namely, the perceived anthropomorphism and animacy were below average. A possible reason for this is that although Baxter is a humanoid robot with anthropomorphic features, it does not look and move like a human, which may explain why these attributes were evaluated as low compared to actual human beings [36, 37]. The perceived likeability was above average for the RH task and around average for the CB task. When considering the performance results, a possible explanation could be the that the robot was considered as more helpful and thus more likable by the individuals for the RH than for the CB task due to a greater need of assistance for the former compared to the latter. In addition, the results revealed that for both tasks, individuals perceived the robotic partner to have an intelligence and safety level greater than average. A greater than average intelligence level is likely due to the planning algorithm which, when engaged, not only affected the performance but also the individuals' perception of the robotic teammate. Finally, the safety of the robot was also perceived as above average for both tasks by the participants, which was expected since this platform does not involve a physical but a virtual system. On the one hand, this is advantageous since this allows one to examine human cognitive-motor performance in a controlled environment without having potential biases due to changes in emotional state. However, this could also be a limitation since a human-robot study conducted with a virtual versus a physical robot may yield different results due to a different safety perception between the former and the latter. However, such a difference could be attenuated if the physical robot is a cobot.

4.3 Conclusions, Limitations, and Future Work

As a whole, this investigation suggests that good usability and workload levels were observed when individuals operated the VTEAM virtual environment while completing alone or with the robotic teammate both the RH and CB maintenance tasks. In addition, even when using fairly simple action sequences, the robotic teammate was able to improve task performance, suggesting that this experimental platform is robust enough to assess human-robot teaming even when executing sequences of moderate complexity. This suggests that this platform can conduct graded experimental manipulations of task demands without extreme contrast as is often used in the cognitive-motor literature (e.g., [1, 33]). In addition, individuals perceived their robotic teammate to have acceptable levels of likeability, intelligence and safety, which are also desirable features for a virtual platform like VTEAM since it may facilitate the engagement of the participants in completing the tasks. Thus, overall, it appears that the VTEAM experimental platform is appropriate for examining human cognitive-motor processes when individuals perform and learn sequential tasks alone or teaming with a robotic partner. The successful implementation of the EEG event markers system will also allow VTEAM to be deployed for examination of human behavioral and cortical dynamics.

This work also had several limitations, of which some could be addressed in future work. First, the perceived anthropomorphism and animacy of the robot by the participants were both rated as below average. Although, this was not of primary interest in this work, an elevation of these ratings could contribute to greater participant engagement in task execution and teaming. These scores could possibly be improved by considering a more biologically plausible control system able to generate human-like movements instead of the more discrete motion currently produced [36, 37]. Currently, VTEAM has only one planning algorithm, however, it would be beneficial to be able to select different planning systems to examine how they will affect the human cognitive-motor states. Moreover, the present platform does not allow specific parametrization for both tasks (e.g., changing the exit location during the RH task completion, creating more complex dependency between the fuses for the electrical panel) as well as the team (e.g., swapping the role between team members, alter the team interdependence in real time, simultaneous teammate movements). While the proposed platform embeds an AI-based robotic teammate, it does not have any explainable AI (XAI) capability which would allow the synthetic partner to explain its behavior to its human teammate. This could be included in the future with the option to engage or not the XAI system to examine its effect on the human neural mechanisms during task performance. Finally, in the longer term, this platform should be merged with a prior virtual environment developed by our research team (VLEARN) which is a web-based system allowing remote execution of human sequential tasks [22]. The combination of both systems would provide a powerful experimental platform allowing onsite or remote examination of human cognitive-motor processes during performance and learning of action sequences when individuals perform alone or in a (human-human, human-robot) teaming context.

Acknowledgment. Work on VLEARN and VTEAM was supported in part by funding from ONR to RG, JR, and GK (N000141912044) and to JP (N000142112821).

References

1. Gevins, A., Smith, M.E., McEvoy, L., Yu, D.: High-resolution EEG mapping of cortical activation related to working memory: effects of task difficulty, type of processing, and practice. Cereb. Cortex **7**(4), 374–385 (1997)
2. Gentili, R.J., et al.: Combined assessment of attentional reserve and cognitive effort under various levels of challenge with a dry EEG system. Psychophys **55**(6), e13059 (2018)
3. Miller, M.W., et al.: The effects of team environment on cerebral cortical processes and attentional reserve. Sport Exerc. Perform. Psychol. **3**(1), 61–74 (2014)
4. Mehta, R.K., Parasuraman, R.: Neuroergonomics: a review of applications to physical and cognitive work. Front. Hum. Neurosci. **7**, 889 (2013)
5. Dehais, F., Lafont, A., Roy, R., Fairclough, S.: A neuroergonomics approach to mental workload, engagement and human performance. Front. Neurosci. **14**, 268 (2020)
6. Ahmad, M.I., Bernotat, J., Lohan, K., Eyssel, F. Trust and cognitive load during human-robot interaction, arXiv:1909.05160 (2019)
7. Ehrlich, S.K., Cheng, G.: A feasibility study for validating robot actions using EEG-based error-related potentials. Int J of Soc Robotics **11**, 271–283 (2019)
8. de Visser, E.J., Beatty, P.J., Estepp, J.R., Kohn, S., Abubshait, A., Fedota, J.R., McDonald, C.G. Learning from the slips of others: neural correlates of trust in automated Agents. Front Hum Neurosci, 12, (2018)
9. Henschel, A., Hortensius, R., Cross, E.S.: Social cognition in the age of human-robot interaction. Trends Neurosci. **43**(6), 373–384 (2020)

10. Hauge, T.C., et al.: A novel application of Levenshtein distance for assessment of high-level motor planning underlying performance during learning of complex motor sequences. J. Mot. Learn. Dev. **8**(1), 67–86 (2019)
11. Hauge, T.C., Katz, G.E., Davis, G.P., Huang, D.W., Reggia, J.A., Gentili, R.J.: High-level motor planning assessment during performance of complex action sequences in humans and a humanoid robot. Int. J. Soc. Robot. **13**, 981–998 (2021)
12. Katz, G., Huang, D.W., Hauge, T., Gentili, R., Reggia, J. A novel parsimonious cause-effect reasoning algorithm for robot imitation and plan recognition. IEEE Trans Cognit Dev Syst PP(99):1–17 (2017)
13. Welsh, M.C., Huizinga, M.: Tower of Hanoi disk-transfer task: influences of strategy knowledge and learning on performance. Learn. Individ. Differ. **15**(4), 283–298 (2005)
14. Wulf, G., Shea, C.H.: Principles derived from the study of simple skills do not generalize to complex skill learning. Psychon. Bull. Rev. **9**(2), 185–211 (2002)
15. Wong, M., et al.: A remote synthetic testbed for human-robot teaming: an iterative design process. Proc Hum Factor Ergonom Soc Ann Meet **65**(1), 781–785 (2021)
16. Raimondo, F.R., et al.: Trailblazing roblox virtual synthetic testbed development for human-robot teaming studies. Proc Hum Factor Ergonom Soc Ann Meet **66**(1), 812–816 (2022)
17. El Makrini, I., Merckaert, K., Lefeber, D. Vanderborght, B. Design of a collaborative architecture for human-robot assembly tasks. Proc. IEEE/RSJ International Conference on Intelligent Robots and Systems (IROS), 1624–1629 (2017)
18. Natarajan, M., et al.: Human-robot teaming: grand challenges. Curr Robot Rep **4**, 81–100 (2023)
19. Cian, L., Dreossi, T., Dovier, A. Modeling and solving the rush hour puzzle. In: 37th Italian Conference on Computational Logic, June 29 - July 1, 2022, Bologna, Italy (2022)
20. Huang, D.W., Katz, G.E., Langsfeld, J.D., Gentili, R.J., Reggia, J.A. A virtual demonstrator environment for robot imitation learning. In: IEEE international conference on technologies for practical robot applications (TePRA), Woburn, MA, USA, pp 1–6 (2015)
21. Huang, D.W., Katz, G.E., Langsfeld, J.D., Oh, H., Gentili, R.J., Reggia J.A. An object-centric paradigm for robot programming by demonstration. In: Schmorrow, D.D., Fidopiastis, C.M. (eds.) Foundations of Augmented Cognition. AC 2015. LNCS, vol 9183. Springer, Cham (2015)
22. Shaver, A.A., Peri, N., Mezebish, R., Matthew, G., Berson, A., Gaskins, C., Davis, G.P., Katz, G.E., Samuel, I., Reinhard, M.J., Costanzo, M.E., Reggia, J.A., Purtilo, J., Gentili, R.J. Assessment of a novel virtual environment for examining human cognitive-motor performance during execution of action sequences. In: Schmorrow, D.D., Fidopiastis, C.M. (eds) Augmented Cognition. HCII 2022. Lecture Notes in Computer Science, vol 13310. Springer, Cham (2022)
23. Flake, G.W., Baum, E.B.: Rush hour is pspace-complete, or "why you should generously tip parking lot attendants." Theoret. Comput. Sci. **270**, 895–911 (2002)
24. Pereira, A.G., Ritt, M., Buriol, L.S.: Pull and pushpull are PSPACE-complete. Theoret. Comput. Sci. **628**, 50–61 (2016)
25. Lewis, J.R.: Psychometric evaluation of the PSSUQ using data from five years of usability studies. International Journal of Human-Computer Interaction **14**(3–4), 463–488 (2002)
26. Bangor, A., Kortum, P.T., Miller, J.T.: An empirical evaluation of the system usability scale. Intl. Int J Hum-Comput Int **24**(6), 574–594 (2008)
27. Sauro, J. Dumas, J. S. Comparison of three one-question, post-task usability questionnaires. In Proceedings of the SIGCHI Conference on Human Factors in Computing Systems (CHI '09). Association for Computing Machinery, New York, NY, USA, 1599–1608 (2009)
28. Kortum, P.T., Bangor, A.: Usability ratings for everyday products measured with the system usability scale. Int J Hum-Comput Int **29**(2), 67–76 (2013)

29. Bangor, A., Kortum, P., Miller, J.: Determining what individual SUS scores mean: adding an adjective rating scale. J. Usability Stud. **4**(3), 114–123 (2009)
30. Sauro, J., Lewis, J.R.: Quantifying the user experience: practical statistics for user research, 2nd edn. Morgan Kaufmann, Cambridge (2016)
31. Barnum, C.N.: Usability testing essentials, 2nd edn. Morgan Kaufmann, Cambridge (2021)
32. Hart, S.G.: NASA-task load index (NASA-TLX); 20 years later. In proceedings of the human factors and ergonomics society annual meeting **50**(9), 904–908 (2006)
33. Shuggi, I.M., Oh, H., Shewokis, P.A., Gentili, R.J.: Mental workload and motor performance dynamics during practice of reaching movements under various levels of task difficulty. Neuroscience **360**, 166–179 (2017)
34. Grier, R.A.: How high is high? A meta-analysis of NASA-TLX global workload scores. Proceedings of the Human Factors and Ergonomics Society Annual Meeting **59**(1), 1727–1731 (2015)
35. Bartneck, C., Kulić, D., Croft, E., Zoghbi, S.: Measurement instruments for the anthropomorphism, animacy, likeability, perceived intelligence, and perceived safety of robots. Int J of Soc Robotics **1**, 71–81 (2009)
36. Kerzel, M., Strahl, E., Magg, S., Navarro-Guerrero, N., Heinrich S., Wermter, S. NICO — Neuro-inspired companion: A developmental humanoid robot platform for multimodal interaction. Proc. 26th IEEE International Symposium on Robot and Human Interactive Communication (ROMAN), pp. 113–120 (2017)
37. Maroto-Gómez, M., Castro-González, Á., Malfaz, M., Salichs, M.Á.: A biologically inspired decision-making system for the autonomous adaptive behavior of social robots. Complex Intell. Syst. **9**, 6661–6679 (2023)

Measuring Cognitive Workload in Augmented Reality Learning Environments Through Pupil Area Analysis

Siddarth Mohanty[1], Jung Hyup Kim[1(✉)], Varun Pulipati[2], Fang Wang[3], Sara Mostowfi[1], Danielle Oprean[4], Yi Wang[1], and Kangwon Seo[1]

[1] Department of Industrial and Systems Engineering, University of Missouri, Columbia, Mo 65211, USA
`{smdqv,kijung,sara.mostowfi,yiwang,seoka}@missouri.edu`
[2] Department of Electrical Engineering and Computer Science, University of Missouri, Columbia, Mo 65211, USA
`vpccn@umsystem.edu`
[3] Department of Engineering and Information Technology, University of Missouri, Columbia, Mo 65211, USA
`wangfan@missouri.edu`
[4] School of Information Science and Learning Technologies, University of Missouri, Columbia, Mo 65211, USA
`opreand@missouri.edu`

Abstract. In the digital learning landscape, Augmented Reality (AR) is revolutionizing instructional methodologies. This study shifts focus to explore the impact of AR-based lectures on pupil dilation as a biomarker of mental demand. By analyzing pupil dilation with cognitive load assessment tools like the NASA Task Load Index, we aim to understand the cognitive implications of prolonged exposure to AR in educational settings. We hypothesize that variations in pupil size can be indicative of cognitive load, correlating with the mental demands imposed by AR lectures. Preliminary findings suggest a significant relationship between increased pupil dilation and heightened mental workload during AR engagements. This study highlights the new way to measure cognitive workload in AR environments using pupil dilation data.

Keywords: Augmented Reality · Cognitive Workload · Pupil Dilation Analysis

1 Introduction

Augmented Reality (AR) has emerged as a transformative tool in educational technology, offering immersive and interactive learning experiences. Despite its growing adoption, understanding the cognitive impact of AR on students remains a critical area of exploration. This study focuses on measuring and analyzing the cognitive load in biomechanics AR lectures.

© The Author(s), under exclusive license to Springer Nature Switzerland AG 2024
D. D. Schmorrow and C. M. Fidopiastis (Eds.): HCII 2024, LNAI 14694, pp. 167–181, 2024.
https://doi.org/10.1007/978-3-031-61569-6_11

Prior studies on AR-based learning have mostly focused on its effectiveness, learning outcomes, and user experience, which has led to a lack of knowledge about the cognitive load it imposes on learners. This study seeks to fill this gap using pupil dilation analysis and comparing mental workload in AR settings. To assess mental demand, we used the NASA Task Load Index (NASA TLX).

We propose that there may be a relationship between changes in pupil size and perceived mental effort, as determined through a combination of objective physiological data and subjective cognitive evaluations. The results of our research aim to provide a comprehensive understanding of the cognitive demands placed on individuals participating in augmented reality (AR) learning settings.

The research problem is twofold: firstly, to measure and quantify the cognitive load experienced by students using eye-tracking technology within AR educational settings, and secondly, to investigate the correlation between pupil area and cognitive load, assessing mental exertion in these settings. By achieving these objectives, this study seeks to provide actionable insights for educators and developers in AR-based learning, enhancing both the effectiveness and efficiency of the learning process. The significance of this research project lies in its potential to bring about transformative advancements in the field of educational technology, particularly in the context of AR-based learning.

This research emphasizes the key elements of assessing and analyzing cognitive load among students in AR educational environments. Developing a technique for gauging mental demand in AR-driven learning presents a new strategy for understanding and enhancing student education. It will help educators customize their teaching methods to boost engagement and productivity, ultimately enhancing the effectiveness of the learning experience. Through an assessment of the mental demand on student learning, we will identify factors that either hinder or facilitate learning outcomes and task execution efficiency in AR settings. Such insights empower researchers to develop interventions that significantly improve learner achievement and overall performance.

To measure cognitive workload in the AR learning environment, we implemented pupil dilation analysis. This physiological response reflects different cognitive states, such as mental workload and demand. To participants' subjective mental demand with the pupil dilation data, we gathered information using the NASA-TLX, a tool for evaluating perceived workload. Research has shown that pupil size tends to increase with the level of cognitive effort [1, 2]. When a task requires more mental demands, such as increased attention, memory, or problem-solving, the pupils may dilate in response to the increased demand for processing resources [3]. Because of this relationship, pupillometry can be used as an objective measure to gauge mental workload. In studies where NASA-TLX is used, pupil dilation measurements can serve as a corroborating physiological marker to support subjective mental demand ratings [4]. While NASA-TLX relies on subjective self-report measures of workload across six dimensions (including mental demand), pupillometry can provide complementary objective data. The combination of subjective ratings with physiological data can enhance the understanding of the actual workload experienced by individuals [5]. Objective measures like pupil dilation can help calibrate the subjective ratings given in the NASA-TLX.

In this study, we hypothesize that there would be a significant difference in eye tracking pupil area when participants are engaged in learning or problem-solving lectures in AR environments. Specifically, we expect to observe a larger pupil dilation during problem-solving tasks compared to the learning tasks, indicative of increased cognitive workload during the experiment. Our hypothesis is based on the premise that more complex cognitive processing is required for problem-solving activities, which will result in higher cognitive workload ratings on the NASA TLX questionnaire.

2 Literature Review

This literature review embarks on an exploration of pivotal research discoveries concerning the measurement of cognitive workload in various applications, with particular attention given to eye tracking, pupil area, and their impact on student performance. Cognitive load theory, as initially propounded by Sweller, Van Merrienboer [6], underscores the paramount importance of overseeing cognitive demands to optimize the learning process. In the area of educational technology, the consideration of cognitive load becomes pivotal, as digital tools and AR applications can either facilitate or impede learning, contingent upon the cognitive resources they consume. Eye tracking technology has gained prominence within cognitive load research, offering insights into the precise areas to which learners direct their visual attention during tasks [7–9]. Previous studies showed that eye tracking serves as a valuable tool for capturing cognitive load by tracking gaze patterns and fixation durations [10–14]. In the context of AR-based learning, eye tracking elucidates how cognitive load fluctuates in response to changing visual stimuli and interactive elements. Pupil dilation could serve as a physiological marker intricately linked to cognitive load [15]. The study done by Ahern and Beatty [16] demonstrated that cognitive tasks demanding heightened mental effort correspond to increased pupil dilation. This implies that pupil area can function as a real-time indicator of cognitive engagement during AR learning experiences. Numerous research endeavors have delved into the intricate relationship between cognitive load and student performance. A met-analysis conducted by Sweller [17] underscored that elevated cognitive load can act as an impediment to the achievement of learning outcomes, ultimately resulting in reduced performance. This accentuates the pivotal role of optimizing cognitive load within AR-based educational settings to augment student accomplishments. AR's potential in the realm of education is vast, providing opportunities for interactive 3D visualizations and simulations. AR has the potential to enrich spatial comprehension, critical thinking, and problem-solving skills [18]. While Augmented Reality (AR) has been increasingly integrated into educational settings, offering promising avenues for enhanced learning experiences, a specific aspect of its impact remains underexplored – the analysis of pupil size as an indicator of cognitive load in AR learning environments. Previous studies have delved into the general effects of AR on learning outcomes and student engagement. For example, research on the application of AR in educational settings has examined its influence on student motivation and performance, as seen in studies done by Braarud [19]. Similarly, the study "AR Learning Environment Integrated with EIA Inquiry Model: Enhancing Scientific Literacy and Reducing Cognitive Load of Students" has underscored the potential of AR in improving scientific literacy and reducing cognitive load, highlighting the EIA (Experience–Inquiry–Application) model's effectiveness in this domain.

However, these studies have not specifically focused on using pupil size as a metric for cognitive load in AR learning environments. This gap presents a unique opportunity for our research. Our study aims to fill this lacuna by leveraging pupillometry – the study of pupil size variation – as a novel approach to gauge cognitive workload in AR-based educational settings. By focusing on the correlation between pupil size and cognitive load, our research endeavors to provide new insights into the physiological responses of learners engaged in AR experiences. This approach is pioneering in its attempt to objectively measure the cognitive impact of AR on learners, a dimension that has been relatively overlooked in existing literature. By doing so, our study not only contributes to the broader understanding of AR's educational implications but also opens new pathways for assessing and optimizing cognitive engagement in digital learning environments.

Mental Demand refers to the amount of mental and perceptual activity required by a task. This can include aspects like thinking, decision making, calculating, remembering, looking, searching, and any other mental activities. NASA-TLX has been used for evaluating the mental exertion and cognitive involvement needed to execute a task, as perceived by the individuals themselves [20–22]. The rating is typically on a scale from low to high. For instance, a task might be considered to have low mental demand if it is simple, straightforward, and requires minimal thought or concentration [23]. Conversely, a task with high mental demand might be complex, challenging, involve intricate decision-making, or require sustained attention and concentration. Understanding the mental demand of a task is crucial for evaluating the potential for cognitive overload, which can occur when the demands of a task exceed an individual's cognitive capacity. It is also important for the design of systems and tasks, especially in ensuring that they are within the capabilities of the user, thereby increasing safety and efficiency. It is used not only in research but also in the design and evaluation of products, in the workplace, and in the assessment of training programs. In a typical NASA-TLX assessment, after completing a task, a participant is asked to reflect on the mental demand it required and to provide a rating. This score is then combined with the ratings from the other five dimensions (Physical Demand, Temporal Demand, Performance, Effort, and Frustration) to calculate an overall workload score Braarud [19]. The outcomes of the mental demand assessment can inform changes to task design, indicate the need for additional training or resources, or suggest modifications to improve user interaction and reduce the potential for errors. By assessing mental demand and the other subscales, the NASA-TLX provides a comprehensive view of workload that can inform improvements in system design.

3   Methodology

3.1   Experimental Design

Twelve participants (average age = 20.6) from University of Missouri were recruited. They were requested to complete a questionnaire encompassing general inquiries regarding their age, gender, academic status, and prior experience with AR. The flowchart shown in Fig. 1. Outlines the procedural steps for a study where participants begin by giving informed consent and providing demographic information via a questionnaire. They then proceed to the setup and calibration of eye-tracking equipment and the

Microsoft HoloLens 2 device. The experiment is conducted in two parts, with a mandatory four-hour gap between them to prevent data interference. Upon completion of each experiment, participants fill out the NASA-TLX form to assess their mental workload. Only after both experiments are completed do participants move on to the data analysis phase. We will explain more details of the data analysis phase in the next section. After that, we conducted a statistical analysis with the experimental data and NASA-TLX forms, aiming to establish a relationship between the measured pupil dilation and the subjective workload reported by the participants. This structured approach ensures a systematic collection and analysis of data pertinent to understanding cognitive load in AR learning environments.

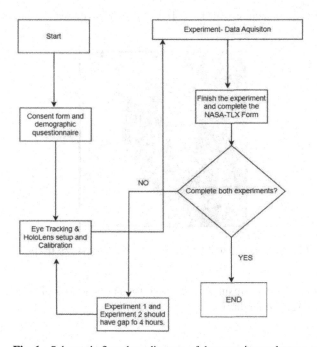

Fig. 1. Schematic flowchart diagram of the experimental setup.

After the experiment was explained, participants were equipped with the Microsoft HoloLens 2 headset, followed by the placement of the Dikablis Eye tracker over their eyes (refer to Fig. 2.), and a powering device was slung across their body (see Fig. 3). After the eye tracker and HoloLens 2 devices were properly placed on the participant, the calibration of both devices had been proceeded to collect accurate eye data.

Two experiments (lecture 1 and lecture 2) were conducted with a minimum time gap of 4 h and maximum 48 h in between. The lecture 1 is a basics Biomechanics and Ergonomics AR learning session while the AR learning in the lecture 2 is more challenging compared to the first lecture, as the participant must make use of the first session's knowledge to solve problems in Biomechanics and Ergonomics [24]. In each

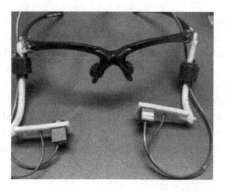

Fig. 2. Dikablis eye tracker & HoloLens and Eye tracker placement.

Fig. 3. Powering unit for the Eye Tracker hung across the body.

learning sessions the participant will be asked to complete multiple modules (7 in first lecture and 8 in second lecture).

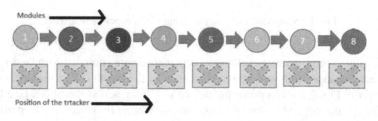

Fig. 4. Experimental setup describing the layout.

We set up a table with an indoor location sensor to trace the participant's location during AR learning [25]. This table also functioned as a navigational tool for transitioning between different AR scenes (see Fig. 4 and 5). We used the Q-Track NFER system for accurate indoor positioning. The NFER system plays a vital role in gathering important information about the participants' movements, facilitating an examination of their interaction with the AR material and their movement within the educational area.

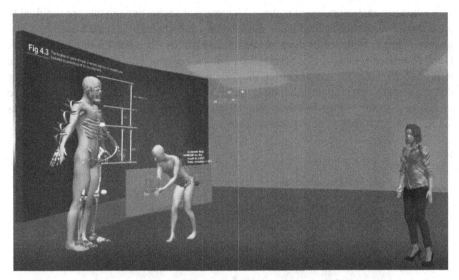

Fig. 5. AR environment setup showing the instructor dictating a biomechanics module.

Our custom-built client program was configured to promptly receive positional data via the locator receiver as soon as participants moved the table to a marked location

Fig. 6. Participant with the laptop along with the location tracking equipped table.

(see Fig. 6). Upon identifying the specific area, the program initiated the Windows Device Portal to execute the corresponding AR application and project the scene onto the HoloLens device.

Following each augmented reality (AR) learning scene, participants are required to answer a quiz question related to the material they just studied. They also need to assess and rate their confidence in their answer. Subsequently, they view a feedback screen. Once they have reviewed this screen, they can proceed to the next location to engage with the following AR scene. During the time when participants are engaging with the AR scene and answering the quiz, their eye pupil movements are tracked and monitored in real time (refer to Fig. 7). After completion of the lecture, the eye tracker data was saved in the DLAB eye tracking software in a CSV file.

Fig. 7. Dikablis eye tracking software interface showing the eye pupil.

3.2 Data Analysis for Pupil Eye Tracking

Once the participant data was gathered, multiple steps were undertaken to cleanse the data for statistical analysis, aiming to uncover its relationship with the NASA TLX Mental Demand parameter. Utilizing the Dikablis scene view camera footage, the eye tracking dataset was segmented into learning and solving phases for each AR scene (7 modules for lecture 1 and 8 modules for lecture 2).

Given the variation in pupil size among individuals, which can range from 800 to 2500 square millimeters, we collected data on the initial size of each participant's pupils before exposing them to the visual stimuli created for this experiment. This baseline measurement acts as a reference for tracking changes in pupil size in response to the AR learning experience.

After that, we applied normalization to the pupil area data using Eq. 1 [26], where Pnorm represents the normalized pupil area, Pi denotes each data point of the pupil area $(i = 1, ..., n)$, min(P) is the smallest pupil area observed in the participant's entire set of data points, and max(P) signifies the largest pupil area from that same set of data

$$P_{norm} = \frac{P_i - \min(P)}{\max(P) - \min(P)} \tag{1}$$

4 Results

4.1 Pupil Dilation Analysis

Upon examining the changes in pupil dilation among participants, we identified a significant pattern between the variations in pupil dilation from baseline to problem-solving phases and the mental demand. Table 1 presents the variations in pupil size from the baseline phase (B) to the problem-solving phase (S), labeled as 'B-S-1' to 'B-S-7'. For instance, 'B-S-1' signifies the difference in pupil area between phases B and S for AR scene 1. These values represent the normalized difference in pupil size when participants were engaged in specific AR scene, compared to their initial pupil size. This data is pivotal as it suggests a quantifiable link between physiological responses and cognitive load. The last column, titled 'Mental Demand', shows a subjective rating of the mental effort as reported by participants, with values ranging from 20 to 80. These values reflect the cognitive demand of the tasks, with higher numbers indicating more demanding tasks. The variation in pupil dilation across tasks—from as low as 0.0010 to as high as 0.2846. By comparing the pupil dilation data with the self-reported mental demand, we were able to find the validity of using pupillometric data as an objective metric for cognitive workload in AR learning environments.

Table 1. Table shows the difference between the absolute value of the normalized pupil data (baseline phase and problem-solving phase).

B-S-1	B-S-2	B-S-3	B-S-4	B-S-5	B-S-6	B-S-7	Mental Demand
0.2380	0.1380	0.2130	0.1990	0.2810	0.1560	0.1700	60
0.0950	0.1396	0.0130	0.0010	0.1190	0.2380	0.0100	50
0.0010	0.2180	0.0260	0.1250	0.0130	0.2140	0.2400	80
0.1990	0.1210	0.0060	0.1260	0.0690	0.0250	0.0220	30
0.1120	0.1160	0.0710	0.1660	0.1470	0.1210	0.1230	50
0.0801	0.0054	0.1046	0.0377	0.1065	0.0080	0.2891	50
0.2000	0.0960	0.0153	0.0780	0.1523	0.0779	0.0078	20
0.1281	0.0759	0.1849	0.1813	0.1311	0.0940	0.1167	50
0.1693	0.1520	0.2698	0.1988	0.0889	0.0248	0.0266	50
0.1775	0.1375	0.0689	0.2945	0.0885	0.0379	0.0893	40
0.2846	0.0725	0.0944	0.0390	0.0891	0.1021	0.0714	70
0.1189	0.0174	0.1848	0.0050	0.0988	0.1586	0.1096	50

4.2 Relation Between Pupil Dilation and Mental Demand

According to the results (see Table 2), we could find the significant relation the pupil dilation and mental demand in AR scenes 1, 2, 3, 5, and 6 in lecture 1.

Table 2. Table shows regression coefficients solving pupil dilation correlated with Mental Demand in the lecture 1.

Term	Estimate	Std Error	t Ratio	Prob > |t|
Intercept	2.548576	10.84765	0.23	0.8236
B-S-1	132.8429	45.02071	2.95	0.0319
B-S-2	57.16934	41.72258	1.37	0.2289
B-S-3	72.32262	27.85889	2.6	0.0485
B-S-5	-154.746	45.48291	-3.4	0.0192
B-S-6	157.9889	36.44966	4.33	0.0075

Figure 8 displays a linear trend illustrating the association between the predicted mental workload and the actual measurements derived from pupil size. There's an ascending trend line depicted, indicating that higher predicted levels of mental workload correlate with increased actual levels. The pink band surrounding the trend line signifies the confidence interval, which provides an estimate of where the actual trend line might fall with a certain level of confidence.

For lecture 1, The RMSE value is noted as 7.3448 (see Fig. 8), serving as an index of the average discrepancy between the model's predictions and the observed values—the smaller this value, the more accurate the model is. An R-squared value of 0.90 signifies a strong correlation, with the model accounting for 90% of the variance in actual mental workload, which demonstrates an excellent model performance. A P-value of 0.0197 indicates a statistically meaningful correlation between the predicted and actual mental workload, as it falls below the conventional threshold of 0.05.

However, there was no significant relation between pupil dilation and mental demand in lecture 2 (see Fig. 9). It was observed that the P-value is 0.3385, which is above the conventional threshold of 0.05 for statistical significance. This P-value suggests that the relationship observed between predicted and actual mental demand might not be statistically significant.

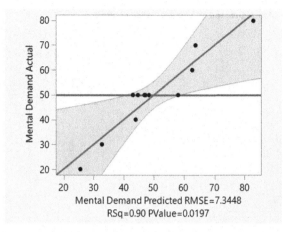

Fig. 8. Relation between the predicted mental load and pupil area for lecture 1.

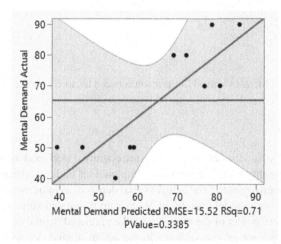

Fig. 9. Relation between the predicted mental load and pupil area for lecture 2.

In terms of mental demand between lecture 1 and lecture 2, there was a notable difference in mental workload between them, as illustrated in Fig. 10. The mental demand of lecture 2 is significantly higher compared to lecture 1. This could imply that the pattern of pupil dilation becomes more unpredictable with increased mental demand.

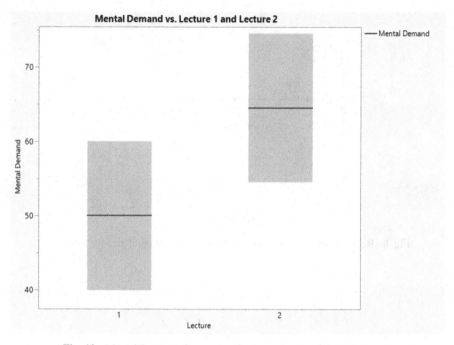

Fig. 10. Mental Demand Comparison between Lecture 1 and Lecture 2.

5 Discussion

This study aimed to find the new way to measure cognitive workload using pupil dilation in an augmented reality (AR) learning environment. Our findings revealed a significant relationship between predicted and actual mental demand, as indicated by the regression results. The regression model (see Table 2), with an R-squared value of 0.90, suggests a strong explanatory power of the model, with the predicted mental demand accounting for a substantial portion of the variance in the actual mental demand measurements. However, it was only shown in lecture 1. There was no significant relationship between predicted and actual mental demand in lecture 2. A potential reason for this discrepancy may lie in the differing levels of workload between the two lectures. Figure 10 illustrates that the mental demand during lecture 2 was substantially higher compared to lecture 1. The AR learning session in lecture 2 posed greater challenges, requiring participants to apply knowledge from the first session to address problems in biomechanics. This increase in task complexity could significantly diminish the predictability of pupil dilation responses. If the task is more demanding than expected, mental demand may rise, leading to increased variability in pupil dilation as participants adapt to the real level of difficulty.

The regression coefficients in the model of lecture 1 indicate the relationship each predictor has with the dependent variable, mental demand. For instance, B-S-1, B-S-3, and B-S-6 are notable for their significant positive relationship with mental demand, suggesting these conditions notably increase cognitive workload. In other words, the positive values of these coefficients suggest that an increase of the pupil dilation difference between baseline phase and problem-solving phase is associated with a corresponding rise in mental demand. While the effect of B-S-2 lacks statistical significance, its inclusion resulted in the highest R-squared value compared to any other combination. B-S-5 shows a notable negative correlation, signifying that as the pupil dilation difference between the baseline and problem-solving phases increases, there is a decrease in mental demand. The statistical significance of the lecture 1 model is reinforced by the P-value of 0.0197, suggesting that the predictors used in the model are indeed relevant to estimating mental demand in an AR setting. Further investigation is necessary to understand why certain AR scenes exhibit a positive relationship between pupil dilation and mental demand, while others demonstrate a negative relationship.

Pupil dilation is widely recognized as an indicator of cognitive load, though finding a strong linear regression model has proven difficult. However, in this study, we have successfully found a strong linear regression pattern at a medium level of participant workload. The model's high predictive validity has practical implications for the development of adaptive AR systems. For instance, real-time monitoring of pupil area could be integrated into AR applications to assess learner engagement and cognitive load, thereby allowing for dynamic adjustments to the complexity of the content. Such adaptability could enhance learning efficiency and reduce cognitive overload, potentially leading to better educational outcomes.

6 Conclusion

In this study, we exam the effects of AR-based lectures on pupil dilation, utilizing it as an indicator of mental demand. By comparing pupil dilation measurements with cognitive load evaluation methods such as the NASA Task Load Index, we find that fluctuations in pupil size could reflect varying cognitive loads, aligning with the mental demands of AR lectures. Initial results reveal a notable link between enlarged pupil dilation and increased cognitive workload in AR settings. This study introduces an innovative approach for assessing cognitive workload in AR environments through the analysis of pupil dilation data. The regression model used in our study reliably identifies pupil dilation as an indicator of cognitive workload in AR learning settings. Our results emphasize the model's effectiveness in detecting variations in mental demand.

As for limitations, our study did not account for how individual differences related to stress and cognitive demand could affect pupil dilation. Some individuals might exhibit more significant pupil dilation as a reaction to increased cognitive demand due to stress, whereas others may not show a physiological response to the same level of demand. This variability could arise from personal differences among learners or from external factors not accounted for in our model. Future studies should aim to include additional physiological or environmental variables to improve the predictive power of the model. Moreover, it is essential to explore how these findings apply across a larger sample size that includes diverse age groups. Further research is needed to refine AR learning environments, ensuring they effectively balance educational engagement with the cognitive demands placed on learners.

Acknowledgments. This study was funded by the National Science Foundation (NSF).

References

1. Holmqvist, K., et al.: Eye tracking: A comprehensive guide to methods and measures. OUP Oxford (2011)
2. Kim, J.H., Yang, X.: Measuring driver's perceived workload using fractal dimension of pupil dilation. In: Proceedings of the Human Factors and Ergonomics Society Annual Meeting (2020). SAGE Publications Sage, Los Angeles, CA
3. Othman, N., Abdullah, U.N., Romli, F.I.: Evaluating mental workload using pupil dilation and nasa-task load index. In: Convergence of Ergonomics and Design: Proceedings of ACED SEANES 2020. Springer (2021). https://doi.org/10.1007/978-3-030-63335-6_26
4. Orlandi, L., Brooks, B.: Measuring mental workload and physiological reactions in marine pilots: Building bridges towards redlines of performance. Appl. Ergon. **69**, 74–92 (2018)
5. Yan, S., Wei, Y., Tran, C.C.: Evaluation and prediction mental workload in user interface of maritime operations using eye response. Int. J. Ind. Ergon. **71**, 117–127 (2019)
6. Sweller, J., Van Merrienboer, J.J., Paas, F.G.: Cognitive architecture and instructional design. Educ. Psychol. Rev. **10**, 251–296 (1998)
7. Shi, C., et al.: Potential benefits of eye tracking within process control monitoring tasks. Hum. Fact. Ergonomic Manufact. Service Indust. **31**(3), 316–326 (2021)
8. Kim, J.H., Yang, X.: Applying fractal analysis to pupil dilation for measuring complexity in a process monitoring task. Appl. Ergon. **65**, 61–69 (2017)
9. Yang, X., Kim, J.H.: Measuring workload in a multitasking environment using fractal dimension of pupil dilation. Inter. J. Hum.-Comput. Interact. **35**(15), 1352–1361 (2019)
10. Kardan, O., et al.: Classifying mental states from eye movements during scene viewing. J. Exp. Psychol. Hum. Percept. Perform. **41**(6), 1502 (2015)
11. Yang, X., Kim, J.H.: Assessing situation awareness in multitasking supervisory control using success rate of self-terminating search. Int. J. Ind. Ergon. **72**, 354–362 (2019)
12. Shotton, T., Kim, J.H.: Assessing differences on eye fixations by attention levels in an assembly environment. In: Advances in Neuroergonomics and Cognitive Engineering: Proceedings of the AHFE 2020 Virtual Conferences on Neuroergonomics and Cognitive Engineering, and Industrial Cognitive Ergonomics and Engineering Psychology, 16–20 July 2020. Springer, Cham (2021). https://doi.org/10.1007/978-3-030-51041-1_55
13. Du, W., Kim, J.H.: An eye inter-fixation analysis of user behavior in a monitoring task. In: IIE Annual Conference. Proceedings. 2015. Institute of Industrial and Systems Engineers (IISE)
14. Kim, J.H., Zhao, X., Du, W.: Assessing the performance of visual identification tasks using time window-based eye inter-fixation duration. Int. J. Ind. Ergon. **64**, 15–22 (2018)
15. Beatty, J.: Task-evoked pupillary responses, processing load, and the structure of processing resources. Psychol. Bull. **91**(2), 276 (1982)
16. Ahern, S., Beatty, J.: Pupillary responses during information processing vary with scholastic aptitude test scores. Science **205**(4412), 1289–1292 (1979)
17. Sweller, J.: Cognitive load theory. In: Psychology of learning and motivation, pp. 37–76. Elsevier (2011)
18. Kerawalla, L., et al.: "Making it real": exploring the potential of augmented reality for teaching primary school science. Virt. Reality **10**, 163–174 (2006)
19. Braarud, P.Ø.: Investigating the validity of subjective workload rating (NASA TLX) and subjective situation awareness rating (SART) for cognitively complex human–machine work. Int. J. Ind. Ergon. **86**, 103233 (2021)

20. Guo, W., Kim, J.H.: How augmented reality influences student workload in engineering education. In: Stephanidis, C., et al. (ed.) HCI International 2020 – Late Breaking Papers: Cognition, Learning and Games. HCII 2020. LNCS, vol. 12425. Springer, Cham (2020). https://doi.org/10.1007/978-3-030-60128-7_29

21. Putri, M., Yang, X., Kim, J.H.: Sensitivity, bias, and mental workload in a multitasking environment. In: Harris, D. (eds) Engineering Psychology and Cognitive Ergonomics. EPCE 2016. LNCS. vol. 9736. Springer, Cham (2016). https://doi.org/10.1007/978-3-319-40030-3_2

22. Kim, J.H., Macht, G.A., Li, S.: Comparison of individual and team-based dynamic decision-making task (anti-air warfare coordinator): consideration of subjective mental workload metacognition. In: Proceedings of the Human Factors and Ergonomics Society Annual Meeting. SAGE Publicationsm Los Angeles, CA (2012)

23. Hart, S.G., Staveland, L.E.: Development of NASA-TLX (Task Load Index): Results of empirical and theoretical research. In: Advances in psychology, pp. 139–183. Elsevier (1988)

24. Mostowfi, S., et al.: The effect of metacognitive judgments on metacognitive awareness in an augmented reality environment. In: International Conference on Human-Computer Interaction. Springer (2023). https://doi.org/10.1007/978-3-031-35017-7_22

25. Yu, C.-Y., et al.: Developing an augmented reality-based interactive learning system with real-time location and motion tracking. In: International Conference on Human-Computer Interaction. Springer (2023). https://doi.org/10.1007/978-3-031-34550-0_16

26. Liang, N., et al.: Using eye-tracking to investigate the effects of pre-takeover visual engagement on situation awareness during automated driving. Accid. Anal. Prev. **157**, 106143 (2021)

Human Performance in Vehicle Recognition with Visual and Infrared Images from Unmanned Aerial Vehicle

Petter Norrblom[✉], Patrik Lif, and Fredrik Näsström

Swedish Defence Research Agency, Linköping, Sweden
`{petter.norrblom,patrik.lif,fredrik.nasstrom}@foi.se`

Abstract. Recognition of vehicles and other objects is important in military operations. Unmanned aerial vehicles (UAVs) equipped with different sensors can provide images from which a human operator can recognise vehicles. Two experiments were carried out to study human performance in recognising vehicle types in visual and thermal long-wavelength infrared images respectively. The effect of vehicle model, stimuli size, and response time limit was studied in both experiments. In the experiments, trained laypeople classified images including different vehicle models, six military and one civilian. The results show that the vehicle model had an effect on both the classification accuracy and the response time. The results for the civilian vehicle stood out in particular as it was classified more accurately and faster than the military vehicles. Using larger stimuli and not limiting the response time generally led to higher classification accuracy and longer response times. There were also interactions between the variables, where for example different vehicle models were affected differently by stimuli size and limiting the response time. The results provide an overall indication of what level of performance can be expected for human vehicle recognition and how vehicle type, stimuli size, and time pressure effect performance.

Keywords: Unmanned aerial vehicle · Vehicle recognition · Visual images · Infrared images · Human performance

1 Introduction

In almost all military operations, there is a need to quickly detect and recognise adversaries imaged by various sensors, cameras and sights. One such way to detect and recognise adversaries is by using sensors and cameras carried by unmanned aerial vehicles (UAVs) [1]. Two examples of this are visual sensors and thermal long-wavelength infrared sensors, the latter of which is referred to in this paper as infrared. The use of UAVs for target detection and recognition is today common practice and is playing a central role in the ongoing war in Ukraine [2, 3]. One common target that can be detected and recognised by using UAVs is vehicles.

UAVs can be operated during both day and night. Therefore, UAVs are often equipped with both visual and infrared sensors. At night, there is limited value in visual sensors, but

© The Author(s), under exclusive license to Springer Nature Switzerland AG 2024
D. D. Schmorrow and C. M. Fidopiastis (Eds.): HCII 2024, LNAI 14694, pp. 182–198, 2024.
https://doi.org/10.1007/978-3-031-61569-6_12

thermal infrared sensors work well as the contrast in thermal infrared images occurs due to differences in temperature and emissivity between objects. In daylight, UAV operators often switch between infrared and visual sensors to obtain as much information about targets as possible.

A UAV operator's ability to recognise targets is affected by several factors, such as light conditions, weather, terrain, and target resolution (distance to targets). In a military setting, the operator might also have limited time to make decisions. Automatic vehicle detection, recognition, and identification is beginning to emerge in both civilian and military use of UAVs [4–6]. The best performing algorithms for real-time detection and recognition of targets in video feeds are currently based on deep neural networks, with three common algorithms being RetinaNet [7], Mask R-CNN [8], and Cascade R-CNN [9]. However, a human operator responsible for target recognition from a UAV must ensure both correct recognition of objects and ensure that inappropriate actions, such as attacking civilian vehicles, are prevented. Thus, research on factors that impact UAV operators' performance is needed, so conditions in which operators can carry out their task successfully can be provided.

Research has been carried out on human vehicle detection, recognition, and identification in both visual and infrared images and videos from military settings. Simulated augmented reality labels were used to support human vehicle identification in infrared images, leading to increased identification accuracy and shorter response times [10]. Also, in the same study limiting both the response time and increasing the distance to the target decreased identification accuracy and increased response times. Visual video sequences led to higher recognition accuracy than infrared video sequences in human vehicle recognition based on video sequences from simulated visual and infrared sensors placed on a UAV, and accuracy varied for different types of vehicles [11]. Target detection in visual video sequences was found to be more accurate and faster compared to detection in infrared video sequences, using video sequences from simulated UAV sensors [12].

In this work, two experiments were carried out. The first experiment studied human ability to recognise vehicles in simulated visual images and the second studied human ability to recognise vehicles in simulated infrared images. The purpose of both studies was to study how accuracy and time for vehicle recognition are affected by vehicle model, stimuli size, and response time limit. The following research questions were formulated:

1. How does vehicle model affect the ability to classify vehicles?
2. How does stimuli size affect the ability to classify vehicles?
3. How does response time limit affect the ability to classify vehicles?

The ability to classify vehicles was primarily measured by classification accuracy, i.e. the portion of correctly classified vehicles. In addition, response time was used as a secondary measure.

2   Experiment 1 – Visual Images

Experiment 1 studied the ability to recognise different types of vehicles in visual images.

2.1   Method

In the experiment, the participants viewed images from a simulated UAV visual sensor. Each image included one vehicle to be classified. The experiment had a 7 (vehicle model) × 2 (stimuli size) × 2 (response time limit) within-group design. The vehicle models and stimuli sizes in the experiment are further described in the stimuli section. The two levels of response time limit were an unlimited response time and a five-second limit. The dependent variables for the experiment were classification accuracy, measured by the proportion of correct classification, and the response time for classifying images.

Participants. In total 15 participants (9 men, 6 women) with an average age of 29 (interval 24–38) participated in the experiment. Two participants had a military background. All participants reported having adequate vision with or without correction. Participants received a cinema ticket for their participation.

Stimuli. The stimuli consisted of seven vehicle models, six military and one civilian. The six military vehicle models used were 2S3, BMP-3, BTR-82, MT-LB, Strela-10, and T-72, and the civilian vehicle model Volvo V70. Figure 1 shows the vehicles and Table 1 provides a brief description of the vehicle models.

The stimuli, i.e. the vehicles, in the images had two different sizes. The small stimuli size ranged from 228–340 pixels, which corresponds to images taken from a UAV from approximately 1300–2200 m, and the large stimuli size ranged from 631–1438 pixels, corresponding to images taken from approximately 650–1100 m. Figure 2 shows one example image for each stimuli size. All vehicles were in open view in different settings, such as fields, forest edges, and lightly built-up areas. The images were selected initially by one author and then reviewed by a second author to judge whether the images were suitable for the experiment. Selection criteria for images were if the vehicle in the image was within either of the previously specified stimuli-size ranges and if the vehicle was judged to be sufficiently visible. The vehicles had to be in open view and not presented directly from the front or back to be considered sufficiently visible, however the vehicles were presented from different angles in different images.

The simulation software program SE-WORKBENCH [13] was used to generate the vehicles and terrain in the images. SE-WORKBENCH-EO can simulate sensor systems in the ultraviolet, visual, and infrared domains. SE-WORKBENCH-EO uses physics-based models for propagation, transmission, reflectance, and absorption. Thermodynamic models are used to calculate the physical surface temperature. MODTRAN [14] was used to model the atmosphere in the images.

Materials and Apparatus. SuperLab 6 [15] was used to present stimuli and record both classifications and response times. The images were displayed on a computer monitor with a 27 inch screen with 2560 × 1440 resolution. The experiment was carried out on a computer.

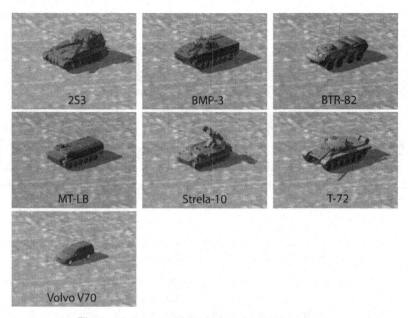

Fig. 1. The seven vehicles included in the experiment.

Table 1. A description of the seven vehicle models included in the experiment.

Name	Description
2S3	A fighting vehicle from the Soviet Union
BMP-3	Infantry fighting vehicle from the Soviet Union
BTR-82	An armoured personnel carrier from the Soviet Union
MT-LB	Often used as simple armoured personal carrier but also as artillery tractor or ambulance from the Soviet Union
Strela-10	A surface-to-air missile system with electro-optical guidance from the Soviet Union
T-72	A battle tank from the Soviet Union
Volvo V70	A passenger car from Sweden

Procedure. The experiment was carried out in person with one participant at a time. After arriving, the participant was informed in writing about the purpose of the experiment, what they would do in the experiment, how data would be managed, and that they could stop their participation at any time. The participant was encouraged to ask questions at any time throughout the experiment if any clarification was needed. After reading the information, the participant filled out an informed consent form, confirming that they had read the information and consented to participate in the experiment. The

Fig. 2. Example images of the vehicle model 2S3 showing the two stimuli sizes, large to the left and small to the right.

participants also filled out a pre-study questionnaire reporting age, gender, whether they had a military background, and whether they had adequate vision.

Thereafter, the participant received training. First, the participant viewed a printed document with images of the seven vehicle models (see Fig. 1) numbered from one to seven. The aim of this training was to learn the numbering for each vehicle model and learn to discriminate the different vehicle models from each other. The experiment leader provided tips regarding differentiating features for the vehicle models, such as whether the vehicle had wheels or continuous tracks and differences in weapon systems, size, and form, to help the participant discriminate the vehicle models from each other.

Thereafter, the training continued with a practice run of the experimental task. In the experimental task, images containing one vehicle each were presented one at a time on a computer screen. For each image the participant classified the presented vehicle using the number keys on a computer keyboard. After each response a visual mask, in the form of an image with a random pattern, was presented for five seconds before the next image was presented to prevent interference from the previously presented stimulus. A given response could not be changed. In the scenario with the time limit, if a response was not provided within five seconds no answer was recorded. A timer or feedback on how much time the participant had left to classify the image was not provided. The participant did not receive feedback on whether they classified images correctly throughout the experiment. The participant was seated in front of the computer screen at about an arm's length during the task but was allowed to move around in the seat and lean forward. The participant had the printed document from the initial training as a support when performing the experimental task.

The practice run was performed in two blocks, one with no response time limit and one with a five-second response time limit. Each block included two images for each of the seven vehicle models in the experiment, resulting in 14 images per block. The stimuli size used in the practice run was the same in all images and was slightly larger than the large stimuli size used in the experiment. The same images were used in each block for all participants, but the order of the images was randomised.

Next, the participant performed the experimental task. The experimental task was performed in two blocks, with a short break in between. In each block the participant classified a batch of 42 images, consisting of three images for each combination of vehicle model and stimuli size. Thus, 84 images were classified in total. Two different batches were used, one for each block, and the order of the batches was balanced using block randomisation. The order of the images in each batch was random. One block was performed with and one without the five-second response time limit. Whether the participant started with or without response time limit was balanced.

After performing the experimental task, the participant was thanked for their participation and received a cinema ticket. The participant did not by default receive feedback on their performance after the experiment, but if the participant asked they were told how many vehicles they classified correctly in the experimental task.

Analysis. Three-way repeated measures ANOVA, 7 (vehicle model) × 2 (stimuli size) × 2 (response time limit), was used to analyse the effect of the independent variables on classification accuracy and response times. Post hoc tests were performed by Tukey HSD. Post hoc tests was only performed for the main effects. Jamovi version 2.3.28 [16] was used for statistical analysis. Mauchly's test of sphericity was used to test the sphericity assumption for all ANOVAs, and Greenhouse-Geisser corrected degrees of freedom and p-value is reported when the sphericity assumption is violated. The significance level was set to .05 for all analyses.

2.2 Results

The results for classification accuracy are presented first, followed by results for response time.

Classification Accuracy. The participants overall classified 78% of the vehicles correctly. For the ANOVA, Mauchly's test of sphericity was significant for vehicle model ($W = 0.038, p = .01$). Greenhouse-Geisser correction was thus applied for this analysis.

All three main effects were significant (vehicle model, $F(3.51, 49.15$; Greenhouse-Geisser corrected) $= 10.79, p < .001$; stimuli size, $F(1,14) = 50.68, p < .001$; and response time limit, $F(1,14) = 9.70, p = .008$).

The post hoc test of the main effect of vehicle model showed that the V70 (98% accuracy) was classified with significantly higher accuracy than all other vehicle models (2S3 86%; BMP-3 66%; BTR-82 72%; MT-LB 67%; T-72 63%) except for Strela-10 (91%). Strela-10 and 2S3 also differed significantly from the BMP-3 and T-72. The reason for the significance of the main effect for stimuli size was that accuracy was lower for the small stimuli size (71%) compared to the large stimuli size (84%). The reason for the significance of the main effect for response time limit was that accuracy was lower with the five-second response time limit (74%) than with no response time limit (82%).

The interaction effect between vehicle model and stimuli size was significant, $F(6,84) = 3.14, p = .008$. No other interaction effects were significant. For the interaction effect between vehicle model and stimuli size, stimuli size made a bigger difference for 2S3 and BMP-3 and smaller for V70 compared to the other vehicle models (see Fig. 3).

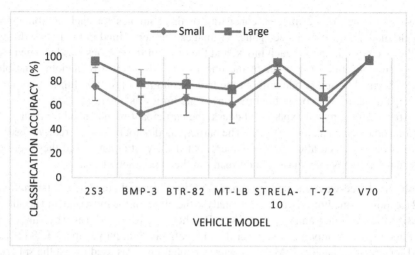

Fig. 3. Estimated marginal means for the interaction between vehicle model and stimuli size classification accuracy. The error bars show 95% confidence intervals.

Response Time. Overall, the average response time was 3.6 s. In the ANOVA the main effect for vehicle model violated the sphericity assumption (Mauchly's $W = 0.057, p = .03$). A Greenhouse-Geisser correction was thus applied for that analysis.

All three main effects were significant (vehicle model, $F(3.26,45.65$; Greenhouse-Geisser corrected$) = 23.25, p < .001$; stimuli size, $F(1,14) = 23.13, p < .001$; response time limit, $F(1,14) = 37.64, p < .001$). The post hoc test of the main effect for vehicle model showed that both Strela-10 (2.7 s) and V70 (2.0 s) were classified significantly faster than all other vehicle models (BMP-3 4.6 s; BTR-82 4.1 s; MT-LB 5.2 s; T-72 3.5 s), except for 2S3 (3.0 s) and each other. Also, 2S3 and T-72 were classified significantly faster than BMP-3 and MT-LB, and 2S3 significantly faster than BTR-82. The reason for the main effect of stimuli size was that response time for the large stimuli size was faster (3.1 s) compared to the small stimuli size (4.1 s). The reason for the main effect of response time limit was that response times were faster with the five-second response time limit (2.6 s) compared to with no limit (4.5 s).

All three two-way interactions were significant (vehicle model × stimuli size, $F(6,84) = 2.46, p = .03$; vehicle model × response time limit, $F(6,84) = 8.39, p < .001$; stimuli size × response time limit, $F(1,14) = 8.46, p = .01$). The three-way interaction was not significant.

For the interaction effect between vehicle model and stimulus size, the difference in response time between stimuli sizes was smaller for BMP-3 and V70 and a bigger for 2S3 and BTR-82 compared to other vehicle models (see Fig. 4). For the interaction effect between vehicle model and response time limit, all vehicle models were classified faster with the five-second response time limit, but the difference in response time with or without the limit was bigger for MT-LB and BMP-3 and smaller for V70 and Strela-10 compared to other vehicle models (see Fig. 5). Lastly, for the interaction effect between stimuli size and response time limit both small and large stimuli were classified faster with the response time limit, but the difference in response time with or without the limit was bigger for the small stimuli (see Fig. 6).

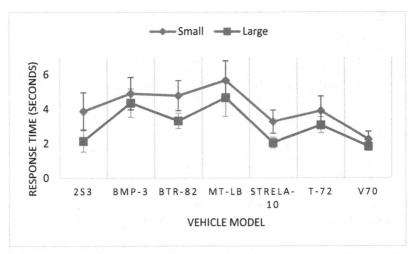

Fig. 4. Estimated marginal means for the interaction between vehicle model and stimuli size on response times. The error bars show 95% confidence intervals.

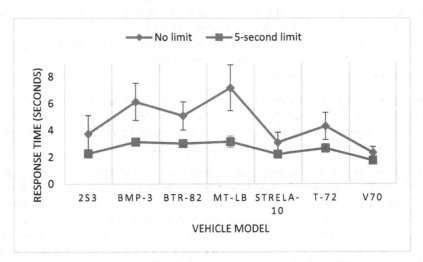

Fig. 5. Estimated marginal means for the interaction between vehicle model and response time limit on response times. The error bars show 95% confidence intervals.

3 Experiment 2 – Infrared Images

Experiment 2 studied the ability to recognise different types of vehicles in infrared images.

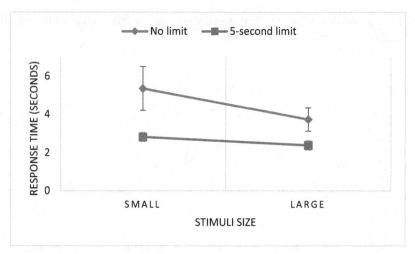

Fig. 6. Estimated marginal means for the interaction between stimuli size and response time limit on response times. The error bars show 95% confidence intervals.

3.1 Method

Overall, the method used in Experiment 2 was similar to the method in Experiment 1. Therefore, readers are referred to Experiment 1 for a description of the method. Thus, this section only describes how the experiments differed.

Experiment 2 was performed with a 6 (vehicle model) × 3 (stimuli size) × 2 (response time limit) instead of the 7 × 2 × 2 design used in Experiment 1 (see the stimuli section for information on the differences).

Participants. Twelve participants (7 men, 5 women) with a mean age of 45 years (interval 29–63) participated. None of the participants had a military background. All participants reported having adequate vision with or without correction. The participants were compensated with a cinema ticket for participating.

Stimuli. In this experiment images and stimuli from a simulated UAV infrared sensor were used. The same vehicle models as in Experiment 1 except for the MT-LB were used. The two stimuli sizes in Experiment 1 were used in Experiment 2, but another smaller stimuli size ranging from 35 to 87 pixels was added, which corresponds to UAV images taken from approximately 2100–2500 m. Thus, the medium stimuli size in this experiment corresponds to the small stimuli size from Experiment 1. Figure 7 shows infrared images of the six vehicle models used in Experiment 2, and Fig. 8 shows one example image of each stimulus size. The same selection criteria as in Experiment 1 was applied. The images were generated as in Experiment 1.

Materials and Apparatus. Overall the same materials and apparatus were used, but the display and computer used differed. In this experiment a Dell Latitude 7240 with a 12.5 inch display with 1366 × 768 resolution was used.

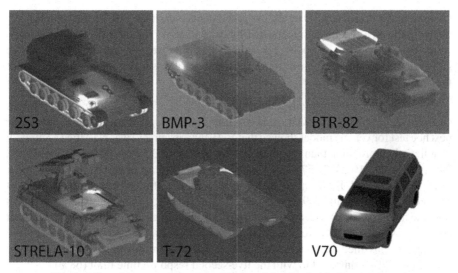

Fig. 7. Infrared images of the six vehicle models included in the experiment.

Fig. 8. Examples of infrared images of the vehicle model T-72 for the three stimuli sizes, from large (left image) to small.

Procedure. The procedure differed from Experiment 1 in that the participants first received training on both a printed document with visual images and a printed document with infrared images before practicing the task on computer. During the experiment, the participants had the printed document with visual images as an aid and not the document with infrared images. Since the experiment was performed with $6 \times 3 \times 2$ design, the participants viewed 54 images (3 images for each combination of vehicle model and stimuli size, i.e. $3 \times 6 \times 3$) in each block rather than 42 images, thus totally 108 images in the two blocks.

Analysis. The analysis was performed as in Experiment 1, although the three-way ANOVAs had a 6 (vehicle model) $\times$ 3 (stimuli size) $\times$ 2 (response time limit) design.

3.2 Results

First results for classification accuracy are presented followed by results for response time.

Classification Accuracy. Overall, the participants classified 74% of the vehicles correctly. In the ANOVA the assumption of sphericity was violated for the three-way interaction (Mauchly's $W = 0.00001$, $p = 0.01$) and for the vehicle model and stimuli size interaction ($W = 0.00001$, $p = 0.02$). A Greenhouse-Geisser correction was applied for these analyses.

All main effects were significant (vehicle model, $F(5,55) = 18.79$, $p < .001$; stimuli size, $F(2,22) = 65.60$, $p < .001$; response time limit, $F(1,11) = 13.32$, $p = .004$). The post hoc test for vehicle model showed that V70 (99% accuracy) was classified accurately significantly more often than all other vehicle models (2S3 59%; BMP-3 67%; BTR-82 79%; Strela-10 81%; T-72 57%). Strela-10 was classified accurately significantly more often than 2S3 and T-72, and BTR-82 than T-72. For stimuli size, the post hoc test showed that large stimuli (89%) was classified accurately significantly more often than both the medium (70%) and small stimuli (62%), and the medium stimuli was classified accurately significantly more often than the small stimuli. For response time limit, the participants classified the images accurately significantly more often without a response time limit (79%) compared to with the five-second response time limit (68%).

Two interaction effects were significant, the vehicle model and stimuli size interaction, $F(4.54,49.91$; Greenhouse-Geisser corrected) $= 4.75$, $p = .002$, and the stimuli size and response time limit interaction, $F(2,22) = 8.50$, $p = .002$. The three-way interaction was not significant with the applied Greenhouse-Geisser correction but was significant without the correction. The vehicle model and response time limit interaction was not significant.

For the vehicle model and stimuli size interaction effect, V70 were classified with nearly the same accuracy for all stimuli sizes (see Fig. 9). T-72 were classified with low accuracy compared to the other vehicle models for the medium and small stimuli, but not to the same degree for large stimuli. Further, Strela-10 was classified with lower accuracy for the medium than for the small stimuli, which was not the case for any other vehicle model. For the stimuli size and response time limit interaction effect, the decrease in accuracy from the five-second response time limit was bigger for the small stimuli size compared to the medium and large stimuli size (see Fig. 10).

Response Time. The average response time was 7.2 s. For the ANOVA, Mauchly's test of sphericity was significant for the vehicle model and stimuli size interaction ($W = 0.000001$, $p < .001$). A Greenhouse-Geisser correction was therefore applied for this analysis.

All three main effects were significant (vehicle model, $F(5,55) = 23.29$, $p < .001$; stimuli size, $F(2,22) = 16.32$, $p < .001$; response time limit, $F(1,11) = 42.94$, $p < .001$). The vehicle model post hoc test show that V70 (2.4 s) was classified significantly faster than all other vehicle models (2S3 8.9 s; BMP-3 10.1 s; BTR-82 6.5 s; Strela-10 5.2 s; T-72 9.8 s). Strela-10 and BTR-82 were also classified significantly faster than BMP-3 and T-72, and Strela-10 significantly faster than 2S3 as well. For the stimuli size post hoc test there was a significant difference between images with large stimuli (5.0 s) compared to both medium (7.8 s) and small stimuli (8.6 s), while the difference between medium and small stimuli was not significant. For the response time limit main effect,

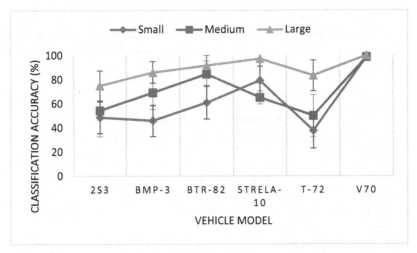

Fig. 9. Estimated marginal means for the interaction between vehicle model and stimuli size for classification accuracy. The error bars show 95% confidence intervals.

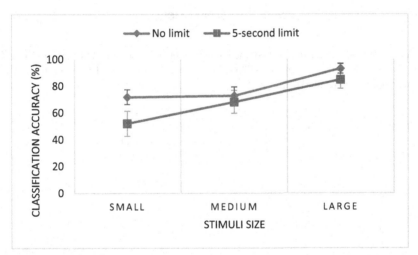

Fig. 10. Estimated marginal means for the interaction between response time limit and stimuli size for classification accuracy. The error bars show 95% confidence intervals.

the average response time was significantly longer with no response time limit (11.6 s) compared to with the five-second response time limit (2.7 s).

Two interaction effects were significant, the vehicle model and response time limit interaction, $F(5,55) = 15.66$, $p < .001$, and the stimuli size and response time limit interaction, $F(2,22) = 13.70$, $p < .001$,. The vehicle model and stimuli size interaction was not significant with the applied Greenhouse-Geisser correction but was significant without the correction. The three-way interaction was not significant.

For the vehicle model and response time limit interaction effect, not having a response time limit increased response times less for V70 and more for 2S3, BMP-3, and T-72 compared to other vehicle models (see Fig. 11). For the stimuli size response time limit interaction effect, response times were longer without a response time limit, however the difference was smaller for large stimuli compared to medium and small stimuli (see Fig. 12).

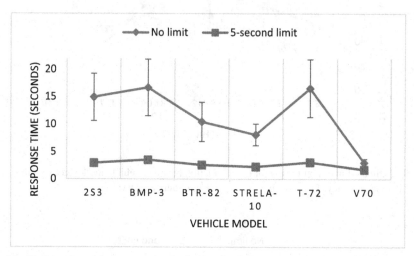

Fig. 11. Estimated marginal means for the interaction between vehicle model and response time limit for response time. The error bars show 95% confidence intervals. The 5-s limit graph error bars are covered by the markers.

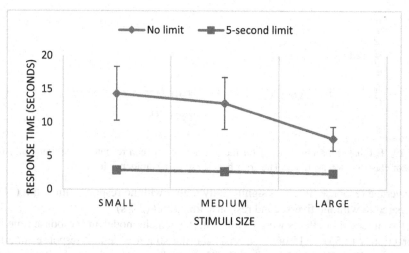

Fig. 12. Estimated marginal means for the interaction between vehicle model and response time limit for response times. The error bars show 95% confidence intervals. The 5-s limit graph error bars are covered by the markers.

4   Discussion

The prevalent use of UAVs in current military conflicts such as the ongoing war in Ukraine [2, 3] demonstrates a need for research on UAVs and performance of human UAV operators. In the experiments presented in this paper, vehicles were recognised with 78% accuracy in visual images in Experiment 1 and with 74% accuracy in infrared images in Experiment 2. The average classification time was 3.6 and 7.2 s in the respective experiments. All independent variables, i.e. vehicle model, stimulus size, and response time limit, had significant effects on classification accuracy and response time, which will be discussed further in relation to the research questions. Both dependent variables, classification accuracy and response time, generally coincided in that, for example, the vehicle models that were classified less accurately also took longer to classify. Also, the different independent variables affected both dependent variables in similar ways.

The results provide an indication of what performance can be expected when recognising vehicles in visual and infrared images and how the independent variables affect performance. Such indications may serve as baselines for evaluating human performance with different types of support, such as decision support systems, or performance of algorithms for vehicle classification. The results may also indicate certain situations where automatic recognition support for human operators, for example by augmented reality as suggested in [10], might be specifically relevant to provide.

Whether performance should be considered good or bad, and how important the independent variables studied in these experiments are, depends on the specific real-life context in which vehicles are to be recognised. For example, if vehicles are recognised in a context where the same action should be taken for all vehicle models, being able to distinguish specific vehicle models would not be important, or if the UAV need to fly at a certain distance from the target stimuli size will be hard to influence. However, in such challenging contexts other factors such as providing the operator with plenty of time to recognise vehicles could be considered to compensate for the challenges and support the operators.

Considering research question 1, how the model of vehicle affects the ability to classify vehicles, the results show significant differences in both classification accuracy and time to classify the different vehicle models in both experiments. Also, the significant interaction effects show that the ability to recognise different vehicle models is affected differently by stimulus size and whether there is limited time to classify the vehicle. Accordingly, providing support for recognising vehicles, for examples by algorithms or training, might be especially relevant for certain types of vehicles. However, from the results of these experiments, the less accurately recognised vehicle models should not be concluded as generally difficult to recognise, since the difficulty of recognising a certain vehicle model was affected by whether other similar vehicle models were included in the experiment.

The only civilian vehicle model, V70, was in both experiments correctly recognised in almost all cases and also classified faster than other vehicle models. Being able to recognise civilian vehicles is important to avoid attacking or causing collateral damage to civilian targets. These results indicate a high ability to distinguish civilian vehicles from military vehicles. However, other civilian vehicle models than V70 might be more difficult to distinguish from military vehicles, and if numerous similar-looking civilian vehicle models were included performance when it comes to identifying civilian vehicles would likely be lower.

Considering research question 2, how stimuli size affects the ability to classify vehicles, smaller stimuli sizes were in both experiments overall classified less accurately and took longer time to classify. This is in line with previous research [10]. Overall, the results indicate what level of performance can be expected from laypeople with limited training. Once again, however, conclusions should not be drawn regarding how stimuli size affected the responses for the specific vehicles used in the experiments, since the experimental setup with certain vehicles resembling each other might have impacted upon classification of small size stimuli for certain vehicles more. Another factor to take into consideration is that stimuli size was based on stimuli resolution. Stimuli for all the vehicle models therefore had the same absolute sizes in the images. However, since some of the vehicle models are comparatively smaller in real life, especially the V70, these vehicle models were larger relative to their real-life sizes when compared to the larger vehicle models, which likely made the smaller vehicle models easier to recognise.

Considering research question 3, how response time limit affect the ability to classify vehicles, vehicles were in both experiments classified more accurately and slower without the five-second response time limit. This is in line with previous research [10]. In a military setting, there may often be limited time to make decisions and targets may only be visible for a short period. Thus, operators may need support from algorithms or information from other sensors to confidently make quick classifications. Considering the response time limit, one question this raises is whether it is the time limit in itself or the pressure added from the response time limit that impaired performance. Since participants without the response time limit took longer than five seconds on average to classify multiple vehicle models in Experiment 1 and all vehicle models but V70 in Experiment 2, five seconds does not appear to be enough time to comfortably classify the vehicles in the experiments.

Comparing the two experiments, the results overall seem to agree. In both experiments similar vehicle models were generally classified more accurately and faster, and both stimuli size and response time limit had similar effects. The differences in experimental design should be kept in mind when comparing results from the experiments, and statistical comparisons between the experiments were not conducted due to these differences. Participants took longer to classify the infrared images in Experiment 2 than the visual images in Experiment 1 when there were no response time limit (11.6 s versus 4.5 s). While similar differences were reported in previous research on infrared versus visual video [11, 12], the difference was larger in this study. The differences in experimental design might have had an effect as well as the differences in sample, where Experiment 1 had a younger sample (average 29 years) than Experiment 2 (average 45 years). However, that these factors would account for the entire difference seems unlikely.

4.1 Limitations and Further Research

One limitation regards the ecological validity of the results, i.e. how well the findings transfer to real-life settings. In both experiments, the sample consisted of laypeople, while operators in real-life settings would likely be military personnel with extensive training and experience of regularly recognising vehicles. Also, the environment in which military operators carry out recognition tasks differ from the environment in these experiments. Thus, an area for further research is to study professional operators' ability to recognise vehicles in real-life settings.

Another limitation identified is the differences in sample and design of the two experiments. Further studies including both visual and infrared images in the same experiments, as conducted previously for video [11, 12], could be performed to study differences in vehicle recognition in visual versus infrared images in greater detail.

Considering the stimuli, one limitation is that the images used were simulated and thus not exactly the same for all vehicles, for example regarding the angle the vehicle was presented from. Including other vehicle models and other types of both military and civilian vehicles, such as trucks, is another avenue for further research. Also, in military settings vehicles would usually not be positioned in open view as they were in these experiments. Further research could therefore be performed to study how concealing elements, such as terrain and forests, affect vehicle recognition.

4.2 Conclusion

Overall, classification accuracy were around 75% for both visual and infrared images, and classification took on average 3.6 s for visual images and 7.2 s for infrared images. Performance varied depending on the vehicle models, with the civilian vehicle Volvo V70 being classified more accurately and faster than the military vehicles. Larger stimuli size overall led to better performance, with both higher accuracy and faster response times. Having a five-second response time limit decreased accuracy and shortened response times compared to not having a response time limit, indicating that five seconds is not sufficient to comfortably recognise vehicles. Comparing both experiments, classification took longer for infrared images than visual images when no response time limit was in place.

These results give an overall indication of human performance in recognising vehicles, identifies differences in performance between different vehicle models, and how stimuli size and a response time limit affect performance. The results also identify differences between recognition in visual and infrared images. Consideration of these factors could help operators to better execute their missions with UAVs.

Acknowledgements. This work was funded by the Swedish Armed Forces R&D programme for Sensors and low observables (FoT SoS, AT.9220424).

Disclosure of Interests. The authors have no competing interests to declare that are relevant to the content of this article.

Ethics Statement. According to local legislation and institutional requirements ethical review and approval was not required for the study Participants provided written informed consent. No personal data was collected.

References

1. Gupta, S.G., Ghonge, M., Jawandhiya, P.M.: Review of unmanned aircraft system (UAS). Int. J. Adv. Res. Comput. Eng. Technol. **2**(4), 1646–1658 (2013). https://doi.org/10.2139/ssrn.3451039
2. Kunertova, D.: The war in Ukraine shows the game-changing effect of drones depends on the game. Bull. Atomic Sci. **79**(2), 95–102 (2023). https://doi.org/10.1080/00963402.2023.2178180
3. Chávez, K., Swed, O.: Emulating underdogs: tactical drones in the Russia-Ukraine war. Contemp. Secur. Policy **44**(4), 592–605 (2023). https://doi.org/10.1080/13523260.2023.2257964
4. Gupta, P., Pareek, B., Singal, G., Rao, D.V.: Edge device based military vehicle detection and classification from UAV. Multimedia Tools Appl. **81**(14), 19813–19834 (2022). https://doi.org/10.1007/s11042-021-11242-y
5. Chen, H.-W., Gross, N., Kapadia, R., Cheah, J., Gharbieh, M.: Advanced automatic target recognition (ATR) with infrared (IR) sensors. In: 2021 IEEE Aerospace Conference (50100), pp 1–13. IEEE, New York (2021). https://doi.org/10.1109/AERO50100.2021.9438143
6. Liu, X., Yang, T., Li, J.: Real-time ground vehicle detection in aerial infrared imagery based on convolutional neural network. Electronics **7**(6), 78 (2018). https://doi.org/10.3390/electronics7060078
7. Lin T.-Y., Goyal, P., Girshick, R., He, K., Dollár, P.: Focal loss for dense object detection. In: 2017 IEEE International Conference on Computer Vision (ICCV), pp. 2999–3007. IEEE, New York (2017). https://doi.org/10.1109/ICCV.2017.324
8. He, K., Gkioxari, G., Dollár, P., Girshick, R.: Mask R-CNN. In: 2017 IEEE International Conference on Computer Vision (ICCV), pp. 2980–2988. IEEE, New York (2017). https://doi.org/10.1109/ICCV.2017.322
9. Cai, Z., Vasconcelos, N.: Cascade R-CNN: delving into high quality object detection. In: 2018 IEEE/CVF Conference on Computer Vision and Pattern Recognition, pp 6154–6162. IEEE, New York (2018). https://doi.org/10.1109/CVPR.2018.00644
10. Graybeal, J.J., Nguyen, R.T.T., Bosq, T.W.D.: Simulating human vehicle identification performance with infrared imagery and augmented reality assistance. In: Holst, G.C., Krapels, K.A. (eds.) Infrared Imaging Systems: Design, Analysis, Modeling, and Testing XXX, SPIE, vol. 11001, p. 110010A. SPIE, Bellingham (2019). https://doi.org/10.1117/12.2518990
11. Lif, P., Näsström, F., Bissmarck, F., Allvar, J.: User performance for vehicle recognition with visual and infrared sensors from an unmanned aerial vehicle. In: Kurosu, M. (ed.) HCI 2018. LNCS, vol. 10901, pp. 295–306. Springer, Cham (2018). https://doi.org/10.1007/978-3-319-91238-7_25
12. Lif, P., Näsström, F., Tolt, G., Hedström, J., Allvar, J.: Visual and IR-based target detection from unmanned aerial vehicle. In: Yamamoto, S. (ed.) HIMI 2017. LNCS, vol. 10273, pp. 136–144. Springer, Cham (2017). https://doi.org/10.1007/978-3-319-58521-5_10
13. OKTAL-SE. https://www.oktal-se.fr/. Accessed 03 Mar 2023
14. Abreu, L.W., Anderson, G.P. (eds.): The MODTRAN 2/3 Report and LOWTRAN 7 MODEL. https://web.gps.caltech.edu/~vijay/pdf/modrept.pdf. Accessed 18 Jan 2024
15. SuperLab 6. https://www.cedrus.com/superlab/index.htm. Accessed 18 Jan 2024
16. Jamovi. https://www.jamovi.org/. Accessed 18 Jan 2024

A Mixed-Methods Approach for the Evaluation of Situational Awareness and User Experience with Augmented Reality Technologies

Stavroula Ntoa[1]([✉])[iD], George Margetis[1][iD], Aikaterini Valakou[1][iD],
Freideriki Makri[3][iD], Nikolaos Dimitriou[2][iD], Iason Karakostas[2][iD],
George Kokkinis[3][iD], Konstantinos C. Apostolakis[1][iD], Dimitrios Tzovaras[2][iD],
and Constantine Stephanidis[1,4][iD]

[1] Institute of Computer Science, Foundation for Research and Technology-Hellas
(FORTH), 70013 Heraklion, Crete, Greece
{stant,gmarget,valakou,cs}@ics.forth.gr
[2] Information Technologies Institute, Centre for Research and Technology Hellas,
57001 Thessaloniki, Greece
{nikdim,iason,dimitrios.tzovaras}@iti.gr
[3] Center for Security Studies – KEMEA Hellenic Ministry of Interior – Public Order
Sector, Athens, Greece
{f.makri,g.kokkinis}@kemea-research.gr
[4] University of Crete, Heraklion, Greece

Abstract. The integration of Augmented Reality (AR) and Artificial
Intelligence (AI) in the field of security has proven to be a game-
changer, enhancing the operational capabilities of agents. Nevertheless,
their adoption in field operations depends on several factors, including
their actual impact in increasing the performance of Law Enforcement
Agencies, as well as their overall User Experience (UX) and acceptance
by target users. This paper introduces a mixed-methods approach to
assess AR wearable solutions with integrated AI techniques, applicable
since the early phases of design, thus ensuring the timely detection of
potential problems and the iterative evaluation of such transformative
technologies following a human-centered design approach. In particular,
the evaluated system, DARLENE, is an ecosystem with AI for activity
recognition and pose estimation, combined with wearable AR for the
visualization of the outcomes of the algorithms, via dynamic content
adaptations based on contextual factors, towards the improvement of
the Situational Awareness (SA) of police officers. The system was tested
with 35 participants from 6 different police organizations, adopting multiple methods to measure perceived and observed SA, workload, UX of
the DARLENE AR User Interface and wearable equipment, and user
acceptance. The methodology employed in this evaluation serves as a
general-purpose approach suitable for the assessment of AI-empowered
AR systems, emphasizing its potential for broader implementation and
adoption not only in the realm of security systems, but also in any application domain.

© The Author(s), under exclusive license to Springer Nature Switzerland AG 2024
D. D. Schmorrow and C. M. Fidopiastis (Eds.): HCII 2024, LNAI 14694, pp. 199–219, 2024.
https://doi.org/10.1007/978-3-031-61569-6_13

Keywords: User-based evaluation · Methodology · Augmented
Reality · Artificial Intelligence · XR simulation · Situational
Awareness · User Experience

1   Introduction

The increasing integration of Augmented Reality (AR) and Artificial Intelligence
(AI) across diverse sectors, including healthcare, manufacturing, and security,
underscores their growing significance in modern society and their potential to
transform interaction. This trend has spurred the transition of AR and AI systems from experimental prototypes to practical, real-world applications. However, before AR and AI systems can be deployed as mainstream applications, it is
essential to ensure that they are designed following a human-centered approach
[26], putting human needs at the forefront. However, this can be a challenging
endeavour with such radically new technologies. More specifically, research highlights that participatory design of AI has turned out to be difficult to achieve,
with AI system designers embracing a proxy-based approach to participation
and employing stand-ins, User Experience (UX) experts, or algorithmic proxies
instead of affected stakeholders [8]. At the same time, a cornerstone activity
of human-centered design is the evaluation of the developed technologies, iteratively, involving representative end users. It is noteworthy that as we transition
from well-established and extensively tested technological paradigms to intelligent environments, evaluation becomes an intricate procedure, whereby it is no
longer sufficient to assess the usability of a system, through studying its effectiveness, efficiency, and user satisfaction [29].

   This work proposes a mixed-methods approach to assess UX, task performance achieved with the system in terms of Situational Awareness (SA) and
workload, as well as technology acceptance, trust in automation, and confidence
in AI decision-making processes. The focus of the conducted evaluation was
the DARLENE system, which integrates AR and AI to assist Law Enforcement Agencies (LEAs) in their day-to-day policing operations. By utilizing an
AR prototype heads-up display (HUD), DARLENE visualizes real-time outputs
from AI and computer vision algorithms. These algorithms perform instance segmentation and activity recognition, identifying individuals or objects of interest
[21,38]. Through AR, essential mission-related information is superimposed onto
the physical environment. The DARLENE AR application employs User Interface (UI) widgets to enhance user SA, providing supplementary details about
individuals and objects flagged by the AI and computer vision systems (for
example, a detected foe, a suspicious object or activity). To further enhance the
user experience, a novel method is proposed for adaptable rendering of these
widgets. This approach takes into account the user's stress levels, the contextual
factors of their environment, and the prevailing environmental conditions [34].
By adjusting the presentation of information accordingly, offering all visualisa-
tion components in three different Levels of Detail, the aim is to optimize the
user's SA depending on the situation at hand. Following a co-creation approach,

LEAs collaborated in defining the requirements of the prototype, ensuring that it aligns closely with their operational needs. A conceptual description of the DARLENE system is provided in Apostolakis et al. [3], illustrating the complete DARLENE system featuring the AR HUD and the wearable computing node.

This paper presents the methodology followed and results of the evaluation of the DARLENE prototype, which involved system trials conducted with the active participation of law enforcement professionals. The evaluation methodology employed is versatile and can be applied to the assessment of similar systems, employing AR and AI technologies. More specifically, the evaluation of the DARLENE technology employed a combination of methods to assess its performance and user experience comprehensively. Specifically, the evaluation focused on parameters such as perceived and observed SA, workload, UX, and user acceptance, exploring participants' attitudes to the use of AI. In this study, 35 participants engaged in testing of the DARLENE prototype, providing valuable feedback through questionnaires administered before, during, and after the testing sessions.

The paper is organized as follows. Section 2 summarises related work and presents relevant evaluation efforts and background for the work reported in this paper. Section 3 analyzes the evaluation methodology, whereas Sect. 4 presents the evaluation results. A discussion on the findings is conducted in Sect. 5, while Sect. 6 concludes the paper and provides directions for future research.

2   Background and Related Work

User-based evaluation is the process through which the users of a product, service, or system evaluate its performance or efficacy. This sort of review involves soliciting feedback from users regarding their experiences with the product, service, or system, and leveraging this data to pinpoint areas for improvement and enact necessary adjustments. The primary aim of user evaluation is to ensure that the assessed product, service, or system fulfills the expectations of its users and delivers a satisfactory and efficient user experience [39].

Many researchers emphasize the significance of formally evaluating AR interfaces as a crucial step in the research process [10]. However, recent studies, as indicated by Dey et al. [9], reveal that less than 10% of the developments presented in scientific publications include user-based evaluations of AR. This disparity in user studies may stem from various factors, including a lack of standardized methods and guidelines for evaluating AR applications [6,20]. Moreover, the assessment of AR systems cannot solely rely on design principles for traditional user interfaces [10]. Researchers commonly employ questionnaires, interviews, inspection methods, and user testing to evaluate such systems [4,32]. Some studies argue that AR can lead to cognitive overload, while others refute this claim entirely [32]. Therefore, assessing cognitive workload is a crucial aspect of evaluating AR systems.

Similarly, systems incorporating AI for decision-making require user evaluation to gauge responses, trust, and acceptance [27]. While numerous techniques exist for assessing such systems, there is a growing consensus on the necessity of conducting evaluations under practical conditions. In this regard, user studies should be conducted with future users in real-world application settings, given the significant influence of the context of use and the environment on the overall UX and user acceptance [31].

Scenario-based trials have emerged as a commonly utilized approach for evaluating AR systems in the literature [10]. By replicating real-world scenarios, these trials allow participants to interact with the technology within contextually relevant environments, thereby providing valuable insights into usability and effectiveness [32]. For complex applications, particularly those involving AI decisions, many researchers advocate for utilizing simulations to supplement user-based evaluations.

On the other hand, evaluation studies aiming to assess systems in potentially hazardous situations, such as driving [7], medical procedures [23], or law enforcement tasks [34], often utilize system simulators. These simulators recreate real-life scenarios within a controlled environment, enabling the training of operators and the development and testing of UIs. By replicating real scenarios in a reproducible and controllable manner, the studies conducted through simulators, mitigate the risks associated with real-world execution, while still gathering valuable feedback from end-users [16,34]. Furthermore, the advantage of utilizing simulators lies in their ability to recreate complex and dynamic situations with precision and repeatability [7]. This reproducibility ensures that experiments can be conducted consistently, allowing for accurate comparisons and analyses.

3   Methodology

The trials took place when an early prototype of the system was available and involved two main parts: (i) XR simulation aimed at allowing users to experience the full-fledged DARLENE functionality and acquire quantitative and qualitative feedback and results, and (ii) scenario-based trials of the AR glasses yielding principally qualitative results. The main reason for adopting an XR simulation was that it empowered the assessment of the full breadth of the system functionality in a controlled environment, allowing the application of experimental methods for controlling participants' stress and measuring observed SA. On the other hand, hands-on experience with the AR glasses using simulated scenarios offered participants the experience of how the actual system will behave, thus achieving the benefits of "in the wild" evaluations [22]. It is noted that the system employed custom-developed AR glasses, offering maximum customisation of the visors to LEAs' equipment.

3.1   XR Simulation

Overview. The simulation approach was adopted in this part of the study, allowing participants to experience the DARLENE system through a video simulation approach. In this regard, participants wore the DARLENE HUD, however, instead of watching real-life scenarios, they watched videos featuring staged terrorist attacks in different situations and contexts retrieved from public videos of police exercises, as summarised in Table 1. The DARLENE system was run on each video, resulting in the production of eight DARLENE-augmented videos.

Table 1. Simulation video situations, contexts, and mapped DARLENE functionalities

Video	DARLENE functionalities	Situation demonstrated	Context
1	Crisis management, health care provision, suspect apprehension, and unattended object identification	Terrorist attacks and injury of citizens	Train station (indoor)
2	Crisis management, health care provision	Terrorist attacks and injury of citizens	Street
3	Crisis management, health care provision, suspect apprehension and LEA identification	Terrorist attacks and injury of citizens	Public library
4	Crisis management, health care provision, suspect apprehension and LEA identification	Bombing and injury of citizens	Mall
5	Crisis management, health care provision, suspect apprehension and LEA identification	Terrorist attacks and injury of citizens	Train station (outdoor)
6	Crisis management, health care provision,	Terrorist and suicide bombing attack	Mall
7	Crisis management, suspect apprehension, LEA identification	Terrorist attacks and hostage situation	Cruise boat
8	Crisis management, health care provision, suspect apprehension and LEA identification	Terrorist attacks and injury of citizens	Public fair event (outdoor)

Experimental Setup. The experimental setup involved a controlled within-subjects study featuring two independent variables: agents' stress levels and DARLENE system usage. This setup led to the establishment of four experimental conditions. To mitigate potential biases such as time-related effects and carryover effects, the order of these conditions was randomized across participants.

This randomization was achieved using a 4×4 Latin square design, enabling the allocation of simulated scenarios to the different experimental conditions. The conditions were categorized as follows: Stressed with the use of DARLENE, Stressed without DARLENE, Not stressed with the use DARLENE, and Not stressed without DARLENE.

Metrics and Hypotheses. The study encompassed several dependent variables and corresponding hypotheses. These variables included perceived SA, observed SA, workload during the DARLENE system usage, overall UX of the DARLENE AR graphical user interface (GUI) and equipment, and user acceptance of the DARLENE system. Hypotheses were formulated to examine the impact of the DARLENE system on these variables in the context of conducted user trials. The hypotheses were structured as follows:

H1: The DARLENE system increases agents' perceived SA.

H1a: The DARLENE system increases agents' perceived SA when stressed.

H1b: The DARLENE system increases agents' perceived SA when not stressed.

H2: The DARLENE system increases agents' observed SA.

H2a: The DARLENE system increases agents' observed SA when stressed.

H2b: The DARLENE system increases agents' observed SA when not stressed.

H3: The DARLENE system does not impose workload on agents.

H3a: The DARLENE system does not impose workload on agents when stressed.

H3b: The DARLENE system does not impose workload on agents when not stressed.

H4: The DARLENE system provides a satisfactory overall UX.

H4a: The DARLENE system provides a satisfactory overall UX when the user is stressed.

H4b: The DARLENE system provides a satisfactory overall UX when the user is not stressed.

H5: The DARLENE equipment is estimated as wearable by the agents.

H6: The DARLENE system is acceptable by the target population.

Overall, the methodology adopted was based on standardised questionnaires and validated methods. In more detail, perceived SA was measured with the use of the SART questionnaire [13], whereas observed SA by means of the SAGAT method [12]. Workload was studied using the NASA Task Load Index (NASA-TLX) questionnaire [18,19], while UX was assessed with the UMUX-Lite questionnaire [25]. However, due to the lack of existing validated questionnaires to assess the wearability of the equipment and the acceptance of the DARLENE system, custom questionnaires were developed. Furthermore, to acquire additional qualitative feedback, an interview was administered at the end of the session of each participant, following a semi-structured approach [1].

SAGAT Queries for Measuring Observed SA. SAGAT is an online probing method based on queries delivered to participants during arbitrary freezes in a simulation [12]. This method has been shown to have a high degree of validity and reliability and is one of the most widely utilised measures of SA [11]. The

SAGAT questions for our application domain were developed for each video individually and were evaluated by 2 LEA experts. The formulated questions aimed to assess all three levels of SA in Endsley's Model [14], and in particular:

- The participants' perception of elements in the environment (Level 1);
- Their comprehension of the current situation (Level 2); and
- Their prediction of the future status of the current situation (Level 3).

During the experiment, questions were administered at arbitrary time points, appearing in the participants' field of view (FOV), during freezes of the simulation videos. Responses to all questions were numbered and participants were asked to respond verbally, while the experiment facilitator took handwritten notes in a recording sheet.

Equipment Wearability. Aiming to assess the ergonomics of the DARLENE equipment, a questionnaire was created focused on ergonomic aspects, the functionalities provided, and the foreseen impact on smart policing [15]. The questionnaire consisted of two main parts, namely minimal anonymous background information, and the main part regarding the wearability of the equipment with questions the ergonomics and weight of the AR HUD and the belt box with the computing node, as well as the health impact of the DARLENE usage and foreseen impact on policiging tasks.

Technology Acceptance. Technology acceptance is a concept often studied in the context of different technological environments. There are several models reported in the literature aiming to predict the factors that influence the acceptance of a given technology by its intended audiences, such as the Technology Acceptance Model (TAM) and the Unified Theory of Acceptance and Use of Technology (UTAUT) [35], while numerous studies have been carried out to extend them in different technological domains [2,42]. However, an important concern regarding measuring user acceptance of the DARLENE technology was that existing questionnaires do not take into account specific features of AI-enabled technology, which may impact its overall adoption by its target users [41]. In particular, major concerns that should be addressed refer to the fact that AI models are black-boxed, they often make errors and are biased, but also that humans are biased and sometimes exhibit algorithmic aversion [41]. In this respect, a questionnaire was developed, based on two already validated approaches, namely UTAUT [40] and the measurement of trust in automation [24]. Based on these, the developed questionnaire entailed the following thematic categories, each explored using a small number of statements, some with positive and others with a negative connotation: performance expectancy, effort expectancy, behavioural intention, system explainability, system reliability, attitude to automation, and trust in automation.

The questionnaire was evaluated by five experts assessing its face and content validity, which determined its readability, clarity, comprehensiveness, and relevance. Face validity assessment focused on the questionnaire's appropriateness for its intended purpose and data collection needs. That is, the assessment of each question "seems to be a reasonable measure of its underlying construct 'on its face"' ([5], p. 54). Each evaluator provided individual feedback on question wording, objectives, and structure, culminating in a revised version based on their recommendations, resolved through consensus-building. All evaluation reports were aggregated, and a revised version of the questionnaire was prepared based on the experts' recommendations. As a result, the questionnaire at that time comprised inquiries concerning several aspects of the system's functionality and usability. These included questions of the system's anticipated performance in policing tasks, the perceived level of effort required to use it, participants' intentions to utilize the system in the future, its explainability and reliability, as well as assessments regarding human biases and trust in automation.

The next phase involved content validity evaluation of the revised version of the questionnaire. Content validity pertains to examining how well an instrument matches the relevant content domain of the construct it is aiming to measure [5]. The evaluators assessed the questionnaire for readability, clarity, comprehensiveness, and relevance [30]. To quantify content validity, the Content Validity Index (CVI) was calculated, with Item-CVI (I-CVI) for each item and Scale-CVI (S-CVI) for the overall scale. Each item received ratings from 1 to 4 for these constructs. I-CVI for each construct per question was computed as the proportion of experts agreeing (rating of 3 or 4), with the final I-CVI being the average across constructs.

The S-CVI score for the entire questionnaire averaged at 94.8%, indicating a very good overall score. While literature suggests an I-CVI of .78 or higher for individual items to indicate good content validity, any questions with ratings below 1.00 in more than one construct were reevaluated based on expert feedback. These questions were revised accordingly, including rephrasing, elimination, renaming categories, and adding new questions. The updated questionnaire achieved an excellent I-CVI score (>0.95) for all questions, resulting in an overall scale validity index of 98.4%, signifying a very high score. Following the final evaluation iteration, the revised questionnaire was deemed suitable for use in the study.

Semi-structured Interview. Semi-structured interviews are interviews based on specific predetermined closed and open-ended questions, followed by why and how questions [1], aimed at assisting the researcher to further pore over the reasons behind the testified negative or positive aspects highlighted by participants. This interviewing method is useful to supplement quantitative methods, such as questionnaires, and user observation studies, shedding light to puzzling issues or issues that need to be further clarified. Their most important benefit, however, is the flexibility they support in allowing the researcher to deviate from the predetermined questions along different directions, depending on the participant's responses. A small number of questions was provisioned, focusing on the following:

- Participants' overall view of the DARLENE experience;
- Feeling of nausea when wearing the DARLENE HUD;
- Perceived SA with the DARLENE system;
- Ease of use of the DARLENE system during field operations;
- Likelihood of using the DARLENE system during field operations.

3.2 Scenario-Based Trials

In the second part of the study, three short action scenarios were instantiated by agents and personnel from the technical partners, simulating policing activities addressed by the DARLENE technologies (for example, a suspect holding a gun and attacking another person). During this scenario-based assessment, participants were wearing the DARLENE equipment. After each short scenario, participants were asked to respond to a short questionnaire regarding the UI components that were visualised on the HUD, aiming to assess: the relevance of the visualised components, their appropriateness for the specific context, the appropriateness of their Level of Detail, the fitness of their placement on the screen, and the overall satisfaction with the provided information. All three scenarios were executed in two hypothetical situations: one in which the agent is stressed and one in which they are not, thus assessing the DARLENE decision-making and visualisations produced in these two experimental conditions.

4 The DARLENE System Evaluation: Applying the Evaluation Protocol

Overall, six trials were conducted using a stable working prototype of the DARLENE system, involving 35 LEAs from different organisations. The trials were conducted after training events, showcasing DARLENE functionalities and ensuring that participants were familiarized with the system, as they would in normal operations.

Out of the 35 LEAs who participated in the pilot trials, one was female. The age range of participants was 35 to 64 years, with the majority (94%) possessing over 10 years of professional experience in various policing tasks and a smaller proportion (6%) having 5 to 10 years of experience. Furthermore, the majority of the participants (94.28%) had no prior experience with AR.

The trials were conducted after participants were introduced to the DARLENE GUI and its functionalities. Divided into two parts, the trial began with the XR simulation, in the format of single-user sessions. Participants were briefed on the study's objectives, testing procedures, and data handling before signing consent forms[1]. Then participants provided background information via a questionnaire and calibrated the DARLENE HUD before testing to ensure viewing comfort.

Once the calibration phase was through and all participants' questions had been responded, the main part of the experiment followed. Before initiating an experimental condition, a stress manipulation task was employed, similar to Stefanidi et al. [34], depending on the stress variable. In more detail, before a *Stress* condition, the participants performed the PASAT test [37] for 5 min, whereas before a *Non-stress* condition, they watched a video featuring nature images

---

[1] It is noted that the research activities that will be conducted in the context of the pilot studies have been approved by the Ethical Committee of CERTH with reference number ETH.COM-69.

and relaxing music for 5 min. Before moving on to the next part of the evaluation, they were asked if they felt stress or relaxed and the stress manipulation method was extended if needed. Then, they watched two simulation videos with or without the system, depending on the condition, during which they answered the corresponding SAGAT queries. At the end of the experimental condition, the participant filled in the SART, NASA-TLX, and UMUX-LITE questionnaires (if the experimental condition involved the DARLENE system). Upon study completion, participants filled out the user acceptance questionnaire and underwent semi-structured interviews. The procedure was coordinated by two experienced facilitators. Each testing session with a participant lasted for approximately 60 min.

The second part involved the acting of the short scenarios in front of three users wearing the DARLENE equipment. After that, the participants completed a questionnaire to assess the visualization of the AR components. Finally, participants were thanked for their contribution and were asked if they had any additional comments or recommendations. Any input offered was recorded through handwritten notes by the evaluation facilitator.

5   Results

5.1   Perceived Situational Awareness

To study the perceived SA of the participants, under stress and non-stress conditions (H1a and H1b), the results from the SART questionnaire were analysed. It is noted that in the SART questionnaire, participants rate their own perception regarding their SA with respect to ten dimensions after the simulation is completed. These ten dimensions are classified into three main subscales: Attentional Demand (AD), Attentional Supply (AS) and Understanding (U). The score for each subscale is calculated as the sum of the participant's rating in each of the subscale's questions. The final SART score is calculated as per Eq. 1 below.

$$SARTscore = U - (AD - AS) \tag{1}$$

The results of the analysis suggest that under stress conditions, the majority of participants assessed their SA as higher when using the DARLENE system when in stress. The same conclusion holds for the majority of participants when they were not stressed. Overall, analysis of the aggregated results indicates that agents' perceived SA was better when using the DARLENE system, either in stress or in non-stress conditions, as well as overall. Table 2 presents the perceived SA results (mean and Confidence Interval [CI]) per experimental condition and overall.

In summary, it turns out that the system improves perceived SA, and therefore hypotheses H1, H1a and H1b are confirmed. In fact, the use of the system improved perceived SA by 15.81% in stress conditions, 16.15% in non-stress conditions and 15.98% overall. A statistical analysis of the results indicated that the differences observed in perceived SA when using the DARLENE system as

Table 2. Perceived SA results for all experimental conditions and overall

Condition	DARLENE	Without DARLENE	Overall
Stress	19.23, CI [16.94, 21.52]	16.74, CI [14.66, 18.83]	19.36, CI [17.85, 20.87]
No Stress	19.49, CI [17.40,21.57]	17.09, CI [14.70, 19.47]	16.91, CI [15.37, 18.46]

opposed to not using it are important both in stress conditions (t(34) = 2.66, p = 0.005) and in non-stress conditions (t(34) = 1.97, p = 0.02).

5.2   Observed Situational Awareness

To calculate the results of the SAGAT query technique, each correct response to a question acquired one score point, whereas erroneous responses did not receive any points. Then, all the individual scores for each participant were accumulated and divided by the total number of questions the participant was asked, acquiring the final SAGAT score, which represents the percentage of their correct responses. Results per participant indicated that for the vast majority of officers, their observed SA was higher when wearing the DARLENE system in stress conditions. In non-stress conditions, a higher percentage of participants, yet not their vast majority, exhibited higher observed SA when wearing the DARLENE system.

Analysis of the aggregated results per experimental condition indicates that agents' observed SA was better when using the DARLENE system in stress conditions, in non-stress conditions, as well as overall. Table 3 presents the observed SA results (mean and CI) per experimental condition and overall.

Table 3. Observed SA results for all experimental conditions and overall

Condition	DARLENE	Without DARLENE	Overall
Stress	0.65, CI [0.61, 0.69]	0.61, CI [0.56, 0.67]	0.63, CI [0.60, 0.66]
No Stress	0.57, CI [0.54, 0.60]	0.58, CI [0.53, 0.63]	0.58, CI [0.55, 0.60]

In summary, it turns out that the system improves observed SA in stress and non-stress conditions as well as overall, and therefore hypotheses H2, H2a and H2b are confirmed. More specifically, DARLENE improves observed SA by 13.13% in stress conditions, 5.19% in non-stress conditions, and 9.20% overall. A statistical analysis of the results indicated that the differences observed in observed SA when using the DARLENE system as opposed to not using it are statistically significant in stress conditions (t(34) = 3.76, p = 0.0003) but not in non-stress conditions (t(34) = 1.14, p = 0.13).

5.3   Workload

The results from the NASA-TLX questionnaire were studied to assess participants' overall workload, as well as workload along six dimensions, namely mental, physical, temporal, performance, effort and frustration [18]. Aiming to have a benchmark against which to compare findings, we adopted the Raw Task Load Index (RTLX) scoring approach of the NASA-TLX questionnaire, comparing raw scores as provided by participants with a relevant study retrieved from the literature, in which workload in the context of "tour" activities was assessed [36], that is during duties on shift hours of a police investigator, including those done immediately after a shift. A comparative analysis of the mean RTLX workload scores for the DARLENE system when in stress and in non-stress conditions, in relation to the aforementioned workload studies of policing tasks, is provided in Table 4. As a result, by comparing the means, it can be concluded that DARLENE (either in stress or in non-stress conditions) does not impose to users higher workload than what they experience in typical policing tasks, thus confirming hypothesis H3, H3a, and H3b.

Table 4. RTLX scores for the DARLENE system and for police investigator "tour" activities

Condition	DARLENE	Without DARLENE	Overall
Stress	0.65, CI [0.61, 0.69]	0.61, CI [0.56, 0.67]	0.63, CI [0.60, 0.66]
No Stress	0.57, CI [0.54, 0.60]	0.58, CI [0.53, 0.63]	0.58, CI [0.55, 0.60]

5.4   User Experience

In order to study the UX of the participants while using the system, under stress and non-stress conditions, the results from the UMUX-Lite questionnaire were analysed. For the vast majority of participants, the DARLENE system was in both conditions assessed as offering a good experience, higher than average. An analysis of the aggregated results along the different dimensions of UX (as these are explored by the UMUX-Lite questionnaire) is provided in Table 5. Therefore, it can be concluded that the DARLENE system provides a satisfactory overall UX (and hence hypotheses H4, H4a, and H4b are confirmed), considering that the average overall UX score is above the midpoint of the UMUX-Lite scale, both in the stress and non-stress conditions. Nevertheless, additional feedback was sought in the participants' feedback provided through the debriefing interview.

Table 5. UX results for stressful, not stressful situations, and overall

Condition	Usable	Useful	Overall UX
Stress	5.13, CI [4.64, 5.62]	4.94, CI [4.43, 5.46]	5.04, CI [4.62, 5.45]
No Stress	4.94, CI [4.43, 5.46]	4.71, CI [4.16, 5.26]	4.83, CI [4.35, 5.31]

5.5 DARLENE Acceptance

The user acceptance questionnaire results were analyzed to assess overall system acceptance. Acceptance was not separately studied for stressful and non-stressful conditions. Overall, most users showed a positive attitude toward the system. Although some users expressed less favorable views, the average acceptance score across all participants was equal to or higher than average, indicating no users had a negative stance. This observation holds true for the general population, confirming that DARLENE is generally acceptable among the target audience, thus supporting hypothesis H6. Notably, all subscales received scores higher than average, with attitude to automation being the lowest. Analysis of the aggregated results along the different subscales of technology acceptance is provided in Table 6.

Table 6. acceptance results

Dimension	Perf.Exp.	Eff.Exp.	Beh.Int.	Sys.Exp.	Sys.Rel.	Att.Aut.	Trt.Aut.	Overall
Mean	4.20	3.81	3.86	3.62	3.48	3.21	3.60	3.60
CI (LL)	3.92	3.50	3.54	3.33	3.23	2.98	3.33	3.33
CI (RL)	4.48	4.13	4.17	3.91	3.74	3.44	3.87	3.87

5.6 Equipment Wearability

Participants provided background information about their role in their agency, their duties, and their habits. Results indicated that 91.67% were police officers, whereas 8.33% were police instructors. The majority (83.33%) do not usually wear a helmet when in service. Responses regarding the ergonomics of the equipment indicated that the ergonomics of the equipment required improvement. In particular, only 10.34% of participants perceived that the DARLENE HUD prototype attached to a helmet was convenient for wearing it, although 65.52% were satisfied with its weight. Further, 41.38% of participants thought that the computing node worn as a belt box was convenient for wearing it, but 79.31% would like it to be smaller and lighter. When asked about the impact of the extra weight of the helmet, 34.88% indicated that it would affect their daily operations in the field, whereas 62,07% believed that it would not, and 3.45% did not respond to this question. Finally, participants were asked about AR-induced sickness, with

79.31% indicating that they did not experience any sickness symptoms, 17.24% experiencing light symptoms, and 3.45% not providing a response. Overall, the analysis of the questionnaires highlighted that there were mixed feelings about the ergonomics of the DARLENE equipment, especially the weight of the helmet. Therefore, this turned out to be an important point of concern for the overall UX of the system which could be further improved in terms of ergonomics. As a result, hypothesis H5 is partially supported (only in terms of the AR GUI, but not with regard to the equipment wearability). However, it should be noted that the majority of participants in this study were not used to wearing helmets in their daily operations and as such this was an expected finding. Future studies should also explore the use of the DARLENE AR HUD not being attached on a helmet, thus supporting a wider variety of policing operations.

5.7 Qualitative Feedback

Semi-structured interviews were conducted alongside quantitative questionnaire assessments to gather qualitative insights from participants on various aspects of the DARLENE system. Interviews covered overall experience, nausea, situational awareness and relevance to their job. Two researchers used inductive coding to analyze interview outcomes, ensuring consistency through cross-examination.

Overall Experience. Participants generally viewed DARLENE positively, citing its effectiveness in policing tasks, handling challenges, and training new officers. They appreciated its ease of use, and ability to enhance visibility and decision-making. Several users identified it as a good tool, helpful, interesting, easy to understand, and empowering the agent to perceive things that would otherwise be difficult to see. However, concerns were raised about the helmet attachment. In addition, some officers emphasized the need to ensure that the system avoids potential information overload, and appropriately prioritizes the highlighting a person or object of interest, depending on the situation at hand. These insights emphasize DARLENE's effectiveness while indicating the need for enhancements in helmet design and user interface clarity. Overall, findings align with conclusions on user experience and wearability.

Situational Awareness. Participants' responses to the question about whether the system could assist them in becoming more situationally aware were mostly positive (80%), with some negative (14.2%) and others indicating occasional usefulness (5.71%). Participants provided explanations for their responses. Those who expressed scepticism or occasional usefulness suggested that the system needs to be more comfortable to wear, it should present information that is critical for the given situation, and that officers need to trust the system first in order to capitalise on the possibilities that it offers. Conversely, those who believed that DARLENE could enhance situational awareness highlighted its assistance in handling complex situations, providing valuable information, aiding decision-making, and increasing self-confidence. These insights reinforce quantitative findings on perceived situational awareness and offer deeper insights into participants' reasons for considering the system helpful in enhancing awareness.

Job Relevance. The subsequent questions examined participants' views on using the system in their daily tasks and operations. Regarding the question about the difficulty of using the system during field operations, some participants expressed concerns about the prototype's ergonomics, citing issues like weight and the need for adjustments to LEA equipment. Others emphasized the importance of training and operation type in determining usability, while those with positive views praised the system's provided information and capabilities. Similarly, responses to whether participants would like to use DARLENE during operations were diverse. Those hesitant cited concerns about the current helmet version, while others highlighted potential benefits for specific tasks or situations, such as education, special operations, or escorting of Very Important Persons (VIPs). Positive responses emphasized the system's ability to enhance situational awareness and provide valuable information to users.

5.8   Results from the Hands-On Evaluation

The hands-on assessment of short scenarios in stressed and non-stressed conditions provided valuable insights for improving the DARLENE system. For each scenario enacted, participants responded to five questions addressing the relevance, appropriateness, level of detail, placement, and satisfaction with the visualized components, thus providing an assessment of the system's decision-making regarding UI adaptability. They were prompted to select from three options (yes, partially, no) and provide further explanations. It is evident that for all aspects explored and for all scenarios, the majority of participants were very satisfied or partially satisfied with the visualised components (Table 7). Overall, participants emphasized the importance of a stable helmet for accurate visualizations and the need for fast, reliable recognitions to build user trust. Suggestions included ensuring the highlighter frame closely follows body shapes. Some participants noted the small scale of the hands-on trials and expressed a desire for more complex situations, indicating the necessity for large-scale pilots. Nonetheless, these small-scale trials were crucial for refining the DARLENE prototype before larger-scale testing, with feedback already integrated into the current system version.

Table 7. Hands-on scenario results

Dimension	High		Partial		SLow	
	Stress	No Stress	Stress	No Stress	Stress	No Stress
Relevance of components	65.30%	71.09%	20.39%	15.61%	14.30%	13.31%
Appropriateness of components	62.66%	63.93%	22.95%	25.33%	14.39%	10.74%
Level of Detail	65.13%	64.94%	17.03%	17.77%	17.84%	17.29%
Placement of components	61.60%	60.48%	27.80%	27.37%	10.60%	12.16%
Information provided	67.60%	67.51%	19.33%	21.49%	13.07%	11.01%

6   Discussion and Lessons Learned

The two-phase small-scale pilot evaluation of the DARLENE system produced valuable findings and insights on different aspects of the system, its impact on policing tasks, as well as limitations that should be addressed for the system to be usable and useful in field operations.

First of all, the evaluation confirmed our hypotheses with regard to the positive impact of the system on LEAs' SA. As it turned out, both perceived and observed SA were improved with the system compared to carrying out the same tasks without the system across both stress conditions. These findings highlight the increased potential of the DARLENE solution in highly complex and stressful situations. Relevant discussions with LEAs revealed among others that participants found the system helpful in handling complex situations, allowing them to perceive information and situations that they otherwise would not, and helping them confirm their own decision-making.

In terms of workload imposed on agents, findings were compared to another study exploring the workload in "tour" policing tasks, demonstrating that the workload imposed by DARLENE is lower than that of typical policing tasks. These findings hold for the overall workload, as well as workload across the different subscales studied, namely mental, physical, temporal, effort, and frustration.

The UX of the system was positive exhibiting higher than the average values for usability, usefulness, and overall UX as well. Further insights were acquired during the interviews, where participants highlighted that the system is helpful, easy to understand, and easy to use, and a generally good tool that offers higher confidence, allows LEAs to perceive things hard to observe, and assists their decision-making, but can also be used as a helpful training tool.

In terms of technology acceptance, for all the subscales as well as the overall acceptance, scores higher than the average values were achieved, thus indicating that the system is acceptable to the target population. In addition, analysis of the interview responses indicated that a substantial percentage of participants found that the system could be used in their everyday tasks (57.15%) and that the majority would like to use it generally or in specific cases (82.85%). Analysis of interview comments revealed that some participants were more hesitant to trust the system and its decision-making, expressing concerns about possible errors of the system or its capability for accurate recognition in long distances. This is also reflected in participants' ratings in the "attitude to automation" subscale which achieved the lowest scores among all technology acceptance subscales (M = 3.21, CI = LL:2.98, RL:3.44).

Detailed discussions with participants on the aforementioned DARLENE dimensions highlighted their likes, dislikes, and suggestions for improvement. The DARLENE features that were most liked were its identification capabilities, the useful information provided, the clear UI, the AR technology employed, as well as its overall potential in the context of policing tasks. On the other hand, participants expressed concerns about the hardware, and in particular the fitting of the helmet to individuals with different physiology and the size of the AR glasses. Another concern was the information offered by the system, which on certain occasions was deemed as superfluous, given the job priorities of officers (e.g. when they need to neutralise a hostile person information about injured civilians is useless and disorienting).

During the hands-on assessment, the different qualities of the system were generally positively evaluated, with participants' responses indicating that the visualised components were generally relevant and appropriate for the given context, presenting information at an appropriate Level of Detail and placement in the wearer's FOV. Features that were highlighted as important for the smooth operation of the system were the need for a stable and well-fitting helmet, accurate and fast recognition, robust highlighter frame close to the shape of the recognised person or object, and stable UI components visualised accurately over the corresponding real-world objects. These findings were aligned with the results from the first evaluation phase. The consistency of findings highlighted the robustness of the methodology followed, but also revealed that specific DARLENE attributes are important for a smooth and effective operation, high-quality UX, and increased technology acceptance.

The limitations of the current study are twofold. One major limitation is that the majority of participants were male, therefore it cannot be claimed with certainty that the observed results hold equally for men and women. Nevertheless, it should be noted that although the sample of participants was heavily imbalanced with regard to gender, it was noted by police experts that it is practically impossible to achieve gender balance in this field, taking into account that anti-terrorist police tactical units are dominated by male agents [17,28]. Another limitation refers to the stress manipulation approach adopted. In particular, although the methods employed have proved their effectiveness [33] in manipulating stress, we did not employ a method to objectively measure stress in the context of the current study, to avoid inducing further complexities. In addition to subjective stress self-assessment, future studies of the system shall employ both objective and subjective stress measurement methods to alleviate this limitation.

7   Conclusions

This paper has presented an evaluation methodology that offers a systematic and comprehensive approach to assessing AR and AI-empowered systems, applicable even in early development phases when a system prototype is available. The methodology put forward was used to assess DARLENE, a security-oriented system, designed to enhance situational awareness for LEAs.

In terms of methodology, the combination of the XR simulation with the hands-on evaluation based on predetermined scenarios, ensured the combination of the benefits of both approaches for the user-based trials, generating quantitative metrics to test several hypotheses, but also acquiring qualitative feedback which was valuable for interpreting the results of quantitative measurements. Therefore, the proposed methodology is suitable even when it is not possible to conduct an in-situ evaluation, garnering valuable feedback from end-users. By using the XR simulation approach, users could evaluate the system in real-life, complex scenarios, which would have been impractical due to safety concerns or infeasible throughout the system development lifecycle when system prototypes are still immature. Furthermore, through the hands-on part, the participants used the DARLENE HUD prototype to evaluate several system functionalities enacted as role-playing scenarios and assess the decision-making algorithm for UI adaptability.

Overall, the evaluation encompassed a range of parameters, including perceived and observed SA, workload, UX, equipment wearability, user acceptance, and UI adaptability decision-making. The applied methodology yielded both quantitative and qualitative results, allowing researchers to both explore specific research questions and study in detail the behavior of the system and acquire insights for improvements. The applied approach and its outcomes underscore the importance of rigorous evaluation processes in advancing the adoption and deployment of AR and AI technologies in real-world settings, ensuring an iterative evaluation approach involving end users from the early phases of design and development. Future work will focus on organizing and conducting in situ pilot evaluations and carrying out a comparative analysis of all methods employed across the studied system attributes.

Acknowledgments. This work has received funding from the European Union's Horizon 2020 research and innovation programme under grant agreement No 883297 (project DARLENE).

References

1. Adams, W.C.: Conducting Semi-Structured Interviews, chap. 19, pp. 492–505. Wiley (2015). https://doi.org/10.1002/9781119171386.ch19. https://onlinelibrary.wiley.com/doi/abs/10.1002/9781119171386.ch19

2. Al-Emran, M., Granić, A.: Is It Still Valid or Outdated? A Bibliometric Analysis of the Technology Acceptance Model and Its Applications From 2010 to 2020, pp. 1–12, March 2021. https://doi.org/10.1007/978-3-030-64987-6_1

3. Apostolakis, K.C., Dimitriou, N., Margetis, G., Ntoa, S., Tzovaras, D., Stephanidis, C.: Darlene - improving situational awareness of European law enforcement agents through a combination of augmented reality and artificial intelligence solutions. Open Research Europe (2022). https://doi.org/10.12688/openreseurope.13715.2

4. Bach, C., Scapin, D.: Obstacles and perspectives for evaluating mixed reality usability, January 2004

5. Bhattacherjee, A.: Social Science Research: Principles, Methods and Practices. Open University Press, Tampa (2012)

6. Billinghurst, M., Clark, A., Lee, G.: A survey of augmented reality. Found. Trends Hum.-Comput. Interact. 8(2-3), 73–272 (2015). https://doi.org/10.1561/1100000049

7. De Winter, J., van Leeuwen, P.M., Happee, R., et al.: Advantages and disadvantages of driving simulators: a discussion. In: Proceedings of Measuring Behavior, vol. 2012, pp. 28–31. Citeseer (2012)

8. Delgado, F., Yang, S., Madaio, M., Yang, Q.: The participatory turn in AI design: theoretical foundations and the current state of practice. In: Proceedings of the 3rd ACM Conference on Equity and Access in Algorithms, Mechanisms, and Optimization, EAAMO 2023, pp. 1–23. Association for Computing Machinery, New York, October 2023. https://doi.org/10.1145/3617694.3623261. https://dl.acm.org/doi/10.1145/3617694.3623261

9. Dey, A., Billinghurst, M., Lindeman, R.W., Swan, J.E.: A systematic review of 10 years of augmented reality usability studies: 2005 to 2014. Front. Robot. AI 5 (2018). https://doi.org/10.3389/frobt.2018.00037. https://www.frontiersin.org/articles/10.3389/frobt.2018.00037

10. Duenser, A., Billinghurst, M.: Evaluating Augmented Reality Systems, pp. 289–307, July 2011. https://doi.org/10.1007/978-1-4614-0064-6_13

11. Endsley, M.: A systematic review and meta-analysis of direct objective measures of situation awareness: a comparison of SAGAT and SPAM. Hum. Factors J. Hum. Factors Ergon. Soc. 63, 124–150 (2021). https://doi.org/10.1177/0018720819875376

12. Endsley, M.R.: Situation awareness global assessment technique (SAGAT). In: Proceedings of the IEEE 1988 National Aerospace and Electronics Conference, vol. 3, pp. 789–795 (1988). https://api.semanticscholar.org/CorpusID:110229616

13. Endsley, M.R.: Measurement of situation awareness in dynamic systems. Hum. Factors J. Hum. Factors Ergon. Soc. 37(1), 65–84 (1995). https://doi.org/10.1518/001872095779049499. http://journals.sagepub.com/doi/10.1518/001872095779049499

14. Endsley, M.R.: Toward a theory of situation awareness in dynamic systems. In: Situational Awareness, pp. 9–42 (2017)

15. Engelbrecht, H., Lukosch, S.G.: Viability of augmented content for field policing. In: 2018 IEEE International Symposium on Mixed and Augmented Reality Adjunct (ISMAR-Adjunct), Munich, Germany, pp. 386–389. IEEE, October 2018. https://doi.org/10.1109/ISMAR-Adjunct.2018.00111. https://ieeexplore.ieee.org/document/8699296/

16. Forsman, V.: Measuring situation awareness in mixed reality simulations (2019)

17. Gidney, J.: The female factor: gender balance in law enforcement. Technical report, Europol (2013). https://shorturl.at/gDOTV

18. Hart, S.: Nasa-task load index (NASA-TLX); 20 years later, vol. 50, October 2006. https://doi.org/10.1177/154193120605000909

19. Hart, S.G., Staveland, L.E.: Development of NASA-TLX (task load index): results of empirical and theoretical research. In: Advances in Psychology, vol. 52, pp. 139–183. Elsevier (1988). https://doi.org/10.1016/S0166-4115(08)62386-9. https://linkinghub.elsevier.com/retrieve/pii/S0166411508623869

20. Huang, T.K., Yang, C.H., Hsieh, Y.H., Wang, J.C., Hung, C.C.: Augmented reality (AR) and virtual reality (VR) applied in dentistry. Kaohsiung J. Med. Sci. 34(4), 243–248 (2018). https://doi.org/10.1016/j.kjms.2018.01.009. https://www.sciencedirect.com/science/article/pii/S1607551X1730815X. Special Issue on Dental Research to celebrate KMUD 60th Anniversary

21. Karakostas, I., et al.: A real-time wearable AR system for egocentric vision on the edge. Virtual Real. (2024). https://doi.org/10.1007/s10055-023-00937-2

22. Kjeldskov, J., Skov, M.B.: Was it worth the hassle? Ten years of mobile HCI research discussions on lab and field evaluations. In: Proceedings of the 16th International Conference on Human-Computer Interaction with Mobile Devices & Services, MobileHCI 2014, pp. 43–52. Association for Computing Machinery, New York (2014). https://doi.org/10.1145/2628363.2628398

23. Kunkler, K.: The role of medical simulation: an overview. Int. J. Med. Robot. Comput. Assist. Surg. **2**(3), 203–210 (2006). https://doi.org/10.1002/rcs.101. https://onlinelibrary.wiley.com/doi/abs/10.1002/rcs.101

24. Körber, M.: Theoretical considerations and development of a questionnaire to measure trust in automation, March 2018

25. Lewis, J.R., Utesch, B.S., Maher, D.E.: UMUX-LITE: when there's no time for the SUS. In: Proceedings of the SIGCHI Conference on Human Factors in Computing Systems, Paris, France, pp. 2099–2102. ACM, April 2013. https://doi.org/10.1145/2470654.2481287. https://dl.acm.org/doi/10.1145/2470654.2481287

26. Margetis, G., Ntoa, S., Antona, M., Stephanidis, C.: Human-centered design of artificial intelligence. In: Handbook of Human Factors and Ergonomics, pp. 1085–1106. Wiley (2021). https://doi.org/10.1002/9781119636113.ch42. https://onlinelibrary.wiley.com/doi/abs/10.1002/9781119636113.ch42

27. Mohseni, S., Zarei, N., Ragan, E.D.: A multidisciplinary survey and framework for design and evaluation of explainable ai systems. ACM Trans. Interact. Intell. Syst. **11**(3-4) (2021). https://doi.org/10.1145/3387166

28. Novović, S., Vla, S., Rakić, N.: Establishing the Southeast Europe women police officers network. Technical report, Southeast Europe Police Chiefs Association, September 2010. https://www.seesac.org/f/tmp/files/publication/827.pdf

29. Ntoa, S., Margetis, G., Antona, M., Stephanidis, C.: User experience evaluation in intelligent environments: a comprehensive framework. Technologies **9**(2), 41 (2021). https://doi.org/10.3390/technologies9020041. https://www.mdpi.com/2227-7080/9/2/41

30. Polit, D., Beck, C., Owen, S.: Is the CVI an acceptable indicator of content validity? Appraisal and recommendations. Res. Nurs. Health **30**, 459–67 (2007). https://doi.org/10.1002/nur.20199

31. Quandt, M., Stern, H., Zeitler, W., Freitag, M.: Human-centered design of cognitive assistance systems for industrial work. Procedia CIRP **107**, 233–238 (2022). https://doi.org/10.1016/j.procir.2022.04.039. https://www.sciencedirect.com/science/article/pii/S2212827122002554, leading manufacturing systems transformation – Proceedings of the 55th CIRP Conference on Manufacturing Systems 2022

32. Sheikh, S., Bin Heyat, M.B., AlShorman, O., Masadeh, M., Alkahatni, F.: A review of usability evaluation techniques for augmented reality systems in education. In: 2021 Innovation and New Trends in Engineering, Science and Technology Education Conference (IETSEC), pp. 1–6 (2021). https://doi.org/10.1109/IETSEC51476.2021.9440506

33. Starcke, K., Wiesen, C., Trotzke, P., Brand, M.: Effects of acute laboratory stress on executive functions. Front. Psychol. **7** (2016). https://doi.org/10.3389/fpsyg.2016.00461. https://www.frontiersin.org/journals/psychology/articles/10.3389/fpsyg.2016.00461

34. Stefanidi, Z., Margetis, G., Ntoa, S., Papagiannakis, G.: Real-time adaptation of context-aware intelligent user interfaces, for enhanced situational awareness. IEEE Access **10**, 23367–23393 (2022). https://doi.org/10.1109/ACCESS.2022.3152743

35. Taherdoost, H.: A review of technology acceptance and adoption models and theories. Procedia Manuf. **22**, 960–967 (2018). https://doi.org/10.1016/j.promfg.2018.03.137

36. Tan, Y., Zalzuli, A., Ang, J., Ho, H., Tan, C.: Understanding the workload of police investigators: a human factors approach. J. Police Crim. Psychol. **37** (2022). https://doi.org/10.1007/s11896-022-09506-w

37. Tombaugh, T.: A comprehensive review of the Paced Auditory Serial Addition Test (PASAT). Arch. Clin. Neuropsychol. **21**(1), 53–76 (2006). https://doi.org/10.1016/j.acn.2005.07.006. https://academic.oup.com/acn/article-lookup/doi/10.1016/j.acn.2005.07.006

38. Tsinikos, V., et al.: Real-time activity recognition for surveillance applications on edge devices. In: Proceedings of the 16th International Conference on PErvasive Technologies Related to Assistive Environments, PETRA 2023, pp. 293–299. Association for Computing Machinery, New York (2023). https://doi.org/10.1145/3594806.3594823

39. Tullis, T., Albert, W.: Measuring the User Experience: Collecting, Analyzing, and Presenting Usability Metrics, 2nd edn. Morgan Kaufmann Publishers Inc., San Francisco (2008)

40. Venkatesh, V., Morris, M.G., Davis, G.B., Davis, F.D.: User acceptance of information technology: toward a unified view. Inst. Transit. Econ. Microecon. Issues eJournal (2003). https://api.semanticscholar.org/CorpusID:14435677

41. Venkatesh, V.: Adoption and use of AI tools: a research agenda grounded in UTAUT. Ann. Oper. Res. **308** (2022). https://doi.org/10.1007/s10479-020-03918-9

42. Yogesh, K.D., Nripendra, P.R., Kuttimani, T., Ramakrishnan, R.: A meta-analysis based modified unified theory of acceptance and use of technology (meta-UTAUT): a review of emerging literature. Curr. Opin. Psychol. **36**, 13–18 (2020). https://doi.org/10.1016/j.copsyc.2020.03.008. https://www.sciencedirect.com/science/article/pii/S2352250X20300373, cyberpsychology

Enhancing Cognition Through Cooperative Learning and Augmented Mentorship

Michael-Brian Ogawa[1]([⊠]), Rita M. Vick[2], Barbara Endicott-Popovsky[1],
Ran J. Hinrichs[3], Alejandro D. Ayala[4], Sean Mosier[1], and Martha E. Crosby[1]

[1] University of Hawai'i at Mānoa, Honolulu, HI 96822, USA
{ogawam,bendicot,smosier,crosby}@hawaii.edu
[2] RMVick Consulting, Trenton, MI 48183, USA
[3] Norwich University, Northfield, VT 05663, USA
rhinrich@norwich.edu
[4] University of Washington, Seattle, WA 98195, USA
aayala@uw.edu

Abstract. With increasing cybercrime, educational institutions are working to create increased opportunities for people to enter the cyber workforce. Some programs are expanding their entry criteria to include those from a wider variety of backgrounds. This two-part study uses augmented cognition approaches to identify how individual differences can influence instructional design for security education. Higher levels of variance and time on task typically led to lower performance. In addition, the design of content (internal and external content) influenced performance and time on task, where external supplemental content led to increased effort and lower outcomes.

Keywords: Security education · augmented cognition · instructional design

1 Introduction

Between 2018 and 2022, the Federal Bureau of Investigation (FBI) reported that cyber-crime increased 380% over the five-year period. They received 3.26 million complaints about cyber-crime, which resulted in a reported loss of $27.6 billion [4]. Of which, $10.3 billion in losses were reported in 2022 alone. These statistics highlight the growing trend in cyber-crime and illustrate that it is continuously growing. Therefore, there is a high need for security professional in the workforce to protect assets of organizations and individuals. There is an approximate need for 1.7 million cyber security professionals in the United States [3]. However, approximately one-third of these positions remain unfilled and is expected to continuously grow based on the rapid growth in cyber-crime [2]. Educational institutions developed cyber security education programs to account for this need starting primarily with master's program and expanding to certificates and other micro credentials.

© The Author(s), under exclusive license to Springer Nature Switzerland AG 2024
D. D. Schmorrow and C. M. Fidopiastis (Eds.): HCII 2024, LNAI 14694, pp. 220–232, 2024.
https://doi.org/10.1007/978-3-031-61569-6_14

1.1 Cybersecurity Education

Approaches to Cyber security education and training includes theoretical models [1, 10] and practical simulation approaches [5, 6]. [1] conducted a meta-analysis of extant literature to identify features that can create learning situations with effective outcomes. These generally included an evaluation of evaluation criteria, conducting a needs assessment, and identifying a match between skill/task and training method. Cognitive modeling in cyber security education was also studied [10], where multiple models such as standalone model (network modeling, pure simulations, hybrid networking emulation), tracing for attacker behavior prediction, and model tracing for automation. They found that these models were more accurate with precise predictions when they were customized to reflect the population's tendencies. Although larger models of education and training like these exist, other studies focused on specific approaches such simulation and game-based mechanics [5, 6]. These approaches typically utilize a directed learning approach focusing on specific objectives followed by task-performance behaviors. These task-performance behaviors may be in the form of educational/serious games within a simulation. Specific approaches tended to improve motivation and learning by melding it with entertainment characteristics. Game-based mechanics such as capture the flag [8], can improve engagement for learners by offering a hands-on cyber challenge that is rooted in real-world scenarios. Many of these scenarios are offered in virtual machine environments to allow learners to attempt real defense and attack scenarios within a safe environment.

In addition to overarching approaches to cyber security education, other studies targeted specific methods of learning computer security concepts [7, 9, 11]. [7] studied the impact of perceptions of risk and secure behaviors. They found that the largest impact on out-of-class secure behaviors came from a combination of mini lectures and active learning tasks. This approach helped to change actual behaviors outside the classroom such as modifying passwords after data breaches. [9] reviewed the different levels of learning using similar constructs with static and animated content. The authors found that static content was generally more effective when paired with more complex concepts such as mathematical content such as encryption. Animated content was generally more useful for practical applications such as visualizing a distributed denial of service attack. [11] researched a specific approach to cyber security education, Present-Test-Practice-Assess (PTPA). This approach used the four major components: 1) Present: target s single set of related concepts, 2) Test: check understanding through an assessment of learning, 3) Practice: opportunities to apply concepts learned and 4) Assess: evaluation of performance on practice tasks. This method of instruction utilized live activities (simulations) to create replicate real-world scenarios. They found that the PTPA was more effective than traditional approaches that added capture the flag activities and hackathons.

These studies highlighted the importance of unveiling instructional approaches that best benefit cyber security education. Due to the large gap between total positions and positions filled, it may be helpful to expand the pool of applicants with individuals from a range of backgrounds. This study aims to distill one of the major approaches to learning, case studies in cyber security education when the participants have a wide range of backgrounds. We focused our efforts on time on task based on individual differences, performance alignment, and how it can influence security education design.

The following questions guided the study:

1. How does students' time on task influence their ability to accomplish assignments?
2. What types of approaches are best aligned with performance?
3. How can student differences influence security education design?

2 Exploratory Analytics

2.1 Setting and Participants

The exploratory study was conducted with students enrolled in a Cybersecurity Education program, CyberEd in a Box. This cybersecurity educational program was designed to build capacity to fill the need for professionals in the cybersecurity workforce. Due to workforce gap and wide range of cybersecurity positions available, this program invites students from any field to enroll, not just computer science. Approximately 20 students are enrolled in the program each year and come from a wide range of academic backgrounds such as Computer Science, Engineering, Information Systems, Business, Management, Marketing, Education, Psychology, and Sociology. The program includes three courses, mentoring and an overarching internship that occurs throughout the program (Fig. 1). Each of the courses includes three major components: 1) tech labs, 2) projects and 3) discussions. Tech labs focus building information technology security skills such as networking, network defense, and ethical hacking. Projects target critical thinking skills in information security and risk management by having students complete case studies to determine appropriate actions in a chief security officer role with a range of security issues such as data breaches and information leakage. Discussions give students the opportunity to build their network by sharing resources with their peers and offering feedback to one another to build the community of practitioners throughout the term. Based on these major areas of each course, the researchers explored the projects portion due to the broad range of critical thinking and learning skills taught.

The initial study included 17 participants enrolled in class 3. These students came from a wide range of educational backgrounds and were at the ending of their program of study, which allowed them to hone their study skills over the course of the CyberEd in a Box program. Therefore, the final class would limit the initial influence of students getting acclimated to a new program of study.

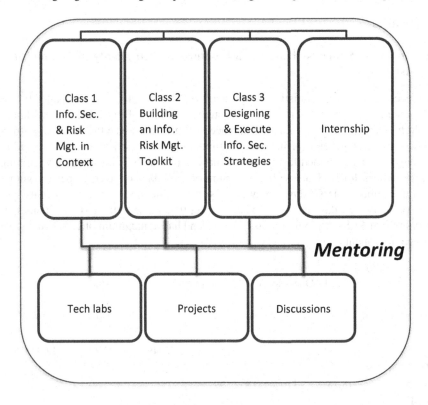

Fig. 1. CyberEd in a Box Program structure

2.2 Project Tasks

The course included five major projects with each project including two to three tasks each based on case study complexity. Data were collected based on initial opening of a case study in the course management system and submission of each assignment. The CyberEd in a Box program is a professional program that assesses assignments on a meets or does not meet professional standards. Thus, data were also collected based on number of submissions to meet the professional standard.

2.3 Analysis

The data were analyzed using a repeated measures design to determine the time on task for each student and how it differed throughout the term. We used an analysis of variance to determine the individual differences between users and identified different clusters based on metrics such as performance, variance, and time on task. Data were aligned with course content analysis to determine difficulty of task and possible approaches to improve cognition through appropriate mentoring and support.

3   Results

3.1   How Does Students' Time on Task Influence Their Ability to Accomplish Assignments?

As expected, there was a statistically significant difference between participants' time on task based on each component of the case studies with p < .001 (Table 1). This finding highlights individual differences and the need to further analyze the data to determine a descriptive background for the data set to identify clusters for performance and the challenge of each assigned task. The summary data (Table 2) illustrates a wide range of time on task for students with a minimum of 1.07 days on average per assignment and a maximum of 18.67 days on average per assignment. On average, students spent approximately 7.34 days per assigned task. Over the course of the term, students spent a minimum of 11.84 days on the class projects and had a maximum of 205.39 days. The average time spent on project tasks was 80.79 days.

Table 1. One-Way ANOVA for time on task for case studies

Source of Variation	SS	df	MS	F	P-value	F crit
Between Groups	5852.248	16	365.7655	2.736949	0.000652	1.703315
Within Groups	22718.78	170	133.6399			
Total	28571.03	186				

We clustered the data by total number of resubmissions by individual to determine performance based on time on task. Three groups emerged, 1) those without any resubmissions, 2) those with a single resubmission, and 3) those with two resubmissions. Based on these groupings, students with the least variance and time on task were in either the no resubmission or one resubmission groupings. Six students in this cluster spent on average one to two days on each task and had a variance less than 10. Two of which had one resubmission while the rest of the group did not resubmit any assignments. Ten of the remaining 11 students had a variance in time over 100. Only one student in this group had a variance of 62. The cluster with the variance mainly above 100 included six students with zero resubmissions, one student with one resubmission, and four students with 2 resubmissions. It appears that the higher the variance in time on each task tended to have participants with increased levels of submission to attain a professional level of performance on case studies.

To determine task challenge, we created a stacked bar chart to identify patterns in the data (Fig. 2). Assignments 3 and 4 appeared to have the greatest range in assignment completion. We conducted an ANOVA on the time spent per assignment, however, the results were not statistically significant (p > .05). The variance for these assignments were the highest of all assignments at 394.56 for assignment 3 and 339.00 for assignment

Table 2. Summary data for time on task across case studies

Groups	Count	Sum	Average	Variance	Resubmission
1	11	132.0029	12.00027	244.9879	0
2	11	18.70464	1.700422	9.141954	0
3	11	76.90679	6.991527	135.2517	0
4	11	14.81988	1.347262	2.273724	1
5	11	72.97556	6.634141	100.5736	0
6	11	205.394	18.67218	199.8102	2
7	11	48.93757	4.44887	101.2293	0
8	11	131.9491	11.99537	291.9185	1
9	11	65.71566	5.974151	140.1004	2
10	11	19.20168	1.745607	1.71381	0
11	11	114.2145	10.38314	121.4065	2
12	11	189.5093	17.22812	609.6	0
13	11	19.67366	1.788514	3.282195	0
14	11	11.84257	1.076597	2.158005	0
15	11	12.53883	1.139894	1.25678	1
16	11	94.91159	8.628326	62.64685	0
17	11	144.0921	13.09928	244.5265	2

4. Interestingly, these two assignments were a part of the same case study. This led the researchers to conduct a content analysis on the case studies to identify major differences which could lead to the disparity in time spent to achieve a professional level submission for this project.

All of the projects included an introduction page (Fig. 3), lecture videos page, case study page and submission page. The introduction page included the learning objectives, workflow details and resources (internal and external). The lecture videos page included each of the videos to support the case study, while the case study page detailed the case and the guidelines for the project. The case study for assignments 3 and 4 included external sites that needed to be utilized to solve the case. Based on a content analysis of all of the case studies, this one in particular included a greater dependency on the use of information external to the course management system. Students needed to search an external site to identify and utilize pertinent information that was not directly discussed in the case study video. Therefore, it appears that requiring the use of external content may have influenced the time spent for individual students on this assignment. This preliminary finding led us to continue this line of research deeper in a subsequent study.

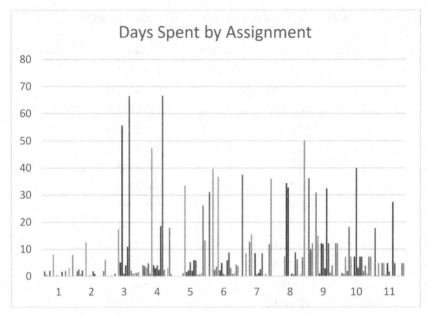

Fig. 2. Average days spent on each case study task

4 External and Internal Content Study

4.1 Background

Since the cyber security education program, we analyzed targeted participants from a wide range of majors, we conducted the follow-up study with a large-enrollment computer science course for non-majors that is a prerequisite for many fields, such as education, business, kinesiology, etc. It is a 101-level course focused on general computer science topics and productivity. The course we examined was a 6-week asynchronous summer session, which has two lecture topics per week that students are quizzed on. In addition, students do lab work utilizing productivity software. One of the units was focused on computer security, where the students were to watch the lecture video which was under 30 min. This video linked out to other videos in the lecture, and students were instructed to pause the lecture video and view the external video, and then return. After watching the video, students would take a quiz on the lecture topics, which included the external video topics. To prevent cheating, the quiz questions were taken as a random draw from a larger question pool.

4.2 What Types of Approaches are Best Aligned with Performance?

We collected user page view data to determine how long each student spent on each question, along with the student scores on the quizzes. We also performed an item analysis on the question to see how difficult it was for students, and how well a question discriminated between the top and bottom scores.

Reading/Resources Assigned - Focus Points

Assigned Resources	Description/Context	Focus Points tied to objectives
Short Lecture: **The Models of this Program: The Decision-Making Model for Capstone**	*Dr. Endicott-Popovsky reviews the thinking models of this program, adding one for decision-making, a managerial model.*	• Explain the program models from Course 1 to Course 3 and derive a personal philosophy on the general application of models in cybersecurity strategy. • Synthesize your thinking about decision-making in the cybersecurity field.
Case Study: Breach of HIPAA Protected Information?	*In this first more complex case, analyze the context of a possible HIPAA breach by studying the case presentation. Video lecture has also been included.* *Come to a decision on whether a HIPAA breach has occurred, and what the resolution should be.*	• Apply case analysis skills to a case involving a possible HIPAA breach. • Practice risk assessment and documentation. • Identify at least three essential questions that framed your approach to the case. • Engage in peer review of others' resolutions. • Compare and contrast your own resolution to the one given by the practitioner.
HIPAA: HHS.gov Health Information Privacy site ⬚	This site provides a search for specific HIPAA questions. For example, you can search for "breach notification requirements" to find notification rules that apply to this case.	• Apply case analysis skills to a case involving a possible HIPAA breach. ○ Conduct strategic research of applicable regulations and requirements.

Fig. 3. Sample resources section of introduction page

We then categorized the content of the lecture material and corresponding questions into recent history, types of criminals, general aspects of security, and typical attacks. Our latter three topics were chosen based on being the topics emphasized in computer security textbooks. Our first category, recent history, was chosen because this can have a strong impact in changing student opinions and practices when they can see how it relates to their lives. We first wanted to see if there was a difference between the performance or time spent on the questions in different content sections. A one-way ANOVA analysis was performed on the performance of different content categories and on the time spent on questions between content areas. The results for the performance are seen in the table below, and showed they were nearing a trend in the difference between content areas with $p = 0.11$ (Tables 3 and 4). The one-way ANOVA for the time spent showed no significant difference in time spent on questions between content areas.

Even though there was no significant difference between the time spent on questions between content areas, we noticed that there was a large amount of time spent on specific questions of the "recent history" category. Based on the descriptive statistics, we could see that the "recent history" category had the lowest performance, but the most amount of time spent. We conducted a one-way ANOVA and found a statistically significant difference between the performance on each question. An examination of the item difficulty and item discrimination value showed that the questions with the worst performance and highest discrimination were based on external video questions (Table 5).

Table 3. Summary data for performance between categories

Groups	Count	Sum	Average	Variance
Recent history	12	10.19874	0.849895	0.028213
Criminal types	4	3.847118	0.961779	0.002502
Aspects of security	3	3	1	0
Typical attacks	6	5.859307	0.976551	0.001567

Table 4. One-way ANOVA on performance between content categories

Source of Variation	SS	df	MS	F	P-value	F crit
Between Groups	0.103987	3	0.034662	2.235038	0.113986	3.072467
Within Groups	0.32568	21	0.015509			
Total	0.429667	24				

As a result, we reviewed questions in this section and identified certain questions that required students to review content from an external video linked in the lecture video, compared to other questions that could be answered solely on the lecture video. We performed a one-way ANOVA (Tables 6 and 7) and found a statistical significance difference between external and internal questions ($P < 0.004$), with external questions only receiving 76% correct, and internal content receiving 94% correct.

We performed the same analyses to examine the time spent on each question, and the time spent on each question in internal and external content. The one-way ANOVA showed a statistically significant difference between time spent on each of the questions in the recent history category ($P = 0.00$) and a statistically significant difference in time spent on each question between internal and external content to the lecture ($P = 0.00$), seen in Tables 8 and 9. The difference here was quite large, with external content taking more than six times as long as internal content.

We performed the same analyses to examine the time spent on each question, and the time spent on each question in internal and external content. The one-way ANOVA showed a statistically significant difference between time spent on each of the questions in the recent history category ($P = 0.00$) and a statistically significant difference in time spent on each question between internal and external content to the lecture ($P = 0.00$), seen in Tables 8 and 9. The difference here was quite large, with external content taking more than six times as long as internal content.

Table 5. Item difficulty and discrimination value of recent history questions

SUMMARY - Score

Groups	Count	Sum	Average	Variance	Discrim
According to the Heartbleed video, a set of open source tools is a common implementation between S.S.L and T.L.S.	23	20	87%	0.118577	0.5
According to the Heartbleed video, how long has Heartbleed been around?	24	12	50%	0.26087	1
According to the Heartbleed video, Open S.S.L runs on _____ percent of the Internet.	17	12	71%	0.220588	1
According to the Heartbleed video, what is in the root of Heartbleed?	25	20	80%	0.166667	.83
According to the Phishing video, what information do they want from you?	16	15	94%	0.0625	.25
A computer on a public university network gets attacked more than 2,000 times a day.	17	17	100%	0	0
According to Google, how many new malicious websites are found every day?	12	11	92%	0.083333	.33
In 2008, how many computer viruses were in circulation?	22	20	91%	0.08658	.33
People who attack public networks look for _____ on computers.	17	12	71%	0.220588	1
Which mobile device has a recorded number of 744,000 viruses?	21	20	95%	0.047619	.2
Which of the following networks is constantly being attacked by hackers?	22	22	100%	0	0
You only need to change your passwords to be safe from Heartbleed.	23	23	100%	0	0

Table 6. Summary data for performance between external and internal content

Groups	Count	Sum	Average	Variance
AveExt	25	19	76%	0.07037
AveInt	23	21.69048	94%	0.012716

4.3 How Can Student Differences Influence Security Education Design?

Examining the results, questions based on content contained within the video required less time to answer and resulted in higher scores for students. Conversely, questions based on content contained in external videos required more time and resulted in lower scores and a higher item discrimination value. While the external videos were integrated to provide additional animated content to increase student engagement with the material, this seems to have been detrimental to student learning. This may have occurred because of the increased cognitive load in having students perform additional tasks.

Alternatively, this may have occurred because students were spending time looking up answers in the lecture and external videos. Using page view statistics, we can see

Table 7. One-way ANOVA on performance between external and internal content

Source of Variation	SS	df	MS	F	P-value	F crit
Between Groups	0.401452	1	0.401452	9.380484	0.003658	4.051749
Within Groups	1.968638	46	0.042796			
Total	2.37009	47				

Table 8. Summary data for time spent per question between internal and external quiz Content

Groups	Count	Sum	Average	Variance
AveExternal	25	1920.3	76.812	824.9162
AveInternal	23	296.4881	12.89079	10.1804

Table 9. One-way ANOVA on time spent per question between internal and external quiz content

Source of Variation	SS	df	MS	F	P-value	F crit
Between Groups	48945.93	1	48945.93	112.4522	0.00	4.051749
Within Groups	20021.96	46	435.2599			
Total	68967.89	47				

some indications of answer-seeking behavior. There were 32 unique views, with only half watching the video in its entirety. Other views spiked at locations we could trace back to answers in the video. This might also indicate that some students may not have watched the external videos prior to starting the quiz or had to go back to check the answers. This would explain the significantly greater time spent on these questions. The item discrimination could also be explained by students who did not watch the external videos at all, as some students already did not watch the internal lecture videos. For example, 35 people took the quiz but page view statistics on the video show that at most only 32 students clicked on the lecture video. Given that watching the external video required more work, even less students may have reviewed the external video.

5 Discussion

5.1 Conclusions and Future Directions

The initial study focused on exploratory analytics from the CyberEd in a Box program that included students from a range of educational backgrounds. The individual differences between students led the research team to identify clusters of students based on performance, time on task, and resubmission rate. These major groupings highlighted the optimal approaches to studying in this environment, spending a consistent amount of time on task for each of the projects. This group spent on average 7.34 days per assignment with a variance under 10 meeting the professional requirements in the first or second submission. The high level of variance in the two-resubmission group led us to our follow-up study to examine the course content and potential underlying reasons for the lower performance.

Our follow-up external and internal content study sought to examine the impact of techniques to reduce variance in time spent with the material and determine its influence on performance. While external videos were implemented to enhance attention, engagement, and learning, the scores and time spent seem to indicate otherwise. While examining the data and potential roadblocks to their learning, we have found that this might have instead made the barrier to entry too high for some, and they did not engage with the content. As a result, we would recommend embedding case study videos or external data within the main course content, since students who are not majoring in computer science may be less willing to view external content than computer science majors. Interestingly, this finding mirrored information in our first study's data set, many students did not click on the external resources provided for many of the case studies.

These complementary studies highlighted the need for further research in computer security education using augmented cognition-based approaches. With the increase in demand for security professionals and computer security programs broadening their entry point to include non-technical individuals, it is vital to consider individual differences amongst students. We would like to conduct further research on embedded learning scenarios to immerse students in their educational experience and optimize their learning. These future studies could be conducted on a range of learning objectives including technical skills, conceptual knowledge, and applied scenarios. Increasing the technical skillset of those enrolled in security programs may take place in simulation-based environments. Many of which include a detailed breakdown of time and click data based on capture-the-flag events. These types of data could be analyzed to determine potential changes to the system to improve long-term learning. Analysis of conceptual learning can take place using a wide range of tools such as quizzes/tests and assignments. Both offer the possibility of utilizing augmented cognition approaches to improve instructional design techniques for assessments and learning material. We are also interested in application of learning through embedded scenarios. Immersive virtual worlds could give students the opportunity to be immersed in learning environments that could be utilized as "live case studies." These worlds may be rich in data and opportunities to augment student development. Computer security education continues to evolve in programmatic opportunities for a wide range of individuals and in its approaches in the learning sciences.

Acknowledgements. This material is based on work that was partially supported by Grant No. 1662487 from the National Science Foundation (NSF) and by Grant No. H98230-22-1-0329 from the National Security Agency (NSA), National Centers of Academic Excellence in Cybersecurity.

References

1. Arthur, W., Bennett, W., Edens, P., Bell, T.: Effectiveness of training in organizations: a meta-analysis of design and evaluation features. J. Appl. Psychol. **88**(2), 234–245 (2003)
2. Cobaj, K., Domingos, D., Kotulski, Z., Respício, A.: Cybersecurity education: evolution of the discipline and analysis of master program. Comput. Secur. **75**, 24–35 (2018)
3. CyberSeek. Cybersecurity supply/demand heat map (2023). https://www.cyberseek.org/heatmap.html
4. Federal Bureau of Investigation (2023). Federal Bureau of Investigation Internet Crime Report (2022). https://www.ic3.gov/
5. Jalali, M., Siegel, M., Madnick, S.: Decision-making and biases in cybersecurity capability development: evidence from a simulation game. J. Strat. Inf. Syst. **28**(1), 66–82 (2019)
6. Jin, G., Tu, M., Kim, T., Heffron, J., White, J.: Game based cybersecurity training for high school students. In: Proceedings of ACM SIGCSE, Baltimore, MD, pp. 68–73 (2018)
7. Ogawa, M.B., Auernheimer, B., Endicott-Popovsky, B., Hinrichs, R., Crosby. M.E.: Privacy and security perceptions in augmented cognition applications. In: Schmorrow, D., Fidopiastis, C. (eds.) Foundations of Augmented Cognition 17th International Conference, AC Proceedings, Proceedings, vol. 17. Springer, Heidelberg (2023). https://doi.org/10.1007/978-3-031-35017-7_27
8. Svabensky, V., Celeda, P., Vykopal, J., Brisakova, S.: Cybersecurity knowledge and skills taught in capture the flag challenges. Comput. Secur. **102**, 1–14 (2021)
9. Taylor, M., Baskett, M., Allen, M., Francis, H., Kifayat, K.: Animation as an aid to support the teaching of cyber security concepts. Innov. Educ. Teach. Int. **55**(5), 532–542 (2018)
10. Veksler, V., Buckler, N., Hoffman, B., Cassenti, D., Sugrim, S.: Simulations in cybersecurity: a review of cognitive modeling of network attackers, defenders, and users. Front. Psychol. **9**, 1–12 (2018)
11. Workman, M.D., Luevanos, J.A., Mai, B.: A study of cybersecurity education using a present-test-practice-assess model. IEEE Trans. Educ. **65**(1), 40–45 (2022)

Digital Twins and Extended Reality for Tailoring Better Adapted Cybersecurity Trainings in Critical Infrastructures

Eloïse Zehnder[1]([envelope]) [ID], Leanne Torgersen[2][ID], Torvald F. Ask[2][ID],
Benjamin J. Knox[2], Holger Morgenstern[3][ID], Jeroen Gaiser[4],
Yannick Naudet[1][ID], Alexeis Garcia Perez[5][ID], and Cristoph Stahl[1][ID]

[1] Luxembourg Institute of Science and Technology, 5 Av. des Hauts-Fourneaux, 4362
Esch-sur-Alzette, Luxembourg
{eloise.zehnder,yannick.naudet,christoph.stahl}@list.lu

[2] Østfold University College, B R A Veien 4, 1757 Halden, Norway
{leanne.torgersen,torvald.f.ask,benjamin.knox}@hiof.no

[3] Hochschule Albstadt-Sigmaringen, Anton-Günther-Straße 51, 72488 Sigmaringen,
Germany
morgenstern@hs-albsig.de

[4] Ministerie van Infrastructuur en Waterstaat, Rijnstraat 8, 2515 XP Den Haag,
Netherlands
jeroen.gaiser@minienw.nl

[5] Aston Business School, Aston University, Birmingham, UK
alexeis.garciaperez@aston.ac.uk

Abstract. Due to their value and interconnected role in our societies, critical infrastructures are vulnerable national assets increasingly becoming targets of cyber-attacks. Despite there being a multitude of training programs in cybersecurity offered, human errors are still accountable for a majority of breaches. As current training and awareness courses are insufficient to meet the current cybersecurity challenges in critical infrastructures, this paper examines how they could be improved with new solutions. In addition to current training programs lacking in effectively addressing human factors, identifying appropriate outcome and performance measures to assess the effectiveness of the program remains an issue. In order to address the uniqueness of an individual's human factors and natural learning trajectory, the need for tailored training programs, to meet the demands of each user and influence a change in cyber-behavior, is proposed. These tailored training programs would be enhanced with the inclusion of training aids such as Digital Twins and Extended Reality. Indeed, recent works started to explore how combining Digital Twins and Augmented or Virtual reality could enhance learning in different contexts. We have studied how some human features could be replicated and used in the digital twin technologies (such as personality, attention, emotions or age and gender), as well as the human factors enhanced in the overall simulated virtual experience (embodiment, engagement, situational awareness, collaboration). However, there

© The Author(s), under exclusive license to Springer Nature Switzerland AG 2024
D. D. Schmorrow and C. M. Fidopiastis (Eds.): HCII 2024, LNAI 14694, pp. 233–252, 2024.
https://doi.org/10.1007/978-3-031-61569-6_15

are still ongoing challenges and ethical concerns with such solutions. We conclude with a discussion of future directions.

Keywords: Cybersecurity training · Extended Reality · Human Factors

1   Introduction

The importance of cybersecurity has grown in the wake of technological advancements, and its criticality is emphasized as the ungoverned Internet of Things (IoT) expands. The ongoing digitalization of critical infrastructures (CI) has been dubbed the fourth industrial revolution [1]. Today's CIs are not isolated environments but "systems-of-systems" connected to the internet, creating an exclusive technical ecosystem with sensors, video surveillance cameras, and computers [2]. The growing role, function, and technological advancement of cyberspace in global security geopolitics means that CIs have become high-value targets and vulnerable to cyber-attacks which have risen in recent years [3]. The cyber-threat to operational technology (OT) systems was first brought to public attention in 2010 by the Stuxnet computer worm attack, which targeted programmable logic controllers used to automate machine processes in Iran's nuclear facilities. Moreover, a growing "community of practice" including a large cross-section of states and private sector actors is emerging in the area of CI protection that is spreading internationally [4]. These attacks can be nation-state sponsored and carried out by highly skilled and well-funded operators. Due to the potential for physical damage and human casualties from cyber-attacks targeting industrial control systems, critical infrastructure protection, has gained increased attention in the worldwide industrial environment. Attacks on CIs have the potential to disrupt and paralyse national resources because of their sensitivity and criticality [5]. Due to their interconnectivity, a disruptive effect on one infrastructure can cause a chain of failures in other CIs [6]. Consequently, the European Parliament has urged EU member states to work cooperatively with their armed forces and cybersecurity measures, along with NATO and other partners. While setting policy goals and implemented programs to secure CIs, the NIS2 directive also explicitly addresses the human factor in cyber-resilience and mandates training [7].

Despite investments being made to promote cyber-resilient practices, human errors still account for 31% of security breaches in industrial firms [8] while stolen data, frequently acquired through social engineering attacks, are the source of 80% of data breaches [9]. These "*major security failures could be the result of not poor security solutions but of security behavior*" (p.2) [10]. Studies have demonstrated the ineffectiveness of security methods that focus only on hardware and software security [12,13] and argued the need for training programs to take human factors into account to increase cybersecurity awareness and cyber-hygiene practices. Indeed, cybercriminals primarily gain access to critical infrastructures through the exploitation of human factors with social engineering, online harassment, identity-related attacks, hacking and/or denial of service or information [14].

The aims of this paper are firstly to discuss what has been offered to date in forms of cybersecurity training while not addressing human factors effectively enough, and the need for tailored and measurable training programs to meet the demands of each user and potentially influence a real change in cyber-behavior. As there is more of a shift towards personalized training, the second objective of this paper is to determine how and which tools and methods (e.g. Digital Twins) could effectively support each individual's cybersecurity training needs and thus address each individual's human factors.

2   The State of Cybersecurity Training

2.1   The Context of Operational Technology

The exposure of an organization to attackers is referred to as the attack surface which includes the human element. Targeting the human element to breach the defenses of organizations is commonplace in IT. Attacks on CI, e.g. in 2015 on the Ukrainian power grid [15], Colonial Pipeline in the US in 2021 [16] and a Pennsylvania water authority in 2023 [17] show that exploiting the human factor is an available vector in OT as well.

It is therefore important to approach resilience in the human factor in OT in the same manner as IT. Most training aimed at increasing resiliency here is focused on the IT environment. Although the underlying technical aspects might be similar (e.g. the use of file transfer, software, and USB drives), the operating environment where OT is implemented is physically very different (e.g. a factory floor, platform at sea, or control room) than an office environment, leading to a form factor to be more resilient to environmental extremes. The use of OT is more homogeneous in relation to an IT environment. For instance, the operation of a bridge is restricted to a very limited set of predictable actions compared to the heterogeneous office environment, where the potential actions of use vary significantly. The systems and interfaces in OT are tailored to predetermined actions focused on reliable operation in a wide range of environmental conditions. Whereas an IT environment is tailored for a wide range of uses in an indoor environment. As a result, simulated training delivered in an office environment will be less recognizable and applicable in the control room of a petrochemical plant. Therefore, training aimed at users of OT should be tailored to the environment in which the lessons learned are applied [18].

2.2   Current Approaches to Cybersecurity Training

Cybersecurity education and training within organizations and to end users have become the norm. There have been a multitude of cyber-training programs offered with the goal of enhancing cybersecurity knowledge, improving cyber-secure skills, and changing the attitudes of its participants to increase cyber-hygiene practices within an organization. Because cybersecurity incidents due to employee misuse or noncompliance continue, the question about the effectiveness of these training programs is raised. Today, multiple cybersecurity training methods are proposed and implemented, including: 1) cybersecurity awareness training, 2) personalized training, 3) cybersecurity education, 4) wargaming approaches including cyber-defense exercises and tabletop exercises, 5) gamification, 6) and those that incorporate extended reality (virtual reality, mixed reality, and augmented reality).

The conventional learning approaches have been referred to as awareness training. This approach ensures an acquisition of core concepts (network security, cryptography, and ethical hacking) and commonly take the form of online courses (MOOC), in-person lectures or presentations, or the distribution of flyers and emails. Awareness campaigns are compliance-based methods that have been criticized for being largely ineffective [19], which can be attributed to a flawed view of employees/users' awareness as the problem as opposed to organizational factors such as culture being conflicting with security goals [19,20]. Indeed, the lack of security awareness is not the issue, but rather other challenges, such as overconfidence, lack of suspicion, and cognitive factors which also applies to IT professionals [21–23].

In comparison, to the previous approaches, the personalized (or human-centric) training approach [19] recognizes that individuals can be at different points in their learning trajectories with different obstacles to surmount on an individual-level (mostly through cognitive factors). Organizational resilience against cyber-threats requires active participation and engagement from all employees [19]. Cybersecurity education has been criticized for not sufficiently addressing the skills needed to meet the cognitive challenges associated with socio-technical working-environments and for its lack of focus on human factor issues [19,24–26]. As a result, educational guidelines and frameworks were proposed by NIST or ENISA [27,28], proposing cybersecurity roles with a set of knowledge, skills, and abilities (KSAs) for each [27], but without specifying the methods for training or the psychological skills related to performing those KSAs. In addition, the inclusion of slow education methods and mentoring were recently recommended, which incorporates the cognitive-psychological components of metacognition, self-regulation, coping, communication, and shared mental modeling [29]. These components are fundamental to the advancement of human performance and key to ensure long-term retention of knowledge, skills, and behavior change [29].

The innovation in cybersecurity training is further evident in simulated cyber-range training. Cyber-ranges are sophisticated, virtual environments that offer safe, controlled spaces for IT professionals to practice and refine their skills against realistic cyber threats. They enable trainees to engage in simulated cyber-warfare, fostering strategic thinking, rapid decision-making skills, and a profound understanding of how different cyber-threats operate and can be mitigated. The simulated nature of these environments ensures that learning is both effective and safe, without repercussions in the context of real-world organisations [30]. The incorporation of game-design elements in cybersecurity trainings not only makes the learning process more engaging but can also significantly enhances information retention and application [31]. Capture-The-Flag (CTF) events are an exemplary instance of this approach, where participants tackle security-related challenges, fostering teamwork, and developing problem-solving skills in game-like settings. For an activity to be intrinsically motivating to a person, it depends on whether they find rewarding reasons to be engaged in the task [32]. For example, a study found males enjoyed game-based cybersecurity learning more than females [33]. As a result, a training program must be tailored to the target population, which requires upfront understanding of what motivates their participants (knowledge acquisition or winning) to remain engaged and interested in further learning.

2.3   Cybersecurity Training and Human Factors

Good cyberdefense decisions are based on human-human communication as the successful mitigation of a cyber-threat situation starts with detecting, analyzing, and reporting on the cyber-threat and from this reporting process, cyberdefense decision-making results. Tensions can arise from asset prioritization between the cyber and physical spaces, and between the tactical and strategic goals during cyberdefense decision-making [34]. For those working at the operational level, focus is given to the technical aspects of cyber-threats. Conversely, individuals at the tactical and strategic levels of an organization may be focused on how cyber-threats affect the daily operations (i.e. maintaining service to their customers and preserving customer relations). Thus, training needs may vary according to their position within the organization hierarchy and thus their decision-making focus. Such an example would be security operations centers (SOCs) with respect to their organizational structure and decision-making hierarchies. In these organizations technical personnel (cyber-analysts), who represent the operational or bottommost level, are tasked with identifying, analyzing, and reporting on cyber-threats, followed by supervisors, managers, and concluding with directors at the upper echelon of the organizational structure and decision-making hierarchy   [35]. While analysts decide what information to impart on threat reports, strategic level decision-makers must decide whether to send or revise these reports. Interactions between individuals at different levels are often bidirectional, with information being 'pushed up' and decisions being 'pushed down' the decision-making hierarchy [35]. Thus, analysts at the operational level monitor ongoing cyber-threats and provide information (reports or alert relevant personnel), while individuals at the tactical and strategic levels use this threat information to make decisions, which can affect daily operations.

During cyber-threat situations, it is crucial for individuals at all levels of the decision-making hierarchy to understand each other's priorities and information needs. Deviations in priorities and knowledge may lead to non-overlapping understanding of the cyber-threat situation between the organizational levels, which could result in negative consequences in how cyber-threat information is received and interpreted [34, 91]. Taking inspiration from computer/cyber-emergency response teams [35, 36], one effective cybersecurity training piece includes participants, from all organizational levels, learning each other's roles and responsibilities and how each approaches, prioritizes, and manages cyber-threats. Thus, the level of knowledge expected from individuals at different organizational levels varies. Operation technicians are focused on the functional operation of the technical equipment they manage, their level of expertise in cyber-resilient practices can vary. Experts, such as IT personnel not only consider all variables and possible code deviations, but also also make decisions based on pattern recognition [37]. Regarding level of experience, reactions to phishing attempts are more influenced by experiential elements (e.g. knowledge, self-efficacy, and online experience) than by dispositional factors (e.g. risk perception and trust) [38]. Therefore, understanding the different knowledge requirements and prioritizing each is a crucial component when creating tailored cybersecurity training .

3   Extended Reality and the Digital Twin

3.1   Extended Reality

The arrival of Extended Reality (XR) technology has allowed users to experience a higher sense of presence in virtual environments. By blurring the lines between the real physical and digitally simulated worlds, XR technology improves the realism of virtual experiences while building a sense of immersion [39]. XR is an umbrella term encapsulating Mixed Reality (MR) and Virtual Reality (VR). (see Fig. 1). MR is further composed of Augmented Reality (AR) and Augmented Virtuality (AV). AR augments the physical world view by adding virtual objects in a real-time display, while AV operates the same way, but with real-world objects added to a virtual setting. MR solutions typically use displays that are video see-through with a headset or a phone camera [40, 41]. AR and AV solutions can be useful when it comes to offering cybersecurity training directly linked to a workplace as it can increase situational awareness and team communication. In [42], a 3D Mixed reality activity of a simulated network attack lead to better communication of cyber-threat information among collaborating dyads while supporting users in being more accurate in their understanding of the network activity and the whole situation's assessment. It can also avoid requiring a total virtual reality replication of that workplace. Finally, with the help of a headset, Virtual Reality (VR) distinguishes itself by isolating users from the real world and immersing them in a fully, three-dimensional virtual setting they can interact with.

VR has already been used in the context of learning in cybersecurity [43, 44], sometimes with video games that have been equally effective but more engaging than traditional methods [45]. VR effects have been compared to other training methods. In the context of workplace safety, a study showed VR groups (compared to the textbook and the desktop one) led to better problem-solving, perceived enjoyment, intrinsic motivation and self-efficacy [46]. A recent immersive

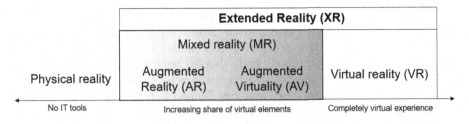

Fig. 1. AR/VR continuum adapted from [40, 41]

reality model (Cognitive Affective Model of Immersive Learning (CAMIL) [47] proposes that because virtual reality environments bring presence and agency in the experience, it will positively influence six cognitive factors such as interest, motivation, cognitive load, self-efficacy, self-regulation and embodiment. Interestingly, VR doesn't really increase factual and conceptual knowledge (bits of information) but is more often used when procedural knowledge is involved (how we do things) [46].

3.2 Digital Twins

The Digital Twin. (DT) concept originates from the aerospace field [48] and has been since implemented in many different domains. From a recent systematic literature review, it can be defined as *"A set of adaptive models that emulate the behavior of a physical system in a virtual system getting real-time data to update itself along its life cycle. The DT replicates the physical system to predict failures and opportunities for change, to prescribe real-time actions for optimizing and/or mitigating unexpected events observing and evaluating the operating profile system"* [49]. In short, it refers to a digital system emulating a physical system (a product, process, building, or even a human), including its structure, states, and behavior. Commonly, it comprises elements allowing visualization of the physical system's states and existing data flows, to serve as decision-aid, and comprises simulation or prediction functions to evaluate new situations and the system's future states. In cybersecurity learning, the DT would allow the replication of a specific CIs' state during a simulated cyber-attack (from doors being opened to a server shutdown).

Human Digital Twins. (HDT) are Digital Twins developed to replicate humans in multiple ways. They can for example help monitor, evaluate, and optimize human ergonomics and performance [50]. In a virtual environment, HDTs can be used to represent users, not as avatars or anonymous virtual humans, but as virtual humans having the same characteristics, behaviors and thought processes as they would have if they were physically present in the virtual world. As digital representations of humans, they have a lot of potential in many domains, the main ones being health and industry [51]. Depending on the use case, HDTs are based on human models attempting to replicate human attributes (physical, physiological, perceptual, cognitive, emotional...) [51]. Some models are developed through the approach of cognitive mimetics [52] in order to imitate or replicate human information processing. In domains such as healthcare, HDTs focus on replicating patients and their tissues, organs and physiological processes. Because a HDT maintains structural and behavioral models of the human it twins, it can be used for, e.g., studying human behavior in a simulation or providing personalized and user-centric services. In training contexts, when classical recommender systems can provide personalized learning content, the use of HDT allows to go a step further, with continuously updated user profiles and the possibility to test reactions to recommendations before actually using them. A HDT with training objectives, a competence or skill map in a specific subject added to the cognitive characteristics of a user, would for example allow the creation of a personalized training program with the help of AI and personal data but also help improve it in real-time and in the future.

3.3 A Combined Use

The combination of DT and XR would enable users to immerse themselves in a virtual and familiar (or not) OT environment, replicated with the help of the DT. Users would then have a virtual twin which would help adapt the training and, which would also be visible for other users in the virtual experience. A DT system combined to XR can then enable visualization, control, and use of all of the collected data and create smooth interaction between users and a context. Thus, real-time synchronized communication can potentially be achieved between users and a digital replica of a critical infrastructure. A few recent studies have worked in the direction of combining DTs and AR/VR [53], with the case for example of a virtual learning application for an electrical laboratory tutorial, a safety and emergency training, industrial robot kinematic control or a workshop digital twin VR synchronization [54–56]. In a study where DTs were combined with VR for asset inspections, users reported feeling immersed and usability scores were high [57], but more human factors still need to be studied. No study yet has been applied to cybersecurity training and its challenges, which leads us to take a closer look at the benefits of this technology combination.

4 Human-Centered Trainings

4.1 Replicable Features

With the help of the DT and XR, training experiences can be adapted. The Digital Twin can replicate, adapt, and be adapted to the user profile based on certain characteristics obtained via real-time data (e.g. eye-tracking, positioning in virtual space) or reported data (e.g. personality, emotions). Based on current research advances, relevant exploitable human characteristics today could be emotions, attention, age and gender, and personality.

Emotions represent an important factor during human experiences in general. They can influence the perception of information [58], attention, learning, memory, judgment, problem-solving [59] and can have a direct impact on behavior [60]. They can also be used by and for HDTs [51,61]. Mixed-evaluation methods (self-reported with questionnaires or interviews, and objective measures with psychophysiological ones) would be the most accurate way of measuring emotional experiences from VR [62,63]. Despite the required time to conduct post-learning interviews or questionnaires, these assessments could also better help predict emotions (with the HDT) during certain contexts for different user profiles, which might even avoid the need for future self-reported measures. However, a recent study showed promising results based on facial expression and body movement recognition [61].

During trainings, emotions can either improve or worsen learning and long-term memory retention [64]. In cybersecurity trainings, fear-inducing techniques are rather inconclusive. They can trigger the desired cybersecurity behaviors but they can also cause fear fatigue, leading to undesirable behaviors [65]. Sadness can result in avoidance instead of compliance [65]. Generally, as opposed to measures that merely act as prohibitions, positive emotions (such as joy and interest) can lead to security behaviours [66]. During attacks, anger, sadness and anxiety are negative emotions that can occur [67]. Finally, because of emotions' influence, cybersecurity trainings could comprise an emotion management aspect.

Attention is an important matter in learning and while dealing with cybersecurity attacks. It is a limited resource used for information processing but also a process of selection of information to be processed with priority [68]. Therefore, during a cybersecurity attack or breach, attention should be directed at the most relevant cues. Eye-tracking has proven to be an efficient way to measure visual attention during learning or training sessions and can be incorporated in VR or XR headsets [69,70]. Saccadic eye movements and fixation duration can indicate where the user focuses their attention, and could help detect whether the training are overloaded with information, or whether a trainee profile is having difficulties during trainings for example. A study also showed that novices and experts have different gaze sequences in regions of interest and may have different gaze behaviors [69].

More generally during cybersecurity breaches, attention should not be overloaded with other job tasks. For example, security warnings with different visuals can help increase attention to those [71] without leading to habituation [72]. Finally, a phishing message particularly relevant to an individual could, for example, lead to attention tunneling and the omission of suspicious cues [73]. Monitoring attention during cybersecurity trainings and trying to adapt it could thus help improve the learning progress of individuals (for example, by increasing warnings and attention to areas of interest for specific profiles).

Age and Gender are human factors that characterize individuals, which should be reflected by HDTs. In cybersecurity, gender is a factor to be considered as it can affect security self-efficacy [74]. Studies have demonstrated that gender variations in computer self-efficacy may vary based on the assessed task (e.g. simple or high level [75]. In another study, gender was not a significant predictor of security behavior, contrary to age as older users appeared less likely to secure their devices (e.g. locking a screen when not in use) and more likely to generate secure passwords with proactive risk awareness contrary to the younger people [76]. However, self-efficacy again was important as it was identified as a mediator between age and cybersecurity behaviors. Between self-reported cybersecurity behaviors and gender, only a minimal effect has been found [74]. Research showed that differences due to age are generally not due to age itself but other predictive factors such as resilience, optimism bias, or learned experience [76]. These indications show that personalization according to age and gender may be relevant, although their links with cybersecurity behaviors need to be nuanced.

Personality appears to be a relevant human factor to take into account when personalizing simulated virtual training experiences in cybersecurity. It has been mentioned in some human digital twin models [51,77] in the same way as physical characteristics or emotions as it helps refine human behavior. Personality has an impact on cybersecurity behavior. With regards to the Five Factors Model [78], individuals with high openness have a higher propensity to perceive the importance of confidentiality and integrity, while a high level of agreeableness hold quite different perceptions regarding the importance of authenticity and accountability. The changes (positive and negative) in the importance perception of confidentiality are very strongly influenced by personality, even more when individuals have no background in engineering [79]. Conscientiousness, agreeableness, and openness are significantly associated with self-reported cybersecurity behaviors [80]. Personality also has an influence on VR training as [81] showed that traits of high agreeableness and low conscientiousness could predict training transferability from the VR environment to a real-world application. However, the work of [82] highlights that there is hardly a consensus on the effects of personality on the sensitivity to social engineering attacks. While exploiting personality with the DT could help adapt trainings, it would potentially also be useful to use it to learn whether and how certain personality profiles behave and react in certain simulated cybersecurity attacks.

4.2   Enhanced and Facilitated Human Factors

XR can enhance and support different human factors which, in turn, can increase learning and raise the awareness of different CIs actors. To this date, XR has shown positive effects on embodiment, situational awareness, collaboration, and engagement.

Embodiment in XR refers to *"the experience of owning a virtual body (body ownership), which can be influenced by the external appearance of the body and the ability to control the actions of the body (agency)"* [47] (p. 946). It is a component of embodied cognition, which proposes that our understanding of our surroundings depends on our sensorimotor system and the physical interactions we have with it [83]. As embodiment can be triggered with XR, its effects are non-negligible in the context of learning. Compared to traditional methods, a setting with enhanced embodiment leads to a higher perceived cooperation process and social flow while learning [84]. To some extent, embodiment could also help memorize training content [85]. Another study showed that embodiment and immersiveness can make learning feel effortless by increasing learners' attention and engagement [86]. Simulating a cybersecurity attack in an XR training enhancing embodiment would also help increase situational awareness, and thus train users to react to emergency situations.

Situational Awareness in cybersecurity refers to *"an individual cyberdefense analyst's (human operator defending an organization from cyber-attacks) awareness of changes to network/system activity that might constitute an attack/breach."* (p.203) [87]. Situational awareness is important in cybersecurity as it is required for identifying, minimizing and stopping cyber-attacks [88]. In a recent study, work showed that VR has the potential to increase cyber-situational awareness and data perception (especially for novice operators) [89]. In our case, VR trainings could potentially help CIs employees to increase their situational awareness in real-life situations to better react to cyber-attacks. In particular, better situational awareness would enable cybersecurity operators to identify security threats and take appropriate action with more accuracy.

Collaboration between cybersecurity experts is crucial to the point it has been standardized, as explained in [90]. It is facilitated in VR as it supports gestures and non-verbal behavior with avatars, although the amount, type and quality of the communication required during a cyber-operation has not precisely been identified and more work is required in this area [91]. Collaboration is rather supported by team cognition, which can be defined "as cognitive processes such as learning, decision making and situation awareness occurring at the team level" (p.206) [87]. Based on the work of [87] on team cognition, we could assume that the collaboration training goals of cybersecurity for a team would be (I) to be able to coordinate behaviors without the need to communicate (shared cognition) (II) knowing who to ask for information (transactive memory) and (III) being able to interactively update individual and team knowledge (interactive shared cognition).

Engagement has often been an important human factor in learning experiences as there is a positive correlation between engagement and achievement [92]. While learning cybersecurity-related issues, it has been shown that VR can increase engagement compared to traditional methods [45,47,103]. Dubovi [92] defines two types of engagement. The first, emotional engagement, refers to a users' emotional involvement in learning activities. Positive emotions during learning include enthusiasm, interest, and enjoyment, while negative emotions include boredom, sadness, and frustration. The second is the cognitive part of engagement, referring to psychological investment. This includes students' mental orientation, cognitive efforts, and focused thoughts during learning tasks. In a few studies, cognitive engagement has been positively linked to motivation and learning achievements [93,94]. Facilitating engagement with the help of VR or

AR can thus help to raise awareness and increase the knowledge in cybersecurity among different levels and types of CIs employees.

5   Discussion

5.1   Ethical Concerns

While solutions like VR and XR systems appear advantageous for learning, their own privacy and security issues have been discussed [95]. VR systems are indeed able to collect a large amount of information such as user movements, biometrics, and usage patterns (hours of personal use, preferences, behaviors). AR and MR have some different privacy and security challenges compared to VR as it can be used with a phone [95].

Ethical considerations simultaneously need to be addressed regarding the DT technology. As DTs assist in the creation of individualized profiles, which contain the knowledge, strengths, and weaknesses specific to an individual, there are heightened vulnerabilities and risks for abuse to that individual. A recent and similar example would be the 23andMe cyber-attack that successfully stole users' ancestry data, which included both private and genetic information as well as shared genetic links to relatives [96]. In addition, some of the stolen genetic data was altered and subsequently published online by hobbyists and genealogists without the knowledge or permission from the concerned individuals [96]. The ethical aspects of 1) the right to privacy and integrity of self, 2) the exposure of or freely giving of an individual's unique and personal vulnerabilities without knowledge of what data is being collected or consenting to the release of that data beforehand; and 3) the vulnerabilities of someone illegally obtaining such a wealth of data on an individual come into light. Knowledge derived from DTs could potentially serve as information for who to target, but more importantly how to target them. Thus, a tool that is supposed to increase the security in an organization could be used to compromise the security instead.

It must be ensured that the Digital Twin's algorithm is created correctly and periodically reassessed as well as the data entered are verified [97]. Also, organizations may mandate using Digital Twin technology for supporting individualized cybersecurity training and education. Once an employee places the equipment on his/her face, data are being collected that would contain an unmistakable identification of that individual [97]. Ethical issues arise regarding the upfront awareness of the employee on what data would be collected, for what purpose, how it would be utilized, and whether the employee consents to the use of his or her data come into question. Thus, an organizational training mandate could run along the delicate lines of coercion without consent.

In addition, digital twins could be easily targeted by adversaries to assist with their identification of potential targets for social engineering type of attacks within an organization as well as the possible manipulation or inflation of the skill levels in vulnerable targets, which would hinder their training needs and potential [97]. Finally, in a currently unregulated metaverse the risk of monitoring, manipulation, and how these converge to mediate our experience and agency should be considered an abject learning environment.

6 Future Work Directions

Despite the mentioned advantages of XR and the DT systems for cybersecurity learning, these solutions remain to be tested and experimented with so they can be optimized. A few questions may already arise. For example, taking into account the Uncanny Valley effect that can occur when interacting with virtual agents in an XR experience, we can ask ourselves what would be the right level of realism and human-likeness. As mentioned earlier, the influence of personality in cybersecurity operations is not well understood. More work in this area could help understand if more factors mediate the effects of personality during cyber-attacks. Social engineering situations could also be precisely simulated through XR and DTs trainings as more human factors linked to social interactions could come into play, especially on the DT side. Indeed, in the context of social engineering, the work proposed by Ferreira and Lenzini [100] combines the principles of persuasion and other studies to represent and explain psychological vulnerabilities. Distraction (focusing on what a victim can gain, need or lose/miss out) is the main phishing tactic being used, followed by authority (obeying the pretense of authority or performing favor for an authority) [100]. In other perspectives, more human factors and vulnerabilities could be addressed to compensate todays' trainings. Common vulnerabilities are security fatigue along with stress and burnout at the workplace [98]. Workload and stress can indeed cause a decrease in performance while countering a cyber-attack and operation fatigue and frustration can occur during the length of a cyber operation [99].

Finally, to date one of the biggest challenges for virtual and tailored trainings, is developing effective and valid outcome measurements (i.e. situational awareness) and performance metrics for individuals tasked with detecting, investigating, and reporting on cyber-threats [101]. While initial efforts have been made to produce incident report templates and questionnaires to measure situational awareness in cyber-threat situations, further development and experimental validation is still needed. Lack of objective outcome measures hinders the ability to effectively assess the efficaciousness of a training. With the exception of awareness training [19], much research on cybersecurity training and education has focused on individuals that either are cybersecurity professionals or in process to becoming one. Also, the cognitive profile of these cybersecurity professionals tended to be unique since they deviated from the norm when assessed and scored [102]. Therefore, to what extent the findings derived from cybersecurity research can be generalized to individuals who are not cybersecurity professionals or the general population is unknown.

7   Conclusion

Cybersecurity in critical infrastructures is a crucial issue as the equilibrium and safety of nation-wide systems depend on it. The collaboration between industry and academia is a cornerstone to ensuring that cybersecurity training remains contemporary and relevant. Recognizing and addressing these limitations with cybersecurity is not just an educational challenge but a strategic imperative. This symbiotic relationship between industry and academia ensures that the training not only imparts knowledge but also inspires a practical skill set that is directly applicable to real-world scenarios. Cybersecurity training solutions must go beyond the current paradigms, integrating psychological insights, behavioral analytics, and social dynamics into the core of cybersecurity education. This collaboration and merging of expertise supports the designing and tailoring of cyber-training programs that are personalized to individuals.

A major part of this state of the art has been to point out what was missing in current cybersecurity training programs, and addressing those missing human factor components through the proposal of combining XR and digital twin technologies. With Digital Twins design and implementation, human factors could be replicated and augmented to give rise to customized and tailored trainings that match the individual's pace at learning, what areas are of specific challenge for each individual, all with the goals of not only improving cybersecurity knowledge and skill development but also with changing in cybersecurity behavior and practice. However, effective human factors and performance measurements with training programs, scalability in design and ethical concerns still remain challenges when designing effective cybersecurity training programs.

As our human factors, that is our personalities, our abilities to handle stress and emotionally regulate and our metacognition, thought processes and decision making capacities are unique, the need to address these human factors through personalized training with the assistance of training aids such as DT, can help us address how to effectively meet the educational, training and cybersecurity safety issues of all. Only by doing so can we develop a holistic defense mechanism that is as adaptable and multifaceted as the human elements it seeks to protect. From these points and with the need for the further inclusion of human factors in cybersecurity training and utilizing DT as a tracking and personalized training aid, the Athena project, funded by Digital Europe, aims to actively address these issues within a critical infrastructure sector (waterways).

Acknowledgement. The project ATHENA is funded by the European Union (Digital Europe Programme) under Grant Agreement No. 101127970 and is supported by the European Cybersecurity Competence Centre. Views and opinions expressed are however those of the author(s) only and do not necessarily reflect those of the European Union or the European Cybersecurity Competence Centre. Neither the European Union nor the European Cybersecurity Competence Centre can be held responsible for them.

References

1. Ardito, L., Petruzzelli, A., Panniello, U., Garavelli, A.: Towards industry 4.0: mapping digital technologies for supply chain management-marketing integration. Bus. Process Manag. J. **25**(2), 323–346 (2019)
2. Galloway, B., Hancke, G.: Introduction to industrial control networks. IEEE Commun. surv. tutorials **15**(2), 860–880 (2012)
3. Lehto, M.: Cyber-attacks against critical infrastructure. In: Lehto, M., Neittaanmäki, P. (eds.) Cyber Security: Critical Infrastructure Protection, pp. 3–42. Springer, Cham (2022). https://doi.org/10.1007/978-3-030-91293-2_1
4. Deibert, R.J., Rohozinski, R.: Risking security: policies and paradoxes of cyberspace security. Int. Polit. Sociol. **4**(1), 15–32 (2010). https://doi.org/10.1111/j.1749-5687.2009.00088.x
5. Cordesman, A.H.: Cyber-Threats, Information Warfare, and Critical Infrastructure Protection: Defending the Us Homeland. Greenwood Publishing Group, CA (2001)
6. Sarwat, A.I., Sundararajan, A., Parvez, I., Moghaddami, M., Moghadasi, A.: Toward a smart city of interdependent critical infrastructure networks. In: Amini, M.H., Boroojeni, K.G., Iyengar, S.S., Pardalos, P.M., Blaabjerg, F., Madni, A.M. (eds.) Sustainable Interdependent Networks. SSDC, vol. 145, pp. 21–45. Springer, Cham (2018). https://doi.org/10.1007/978-3-319-74412-4_3
7. European Commission: Directive (EU) 2022/2555 of the European Parliament and of the Council of 14 December 2022 on measures for a high common level of cybersecurity across the Union, amending Regulation (EU) No 910/2014 and Directive (EU) 2018/1972, and repealing Directive (EU) 2016/1148 (NIS 2 Directive) 2022. https://eur-lex.europa.eu/eli/dir/2022/2555. Accessed 22 Jan 2024
8. Chowdhury, N., Gkioulos, V.: Key competencies for critical infrastructure cybersecurity: a systematic literature review. Inf. Comput. Secur. **29**(5), 697–723 (2021)
9. Alsharif, M., Mishra, S., AlShehri, M.: Impact of human vulnerabilities on cybersecurity. Comput. Syst. Sci. Eng. **40**(3), 1153–1166 (2022). https://doi.org/10.32604/csse.2022.019938
10. Leach, J.: Improving user security behaviour. Comput. Secur. **22**(8), 685–692 (2003)
11. Ratchford, M. M., Wang, Y.: BYOD-insure: a security assessment model for enterprise byod. In: 2019 Fifth Conference on Mobile and Secure Services (MobiSecServ), pp. 1–10. IEEE, Miami Beach, FL, USA (2019)
12. Crossler, R., Bélanger, F.: An extended perspective on individual security behaviors: protection motivation theory and a unified security practices (USP) instrument. ACM SIGMIS Database: DATABASE Adv. Inf. Syst. **45**(4), 51–71 (2014)
13. Alohali, M., Clarke, N., Furnell, S., Albakri, S.: Information security behavior: recognizing the influencers. In: 2017 Computing Conference, pp. 844–853. IEEE, London, UK (2017)
14. Nurse, J. R.: Cybercrime and you: how criminals attack and the human factors that they seek to exploit. arXiv preprint arXiv:1811.0662 (2018)
15. Case, D. U.: Analysis of the cyber attack on the Ukrainian power grid. Electricity Inf. Sharing Anal. Cent. (E-ISAC) **388**, 1–29 (2016)
16. The attack on Colonial pipeline: what we've learned & what we've done over the past two years. https://www.cisa.gov/news-events/news/attack-colonial-pipeline-what-weve-learned-what-weve-done-over-past-two-years. Accessed 29 Jan 2024

17. IRGC-affiliated cyber actors exploit PLCs in multiple sectors, including U.S. water and wastewater systems facilities. https://www.cisa.gov/news-events/cybersecurity-advisories/aa23-335a. Accessed 29 Jan 2024

18. Morelli, U., Nicolodi, L., Ranise, S.: An open and flexible cybersecurity training laboratory in IT/OT infrastructures. In: Fournaris, A.P., et al. (eds.) IOSEC/MSTEC/FINSEC -2019. LNCS, vol. 11981, pp. 140–155. Springer, Cham (2020). https://doi.org/10.1007/978-3-030-42051-2_10

19. Drogkaris, P., Bourka, A.: European Union Agency for Cybersecurity: Cybersecurity culture guidelines - Behavioural aspects of cybersecurity, Drogkaris, P.(eds.), Bourka, A.(editor), European Network and Information Security Agency (2018). https://doi.org/10.2824/324042

20. McMahon, C.: In Defence of the human factor. Front. Psychol. **11**, 1390 (2020)

21. Canham, M.: Repeat clicking: a lack of awareness is not the problem. In: HCI International 2023 - Late Breaking Papers: 25th International Conference on Human-Computer Interaction, pp. 325–342. Copenhagen, Denmark (2023)

22. Sütterlin, S., et al.: The role of IT background for metacognitive accuracy, confidence and overestimation of deep fake recognition skills. In: International Conference on Human-Computer Interaction, pp. 103–119. Springer International Publishing, Cham (2022). https://doi.org/10.1007/978-3-031-05457-0_9

23. Sütterlin, S., et al.: Individual deep fake recognition skills are affected by viewer's political orientation, agreement with content and device used. In: International Conference on Human-Computer Interaction, pp. 269–284. Springer Nature Switzerland, Copenhagen, Denmark, Cham (2023). https://doi.org/10.1007/978-3-031-35017-7_18

24. Lif, P., Sommestad, T.: Human factors related to the performance of intrusion detection operators. HAISA, pp. 265–275 (2015)

25. Pirta-Dreimane, R., et al.: Application of intervention mapping in cybersecurity education design. Front. Educ. **7**, 998335 (2022)

26. Ruh, P., Morgenstern, H.: Establishing cyberpsychology at universities in the area of cyber security. In: Stephanidis, C., Antona, M., Ntoa, S. (eds.) HCII 2021. CCIS, vol. 1499, pp. 294–301. Springer, Cham (2021). https://doi.org/10.1007/978-3-030-90179-0_38

27. European cybersecurity skills framework role profiles. https://www.enisa.europa.eu/publications/european-cybersecurity-skills-framework-role-profiles. Accessed 29 Jan 2024

28. Newhouse, W., Keith, S., Scribner, B., Witte, G.: National initiative for cybersecurity education (NICE) cybersecurity workforce framework. NIST Spec. Publ. **800**(2017), 181 (2017)

29. Knox, B.J., Lugo, R.G., Sütterlin, S.: Cognisance as a human factor in military cyber Defence education. IFAC-Pap. OnLine **52**(19), 163–168 (2019)

30. Huff, P., Leiterman, S., Springer, J.: Cyber arena: an open-source solution for scalable cybersecurity labs in the cloud. In: Proceedings of the 54th ACM Technical Symposium on Computer Science Education V. 1, pp. 221–227. ACM, Toronto, Canada (2023)

31. Jelo, M., Helebrandt, P.: Gamification of cyber ranges in cybersecurity education. In: 2022 20th International Conference on Emerging eLearning Technologies and Applications (ICETA), pp. 280–285. IEEE, Stary Smokovec, Slovakia (2022)

32. Di Domenico, S.I., Ryan, R.M.: The emerging neuroscience of intrinsic motivation: a new frontier in self-determination research. Front. Hum. Neurosci. **11**, 145 (2017)

33. Jin, G., Tu, M., Kim, T.-H., Heffron, J., White, J.: Evaluation of game-based learning in cybersecurity education for high school students. J. Educ. Learn. **12**, 150 (2018)

34. Jøsok, Ø., Knox, B.J., Helkala, K., Lugo, R.G., Sütterlin, S., Ward, P.: Exploring the hybrid space. In: Schmorrow, D.D.D., Fidopiastis, C.M.M. (eds.) AC 2016. LNCS (LNAI), vol. 9744, pp. 178–188. Springer, Cham (2016). https://doi.org/10.1007/978-3-319-39952-2_18

35. Staheli, D., et al.: Collaborative data analysis and discovery for cyber security. In: Twelfth Symposium on Usable Privacy and Security (SOUPS 2016) (2016)

36. Steinke, J., et al.: Improving cybersecurity incident response team effectiveness using teams-based research. IEEE Secur. Priv. **13**(4), 20–29 (2015)

37. Klein, G.A., Calderwood, R.: Decision models: some lessons from the field. IEEE Trans. Syst. Man Cybernet. **21**, 1018–1026 (1991)

38. Wright, R.T., Jensen, M.L., Thatcher, J.B., Dinger, M., Marett, K.: Research note-influence techniques in phishing attacks: an examination of vulnerability and resistance. Inf. Syst. Res. **25**(2), 385–400 (2014)

39. Suh, A., Prophet, J.: The state of immersive technology research: a literature analysis. Comput. Hum. Behav. **86**, 77–90 (2018)

40. Milgram, P., Kishino, F.: A taxonomy of mixed reality visual displays. IEICE Trans. Inf. Syst. **77**(12), 1321–1329 (1994)

41. Knoll, M., Stieglitz, S.: Augmented Reality und Virtual Reality-Einsatz im Kontext von Arbeit, Forschung und Lehre. HMD Praxis der Wirtschaftsinformatik **59**(1), 6–22 (2022)

42. Ask, T.F., Kullman, K., Sütterlin, S., Knox, B.J., Engel, D., Lugo, R.G.: A 3D mixed reality visualization of network topology and activity results in better dyadic cyber team communication and cyber situational awareness. Front. Big Data **6**, 1042783 (2023)

43. Seo, J.H., Bruner, M., Payne, A., Gober, N., McMullen, D., Chakravorty, D.K.: Using virtual reality to enforce principles of cybersecurity. J. Comput. D Sci. Educ. **10**(1), 81–87 (2019)

44. Anwar, M. S., et al.: Immersive learning and AR/VR-based education: cybersecurity measures and risk management. In: Cybersecurity Management in Education Technologies, pp. 1–22. CRC Press (2023)

45. Veneruso, S.V., Ferro, L.S., Marrella, A., Mecella, M., Catarci, T.: CyberVR: an interactive learning experience in virtual reality for cybersecurity related issues. In: Proceedings of the International Conference on Advanced Visual Interfaces, pp. 1–8. ACM, Salerno, Italy (2020)

46. Makransky, G., Borre-Gude, S., Mayer, R.E.: Motivational and cognitive benefits of training in immersive virtual reality based on multiple assessments. J. Comput. Assist. Learn. **35**(6), 691–707 (2019)

47. Makransky, G., Petersen, G.B.: The cognitive affective model of immersive learning (CAMIL): a theoretical research-based model of learning in immersive virtual reality. Educ. Psychol. Rev. **33**, 937–958 (2021)

48. Shafto, M., et al.: Draft modeling, simulation, information technology & processing roadmap. Technol. Area **11**, 1–32 (2010)

49. Semeraro, C., Lezoche, M., Panetto, H., Dassisti, M.: Digital twin paradigm: a systematic literature review. Comput. Ind. **130**, 103469 (2021)

50. Löcklin, A., Jung, T., Jazdi, N., Ruppert, T., Weyrich, M.: Architecture of a human-digital twin as common interface for operator 4.0 applications. Procedia CIRP **104**, 458–463 (2021)

51. Naudet, Y., Baudet, A., Risse, M.: Human digital twin in industry 4.0: concept and preliminary model. In: IN4PL, pp. 137–144. ISBN (2021)
52. Karvonen, A., Saariluoma, P.: Cognitive mimetics and human digital twins: towards holistic AI design. ERCIM News **2023**(132), 17–18 (2023)
53. Yin, Y., Zheng, P., Li, C., Wang, L.: A state-of-the-art survey on augmented reality-assisted digital twin for futuristic human-centric industry transformation. Robot. Comput. Integr. Manuf. **81**, 102515 (2023)
54. Kaarlela, T., Pieskä, S., Pitkäaho, T.: Digital twin and virtual reality for safety training. In: 2020 11th IEEE International Conference on Cognitive Infocommunications (CogInfoCom), pp. 000115–000120. IEEE, Mariehamn, Finland (2020)
55. Tähemaa, T., Bondarenko, Y.: Digital twin based Synchronised control and simulation of the industrial robotic cell using virtual reality. J. Mach. Eng. **19**(1), 128–144 (2019)
56. Wu, P., Qi, M., Gao, L., Zou, W., Miao, Q., Liu, L.L.: Research on the virtual reality synchronization of workshop digital twin. In: 2019 IEEE 8th Joint International Information Technology and Artificial Intelligence Conference (ITAIC), pp. 875–879. IEEE, Chongqing, China (2019)
57. Voordijk, H., Vahdatikhaki, F., Hesselink, L.: Digital twin-based asset inspection and user-technology interactions. J. Eng. Des. Technol. (2023)
58. McConnell, M.M., Eva, K.W.: The role of emotion in the learning and transfer of clinical skills and knowledge. Acad. Med. J. Assoc. Am. Med. Coll. **87**(10), 1316–1322 (2012)
59. Brosch, T., Scherer, K., Grandjean, D., Sander, D.: The impact of emotion on perception, attention, memory, and decision-making. Swiss Med. Wkly. **143**(1920), w13786–w13786 (2013)
60. Lerner, J.S., Keltner, D.: Beyond valence: toward a model of emotion-specific influences on judgement and choice. Cogn. Emot. **14**(4), 473–493 (2000)
61. Amara, K., Kerdjidj, O., Ramzan, N.: Emotion recognition for affective human digital twin by means of virtual reality enabling technologies. IEEE Access **11**, 74216–74227 (2023)
62. Magalhães, M., Coelho, A., Melo, M., Bessa, M.: Measuring users' emotional responses in multisensory virtual reality: a systematic literature review. Multimed. Tools Appl. **83**, 1–41 (2023)
63. Greenfeld, A., Lugmayr, A., Lamont, W.: Comparative reality: measuring user experience and emotion in immersive virtual environments. In: 2018 IEEE International Conference on Artificial Intelligence and Virtual Reality (AIVR), pp. 204-209. IEEE, Taichung, Taiwan (2018)
64. Tyng, C.M., Amin, H.U., Saad, M.N., Malik, A.S.: The influences of emotion on learning and memory. Front. Psychol. **8**, 1454 (2017)
65. Zhang, X.A., Borden, J.: How to communicate cyber-risk? An examination of behavioral recommendations in cybersecurity crises. J. Risk Res. **23**(10), 1336–1352 (2020)
66. Gulenko, I.: Improving passwords: influence of emotions on security behaviour. Inf. Manag. Comput. Secur. **22**(2), 167–178 (2014)
67. Bachura, E., Valecha, R., Chen, R., Rao, H.R.: The OPM data breach: an investigation of shared emotional reactions on Twitter. MIS Q. **46**(2), 881–910 (2022)
68. Oberauer, K.: Working memory and attention - a conceptual analysis and review. J. Cogn. **2**(1), 1–23 (2019)
69. Wang, C.C., Hung, J.C., Chen, H.C.: How prior knowledge affects visual attention of Japanese mimicry and onomatopoeia and learning outcomes: evidence from virtual reality eye tracking. Sustain. **13**(19), 1–28 (2021)

70. Mirault, J., Albrand, J.P., Lassault, J., Grainger, J., Ziegler, J.C.: Using virtual reality to assess reading fluency in children. Fronti. Educ. **6**, 693355 (2021)
71. Al'Absi, M., Hugdahl, K., Lovallo, W.R.: Adrenocortical stress responses and altered working memory performance. Psychophysiol. **39**(1), 95–99 (2002)
72. Anderson, B.B., Kirwan, C.B., Jenkins, J.L., Eargle, D., Howard, S., Vance, A.: How polymorphic warnings reduce habituation in the brain: insights from an fMRI study. In: Proceedings of the 33rd Annual ACM Conference on Human Factors in Computing Systems, pp. 2883–2892. ACM, Seoul, Korea (2015)
73. Montañez, R., Golob, E., Xu, S.: Human cognition through the lens of social engineering cyberattacks. Front. Psychol. **11**, 1755 (2020)
74. Anwar, M., He, W., Ash, I., Yuan, X., Li, L., Xu, L.: Gender difference and employees' cybersecurity behaviors. Comput. Hum. Behav. **69**, 437–443 (2017)
75. Tømte, C., Hatlevik, O.E.: Gender-differences in self-efficacy ICT related to various ICT-user profiles in Finland and Norway. How do self-efficacy, gender and ICT-user profiles relate to findings from PISA 2006. Comput. Educ. **57**(1), 1416–1424 (2011)
76. Branley-Bell, D., Coventry, L., Dixon, M., Joinson, A., Briggs, P.: Exploring age and gender differences in ICT cybersecurity behaviour. Hum. Behav. Emerg. Technol. **2022**, 1–10 (2022)
77. Miller, M.E., Spatz, E.: A unified view of a human digital twin. Hum. Intell. Syst. Integr. 4(1–2), 23–33 (2022)
78. Rammstedt, B., John, O.P.: Measuring personality in one minute or less: a 10-item short version of the big five inventory in English and German. J. Res. Pers. **41**(1), 203–212 (2007)
79. Condori-Fernandez, N., Suni-Lopez, F., Muñante, D., Daneva, M.: How can personality influence perception on security of context-aware applications? In: Groß, T., Viganò, L. (eds.) STAST 2020. LNCS, vol. 12812, pp. 3–22. Springer, Cham (2021). https://doi.org/10.1007/978-3-030-79318-0_1
80. Shappie, A.T., Dawson, C.A., Debb, S.M.: Personality as a predictor of cybersecurity behavior. Psychol. Popular Media **9**(4), 475 (2020)
81. Thorp, S.O., Rimol, L.M., Grassini, S.: Association of the big five personality traits with training effectiveness, sense of presence, and cybersickness in virtual reality. Multimodal Technol. Interact. **7**(2), 11 (2023)
82. Montañez, R., Atyabi, A., Xu, S.: Social engineering attacks and defenses in the physical world vs. cyberspace: a contrast study. In: Cybersecurity and Cognitive Science, pp. 3–41. Academic Press (2022)
83. Wilson, M.: Six views of embodied cognition. Psychon. Bull. Rev. **9**(4), 625–636 (2002)
84. Wei, C.W., Chen, H.H., Chen, N.S.: Effects of embodiment-based learning on perceived cooperation process and social flow. Procedia. Soc. Behav. Sci. **197**, 608–613 (2015)
85. Marre, Q., Huet, N., Labeye, E.: Embodied mental imagery improves memory. Q. J. Exp. Psychol. **74**(8), 1396–1405 (2021)
86. Harackiewicz, J.M., Smith, J.L., Priniski, S.J.: Interest matters: the importance of promoting interest in education. Policy Insights Behav. Brain Sci. **3**(2), 220–227 (2016)
87. Rajivan, P., Cooke, N.: Impact of team collaboration on cybersecurity situational awareness. Theory Models Cyber Situation Awareness, pp. 203–226 (2017)
88. Dykstra, J., Rowe, N., Shimeall, T., Horneman, A., Midler, M.: Introduction: on the nature of situational awareness. Digital Threats Res. Pract. **2**(4), 1–3 (2021)

89. Munsinger, B., Beebe, N., Richardson, T.: Virtual reality for improving cyber situational awareness in security operations centers. Comput. Secur. **132**, 103368 (2023)

90. Kabil, A., Duval, T., Cuppens, N., Le Comte, G., Halgand, Y., Ponchel, C.: From cyber security activities to collaborative virtual environments practices through the 3D CyberCOP platform. In: Ganapathy, V., Jaeger, T., Shyama-sundar, R.K. (eds.) ICISS 2018. LNCS, vol. 11281, pp. 272–287. Springer, Cham (2018). https://doi.org/10.1007/978-3-030-05171-6_14

91. Ask, T.F., Lugo, R.G., Knox, B.J., Sütterlin, S.: Human-human communication in cyber threat situations: a systematic review. In: Stephanidis, C., et al. (eds.) HCII 2021. LNCS, vol. 13096, pp. 21–43. Springer, Cham (2021). https://doi.org/10.1007/978-3-030-90328-2_2

92. Dubovi, I.: Cognitive and emotional engagement while learning with VR: the perspective of multimodal methodology. Comput. Educ. **183**, 104495 (2022)

93. Chi, M.T., Wylie, R.: The ICAP framework: linking cognitive engagement to active learning outcomes. Educ. Psychol. **49**(4), 219–243 (2014)

94. Greene, B.A.: Measuring cognitive engagement with self-report scales: reflections from over 20 years of research. Educ. Psychol. **50**(1), 14–30 (2015)

95. Giaretta, A.: Security and privacy in virtual reality–a literature survey (2022). arXiv preprint arXiv:2205.00208

96. 23andMe confirms hackers stole ancestry data on 6.9 million users. https://tcrn.ch/47Hzimn. Accessed 21 Jan 2024

97. Braun, M., Krutzinna, J.: Digital twins and the ethics of health decision-making concerning children. Patterns (NY) **3**(4), 100469 (2022)

98. Stanton, B., Theofanos, M.F., Prettyman, S.S., Furman, S.: Security fatigue. IT Prof. **18**(5), 26–32 (2016)

99. Dykstra, J., Paul, C. L.: Cyber operations stress survey (COSS): studying fatigue, frustration, and cognitive workload in cybersecurity operations. In: Proceedings of the 11th USENIX Workshop on Cyber Security Experimentation and Test (CSET 18), pp. 1–8. ACM, Baltimore, USA (2018)

100. Ferreira, A., Lenzini, G.: An analysis of social engineering principles in effective phishing. In: 2015 Workshop on Socio-Technical Aspects in Security and Trust, pp. 9–16. IEEE, Verona, Italy (2015)

101. Agyepong, E., Cherdantseva, Y., Reinecke, P., Burnap, P.: Challenges and performance metrics for security operations center analysts: a systematic review. J. Cyber Secur. Technol. **4**, 125–152 (2020)

102. Lugo, R.G., Sütterlin, S.: Cyber officer profiles and performance factors. In: Harris, D. (ed.) EPCE 2018. LNCS (LNAI), vol. 10906, pp. 181–190. Springer, Cham (2018). https://doi.org/10.1007/978-3-319-91122-9_16

103. Childs, E., et al.: An overview of enhancing distance learning through augmented and virtual reality technologies. arXiv Preprint arXiv:2101.11000 (2021). https://doi.org/10.48550/arXiv.2101.11000

Author Index

© The Editor(s) (if applicable) and The Author(s), under exclusive license
to Springer Nature Switzerland AG 2024
D. D. Schmorrow and C. M. Fidopiastis (Eds.): HCII 2024, LNAI 14694, pp. 253–255, 2024.
https://doi.org/10.1007/978-3-031-61569-6

Printed in the United States
by Baker & Taylor Publisher Services